ORGANIZATIONAL BEHAVIOR 6

T0304193

ORGANIZATIONAL BEHAVIOR 6

INTEGRATED THEORY DEVELOPMENT AND THE ROLE OF THE UNCONSCIOUS

JOHN B. MINER

Routledge
Taylor & Francis Group

LONDON AND NEW YORK

First published 2011 by M.E. Sharpe

Published 2015 by Routledge
2 Park Square, Milton Park, Abingdon, Oxon OX14 4RN
711 Third Avenue, New York, NY, 10017, USA

Routledge is an imprint of the Taylor & Francis Group, an informa business

Library of Congress Cataloging-in-Publication Data

Miner, John B.
  Organizational behavior 1. Essential theories of motivation and leadership
  Organizational behavior 2. Essential theories of process and structure
  Organizational behavior 3. Historical origins, theoretical foundations, and the future
  Organizational behavior 4. From theory to practice
  Organizational behavior 5. From unconscious motivation to role-motivated leadership
  Organizational behavior 6. Integrated theory development and the role of the unconscious
  by John B. Miner.
    p. cm.
  Includes bibliographical references and index.
  Vol. 1: ISBN 0-7656-1523-1 (cloth : alk. paper)—ISBN 0-7656-1524-X (pbk : alk. paper)
  Vol. 2: ISBN 0-7656-1525-8 (cloth : alk. paper)—ISBN 0-7656-1526-6 (pbk : alk. paper)
  Vol. 3: ISBN 0-7656-1527-4 (cloth : alk. paper)—ISBN 0-7656-1528-2 (pbk : alk. paper)
  Vol. 4: ISBN 978-0-7656-1529-9 (cloth : alk. paper)—ISBN 978-0-7656-1530-5 (pbk : alk. paper)
  Vol. 5: ISBN 978-0-7656-1990-7 (cloth : alk. paper)—ISBN 978-0-7656-1991-4 (pbk : alk. paper)
  Vol. 6: ISBN 978-0-7656-1992-1 (cloth : alk. paper)—ISBN 978-0-7656-1993-8 (pabk. : alk. paper)

1. Employee motivation. 2. Leadership. 3. Organizational behavior. I. Title: Organizational behavior one.
Essential theories of motivation and leadership. II. Title: Organizational behavior. 1. Essential theories of
motivation and leadership. III. Title: Essential theories of motivation and leadership. IV. Title.

HF5549.5.M63M5638 2005
302.3′5—dc22   200500

ISBN 13: 9780765619938 (pbk)
ISBN 13: 9780765619921 (hbk)

To my wife,

Barbara

Building on Miner's *Organizational Behavior: Foundations, Theories, and Analyses,* the M.E. Sharpe Organizational Behavior series consists of the following volumes—

1. Essential Theories of Motivation and Leadership (2005)
2. Essential Theories of Process and Structure (2006)
3. Historical Origins, Theoretical Foundations, and the Future (2006)
4. From Theory to Practice (2007)
5. From Unconscious Motivation to Role-Motivated Leadership (2008)
6. Integrated Theory Development and the Role of the Unconscious (2011)

CONTENTS

PART I.   THEORIES OF MOTIVATION

PART II.   THEORIES OF LEADERSHIP

PART III.   ORGANIZATIONAL DECISION MAKING

LIST OF TABLES AND FIGURES

TABLES

FIGURES

PREFACE

This book utilizes an approach that I have followed frequently in the past—to combine disparate disciplines in search of new ideas that might operate to advance the science of organizational behavior. In this case the new discipline is the *new unconscious* perspective produced by an amalgam of social psychology, experimental psychology, and personality theory. This literature, and the research inherent in it, is added to my previous background, as well as my training in personality theory, clinical psychology, psychoanalysis, and more recently in industrial and organizational psychology. Recently, the new unconscious perspective has been fashioned out of research on the subject and is in many respects a new way of thinking. I hope that by adding it to my previous background, I will be able to construct some innovative ways of looking at the theories of organizational behavior.

Let me explain what I mean by combining disparate disciplines, in the anticipation that by providing examples from my own experience I may help others to understand what is involved. As I entered the then-forming field of organizational behavior in the early 1960s, I came head-to-head with an extensive sociological literature that previously had been unknown to me. This dealt with Weber's thinking and with the field of entrepreneurship (as interpreted to me by Norman Smith, who served with me on the faculty of the University of Oregon as a scholar in marketing and entrepreneurship). The result of this experience combining sociology into my previous knowledge base is described in Miner 2006b, Chapter 16. Much the same thing was involved in my diversifying into educational administration and into policy/strategy (the latter with the assistance of George Steiner). In both instances I found a new disciplinary literature to link with my existing background (see Miner 1993a); I believe that in each such instance my thinking was enriched and a catalytic role was served. There is something in the process of switching analytical mindsets recommended by Zyphur (2009) in all of this.

A rating system is used to evaluate the various theories that might benefit from the application of the new unconscious perspective. These theories are considered in the order of their estimated validity within content areas. Thus five-star theories are considered first, then four-star theories, and finally three-star theories. Because I was interested in concentrating on the more valid theories, no theory rated at the two- or one-star levels was introduced into this analysis. This was done for the micro theories of motivation and leadership separately; there are 21 such theories in all. Similarly the macro theories dealing with decision making, systems concepts of organizations, bureaucracy-related concepts, and sociological concepts of organization are handled in the same manner; there are 20 such theories. Overall the book devotes about the same number of pages to micro and macro types of theory. These two approaches essentially parallel books 1 and 2 (Miner 2005, 2006a) in this series, but the theories themselves are not always the same, because the criteria applied differ. More detail on the theories selected, and not selected, is contained in Chapters 17 and 18 of Miner (2006b). Book 6 also includes an Introduction, which deals with the historical features involved and with the pluses and/or minuses of operating from the unconscious perspective, as well as a final Conclusions on Conclusions chapter, which deals with aspects of the theory evaluations, projective techniques, and the relevant literature on the consciousness/unconsciousness disparity.

A feature of the current volume is that the literature involved, particularly as it relates to the new unconscious perspective and the research on it, is continuing (see Milkman, Chugh, and Bazerman 2009). I have handled this fact on occasion by introducing corrections to past discussions as the new literature emerged; thus a reliance on the indexes may be more appropriate than utilizing the table of contents to identify where in the book particular subjects are treated. This becomes most evident in the case of articles dealing with mainstream organizational behavior applications to unconscious subject matter. Publications of this type, often involving the early full-scale adoptions of the new unconscious approach by the journals of the field, begin to emerge toward the end of the book, from Chapter 38 on. This thrust continues into the last chapter, which provides an addendum on the value of projective techniques for identifying unconscious materials, and the deficiencies of self-report measures for such purposes (see Dunning, Heath, and Suls 2004; Wilson 2009) as previously presented in Chapter 1 of Miner (2008).

Several other features of this book may prove worthy of note. For one thing I include numerous quotations, usually involving the current literature. My objective is to provide authenticity to the particular research and theorization cited. I want you to experience firsthand what the particular researchers or theorists did and said. Many of these quotes are subject to the criticism that they are taken out of context. Although this is indeed true, I have tried wherever possible to give specific page citations so that the reader may fill in the context if this is desired.

Furthermore I have cited meta-analytic studies related to particular theories to the extent these are available. Unfortunately there are instances where meta-analysis has not been applied to test certain theories—either because of the nature of the theory or because of limitations of research availability; clearly there are instances in which meta-analyses are not to be had. Finally I have bunched the references at the end of the book. These include extensive citations to the new unconscious literature, as well as an updating to the coverage of the various theories extending beyond what was included in previous books of this series on the theories of organizational behavior. These references, and the treatment here, extend up through the first quarter of 2010.

John B. Miner
Eugene, Oregon

ACKNOWLEDGMENTS

I am indebted to Oxford University Press for giving me permission to use material from my *Organizational Behavior: Foundations, Theories, and Analyses* (2002) wherever in the present volume it proved appropriate. Also, I am similarly indebted to M.E. Sharpe for giving me permission to reproduce material from my five previously published volumes in this series.

Harry Briggs at M.E. Sharpe has shown himself to be both a very helpful person and a highly proficient editor. It has been a pleasure to work with him. Stacey Victor, my project editor, has been equally helpful.

In the absence of any university support, my wife, Barbara, has taken on all the numerous tasks involved in the preparation of this book, other than writing it. I thank her not only for her dedication and efficiency, but for her support and love.

INTRODUCTION

This is a book about consciousness and unconsciousness, how they interlock, and how they relate to the "goodness" of theories in organizational behavior developed during the latter part of the twentieth century. My original idea in writing such a book was to integrate the various theories of a micro (Miner 2005) and macro (Miner 2006a) nature and thus to bring them all together into a homogeneous whole that would have the appeal of a multifaceted theoretical approach. I have grappled with this goal for a considerable period, as I know many others have done in various alternative ways. My conclusion is that this goal is not achievable; either by me or anyone else based on the present state of knowledge, although certain links between various theories are in evidence. The problem, as I see it now, is that unconscious considerations have not been adequately integrated into either our theories or the research that attempts to test them. Thus we are left with such a large segment of "I don't know" phenomena that it becomes insurmountable. We simply do not, in fact, have the research evidence to fully test our theories; the introjections of evidence from both the "cleaning up" of projective techniques and the development of "the new unconscious" perspective from psychology has created sufficient uncertainty to make for serious doubt as to where we currently stand within the theoretical framework of organizational behavior (see Miner 2008, Chapters 1 and 2).

Rather than produce the ideal theoretical framework that I originally envisaged, I am limited to developing conceptions of how the various views of unconscious considerations have, and might, interact with organizational behavior's seemingly better theories to produce improved empirical results. This is a first step to generate the research that might serve, at this point in time as of 2010, as a basis for developing a truly integrated theory.

CONSCIOUSNESS AS A PREDOMINANT VIEW

William James was an extremely influential psychologist-philosopher who championed the role of conscious thought (see Boring 1950; Bargh 2005; Fiske 2008). His views on the subject were perpetuated over the years and came to influence many of the theories of organizational behavior. James's writings emphasized the importance of two particular points: (1) the conscious will operating from choice, and (2) the focus of attention. The rational emphasis of his views is to be found throughout his extensive publications and is perhaps best epitomized by a chapter entitled "The Stream of Consciousness," which appears frequently in various sources (James 1890, 1892, 1921). Thus the predominance of a stress on consciousness and volition has a long history in psychology and via this route has entered organizational behavior; it accounts for the present-day preoccupation with self-report measures within the field, and in industrial/organizational psychology as well. Brain studies seem to indicate that decision making and the more rational cognitive processes have their primary locus in the cortical area (Rule and Ambady 2008); there is physiological evidence for the existence of consciousness. Also there is reason to believe brain glycogen expenditure may be linked to these processes (Gailliot 2008).

THE RISE OF THE NEW UNCONSCIOUS PERSPECTIVE

Given that the psychoanalytic view was widely disparaged and that projective techniques were held in equal disregard for more than nine decades, it was not until the early 1980s that this characteristic dedication to consciousness began to erode. Using the PsychInfo database, publications that referred to topics of interest to "The New Unconscious" perspective were tracked from 1980 on. Although that perspective emerged in the early 1980s, it did not manifest itself with any meaningful frequency until the later 1990s (see Wittenbrink 2007). However, by 2000 there were more than 20 such publications listed and by 2005 over 90. This growth has been astronomical, and to date it appears to be increasingly expanding. Two primary reasons exist for the increase:

> The first is that implicit measures promise to address a long-standing and fundamental problem with standard self-report measures of attitudes: people do not necessarily tell the truth, when asked about their attitudes toward socially sensitive issues.
>
> A second important factor driving the interest in implicit measures concerns the popularity of the specific process argument on which implicit measures are based; namely that evaluations can occur automatically without any deliberation. Indeed, all contemporary accounts of how attitudes influence judgment and behavior argue that evaluations vary in the extent to which they are deliberate and effortful. . . . Attitude research has been paying increasing attention to the circumstances under which evaluations occur without deliberation (Wittenbrink 2007, 19).

THE CURRENT STATE OF AFFAIRS

Not all disciplines have absorbed the advent of research on the unconscious perspective in the same way and to the same degree. Social psychology, experimental psychology, and personality theory are at the forefront of the rise; organizational behavior is in process, but well behind the leaders (see Dane and Pratt 2007). Postmodernism as applied to organizational science acknowledges the modernist focus on rationality—a focus reflected in the expectancy theory of motivation and path-goal theory of leadership—but it fails to incorporate unconscious considerations. In fact it contends that "most contemporary theory and practice in organization science is still conducted within a modernist framework" (Gergen and Thatchenkery 2004, 234) and thus with a focus on rationality. Certainly "conscious/rationalist conceptions" have dominated (Skowronski, Carlston, and Hartnett 2008, 316) organization science; and they continue to do so.

Realistically one must accept the fact that the current state of affairs depends as much on the discipline that is being considered as it does on the evidence. Yet the evidence is incontrovertible. As Baumeister (2008) has indicated, "The processes that create these forms of free will may be biologically costly and therefore are only used occasionally, so that people are likely to remain only incompletely self-disciplined, virtuous, and rational" (14). As Bargh and Morsella (2008) put it, "The unconscious is not identifiably less flexible, complex, controlling, deliberative, or action-oriented than is its counterpart. . . . Research has demonstrated the existence of several independent unconscious behavioral guidance systems: perceptual, evaluative, and motivational. . . . Empirical tests have not been kind to the specifics of the Freudian model, though in broad-brush terms the cognitive and social psychological evidence does support Freud as to the existence of unconscious motivation and its potential to impact judgments and behavior. . . . Freud's historic importance in championing the powers of the unconscious mind is beyond any doubt" (73).

Accordingly we come down to the existence of both conscious and unconscious processes, and thus to some type of dual process theorizing. "Human reasoning has been characterized as an interplay between an automatic belief-based system and a demanding logic-based reasoning system" (De Neys 2006, 428). Such dual process theories come in several different varieties, but they always encompass some kind of unconscious process. The two systems can be in conflict with one another, but this is rarely the case. De Neys (2006, 433) concludes: "This study provides clear evidence that all reasoners have access to both an automatic, heuristic reasoning system and an executive, analytic reasoning system. In sum the reasoning systems differ, but the reasoner does not." I subscribe to such a view and it forms the basis of this presentation. Interestingly this dual process view represents a juncture of both the new unconscious perspective and that derived from projective techniques.

TERMINOLOGY AND FEATURES

As has become evident, there is a considerable variation in the terminology used to indicate unconscious processes, and conscious too. My own concern is to indicate how the advent of research on processes that extend beyond awareness has created changes in the evidential demands of our science. However, various writers have brought different terms to bear in speaking of such matters, and I have followed these leads on occasion as well. To be sure that we are on the same page here, I need to deal with these terminological differences. Other researchers, such as Scherer (2005), have faced this issue and proposed solutions as follows:

Unconscious	Conscious
implicit	explicit
automatic	controlled
effortless	effortful
schematic	conceptual/propositional

McClelland, Koestner, and Weinberger (1989) introduced the implicit-explicit differentiation and tied projective techniques to the former and self-report measures to the latter (see Miner 2008, Chapter 1). Implicit measures typically are said to have the same features as automatic (see De Houwer and Moors 2007).

Bargh (1994) describes the "four horsemen of automaticity" as efficiency, lack of awareness, lack of control, and lack of intention. These features are reiterated somewhat later by Lillard and Skibbe (2005). Yet Moors and De Houwer (2006) specify the following features for automaticity: unintentional, uncontrolled/uncontrollable, goal independent, autonomous, purely stimulus driven, unconscious, efficient, and fast; they argue that these features should be investigated separately to the extent possible. The major disparity here occurs with respect to goals. However, at a later point in writing about the features of automaticity, Moors and De Houwer (2007, 39) indicate that "attention may not only be directed by conscious goals, but also by unconscious goals." This dual emphasis is much more aligned with the empirical evidence.

In addition such terms as "executive control" or "executive functioning" are often used to refer to conscious processes (see Gailliot 2008). In short a wide range of terms are used in this literature; these terms are roughly correlated around unconscious and conscious, but they are not always used with great precision. This is a new area of research, and it has not yet had time to come to a highly specific descriptive terminology. Thus the reader should be alert to the diversity of terms and their uses.

ON MALCOLM GLADWELL'S *BLINK*

Malcolm Gladwell wrote a book entitled *Blink: The Power of Thinking without Thinking* (2005) that became a best seller; it and he have had wide exposure and these facts are worthy of some commentary.

Who Is Gladwell?

Gladwell served for a while on the staff of the *Washington Post* and later wrote for the *New Yorker.* He has written several best-selling books, but *Blink* is the only one that deals specifically with the unconscious. Gladwell views himself as a journalist and a storyteller; both are true. He is not an academic, and his training in psychology and organizational behavior is all of a self-taught nature. His stories tend to popularize, to simplify, and to synthesize the ideas of others, and in the process he does take some liberties. Although Gladwell is more a reflector of others' works, he carries out his journalistic feats in ways that make them very attractive to read. Biographical information on Gladwell is contained in Novotney (2008); an interview, dealing mostly with his approach to storytelling, appears in Gruber (2006).

What Is *Blink*?

As a book *Blink* is like a series of well-connected essays (Gladwell's stories). The central theme is the role of a cognitive phenomenon called thin-slicing—"the ability of our unconscious to find patterns in situations and behavior based on very narrow slices of experience" (Gladwell 2005, 23). In presenting this theme Gladwell espouses the view that people draw upon both conscious thought and unconscious processes depending on the situation; this is essentially the dual process view to which I subscribe in this volume, "that truly successful decision making relies on a balance between deliberate and instinctive thinking" (141).

Many of Gladwell's stories—so cleverly interwoven in *Blink*—deal with actual instances from the domain of this volume. There is considerable discussion of John Bargh and his priming research. The studies by Anthony Greenwald, Mahzarin Banaji, and Brian Nosek on the Implicit Association Test (IAT)—a particularly good example of thin-slicing—are treated at some length. The work of Silvan Tomkins and of Paul Ekman on reading emotions from facial expressions is explained. In these and many other instances human interest details are added to make the stories more compelling. This book is widely read, and accordingly should be placed in context for those who may have heard about it. Furthermore it is a good beginning for those who are as yet neophytes to empirical research on unconscious processes.

THE EVALUATIVE DIMENSION

Several different types of evaluation are brought to bear in writing the chapters of this volume.

Estimated Scientific Validity

The most appropriate source on this validity variable is Miner (2006b), Chapter 17 on methodology. Chapter 18 in that volume contains findings from the validity analysis as well. Table 17.1 presents the raw data. In the following chapters I have combined some of the theories to create types, and thus not always individual theories. The ordering of chapters within each category (motivation, leadership, decision making, systems, bureaucracy-related, and sociological) is determined by the validity rating running from 5 to 4 to 3; theories with an estimated validity of 2 or 1 are not included for discussion on the grounds that they either lack validity or have not been studied sufficiently to justify a higher rating. Where theories with similar titles are combined in a given chapter, the estimated scientific validity used is determined based on the particular type of theory deemed to be the most influential.

The validity estimates are my own, but whenever possible they are based on the opinions of knowledgeable scholars in the particular area. This means that they are based on reviews, on commentaries, and in particular on meta-analyses, as proposed by Locke and Latham (2004) in their first recommendation with regard to motivation theories. I have drawn upon descriptions of meta-analyses presented by experts such as Le, Oh, Shaffer, and Schmidt (2007). To combine studies and multiple meta-analyses I have used quality weighting to bring together "four point scales as practical and valuable, and up to nine points as useful in some circumstances" (Rosenthal and DiMatteo 2001, 67).

Miner (2007) has been devoted to the practical usefulness of a number of theories, and thus in the present book this aspect is given relatively little attention; the primary concern here is with validity.

Rated Importance of Theories

The importance ratings are treated as given by organizational behavior scholars in Miner (2006b). Again the methodology is considered in Chapter 17 and the related findings in Chapter 18. Table 17.1 presents the raw data. Table 18.1 contains data on how the importance ratings relate to validity; I present more detail in this regard in the chapters that follow.

Institutionalization Score

Miner (2006b) contains in Chapter 19 a presentation regarding the nature of institutionalization. The methodology of how this score was computed from the importance ratings is contained in Chapter 20, and Chapter 21 presents the findings. Table 21.1 takes up the specifics of the institutionalization scores and indicates which theories have indeed become institutionalized.

The Degree to Which Theories Are Conscious or Unconscious

This is a three-way description of the degree to which the type of theory can be categorized as conscious, unconscious, or balanced. The conscious designation is quite simple in that the theory does not at any point recognize or is not represented by unconscious factors; there may well be instances where I believe unconscious considerations could be brought to the fore, but the theory does not actually do this. In such cases numerous instances of rational, conscious ways of thought are typically in evidence. The literature in general defines the theory as conscious in nature, and self-report measures tend to confirm this classification. The unconscious designation is somewhat more forgiving in that only a limited description of the theory as unconscious is required. The measures actually employed may or may not reflect the unconscious specification. The key point here is that in addition to any rational explications, there is some indication that the theory recognizes unconscious processes.

The balanced description is between these two and clearly takes conscious and unconscious features into account in certain aspects. This becomes most difficult to score in distinguishing between the unconscious and balanced designations. However, the typical such theory possesses aspects that both recommend it and dismiss it, or in some few instances the theory has both conscious and unconscious considerations given priority at the same time and in contradistinction to one another. As we will see this way of classifying the theories by type requires looking into the nature of each specific theory; there are differences.

THE OPPOSING SIDE

Throughout this book, and in Miner (2008) as well, I espouse the positive side of unconscious processes and show how these processes are used, or might be used, to amplify our understanding of what have been assumed to be the more effective and valid theories of organizational behavior. However, in all honesty one has to admit that there is an opposing side to this view. In science there always seems to be an opposing side. I will accordingly devote this section to exploring this type of thought and to what has been said in criticism of the new unconscious perspective. Nevertheless, I do want to preface this critique with the following quote, reflecting my own conviction from a study of the research and literature overall: "Priming measures should, under most circumstances, provide an effective means to assess attitudes free of intentional distortions" (Wittenbrink 2007, 46).

On Partial Awareness

Kouider and Dupoux (2004) present evidence that they have identified a type of partial awareness based on a perceptual illusion. Partial awareness would appear to remove some results from the unconscious condition and place them in the conscious condition. However, it does not serve to explain away all unconscious priming; this phenomenon clearly does operate under the appropriate circumstances.

On Discrepancies between Implicit and Explicit Self-Esteem

Olson, Fazio, and Hermann (2007) also bring evidence to bear with regard to their critique. They indicate that discrepancies between implicit and explicit measures of self-esteem are a function of reporting tendencies, that a distinction must be made between awareness of one's attitudes and awareness of their influence. The authors certainly believe that limits to consciousness do exist, however, they do not believe that people are always aware of the influence of their automatic responses. "What they are more likely to lack is awareness of the influence that these automatically activated attitudes are exerting in any given judgment situation" (290).

On the Assumptions behind Implicit Measures

This article does not contain original empirical evidence; it is a think piece. The point addressed is that the validity of three assumptions with regard to unconscious processes should not be assumed. The particular assumptions that are placed in doubt are as follows:

1. Implicit measures reflect unconscious or introspectively inaccessible representations.
2. The major difference between implicit measures and self-reports is that implicit measures are resistant or less susceptible to social desirability.
3. Implicit measures reflect highly stable, older representations that have their roots in long-term socialization experiences (Gawronski, LeBel, and Peters 2007, 181).

These assumptions are not said to be incorrect, but their validity is viewed as uncertain; this is the case argued. To some degree this case is argued selectively without adequate attention to refuting data. In particular it is noteworthy that neither the McClelland, Koestner, and Weinberger (1989) findings nor any other sources of information on projective techniques are cited. There are other instances of questionable reporting (see for instances the incorrect view that implicit and explicit measures are indeed highly correlated when methodological errors are corrected). Elsewhere the lead author says "IAT performance is influenced by automatic and controlled processes" (Gawronski and Bodenhausen 2007, 279). This would seem to be directly in conflict with the stated Proposition 1. All in all, without evidence to the contrary, I find this presentation seriously lacking.

On the Indeterminacy of Valence

Charland (2005, 249) argues that "strictly speaking, there is no such thing as unconscious or nonconscious affect valence. There is no scientific sense in which valence can be said to reside intrinsically in mental or physical states that fall outside of the active range of attention." Such a thesis has long been the prevailing psychoanalytic view as well. Yet later Charland (2005, 249) says "there appear to be fixed and determinate unconscious affective processes in emotion experience . . . a sort of proto-valence but not valence itself. . . . Perhaps not all aspects of affect valence are equally permeable to attention." There appears to be a degree to which the author is backing away from his main thesis here.

But in the same book other authors do more than back away: They reject the idea that unconscious emotion is a non sequitur (see, for instance, Barrett 2005). Winkielman, Berridge, and Wilbarger (2005) present evidence, including some of their own, that argues convincingly for the operation of implicit valence. They say, "These data again suggest that the impact of affective stimuli on basic behavioral responses can be dissociated from conscious responses to the same stimuli," (345) and again, "We argued for the existence of verifiable but unconscious emotional reactions" (356).

On Sins in the Study of Unconscious Affect

This chapter in the same book, written by Clore, Storbeck, Robinson, and Centerbar (2005), is generally acknowledged to fall in "the opposing side" category. Yet it is introduced with the following: "most bodily, cognitive, and psychological processes occur unconsciously. Affective processes too are largely unavailable to consciousness" (385). As this quote suggests the seven sins are accordingly discussed with a degree of equivocality that often makes it difficult to follow the argument, and thus to understand where the authors stand. Terminological distinctions often serve to dilute the sins to an uncertain degree.

The seven sins are set forth as follows: "The goal was to be provocative in the faith that stirring things up is often useful. With more humility than our presumptuous title suggests, we hope that a critical stance toward some assumptions of our own and others may be helpful, as we collectively stumble toward a coherent understanding of emotion. . . . Our candidates for the seven sins" (384, 386) are:

1. There are unconscious emotions.
2. Unconscious emotional stimuli are stronger than conscious ones.
3. Conscious feelings cause liking.
4. Preferences precede inferences.
5. Expressive actions have fixed effects.
6. "Low route" stimulation causes human emotion.
7. Emotions occur too quickly to require appraisals.

Several quotes from the ensuing discussion should then be noted—

Unconscious emotion may simply be a catchall term to connote processes united only by not being conscious. (387)

Briefer, less intense stimulation can be registered without conscious awareness. (388)

Unconscious primes and other stimuli are weaker, not stronger than conscious ones. (390)

Some investigators . . . present compelling data that the affective guidance of attention occurs unconsciously. (393)

Affective reactions, even those that are presumed to be automatic and to reflect unconscious content, are contingent on the cognitive context. (399)

Although most emotional *processes* are unconscious, properly speaking, there are not unconscious emotions, per se. (403–404)

There is every reason to believe that conscious affect is more potent than unconscious affect. (404)

Emotions necessarily require appraisals, and these are typically fast, unconscious, and based on simple associations. (404)

Admittedly these quotes are given out of context, but together they do serve to make a point.

On Levels of Consciousness (and Unconsciousness)

Carroll Izard (2009), writing in the *Annual Review of Psychology,* is widely recognized as an authority on emotion. He defines levels of awareness as "ranging from phenomenal consciousness to access (verbally reportable) and reflective consciousness, which support the processes in higher-order cognition-emotion schemas" (3). "Feeling an emotion does not guarantee that it will be labeled, articulated, or sensed in reflective consciousness or at a high level of awareness" (6). "Emotion schemas are causal as mediating processes that consist of emotion and cognition continually interacting dynamically to influence mind and behavior" (10). Thus Izard takes a position that emotion feelings occur in some level of consciousness (in phenomenal consciousness), but not with certainty in the unconscious. "Emotion feelings can operate in phenomenal consciousness with little or no cognitive content" (13). Izard (2009) rejects most, but not all, of the conclusions reached in Barrett, Niedenthal, and Winkielman (2005).

Izard considers the idea of the unconscious to be vague and ill defined; he states that there is no consensus on the contents and functioning of the unconscious (17). As a result the idea of unconscious emotion comes down to a definitional issue. "An enormous amount of information processing proceeds very well in the realm of the unconscious, but I propose that the functionality of emotion feelings (that are not in access or reflective consciousness) might be explained better in terms of phenomenal or other levels of consciousness" (Izard 2009, 12–13). Thus, it is not the existence of the unconscious that is at issue, but the definition used with regard to emotions; the level of consciousness (or unconsciousness) brought to bear on what is known at the present time.

In any event this opposing position does not strike me as being as antagonistic to the unconscious perspectives as it might seem initially.

CONCLUSIONS

I take up a wide variety of topics in this introductory chapter. These are topics that need to be given consideration as we begin upon our journey. Initially I talk about the prevalence of conscious processes, then the rise of the unconscious perspective, and I end with an assessment of the current state of affairs. At this point the varied terminology that has come to permeate the field is discussed. The book *Blink* and its author Malcolm Gladwell are treated also as an early way into research on unconscious processes.

The next section takes up the ways in which I have evaluated the various theories considered. Much of this has been explained previously in Miner (2005, 2006a, 2006b, and 2007). However, new data are provided for the degree to which a theory is considered conscious, unconscious, or balanced.

The final section of this introduction is devoted to a discussion of six instances where the authors take an opposing view to my advocacy of unconscious processes. These are all the instances of this kind that I have been able to locate; there must be more, but I am not aware of them. In any event this listing should provide a good idea of where, and to what extent, problems are in evidence.

PART I

THEORIES OF MOTIVATION

EXPECTANCY THEORIES

Among the various expectancy theories, the one set forth by Vroom (1964) stands out on a number of grounds. It is rated in terms of validity at the five-star level (the highest) (see Miner 2005, Chapter 7). In the same source its importance rating is reported as 5.96, based on the judgments of organizational behavior specialists, and it is the only one among the expectancy theories that appears to have achieved institutional status (Miner 2006b). Meta-analyses have yielded consistent support (Miner 2005, 2007), as have extensive nonquantitative reviews. All in all the evidence for the validity of some version of expectancy theory, particularly the Vroom version, is quite impressive; to an only slightly lesser extent this support extends to the Porter and Lawler (1968) version as well.

EXPECTANCY THEORY AS A PREDOMINANTLY CONSCIOUS SET OF CONSTRUCTS

Vroom's theory and its various derivatives or variants are primarily a rational or conscious construction. There is no guarantee the calculation actually occurs as specified, but the reality provided by heuristics and bounded rationality clearly does achieve a result that closely approximates the theoretical expectations; people may not actually think as expectancy theory specifies, but they follow a process that yields essentially the same kind of validity.

Evidence for a Conscious Process

The idea of expectancy assumes that people think and express their motives in ways that take the probability of occurrence of an event into account; they have expectations with regard to the likelihood that things will happen, and they use these likelihood assumptions to reach conclusions with regard to what they should and will do. Thus various formulae are posited that require mathematical calculations, as for instance the following:

Motivation = Effort-to-performance expectancy × the sum of all operating factors (performance-to-outcome expectancies × their valences).

In writing regarding the theory more recently, Vroom (2005) has the following to say in this regard:

> I would make changes if I were to revise it today. . . . First and foremost I would certainly eliminate the mathematization and formalization of the theory. I was probably unduly influenced by the mathematical zeitgeist at Penn at the time. Unfortunately I believe that my mathematical formulation contributed to many ill-advised attempts to test the theory using measures lacking the ratio/scale properties necessary (254).

It is noteworthy that unconscious processes characteristically make little use of mathematical calculations (see Hassin 2005) in such a manner, thus once again reinforcing the highly rational nature of Vroom's expectancy theory as currently written.

The measurement procedures used in testing the theory also point to its preoccupation with conscious processes. Without exception, these have been of a self-report nature. In whatever form expectancy theory has taken, the constituent variables have been measured by questionnaires that are constituted of entirely conscious self-reports; no uses of projective techniques or other procedures that tap unconscious motives have been reported. Insofar as comprehensive personality indexes have been utilized, they continue to rely on self-report approaches—as for instance the "big five" traits (Judge and Ilies 2002).

The Rationality of Implications for Practice

In reviewing the implications of expectancy theory for practice, I conclude that the domain of the theory is limited to structured, rational, and conscious thought processes (Miner 2007, 77). In such a theory-friendly organization people are recognized and rewarded relative to the excellence of their performance, merit salary increases are an accurate reflection of relative performance, and the promotion system operates to help the best person to get to the top. Given the rational emphasis of the theory, individuals with an internal locus of control—those who believe that events in their lives are subject to their own influence—emerge as having particularly high motivation. The idea of selecting people to be congruent with an expectancy theory context receives strong support from research (Miller and Grush 1988).

Much of the work on the practical applications of expectancy theory has been provided not by Vroom, but by Edward Lawler; it is he who has given this work much of its rational thrust. Writing recently in this area (Worley and Lawler 2006), he has emphasized paying the person rather than the job, reinforcing a culture that values growth and personal development, and utilizing performance-based information systems. "Bonus systems can be particularly effective motivators during periods of change by establishing a clear line of sight between results and rewards" (20). Not all of what is said in this regard derives from expectancy theory, but much of it does, and thus continues the emphasis on rationality and conscious processes in the practical domain.

A New Vroom

Although Vroom has not to date, as of 2010, revised his version of expectancy theory, he has given hints as to the direction such a revision might take. In this connection he has the following to say:

> A new expectancy theory would have to acknowledge a "cognitive revolution" which has taken place in the field of psychology during the past several decades. I first became aware of an information-processing perspective to cognition through discussion with Herb Simon on my move to Carnegie in the 1960s. . . . To use Simon's language, [people] "satisficed," rather than optimized, searching until an alternative reaching a level of aspiration was found. Furthermore, they evaluated alternatives sequentially and at a relatively slow speed with no suggestion of the exhaustive multiplication over all outcomes built into my propositions. . . .
>
> The development of prospect theory (Kahneman, Slovic, and Tversky 1982) also exposed limitations of expectancy theory even in the realm of choice behavior. Human choices are led astray from subjective rationality by a number of identifiable heuristics and biases, including the manner in which the alternatives have been framed (Vroom 2005, 255).

A new Vroom would clearly tackle the realm of the unconscious, to which this book devotes itself, or at the very least he would attempt to deal with such issues. To his credit Vroom recognizes the need for work of this kind to redress the changes that have occurred over the past twenty-five years; yet he does not actually move to face the challenges that scientific change now presents.

CONSTRUCTS INTRODUCED BY EXPECTANCY THEORY VARIANTS BEYOND VROOM

Certain constructs have found their way into expectancy theory through routes other than those provided by Vroom. Historically one such construct preceded Vroom, and probably influenced him to some extent. This is the goal construct as introduced by Georgopoulos, Mahoney, and Jones (1957), a formulation that has been shown to have the capability to bring unconscious motivation into the human repertoire (Miner 2008). Unfortunately, however, this potential was not immediately recognized: In the particular study that involved goals they were measured via a self-report questionnaire that tapped into conscious processes only, thus leaving unconscious goal setting entirely outside of the theoretical loop.

A second construct that moves beyond Vroom, and at the same time brings in the possibility of unconscious motivation, is the introduction of role perceptions into the theoretical mix. Constructs of this kind are inherent in the formulations of Porter and Lawler (1968) and in the version of expectancy theory set forth by Graen (1969). In both instances, roles, and perceptions of them, are central to the theoretical formulations. Unconscious motivation comes in by virtue of the fact that roles which establish job behavior (and motivation) can be a product of social constructions regarding how individuals should act in a particular position even without being aware of the role prescriptions acting on them (Miner 2008). Unfortunately once again the theorists used self-reports in testing their views, and thus by relying entirely on conscious measures negated any possible unconscious factors that might have been involved and unearthed.

We will return to the matter of how goals and roles may manifest themselves at the unconscious level as we take up these matters in much greater detail in subsequent chapters.

WAYS IN WHICH UNCONSCIOUS CONSIDERATIONS MIGHT INFLUENCE VROOM'S CONSTRUCTS

On page 101 of Miner (2005a), Figure 7.2 presents the basic expectancy theory model. The variables considered all involve some perceived probability (or expectancy) to be used in the calculations, with the exception of approach-avoidance valence. This leaves only valence as a possible source of unconscious factors—either motives or emotions. Vroom (2005) indicates that he originally borrowed his ideas of valence, and force as well, from Lewin, but in this instance they became attached to outcomes specifically.

Conscious Valence and Emotions

Both Lewin and Vroom were concerned with a valence that was of emotional origin and that yielded either a positive or a negative thrust. As used, valence was a broad-brush construct that served to summarize the directionality of a process but did little to specify the actual nature of what was involved. This kind of approach-avoidance distinction has been found in a wide range of areas. Early work with the Thematic Apperception Test (TAT) focused on the need for affiliation and explored how motivation of this kind either served to attract people to one another or brought about an avoidance response (sociophilia vs. sociophobia).

> The neurobiological evidence provides a possible reason for the consistent emergence of the approach-avoidance distinction in motivation. . . . [This] distinction has a long and prolific history; it emerges in several theories of motivation and goal processes; and physiological evidence supports the existence of neuroanatomical correlates for it. The two systems are functionally independent of one another and thus are correlated with different environmental stimuli and may operate through different processes (Gable and Strachman 2008, 564–565).

For many years identification of the emotions involved in approach-avoidance valence was achieved by asking people to describe their feelings. Thus the existence of emotion was dependent on conscious processes (Barrett, Mesquita, Ochsner, and Gross 2007); unconscious emotion was not a contributor to scientific knowledge regarding how emotions and valence operate. Research evidence, obtained largely from this type of consciously driven study, yielded a conclusion that a negativity bias predominated, and this bias emerged as early as the second half of the first year of life (Vaish, Grossmann, and Woodward 2008):

> Negative stimuli are hypothesized to carry greater informational value than positive stimuli and thus to require greater attention and cognitive processing. . . . Adults spend more time looking at negative than positive stimuli, perceive negative stimuli to be more complex than positive ones, and form more complex cognitive representations of negative than of positive stimuli. . . . When making judgments, people consistently weight the negative aspects of an event or stimulus more heavily than the positive aspects (Kahneman and Tversky 1984, 383).

The negativity bias is thought to serve the evolutionarily adaptive purpose of helping us safely explore the environment while appropriately avoiding harmful situations (395).

Unconscious Emotions

More recent studies have shown clearly that unconscious emotions of a kind powerful enough to alter behavior without reaching the level of awareness, even when conscious processes are directed to feelings, do exist (see Winkielman and Berridge 2004). Thus valence can be a result of unconscious emotions (Ruys and Stapel 2008; Ferguson, Hassin, and Bargh 2008). Some event or stimulus, in most cases external, triggers an emotion; that emotion in turn automatically yields a complex set of changes in the brain and body that constitutes an emotional response (Barrett, Ochsner, and Gross 2007). Thus through a process of unconscious priming, which operates so quickly as to be incapable of activating consciousness, various consequences for subsequent judgment, emotion, and behavior are set off (Ferguson 2007). Such effects may be activated at as quickly as 100 ms. (Willis and Todorov 2006). The emotion created in this way can produce biases by virtue of an overweighting of emotion-congruent events, with emotion acting in lieu of information (Crano and Prislin 2006; Peters, Hess, Västfjäll, and Auman 2007). In addition to priming indexes, similar measures may be obtained from pop out, inattentional blindness, redundant target presentations, and masking (deGelder 2005).

Brain Mechanisms Involved

The part of the brain most likely to be activated by emotion is the amygdala (Phelps 2006); this is equally true of unconscious emotion (Ito and Cacioppo 2007; Kensinger 2007; Cunningham, Van Bavel, and Johnson 2008). Neuroimaging has been extremely helpful in providing information in this regard. This line of research provides continuing evidence for a negativity bias but now extends it to unconscious emotion. Much of this research has utilized the emotional expression in faces to manipulate the experimental variables (Olsson and Phelps 2007). Automatic emotions thus produced tend to be more context dependent than more deliberately generated conscious attitudes and valences (Ferguson and Bargh 2007).

The extent to which consciousness is distinct from unconscious process, and thus whether the two run together in one continuous phenomenon, is a matter of some debate and uncertainty at this point. There is evidence of both continuous and discontinuous processing. The evidence favoring the former provides a more parsimonious view, but there are experimental findings that suggest a bifurcation in neural activity that underlies the distinction between conscious and unconscious processing. Thus conscious access could be characterized by dynamic phenomena, which might ultimately be described mathematically using catastrophe theory (Sergent and Dehaene 2004, 727).

The State of Knowledge vis-à-vis Valence

Among the expectancy theory variables, valence is particularly likely to yield advances in the development of the theory, but the research evidence from the "new unconscious" perspective remains too disjointed to indicate exactly what course such theory development might take. In Chapter 27 of Book 5 within this series (Miner 2008) we emphasized that the "I don't know" response to questions in science can indeed be advantageous to the science involved;

in the early stages of the development of an area it becomes essential. These are the stages at which unconscious motivation and emotion are now operating. Thus this field consists of a variety of bits of information that derive from segmented research that is not yet tied together adequately by coherent theory. Surely the "new unconscious" perspective does not lack for theory intended to achieve such integration, but validated theory is not yet sufficient to lead the way to understanding.

Let me provide some examples: In one instance it has been found that when making evaluations people automatically (unconsciously) conclude that bright objects are good (i.e., have positive valences) and dark objects are bad (have negative valences); any mismatch between color and valence interferes with affective categorization (Meier, Robinson, and Clore 2004, 85).

In another research study within the context of "terror management," where participants are exposed to stimuli intended to elicit the contemplation of death and morbidity, an unconscious search for pleasant, positive emotion actually ensued. As people approach advancing age (and death) their cognitive processes shift to an emphasis on positive emotion; they unconsciously adopt a defensive stance to prevent the terror of thinking about the reality of their situation. The automatic system searches for happy thoughts—immediately and beyond awareness, contrary to any prediction of a conscious reaction of emotional distress (DeWall and Baumeister 2007, 989). Thus an emotional contradiction, or bias, is introduced into valence calculations.

It is hard to reconcile these bits of research information. They stand alone at present, waiting to fill in the dots with many more bits of research information. The relationships involved remain in search of valid theories; for the present we are left with a whole host of "I don't know" questions. Faced with this situation, "some researchers prefer to avoid theorizing about emotion altogether" (Barrett, Niedenthal, and Winkielman 2005, 17).

THE PLACEBO EFFECT

> The archetypical event occurs in a medical setting. A physician gives a patient a pill, that unbeknownst to the patient, is merely a sugar pill. This is the placebo. Presently, the patient's health improves, apparently because of the belief that the pill was a pharmacological agent, effective for the condition. This is the placebo effect. . . . A placebo effect is a genuine psychological or physiological effect in a human or another animal, which is attributable to receiving a substance or undergoing a procedure but is not due to the inherent powers of that substance or procedure. . . . The placebo effect is a genuine and potentially important phenomenon (Stewart-Williams and Podd 2004a, 326).

An example from a meta-analysis of nineteen studies of antidepressant medications' placebo effect was a d value of .79. Such responses are produced in large part because the recipient expects them. They can be explained equally well by expectancy theory and by classical conditioning. In either case the placebo effect clearly results from conscious expectancies, but "there is also evidence that some placebo effects in humans are not mediated by conscious cognition. As such a complete model of the placebo effect must include both noncognitive learning mechanisms and conscious expectancies" (Stewart-Williams and Podd 2004a, 338).

Controversy

Kirsch (2004) has downplayed the importance of nonconscious learning processes in placebo responses; such effects are said to be relatively rare. Yet Stewart-Williams and Podd (2004b) continue to contend that they are important. "There are likely to be limits to the extent that cognition can override automatic, nonconscious processes" (345). The very fact that humans have such nonconscious capabilities would seem to suggest a degree of significance. Thus within expectancy theory meaningful degrees of unconscious phenomena do appear to exist, extending beyond valence considerations.

Medical Theory and the Placebo Response

Richard Kradin (2008), in developing his theory of the placebo effect, provides evidence for such a position. He provides extensive data to support both the fact that the placebo effect is real and that it is associated with unconscious processes. Kradin notes that in the studies of antidepressant medication, the brains of the placebo responders showed changes in activity comparable to what was found in the medicated group. He cites evidence that placebos have proved therapeutically effective 35 percent of the time and that sham surgeries when used as placebos have worked just as well as the completed surgical procedures themselves.

Conscious expectancies and behavioral conditioning are credited with placebo effects; a large number of physiological and anatomical phenomena are thought to be involved in placebo responses, including the operation of various opioid pathways and the activation of brain regions, specifically the amygdala (see also Price, Finniss, and Benedetti 2008). With regard to his medical theorizing Kradin (2008, 109) says, "Aspects of what will be proposed find direct support in observation, whereas others are more speculative," and he typically fails to tie specific findings together, noting only similar effects and parallel findings. He notes that the proposed model is explanatory but clearly lacks detail; thus the Kradin theory invokes a number of phenomena that should be considered in dealing with placebos but at the same time fails to develop a fully integrated medical theory. Yet the theory clearly and repeatedly introduces unconscious processes to explain placebo effects (Kradin 2008, 133, 241). Accordingly it provides a good example of how the unconscious may operate in the production of expectancies.

CONCLUSIONS

As indicated at the beginning of this chapter, expectancy theory (the Vroom version) has an estimated validity of five stars and an importance rating (as given by organizational behavior scholars) of 5.96. When the second value is divided by the first, the result is a value of 1.19, suggesting that the importance ratings tend to overestimate the presumed validity of the theory.

Expectancy theory is shown to be a predominantly conscious or rational theory. However, the theory is vulnerable to unconscious processes and would benefit from being studied with measures of this type. This is particularly true in the area of valence. Also the placebo effects imply that some indexes of expectancy may be activated unconsciously.

CHAPTER 2

GOAL-SETTING THEORY

Goal-setting theory is rated at the five-star level on validity (Miner 2005, Chapter 10) and is included among the eleven theories that have become institutionalized (Miner 2006b). Its importance rating is a hefty 5.97 based on the assessments provided by seventy-one organizational behavior specialists. A large number of meta-analyses have been reported, almost all yielding support for the formulation of goal-setting theory; this is what might be expected given that Locke and Latham (2004, 389) strongly endorse the "use of the results of existing meta-analyses to integrate valid aspects of extant theories." Other, less quantitative evaluations are equally supportive of the theory. Although the Locke and Latham (1990) presentation is by far the most prominent in the goal-setting domain, there exist alternatives.

GOAL-SETTING THEORY IN THE CONTEXT OF CONSCIOUS
AND UNCONSCIOUS MOTIVES

It would be difficult to argue that goal-setting theory has not adopted unconscious motivation as an essential ingredient, particularly given the findings from Stajkovic, Locke, and Blair (2006) as reported in Miner (2008, Chapter 2). Over the history of the theory, however, there has been considerable variability on this score. Given that the authors have frequently advocated attention to unconscious factors, and provided research support for this position, one would have to come down on the side of unconscious motivation as a distinctive factor in goal-setting theory. Yet the authors' writings have not always been consistent in this regard, suggesting some degree of ambivalence. Let us start with the evidence for unconscious processes within the theory.

Recent Advocacy of Unconscious Processes

Most of the endorsement of unconscious processes seems to have come about as a consequence of the research by Stajkovic, Locke, and Blair (2006). The first presentation of these findings that I am aware of was at a Society for Industrial and Organizational Psychology (SIOP) meeting in 2005. From 2004 on there was a burst of advocacy on this score (Locke and Latham 2004, 2005, 2006; Latham and Pinder 2005; Latham 2007; Locke 2007). In discussing Sigmund Freud's contributions, Locke (2007, 889) states, "I believe that there is evidence for the phenomenon of repression, but this has to be detached from the rest of the theory." Thus the commitment to unconscious processes seems quite pronounced at this point.

Also certain alternatives to the Locke/Latham theorizing would seem to foster interpretation in terms of unconscious factors. Perceptual control theory seems to introduce findings which are best explained by virtue of priming and the unconscious motives thus incorporated in the goal-setting process (see Vancouver, Thompson, and Williams 2001; Vancouver, Thompson, Tischner, and Putka 2002; Bandura and Locke 2003), although this is not the position Locke takes on the issue. See Miner (2005) for a discussion on this matter.

This same tendency to foster an interpretation of goal setting in terms of unconscious processes is manifest in Kayes's (2005) description of what has happened as mountain climbers pursued the goal of conquering Mt. Everest:

> I now believe the climbers and other groups I studied pursued goals to their own detriment because of an inherent limitation in the goal-setting process itself. The destructive pursuit of goals emerges from idealized features. . . . When the setters identify too closely with the future goals, the normally functional process of goal setting goes awry. . . . Goals allow leaders to take chances, justify risky behavior, and avoid normal accountability. . . . Even well-intended goals carry unintended consequences, [while] stringent and demanding goals may actually encourage unethical behavior. . . . The unbridled pursuit of idealized goals often leads to obsessive destruction. . . . The unintended consequences of these actions deserve greater attention (392–399).

In situations such as this, goal-setting theory may foster not only unconscious motivation (unintended consequences), but also obsessive destruction. Outcomes of this kind are not exactly what Locke and Latham intended to encourage; yet they can reflect the operation of unconscious factors.

Unconscious Factors in Goal Setting over the Years

Goal-setting theory had its origins in the mid-1960s, although at that point in time it could hardly be said to qualify as a theory. Yet early on (Bryan and Locke 1967) subconscious goals were envisioned, "This goal-setting can vary widely in the degree to which it is conscious or subconscious, explicit or implicit . . . but once the goal is set, it is argued that effort and performance level will be regulated by and with reference to this goal" (260). After this, few references to unconscious goal-setting are to be found in the writing of Locke, or Latham either. But such references do occur, although typically as an aside, referring to "automatic" or as "automatized" behavior (Locke and Latham 1990). By 2002, influenced by the literature on the "new unconscious," more direct statements on the subject began to emerge—"There can be no doubt that the subconscious is a storehouse of knowledge and values beyond that which is in focal awareness at any given time" (Murphy 2001). "People can take action without being fully aware of what is motivating them or what stored knowledge is affecting their choices. The lack of focus on the subconscious is a limitation of goal-setting theory" (Locke and Latham 2002, 708). And indeed up to that point, and perhaps a couple of years later, the theory had little to say on the subject of unconscious factors. However, a recent major study by Shantz and Latham (2009) returns to unconscious goal setting via the priming manipulation, with results paralleling those of Stajkovic, Locke, and Blair (2006).

Conscious Goal Setting

The guiding formulation during the early years of goal-setting theory went as follows (Miner 2007, 113):

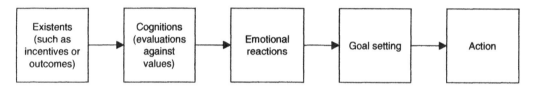

Here the person cognitively compares the existents against standards established by relevant values; the process runs off in a completely rational and conscious manner. Practical applications are described in a comparable way, using self-reports as the method of measurement and multiplication calculations to establish priorities among goals.

Just as goals and intentions are consciously held and processed, task strategies are introduced to plan out ways to deal with tasks, and in particular complex tasks. The bonding that occurred between social learning theory, social information processing, self-efficacy, and goal-setting theory served to further emphasize the commitment to rational thought (see Bandura 1982, 1997).

Furthermore, during a period when unconscious motivation was establishing itself elsewhere as a sound component of goal-setting theory, a number of articles and chapters appeared emphasizing the ties to conscious thought, and typically ignoring unconscious processes (Avolio and Locke 2002; Locke 2003, 2004; Shane, Locke, and Collins 2003; Latham and Locke 2006; Locke and Baum 2007; Quigley, Tesluk, Locke, and Bartol 2007). Perhaps this is a function of coming at a phenomenon from different directions and points of view, but it would seem to indicate a substantial degree of ambivalence.

Individual Differences

Over the years, as goal setting has evolved, it has moved from a position that served largely to ignore individual differences to a rather marked degree of commitment to them (see Miner 2005). This trend raises the possibility that unconscious processes may become involved; theories such as those of Maslow, McClelland, and Miner, which do involve unconscious aspects to varying degrees, are securely integrated into goal-setting formulations (see Figure 10.2 on page 118 of Miner 2007).

As goal-setting theory has moved toward individual differences, it has made efforts to adopt certain projective techniques as well (specifically, the Thematic Apperception Test [TAT] and the Miner Sentence Completion Scale [MSCS]), although to my knowledge neither Locke nor Latham has actually learned how to score either of these procedures. This has not been a very successful effort, and accordingly there has been little, if any, contribution to knowledge from this source, but it does represent an additional manifestation of the unconscious thrust in goal-setting theory. Let me refer the reader to Miner (2008), especially pages 12 (TAT) and 331–332 (MSCS) for confirmatory data on how these measures may fail.

ON CONSCIOUS PROCESSES AND THEIR RELEVANCE FOR GOAL SETTING

"No one yet has provided a convincing answer to the question of why we have consciousness and neither will we" (Dijksterhuis, Chartrand, and Aarts 2007, 113). Yet it clearly is a fact that we do have consciousness, and goal setting often is involved in that process. Locke and Latham, although accepting unconscious goals, are somewhat predisposed toward conscious goal setting; others have demonstrated a similar proclivity (De Houwer and Moors 2007). Furthermore this goal-setting process is widely dispersed across disciplines, and activities in one area tend to be quite independent of those in another (see Elliott and Fryer 2008). I believe that, even when restricted to the conscious domain, the Locke/Latham formulations might benefit from extension into other ways of thinking about goal setting.

Mastery Goals

> When pursuing performance goals, people try to validate their ability for outperforming peers, and so they define success versus failure with normative standards. When pursuing mastery goals, they instead try to develop their ability, and so they define success versus failure with self-referential standards. . . . Performance goals should produce outcomes similar to or worse than mastery goals, but never better (Dweck and Leggett 1988). . . . Studies typically show that mastery and performance goals are uncorrelated. . . . The two goals may produce independent effects on separate outcomes (e.g., grades and interest) (Senko, Durik, and Harackiewicz 2008, 100–101).

Although Locke and Latham have given performance goals considerable attention, they have not devoted nearly as much research and thought to mastery goals; my belief is that thus drawing upon certain formulations from the field of education would yield considerable benefit, and it would extend their treatment of learning goals, as well as perhaps help deal with obsessive performance goals.

Possible Selves

Possible selves include alternatives to a person's current self; such imaged alternatives may be in the form of what one hopes to become, or they may represent undesirable selves that are feared because they could involve something that the person might become. Selves of this kind can serve to motivate a change in behavior and establish commitment to goals. In much the same way, "counterfactuals involve thoughts about more positive selves that one just missed becoming or more negative selves that one just managed to avoid becoming" (Lockwood and Pinkus 2008, 253). Goal setting that introduces these kinds of possible selves can well have a substantial influence on the goals that result.

UNCONSCIOUS PROCESSES

A number of ways in which unconscious processes can operate to affect goal setting have been established through research. Although the authors of the theory have conducted their own research on the subject, and have contemplated implications of the research for their formulations, it is still true that any real integration of unconscious considerations with goal-setting theory remains to be accomplished in the future (see Latham 2007). I will try, however, to point up some of the directions such as integration might take.

Priming

Much of the research on unconscious factors in goal setting has involved some variant of a priming design. Although I have reviewed how such designs operate (see Miner 2008, Chapter 2), it may prove helpful to discuss another example here:

> Participants in this experiment were first given the task of solving scrambled sentences; unscrambled, these sentences included positive or negative personality traits (e.g., reckless vs. adventurous). Afterward, participants were given a short description of a person named "Donald." This description was ambiguous, as some of Donald's deeds (e.g., climbing Mt. McKinley) could be construed as either adventurous or reckless. The outcome variable of interest was participants' impression of Donald. As expected, when participants' were primed with positive traits (adventurous), they reported a favorable impression of Donald; however, when they were primed with negative traits (reckless), they reported unfavorable impressions of Donald. Clearly, the activation of the negative and positive concepts prepared, or laid the groundwork, for participants' interpretation of Donald's behavior and the resulting first impression.

Out of such situations, abstract trait primes produce assimilative first impressions, thus supporting the prime introduction; exemplar trait primes (of figures such as Adolf Hitler or Mohandas Gandhi) tend to produce contrasting first impressions (and thus the opposite of what was primed) (Weisbuch, Unkelbach, and Fiedler 2008, 290–291, 295). These outcomes exhibit some variability and cannot always be expected, since there are a number of moderators that may enter in, but this represents the typical result.

Through priming processes the whole panoply of goal operations can be shown to occur outside of conscious awareness (Fitzsimons and Bargh 2004); this is true even of cognitive processes such as memory and attention. Nonconscious goals can be activated by environmental cues and then proceed to govern cognition, emotion, and actions.

Implementation Intentions

Implementation intentions involve the use of if-then plans that indicate how a goal is to be realized; they create heightened accessibility. "By forming implementation intentions people can strategically switch from conscious and effortful action initiation (guided by goal intentions) to having their goal-directed actions effortlessly elicited by the specified situational cues" (Gollwitzer, Bayer, and McCulloch 2005, 488); a mental link is formed involving a particular future situation and a goal-directed response. Thus both conscious and unconscious factors operate when implementation intentions are set in motion, and accordingly control of behavior is delegated to situational cues. The automatic processes are not available to awareness (Bargh 1990; Gollwitzer, Parks-Stamm, Jaudas, and Sheeran 2008). In this way attentional resources are preserved for alternative goal-directed activities; also people can protect their goal activities from becoming prey to adverse self-states. Thus putting implementation intentions in place can serve to facilitate many aspects of goal setting. The Locke/Latham theory should benefit from giving such matters considerable attention, especially on complex tasks.

Goal Shielding

As with implementation intentions, goal shielding may operate to protect goals to which an individual is highly committed so that in such instances the importance of a goal is enhanced (Shah and Kruglanski 2008). Emotional states can serve to advance goal shielding, as in the case of anxiety, or hinder it, as in the case of depression. Playing tennis may inhibit jogging in that both activities implement the superordinate goal of keeping in shape; it depends on the individual's specific goal structure. All these processes can occur outside a person's awareness, and thus unconsciously.

Significant benefits may be achieved by priming alternative goals. "Goal shielding may serve important self-regulatory functions in that it has distinct consequences for how intensely goals are pursued and how likely they are to be attained (Shah 2005, 12).

Environmental Goal Activation

Environmental goal pursuit in the presence of unconscious factors may be depicted as follows:

If a goal is activated often in a particular environment, then aspects of that environment are likely to become linked to the goal—activating one serves to activate the others (Chartrand, Dalton, and Cheng 2008). Thus, aspects of the environment serve in lieu of semantic associates to trigger and consequently prime goal activation in unconscious memory.

Indeed, this kind of nonconscious goal processing can facilitate learning of completely novel environments (Eitam, Hassin, and Schul 2008). Accordingly this may become an "adaptive way of ensuring effective goal pursuit even under new, complex, or difficult circumstances" (Bargh, Gollwitzer, Lee-Chai, Barndollar, and Trötschel 2001, 1025); the regulation of goal pursuit is shifted from conscious to unconscious operation and behaves much as with conscious processes (Hassin 2005). Consequently through nonconscious control people are allowed to flexibly adapt their behavior and thought to their environments; the amygdala has been implicated in mobilizing this flexibility (Cunningham, Van Bavel, and Johnsen 2008).

Goal Contagion

Goal contagion occurs when an individual has an existing goal activated unconsciously by another person in the environment who possesses the same goal; in this way priming occurs

(Aarts, Dijksterhuis, and Dik 2008). Accordingly goals are inferred from others' actions; the goal to help other people may be transferred in this way, for instance. Normally such priming serves to accentuate a goal, thus strengthening it.

However, exposing people to negative goal-related cues, as in the presence of negative affect, can operate to thwart goal contagion; accordingly goal contagion is not always inevitable. It all depends on how similarity processes align themselves, and thus on whether nonconscious mimicry occurs (Chartrand, Maddux, and Lakin 2005; Markman and Gentner 2005).

Counteractive Control

Counteractive control may be exercised consciously, but also without awareness. It "is exercised only when there is a threat to important long-term goals, when these goals are achievable, before rather than after the achievement of these goals, and when social controls are absent. . . . exercising self-control in one task depletes a person's ability to exercise self-control in a subsequent task" (Trope and Fishbach 2005, 554–555). Only when important goals are at issue do counteractive controls come into play; they tend to become unconscious with repeated and successful employment (Fishbach and Trope 2008). Goal shielding may well be involved on occasion; the mechanism that is activated is set in motion typically when low-order temptations intervene in carrying out high-order intentions.

ADDENDUM ON NEGATIVE EFFECTS OF GOAL SETTING

Toward the beginning of this chapter I noted certain negative effects of goal setting that appeared to stem from unconscious factors. Very recently this tendency has reemerged with a vengeance (see Ordóñez, Schweitzer, Galinsky, and Bazerman 2009a) and has created considerable controversy (Locke and Latham 2009). As Locke and Latham point out, the original article relied heavily on anecdotal evidence, and selected incidents of this type cannot be appropriately applied to test theory. However, they can be used to construct theory, and there is indeed some movement in that direction by Ordóñez et al.

I am reminded here of the Spreier, Fontaine, and Malloy (2006) article on the destructive effects of achievement motivation (see Chapter 4 in this volume). Also I remember a conversation with Ed Locke and Gary Latham in which we planned a publication highlighting the negative effects of management by objectives (MBO)—a publication that somehow never reached fruition. Perhaps, building on the various sources involved, it may be helpful to broaden the issue and construct a general theory of the negative effects of motivational procedures, not just goal setting. Such a theory would, however, need to be testable; for it to work I submit that unconscious motivation must be invoked. Strangely neither of the sets of antagonists raises this issue. In particular I wonder why it is not incorporated by Locke and Latham, given their past involvement with unconscious motivation research.

CONCLUSIONS

Goal-setting theory comes in with a validity rating at the five-star level and an importance rating of 5.97; this is what was indicated early in this chapter. Dividing the second figure by the first one obtains a ratio of 1.19, the same as was reported by Vroom's expectancy theory. Thus again it appears that the importance rating overrates the theory to a degree as an index of validity.

I have designated goal-setting theory as being largely of the unconscious type based on the evidence extending over many years. This is not to say that, consistent with the theme of this book, it does not incorporate much on conscious motivation as well. This latter, conscious process could be extended into new types of goal setting. Also the theory might move more broadly into the unconscious domain; this might include research on implementation intentions, goal shielding, environmental goal activation, goal contagion, counteractive control, and negative effects of goal setting.

CHAPTER 3

KURT LEWIN'S SOCIAL PSYCHOLOGY

Kurt Lewin's influence extends well beyond organizational behavior; it has been particularly significant in various areas of psychology, including especially personality theory and social psychology. The overlap with organizational behavior came toward the end of Lewin's life and was most pronounced in the area of social psychology. This work was devoted primarily to the analysis of group processes and to action research (Lewin 1948). Consonant with Lewin's wide recognition, he is counted among those whose writings have been institutionalized by organizational behavior, and his importance rating averages at 5.31. I have given his theory a four-star validity rating, just below the level attained by the previous scholars. His advocacy of democratic group processes and participative management falls somewhat short of what might be hoped for. Meta-analyses of his ideas on leadership sometimes match expectations (in the case of a laissez-faire style—see Eagly, Johannesen-Schmidt, and van Engen 2003) but sometimes do not (in the area of participative management—see Sagie 1994; Locke, Alavi, and Wagner 1997). All in all within organizational behavior this represents a distinguished contribution. Details on Lewin's work are contained in Miner (2005, Chapter 3; 2006b, Chapter 8; and 2007, Chapter 3).

CONSCIOUS THOUGHT

Although Lewin made major contributions to personality theory (see Hall and Lindzey 1957), he appears to have been uninfluenced by psychoanalysis or any other approach that included unconscious factors. His primary orientation within psychology was to Gestalt psychology. Thus his predisposition was toward conscious thought; along with many similar formulations, he viewed behavior as primarily a function of conscious intentions—certainly his views on level of aspiration are of this nature. Yet recent meta-analyses have shown that a medium to large change in intention (d = .66) is joined by a small to medium change in behavior (d = .36) (Webb and Sheeran 2006). The discrepancy suggests a major role for unconscious factors in addition to conscious. As the authors conclude, "The present findings also suggest, however, that future behavior change efforts might do well to give greater consideration to nonintentional routes to action such as prototype perceptions (e.g. Gibbons, Gerrard, and Lane 2003) and automotives (Gollwitzer and Bargh 2005)" (263).

That Lewin may have been unduly concerned with conscious processes is attested to by the recent literature on his work which emphasizes his use of group decision, self-management, changing stereotypes, resistance to change, and leadership training that facilitates new thinking (see Coghlan and Jacobs 2005; Burnes 2007).

ADDING IN UNCONSCIOUS PROCESSES

Lewin (1951) stressed that a person cannot give or induce in another person any goal not already possessed; thus goals are not capable of activation unconsciously from scratch, but existing goals may be primed by aspects of the environment. Accordingly all features of goal setting noted in Chapter 2 of this volume may be applied here as well. The level of aspiration formulations is particularly implicated.

Group Norms

Change processes involving groups were a major concern for Lewin. Studies of group norms regarding absenteeism behavior, and the development of an absence culture within a work group, are exactly the kind of thing on which he would have focused (see, for example, Bamberger and Biron 2007). However, he did not consider the role that unconscious factors may play in the transmission of group norms in such situations. His theory of how change processes can be affected by consideration of what we now know about developments outside the realm of awareness surely would have benefited from the current research. It appears that much of the transmission of group norms from environmental cues to individual group members occurs unconsciously. People typically have no understanding of why they acquiesce to norms and the dictates of culture (Fitzsimons and Bargh 2004), but priming studies indicate that research of this kind is directly relevant.

Action Research and Sensitivity Training

Lewin created both sensitivity training and action research; both represent possible routes to collaborative leadership and group decision making (see Raelin 2006). Sensitivity training in particular was a very effective way to unfreeze members of a group; it got them to think in very different and new ways about group interaction. Perhaps its effectiveness at unfreezing was its own undoing, but there seems little doubt, in any event, that it unleashed many unconscious processes. Unfortunately research that would deal with these processes in detail has not been conducted, nor has it been of concern either to "the new unconscious" researchers or to sensitivity training advocates. However, the matter of how this type of training affects and unleashes factors outside of awareness certainly would be an important area for scientific investigation in the future.

Leadership Climates and the Conditional Reasoning Approach to Aggression

Lewin's leadership climate research produced mixed results in the authoritarian group on manifestations of aggression—in some cases aggression was frequent and in other cases it was not. Democratic leadership produced mid-range levels of aggression; laissez-faire leadership was associated with rather high levels of aggression. Overall, the findings did not accord well with the hypotheses and were in need of explanation.

Evidence in this regard is provided by a recently evolved technique to assess unconscious aggressive propensity (James and Mazerolle 2002) using the conditional reasoning approach. This approach relies on four propositions:

1. Aggressive individuals often engage in the use of implicit reasoning biases to enhance the rational appeal of their aggressive behavior.
2. Reasoning based on justification mechanisms for aggression is often not convincing or logically persuasive to nonaggressive individuals.
3. The proclivity to see reasoning based on justification mechanisms as logically more persuasive than reasoning based on more conventional assumptions can be measured indirectly through a modification of traditional inductive reasoning problems.
4. A propensity to select alternatives (over multiple conditional reasoning problems) based on implicit cognitive biases that enhance the rational appeal of aggression (i.e. justification mechanisms) indicates an "implicit cognitive readiness" to engage in some form of aggression in the future (139–151).

Thus a defensive rationale emphasizing rationalization defined in terms of justification mechanisms is utilized. These latter are specified through the identification of six biases by James and Mazerolle (2002)—hostile attribution, derogation of target, retribution, victimization by powerful others, potency, and social discounting.

Items present alternatives in terms of the usual multiple choice format, but without using self-reports. Examples of aggressive responses are:

1. Using a stem comparing American and Japanese cars—
   American carmakers built cars to wear out 15 years ago so that they could make a lot of money selling parts.
2. Using a stem citing the saying "an eye for an eye" and asking for the biggest problem with this—
   People have to wait until they are attacked before they can strike (149).

Initial evidence on reliability seems quite satisfactory and suggests a value in the low .80s. Validity is given for eight studies and has a median value of .43; for the four predictive studies, this value is .36 (James and Mazerolle 2002, 156–157). A subsequent report (Bing, Stewart, Davison, Green, McIntyre, and James 2007) presents a similar reliability but notes only five validity studies, two of which are new; here the median validity was .38. At about the same time validities for eleven studies were reported, and the average value was said to be .44 (LeBreton, Barksdale, Robin, and James 2007); in no case were any details of the eleven validity studies provided. This value of .44 for eleven studies is repeated in Frost, Ko, and James (2007), again without any elaboration. This latter report contains correlations between the conditional reasoning approach to aggression and various indexes of aggressiveness that range from –.03 to .61. It is not apparent whether, and how, these figures may have been included in the eleven studies noted previously. Overall there is considerable confusion regarding the reporting of the validity of the conditional reasoning test; however, the actual value must have been in the high .30s, and it probably extended into the .40s. Thus, this does appear to be a useful implicit measure that could be used to disentangle some of Lewin's findings on leadership climates.

A Conditional Reasoning Approach to Achievement

Obviously how significant the conditional reasoning approach becomes is a function of how many different such measures are constructed. Although a number of these measures have been considered, the only one that has been reported on adequately, beyond the aggressiveness index, is a test for achievement. Using performance on the in-basket exercise of an assessment center, a validity coefficient of .39 was obtained. The conditional reasoning measure deals with both achievement motivation (positive) and fear of failure (negative). Using a GPA result, the findings appear positive, but statistical data are not provided (James and Mazerolle 2002). On the evidence available the conditional reasoning approach to achievement motivation appears to be the equal of the conditional reasoning approach to aggression, and significance is present in both instances.

The Lewin leadership climates results also fail to match up with expectations here; the achievement levels under democratic leadership were not as high (relative to authoritarian leadership) as hypothesized. Again the conditional reasoning approach may provide an answer. Yet it is not clear that the construct involved in terms of achievement motivation is the same. We need more research in this regard.

Contrast with Projective Indexes

The work of James and Mazerolle (2002) and the other reports on the conditional reasoning approach are adamant in their rejection of any and all projective techniques; presumably this represents an attempt to promote their own approach to unconscious measurement, but it appears to be a genuine belief as well. The question remains whether this belief is justified. Are their measures really dramatically superior to the results obtained with projectives? To deal with this question I cite results presented in Miner (2008) on the Miner Sentence Completion Scale (MSCS), which is indeed a projective technique.

On Form T of the MSCS (Miner 2008, Chapter 29) validity coefficients were obtained from five studies using career indexes as criteria; the weighted value was .67. In other studies the criteria were of a performance nature and the seventeen of these available yielded a median correlation of .35.

On Form H of the MSCS (Miner 2008, Chapter 30) similar coefficients were obtained from four studies using career measures as criteria and the weighted value was .61. Other studies relied on some thirty-six criteria such as managerial performance, position level, compensation level, job satisfaction, turnover, and the like. Here the median correlation was .29.

On Form P of the MSCS (Miner 2008, Chapter 31) there were three studies having career information as the validity criterion; the weighted correlation obtained was .75. Using the nineteen correlations of a noncareer nature (all based on professional performance and criteria), a median validity of .35 was obtained.

Using appropriate measures of reliability, the results were at least as good as those reported by James and Mazerolle (2002), with median values for total scores on the MSCSs running in the .80s (scorer reliabilities were typically in the .90s) (Miner 1993b).

None of the publications involving James make mention of the Miner research; I take this to represent an intent to ignore, given that the MSCS publications span almost 50 years (as presented in Miner 2008). But what about the comparability of the Conditional Reasoning and the MSCS measures? On the record provided, I believe that the two tests appear to be essentially the same; certainly the projective index is not inferior, and the career data suggest that it may be somewhat more valid. I believe that James et al. should acknowledge this. Yet in a rather delayed presentation James and LeBreton (2010, 34) do invoke the construct of implicit measurement. Further they add a muted position on projective techniques, asking, "By what processes do justification mechanisms influence reasoning, and are these processes similar to what is assessed by traditional projective tests?" Perhaps, however, this position is attributable to the source for which they are writing.

However, I do believe that the conditional reasoning approach, especially to date as it involves the measurement of aggression, is effective. It can be used appropriately, to wit to measure aggression as reflected in the Lewin climate study. My intent in comparing it to projectives is not to denigrate this work, but rather to place it in perspective, to frame it appropriately.

Other Measures

It is not my intention to imply that conditional reasoning and the MSCS are the only measures of unconscious factors available. There are several such, and I will deal with them subsequently. Here, I note the concept of implicit trait policy (Motowidlo, Hooper, and Jackson 2006), which has produced adequate validity approximately half of the time, but then with correlations in the mid-.30s and thus very similar to the figures previously cited. This may be a measure that with further development can also add to the armamentarium of valid indexes of implicit processes; to date it has been applied to agreeableness, extraversion, and conscientiousness.

CONCLUSIONS

Using the data given earlier, the estimated validity of Lewin's theorizing is at four stars and the importance rating is 5.31. Dividing as appropriate, these figures yield a value of 1.33. This suggests that the importance rating tends to overestimate the validity of Lewin's theorizing in a manner consistent with the theory's institutional status.

Lewin's social psychology emerges as a distinctly conscious approach, although there are points at which the mobilization of unconscious processes might be justified. Among these are the work on group norms, action research, sensitivity training, and leadership climates. The conditional reasoning approach as promoted by James appears to be an appropriate procedure to apply under these circumstances, although certain projectives may work at least as well.

ACHIEVEMENT MOTIVATION THEORY

David McClelland's achievement motivation theory is really a concatenation of theories having to do with human needs. These needs are characteristically measured via the Thematic Apperception Test (TAT), a projective test that assesses both conscious and unconscious motives (see Miner 2005, Chapter 4; 2007, Chapter 4; and 2008, Chapter 1). As a projective, it gives special attention to unconscious considerations and this fact as well as the nature of the theorizing serves to classify achievement motivation theory as essentially unconscious in nature. The theory is rated at the four-star level of validity, and its importance rating averages out at 5.15. The validity of the theory is attested to both by meta-analyses (see Spangler 1992) and by a large number of reviews of a nonquantitative nature. That the TAT incorporates unconscious as well as conscious motives is demonstrated by Spangler's (1992) finding that it adds variance above and beyond what is obtained using conscious motivation alone (from self-report indexes).

NEEDS

Aside from the need for achievement, the needs measured by the TAT and incorporated in the theory deal as well with power and affiliation (Winter 2002).

Achievement Motivation

Achievement needs are particularly important for entrepreneurial leadership. When strong among corporate managers, and they often are, achievement needs tend to become obsessive in the same manner as the strong goals noted in Chapter 2 of this volume. They lead to destructive outcomes, often in an unconscious form, just as Kayes (2005) described for Mt. Everest climbers. Overachievers of this kind tend to run amok (Spreier, Fontaine, and Malloy 2006). Another manifestation of this tendency has been observed after leaders have been exposed to successful achievement motivation training. Such individuals often push too hard for results without realizing that they are antagonizing others; they may well end by losing their employment entirely.

Power Motivation

Successful leadership in the corporate setting, or any bureaucratic context, is associated with the need for power, particularly for socialized power. McClelland (1987) indicates that the need for power is a fundamental human motive. Research demonstrates that unconscious power motivation (induced by priming) tends to cause people to react forcefully to an increase in power; they also resist power losses and persist in acting as if they have power even when they do not (Sivanathan, Pillutla, and Murnighan 2008).

In line with the hierarchic nature of bureaucratic organizations, dominant individuals (read those with strong power motivation) are more likely to unconsciously favor vertical locations in visual space; these people are particularly inclined to follow top-down spatial attention processes (Moeller, Robinson, and Zabelina 2008). Thus bureaucratic processes are linked by their very nature to a need for power.

Affiliation Motivation

Winter (2002) also indicates that the McClelland theory is concerned with affiliation motivation and that strong needs of this kind are unrelated (or even negatively related) to successful bureaucratic leadership. Social motives like affiliation are in fact most likely to manifest themselves in the successful leadership of group systems such as those involving autonomous work groups.

Self-Actualization Motivation

There are other needs that characterize particular organizational systems and contribute to successful leadership of them. Among them is the need for self-actualization, which is "directed toward growth and expansion of the self. Consequently, people may strive for self-worth not only to minimize anxiety, but also to maximize their competencies and potential" (Greenberg 2008, 52). Self-actualization motivation may operate unconsciously, and it is associated with the successful leadership of professional organizations and units.

Other Effects of Priming Unconscious Needs

Research has demonstrated numerous other needs that operate unconsciously, along with the various effects of priming and their associated unconscious processes. For example, explicit and implicit processes (the latter involving priming) have been found to be most effective at different times of the day, thus serving further to differentiate the conscious from the unconscious (May, Hasher, and Foong 2005). Other priming effects show that "nonconscious processes appear to serve a default, background regulatory function, freeing the conscious mind from the concerns of the immediate environment" (Bargh and Williams 2006, 1).

Prosocial needs are activated implicitly even when the behavior is anonymous and directed toward strangers. The form these prosocial needs take was to allocate money to others; the prime involved served to activate various God concepts (Shariff and Norenzayan 2007). Similarly the manifestations of aggression-related cues may be muted by pairing them with prosocial thoughts (Meier, Robinson, and Wilkowski 2006):

> In Study 1, we found that priming with aggression-related cues increases aggressive behavior, but only among individuals low on agreeableness. Study 2 showed that aggression-related cues activated prosocial thoughts among individuals high in agreeable affect (a component of agreeableness). These results reveal that agreeable individuals are able to short-circuit the cue-aggression sequence (136).

Other needs are primed by other environmental cues; for instance, the need for competitiveness can be primed by business-related pictures and objects such as briefcases and boardroom tables. These accoutrements of capitalism can serve as "material primes" that create automatic, unconscious, and on occasion unwanted effects, thus serving to bring about conflicts between conscious and unconscious processes (Kay, Wheeler, Bargh, and Ross 2004). Primes of this kind exert their largest effects in less structured or more ambiguous contexts where normative demands are less explicit. Faced with such primes individuals tend to feel more competitive, consider competition more appropriate, and tend generally to escalate the competitiveness of negotiations.

THE TAT

Achievement motivation theory appropriately matches its use of unconscious processes with an instrument that similarly taps these processes (the TAT). However, we need to look at how well the TAT serves this purpose, since organizational behavior has only limited familiarity with projective techniques of this kind; also the author's qualifications to make judgments in this regard need to be assessed.

I learned about the TAT from Silvan Tomkins, an expert on the subject who worked with Henry Murray at the Harvard Psychological Clinic as the TAT was developed there. Tomkins (1947) published a book on the scoring of the test and made several original contributions to the process involved. I carried out a TAT study of alcoholism under his guidance and used the test in several subsequent studies (see Miner 1956; also 1962). However, my work with projectives more recently has been with the Tomkins-Horn Picture Arrangement Test (Tomkins and Miner 1957, 1959) and with sentence completion measures (Miner 2008).

Prior Treatments

From the 1960s until relatively recently the McClelland approach to scoring the TAT has yielded the best results (see, for example, McClelland and Winter 1969). To a large extent work with the test in the early period was dominated by a clinical approach, which often gave insufficient attention to psychometric concerns. This situation may be summarized as follows:

> The TAT's critics gave relatively favorable grades to the test as compared with other projectives, especially when McClelland's applications were involved. This fits well with my own views (see Chapter 4 of Miner 2005 and Chapter 4 of Miner 2007). I find that the evidence in favor of McClelland's theory, much of which derives from TAT studies, is predominantly supportive. This result was achieved largely because of the development of a scoring procedure that emphasized standardization and systematic procedures. Recent research building on these strengths has introduced further improvements in reliability and validity along with certain changes in the format and conduct of the TAT (see Langan-Fox and Grant 2006; Blankenship, Vega, Ramos, Romero, Warren, Keenan, Rosenow, Vasquez, and Sullivan 2006; and Schmalt 2005) (Miner 2008, 12).

My impression from a reading of the literature is that the current research involving the TAT represents a quantum advance over previous years.

Manualized Scoring Systems for the TAT Included in Jenkins (2008)

A recent handbook covering data on nineteen manualized scoring systems for the TAT provides evidence as to the effectiveness of a number of systems (Jenkins 2008). These nineteen are characterized by:

1. Some evidence regarding reliability, particularly scorer reliability.
2. Some evidence of validity, usually using pathological groups as a criterion.

The studies reported use a variety of TAT cards, but ten are recommended as a minimum. A number apply the originally intended twenty cards, extending up to twenty-seven. More cards normally make for greater reliability. A transcendence index has been developed which is presumed to measure the amount of projection present in a TAT protocol. This index "is calculated by scoring the number of ways that a narrative exceeds pure description of the stimuli present in the picture" (Chapman 2008, 89).

Although the majority of the scoring systems are intended for, and validated against, use with various pathological groups, several seem suitable for application within the field of organizational behavior. Most suitable for this purpose are Harder and Greenwald's (2008) ambitious-narcissistic style scale and Ephraim's (2008) psychocultural system. Given that the Jenkins (2008) book does not contain McClelland's system for scoring the TAT, these two come closest to providing such a procedure.

Implications of the Jenkins (2008) Book for McClelland's System

What do the Jenkins (2008) data indicate insofar as the scorer reliability of the TAT is concerned? A wide range of correlation coefficients is reported for the different scoring systems. In some cases extensive training and high standards are indicated; when this is the case scorer reliability in the .90s is often obtained. However, not infrequently such efforts have apparently settled upon a goal of .70 reliability or above as a standard for acceptability, and that is what is reported. Thus the majority of coefficients fall in the .70s and .80s, although more frequently in the .80s. To my mind this is unacceptably low; scorer reliabilities should be in the .90s, and indeed this is what is reported for the McClelland system. On this score the people working with McClelland do quite well. The commonly accepted figure of .70 as the minimum standard for content reliability scoring should not apply to the TAT.

In other respects the McClelland system does not do as well. Ephraim (2008, 740) notes that "the McClelland and Atkinson tradition tended to generate more constrained and stereotyped narratives when scored with the Psychocultural System." The cards used by McClelland do not generate as rich a flow of fantasy as might be desired. Also the number of cards utilized tends—in my opinion, and Jenkins's (2008) too—to be below what is usually considered acceptable. More cards, up to at least ten, should produce greater test reliability.

Certainly the Jenkins (2008) book is indicative of much more psychometric precision for the TAT than existed previously. However, mention should be made of the fact that neither this book, nor the numerous positive findings beyond McClelland, Koestner, and Weinberger (1989) contained in this chapter, is mentioned in a brief but lukewarm review of the TAT presented recently by De Houwer, Tiege-Mocigemba, Spruyt, and Moors (2009).

Projection and the Unconscious

Projection comes in a variety of forms, but whatever the form experimental evidence indicates that it may occur without awareness. Goals activated outside awareness affect perception and behavior just as they do trait constructs. Indeed the studies indicate that both explicit and implicit goals are projected, as the TAT anticipates. Both positive and negative goals are projected, implying that goal projection can serve both self-defensive and self-enhancing purposes; the defensive properties of projection as proposed by psychoanalysis are confirmed. Both implicitly activated and explicitly assigned goals are projected onto others to a similar extent (Kawada, Oettingen, Gollwitzer, and Bargh 2004).

PROJECTIVE TECHNIQUES VS. SELF-REPORT MEASURES

In Chapter 1 of Miner (2008), McClelland, Koestner, and Weinberger (1989) set forth certain theoretical distinctions between projective (implicit) and self-report (explicit) measures. These distinctions are predicated on the assumption that the two types of measures are basically unrelated—that the correlation is essentially .00. The data in which this assumption is rooted derive from a limited number of studies, but they are what the authors had available at the time.

The Miner Data

Miner (1993b, Chapter 9) contains information on the relationships that link projective and self-report measures, of which 140 are noted. These correlations range from –.19 to .59; the median correlation is .15. The self-report indexes are single-item measures, and the projectives are the subscales and total scores of the Miner Sentence Completion Scale–Form H (MSCS–H).

Comparable data are given in a later source by Miner (2008, Chapter 28). There are 52 correlations ranging from –.09 to .45; the median value is .14. The projectives are subscale scores and total scores from Forms T, H, and P of the MSCS; the self-report measures derive from the Lynn Achievement Motivation Questionnaire, the Elizur Achievement Motivation

Index, the Ghiselli Self-Description Inventory (SDI), the Rowe-Mason Decision Style Inventory (DSI), the Slocum-Hellriegel PSQ (Problem Solving Questionnaire), the Shure-Meeker Risk Avoidance Scale, the Kuder Preference Record—Vocational, and Fiedler's LPC (Least Preferred Coworker) Score. All of these indexes are multi-item.

The Implicit Association Test (IAT) Data

Probably the most widely used approach to correlating explicit and implicit data on the same phenomenon is the IAT (Nosek, Greenwald, and Banaji 2007).

> This measure assesses the degree to which people implicitly associate a class of objects with pleasant versus unpleasant stimuli. . . . In this task participants are asked to perform two sorting tasks that are counterbalanced. If researchers want to gauge participants' automatic attitudes toward women versus men, for example, one sorting task would be to press a certain response key if the stimulus that appears on the computer is a member of the category "female names" (e.g. Linda) or a member of the positively valenced category "flowers" (e.g. daffodil). Participants are asked to press a different response key if the stimulus is a member of the category "male names" (e.g. Frank) or a member of the negatively valenced category "bugs" (e.g. roach). The second sorting task is a reversal of the first one, and participants are asked to group female names with bugs and male names with flowers. Researchers can then assess via response latencies and error data the relative ease of the two sorting tasks in order to infer whether participants are faster to group female names with flowers versus bugs, compared to male names. If it is generally easier to group female names with flowers, then it is assumed that participants more strongly associate women (versus men) with positive versus negative information (Ferguson 2007, 225).

> In other words, participants who find it easier to sort men with good (and women with bad) compared to sorting men with bad (and women with good) are said to implicitly prefer males to females (Nosek, Greenwald and Banaji 2007, 271).

> This research demonstrates that people unintentionally and seemingly nonconsciously can form both explicit and automatic attitudes. . . . Even though automatic evaluative acts last only a fraction of a second and occur without the person's intention or awareness they have a host of downstream outcomes (Ferguson 2007, 235, 239).

When results obtained with the IAT are correlated with explicit (conscious) data, the consequence can take somewhat different forms depending on the focus of the study and the particular studies included in a meta-analysis. One data set produced correlations ranging from .13 to .75 with a median of .22. In another meta-analytic study the range was −.25 to .60 and the average .19 (Lane, Banaji, Nosek, and Greenwald 2007, 77).

Imperfections of the IAT

Other such data are presented indicating variations in correlations ranging from almost .00 to above .75 with a median of .48 (Nosek 2007). Here the fact of negative correlations is not recognized, and "correlations . . . can be quite large in domains of consumer brand preferences and political candidate preferences" (Greenwald, Nosek, and Sriram 2006, 59); the McClelland et al. (1989) and the Nosek (2007) data differ widely in these regards.

Furthermore the IAT has been the subject of considerable controversy in spite of its wide usage (see Blanton and Jaccard 2006; Greenwald, Nosek, and Sriram 2006). There have been pleas for more research (Wentura and Rothermund 2007). The test-retest reliability across a number of studies is only .50 (Lane, Banaji, Nosek, and Greenwald 2007).

All in all, although the dissociation between self-report and implicit measures appears warranted, the correlation—with personality variables of the kind McClelland used—is definitely positive, and in some instances can depart meaningfully from the zero point; a case in point is particularly evident with regard to dependency (Cogswell 2008).

THE TRAINING RESEARCH

McClelland and his coworkers developed achievement motivation by conducting training that included, in one aspect, learning to score TAT protocols for n Achievement (McClelland and Winter 1969). Thus participants in training came to bring previously unconscious material into consciousness, thereby exposing it to understanding and introspection. This is what many psychotherapists, including psychoanalysts, attempt to do—to get previously unconscious phenomena and impulses under conscious control. The McClelland researchers were in their own way using interpretation to make the previously unconscious part of the TAT content conscious. Much the same process is involved in role motivation training (Miner 2008, Chapter 3). The question remains, Is the assumption behind such practices warranted?

Experimental Evidence

"It has been well documented that current conscious purposes are capable of overriding automatically suggested responses if the two are in conflict" (Bargh 1990, 95). "It is only when we are unaware of the activation of a motive or goal that we cannot counter its influence. . . . We may not *know* that certain of our motives have been activated, but we can assume that they have been and can take this into account when making decisions" (121).

Elsewhere Payne, Jacoby, and Lambert (2005, 407) add the following:

> People may be able to become aware of a process that is initially unconscious. As suggested by the psychodynamic tradition, achieving awareness of a mental process can provide a basis for controlling it. An experiment has shown that people can harness their biases strategically if they are made aware of them.

In Chapter 1 we noted that unconscious emotion can often be traced to activity in the amygdala. As conscious thought becomes involved, the frontal and prefrontal cortices are activated. Thus physiological processes in the brain can be shown to follow the move from unconscious to conscious as these processes unfold (Rule and Ambady 2008). The mapping is found to match expectations.

Applications to Entrepreneurship

A better understanding of this bringing-to-consciousness phenomenon may be gained from the entrepreneurship literature. "Entrepreneurial intuition is defined to be the dynamic process by which entrepreneurial alertness cognitions interact with domain competence (e.g., culture, industry, specific circumstances, technology, etc.) to bring to consciousness an opportunity to create new value" (Mitchell, Friga, and Mitchell 2005, 671). Thus the ultimate objective involved is to establish an entirely conscious result; improving intuition in this manner should be teachable (as achievement motivation training does).

The recommended approach to measuring the movement of intuitive processes from essentially unconscious to completely conscious, and thus under executive control, is conjoint analysis (Shepherd, Zacharakis, and Baron 2003; Choi and Shepherd 2004). This technique has many advantages, including high reliability and controlling for various sources of bias. However, it weights the measurements of conscious processes very heavily—to the point where it does not seem justified to conclude that unconscious processes are ever truly measured. Some of the reported findings can be explained as well in terms of variations in cognitive load and thus are independent of any effects of unconscious factors. In short conjoint analysis alone does not, at least as described, appear capable of substituting for priming methods, projective techniques, and conditional reasoning approaches.

A Disclaimer from Clinicians

Moving unconscious processes to the conscious level, as in McClelland's achievement motivation training, although it has advantages for some purposes, can produce certain negative consequences for other purposes.

The following quote from Karon (2008, 362) makes this point:

> Teaching clients the scoring system (cf. McClelland and Winter 1969) would be a bad intervention, because it would make it impossible to assess pathogenesis accurately, if the individual did not wish to be assessed accurately. As Tomkins (1949) pointed out, anything of which the subject is fully aware and which they do not wish to disclose can be kept out of the TAT. Knowledge of the scoring system would allow individuals to fake stories that would score low on pathogenesis. At the present time the scoring rationale is not widely known among patients or therapists and therefore yields valid scores.

It all depends on what the TAT is being used to accomplish.

CONCLUSIONS

As data presented early on in this chapter note, achievement motivation theory has a presumed validity of four stars, with organizational behavior specialists awarding it an importance rating of 5.15. When the latter figure is divided by the former, this yields a figure of 1.29. This appears to indicate that the importance rating somewhat overestimates the validity of the theory; organizational behavior tends to view achievement motivation as more valid than it really is, at least to a degree.

Clearly the theory is best categorized as unconscious, although it does incorporate conscious considerations as well. The nature of the needs involved, such as achievement, power, and affiliation motivation, attest to the unconscious grounding; the use of the TAT as an appropriate measure is thus justified. Data are presented as to the psychometric soundness of the TAT, especially as it has been used in the recent period. Data are also given on how unconscious measures, such as the MSCSs and the IAT, correlate with entirely conscious self-report indexes; the figure appears to average at about .15 or perhaps somewhat higher. Training procedures serve to open up unconscious motives to conscious censoring, but doing this, as McClelland and his collaborators have done, may compromise available clinical applications.

CHAPTER 5

JOB CHARACTERISTICS THEORY

Job characteristics theory is an amalgam of ideas developed by Greg Oldham from the climate then existing at Yale University, the group concepts of Richard Hackman, and the expectancy theory of Edward Lawler (Oldham and Hackman 2005). It also has turned out, as a result of later research, to be a consequence of transformational leadership, and to be positively moderated by perceived high-quality leader-member exchange (Piccolo and Colquitt 2006). This theory is rated as to validity at the four-star level (Miner 2005, Chapter 6; Miner 2007, Chapter 6) with several supporting meta-analyses and other favorable reviews, plus an importance rating from organizational behavior peers of 5.61. Yet the authors themselves say of the theory and its key motivating potential score that it "does indeed make conceptual sense, but it is a psychometrics disaster" (Oldham and Hackman 2005, 168). The problems inherent in this latter evaluation seem to result from the imposition of an essentially conscious and rational theory on a phenomenon that inherently involves unconscious factors as well.

CONSCIOUS AND UNCONSCIOUS THEORY

Dijksterhuis, Aarts, and Smith (2005, 77–78) note "the extraordinary antipathy some people still have towards the idea that we might be influenced by things of which we are unaware. . . . The idea that our behavior—or our functioning in general—is driven by unconscious perception makes many people uncomfortable." This antipathy has permeated organizational behavior and in the process job characteristics theory. Yet goals set in motion by environmental cues, and thus primed, serve as well as those that are consciously chosen (Bargh, Gollwitzer, Lee-Chai, Barndollar, and Trötschel 2001).

Accordingly the critique of job characteristics theory mounted from the social information-processing perspective (Salancik and Pfeffer 1977, 1978) gains considerable credence. Although this critique does not draw upon unconscious processes as such, it does attribute much of the evidence favoring job characteristics theory to environmental priming processes,

31

and thus by inference to implicit motivation. The potential for reinterpreting the theory in terms of unconscious mechanisms certainly is raised by the Salancik and Pfeffer critique, even though the latter authors have never actually taken this route.

Like expectancy theory and consistent with Lawler's involvement (see Chapter 1 of this volume), job characteristics theory uses mathematical calculations; calculations of this kind are more typically found in these kinds of conscious theorizing, less typically in the unconscious realm. But once again the imposition of conscious theory on unconscious phenomena seems to have created difficulties for the theory. The self-report nature of the measures used for the theory's variables appears to confirm the commitment to rational thought, but it too, like the use of mathematical relationships, seems inconsistent with unconscious processes. As a result the findings from research tend to be somewhat unstable, and reliabilities for variables are not as high as they could be (see Miner 2005, 2007). Would it not have been preferable to incorporate more of the unconscious in the theorizing?

GROWTH NEED STRENGTH AND SELF-ACTUALIZATION

The need for self-actualization was noted in Chapter 4 of this volume; it is measurable via the Thematic Apperception Test (TAT). Self-actualization is part of the growth need category, and in some contexts it is the essence of that category. Terminology of this kind has a long history in the social sciences, including such names as Kurt Goldstein (1939), Abraham Maslow (1954), Clayton Alderfer (1972), and various writers of a psychoanalytic orientation. Alderfer was presumably the immediate stimulus for the use of the term here, given the focus on theorists residing at Yale when job characteristics theory was created.

Aspects of the Self

Leary (2007) provides a useful comparison and disentangling of the terminology that has developed regarding various aspects of the self. In some instances, he notes, such self-concepts operate automatically and thus without awareness, but when people are required to think deliberately this effect tends to disappear. Yet when a person is placed under cognitive load, the automatic processes reappear. "A major reason why it is adaptive for consciousness to be deployed only when needed is its limited-capacity nature, as shown best by findings of the dramatic 'ego-depleting' consequences of even minimal conscious choice and regulatory processes" (Bargh 2005, 53).

Unconscious Self-Actualization

As indicated previously self-actualization motivation may operate unconsciously (Greenberg 2008; Pelham, Carvallo, and Jones 2005). However, within job characteristics theory self-actualization is employed as a key moderator and is treated as a conscious process measured invariably by self-report procedures; this is something of a non-sequitur—an inconsistency between existing reality and theoretical (and measurement) interpretations. Most phenomena of interest to organizational behavior are governed by a combination of automatic and controlled processes (Uleman, Blader, and Todorov 2005): This holds for needs as well as most other phenomena. Consequently incorporating measures of the unconscious to get at the need for self-actualization (or growth) would seem to be not only warranted for job characteristics theory but absolutely essential, indicating a need to replace the self-report instruments with projectives or some such measure. Book 5 of this series (Miner 2008) provides a detailed exposition of how this might be accomplished through the use of sentence completion instruments. By providing for a fit between theory and measured data in this way, many of the shortcomings of research on job characteristics theory might be eliminated.

SOCIAL AND AFFILIATION MOTIVATION

Many of the variables of job characteristics theory are posited as conscious and measured as such, thus using self-report measures. But in addition to growth need strength (self-actualization), when the theory is applied to group tasks, social needs (the need for affiliation) are brought into play, and so a different class of variables is introduced. Once again the theory faces certain deficiencies, and unconscious motivation appears to offer some solutions. We need to look at some new data here.

Similarity and Unconscious Mimicry

Similarity processes represent one type that must be considered:

> These similarity processes are always active. In particular the comparison process that influences metacognitive judgments need not be under conscious control, and need not yield products that are consciously accessible. Thus the presence of similarities among items may have unintended influences on higher level cognitive processes, because intentional resources may be allocated on the basis of nonintentional similarity comparisons (Markman and Gentner 2005, 131).

Evidence of this type on similarity has led to research on unconscious mimicry. The latter, too, turns out to be a fact. Mimicry of this kind extends to speech expressions, facial positioning, postures, gestures, and mannerisms (Dijksterhuis, Chartrand, and Aarts 2007). It appears to serve a social purpose. Unconscious mimicry of another's behavior operates to foster affiliative goals and thus to cement rapport (Chartrand, Maddux, and Lakin 2005). These effects "are not simply due to increased liking for the mimicker, but are due to increased prosocial orientation in general" (van Baaren, Holland, Kawakami, and van Knippenberg 2004, 71). This latter is a strong finding.

Positive and Negative Transferences

In Chapter 2 of Book 5 in this series I had the following to say regarding transference. This material bears repeating here because it is relevant to social motivation (Miner 2008, 22–23):

> Significant others are conceptualized as those having an impact on a person and with whom that person is emotionally invested—parents, siblings, certain members of any extended family, lovers, spouses, best friends, mentors, close colleagues, and psychotherapists. Aspects of such relationships tend to be called to the fore in new relationship situations and this is called transference (a term derived from psychoanalysis wherein therapists are seen to take on the positive and negative emotionality invested in a parent).
> The authors of a chapter on these phenomena report the following:

We present a wide array of findings that address these issues and support four main conclusions about the unconscious self:

1. Significant-other representations are activated automatically in transference.
2. Affect arises relatively automatically in transference when the significant-other representation is activated.
3. The relational self is activated automatically when the significant-other representation is activated.
4. Some self-regulatory processes in the relational self are evoked in response to "threat" (e.g., negative cues) in transference and may be automatic (Susan Andersen, Inga Reznick, and Noah Glassman in Hassin, Uleman, and Bargh 2005, 423).

The authors indicate that they have direct evidence that significant-other representations can be activated unconsciously and with little or no effort; these representations have a high level of activation readiness. Unconscious transferences can operate to produce rigidity, however, and become maladaptive. At such times the introduction of conscious processes to achieve control may well become desirable.

Numerous reports may be cited as to the unconscious nature of transference relationships (see, for example, Reis and Collins 2004; Shah 2005; Chen, Fitzsimons, and Andersen 2007). Such effects are often treated as aspects of the context on social relationships as well (Smith and Conrey 2007). Kruglanski and Pierro (2008) present evidence that these transference implications hold for variations in circadian rhythms as to the time of day involved. Although not tied to experimental findings, Maccoby (2004) explains the psychoanalytic view of transference and how it relates to corporate leadership.

"There is no reason to believe that implicit impressions are immune from . . . errors and biases. . . . Findings suggest that trait transference—misattributing implied traits to the wrong person—is more likely under spontaneous than intentional inference conditions" (Uleman, Blader, and Todorov 2005, 382–383).

More on Unconscious Social Motivation

Mimicry and transference may operate without awareness and thus have an influence on how job characteristics theory in its social variants is carried out. Other unconscious processes may serve to affect social motivation, however. One of these is the accuracy of first impressions, which has been studied extensively in the laboratory (Hall and Andrzejewski 2008), and uses nonverbal cues from the face or body, as well as verbal cues intended to be highly ambiguous. Are those, among those studied, who exhibit marked accuracy in their first impressions more likely to get along well in their social relationships? The answer here seems to be yes; they reap various social benefits, including a much greater popularity.

Another such manifestation of social motivation involves priming the mating goal and thus activating it unconsciously (Huang and Bargh 2008). Once again a particular aspect of social functioning is specified which operates to influence human behavior. My point in all of these instances is that a variety of processes occur beyond human awareness—processes that were not considered by the authors of job characteristics theory and yet could well serve to affect the research results and their interpretations.

Perhaps these findings have relevance for the "romance of teams," whereby evidence regarding the effectiveness of teams is shown to be far below what many believe their effectiveness to be—"a faith in the effectiveness of team-based work that is not supported by, or even inconsistent with, relevant empirical evidence; . . . this faith is commonly—although, obviously, not universally—held among managers, their employees, and the general lay population" (Allen and Hecht 2004, 440). In any event somewhere in the findings on unconsciously motivated social processes would seem to be solutions for the shortcomings of job characteristics theory as applied to groups.

CREATIVE OUTCOMES

Oldham (2003), going beyond the originally stated list of outcomes from job characteristics theory, has specified that the core characteristics operating through aroused emotions of a positive nature serve to generate creative ideas as a class of outcomes. This is entirely consistent with the specification of self-actualization, or growth need strength, as a moderator for the effective operation of the theory.

Facilitating Creativity

The various factors that facilitate creativity are not fully understood at present; in fact the area is something of a jumble. However, there is evidence to the effect that unconscious as well as conscious processes are involved in some mix (see Vance, Groves, Paik, and Kindler 2007; Sadler-Smith and Shefy 2007); this type of activation appears to be mediated via intuition. This research is not as focused in its handling of unconscious factors as it might be, nor is it as precise from a design viewpoint. Emotions, and unconscious emotions (see Chapter 1 of this volume), would seem to be involved in the creative process. Using self-reports, and thus conscious processes, the evidence seems to favor positive affect as most supportive of creative thinking (Amabile, Barsade, Mueller, and Staw 2005; George and Zhou 2007). However, this is not always without an assist from negative emotion. Sometimes it is emotional ambivalence that seems to work best (Fong 2006), although in this instance the possibility of the existence of labile affect is not adequately considered. Another study (Elsbach and Hargadon 2006) argues for mindless work where both low cognitive difficulty and low performance pressure serve to foster high creativity. Here creativity may be encouraged by mere play, yet this reduced conscious load may induce unconscious processes (which were not taken into consideration). Thus creativity may be facilitated best by some combination of conscious and unconscious factors. Without a fully unconscious measure this alternative cannot be evaluated, and the role of unconscious emotion cannot be determined. Goals help creative effort, but it is not clear in what mix they should be activated. This, again, appears to be a consequence of giving insufficient attention to unconscious factors (see Madjar and Shalley 2008).

Blocking Creativity

There are also various blocks to creative effort involved that appear to unconsciously elicit guilt and a prevention focus in the creative context (Higgins 2005; Leung, Maddux, Galinsky, and Chiu 2008). Such blocking processes may be identified as operating without awareness through priming, or they serve in the role of side effects from conscious strategic processes that are involved in creative thought. In any event any evaluation of Oldham's (2003) hypothesis needs to take both negative processes that may serve to inhibit creative ideas and unconscious considerations into account. Clearly we are far from understanding what goes on when creativity is mobilized, and unconscious considerations must be interjected more fully into the deliberations here if some degree of understanding is to be achieved. The need in particular to give consideration to unconscious factors, which have so frequently been ignored, is paramount.

CONCLUSIONS

Job characteristics theory, as previously indicated, carries a four-star rating on validity and an importance rating from organizational behavior scholars of 5.61. Dividing, as appropriate, yields a very respectable value of 1.40. This provides evidence of a considerable overinflation by organizational behavior insofar as the validity of the theory is concerned. The authors, in fact, ultimately came to recognize this inflation of the theory's popularity themselves.

As stated, job characteristics theory represents a thoroughly conscious approach, with extensive use of self-report measures, in the tradition of expectancy theory. Yet there are numerous points at which this perspective might be modified to incorporate unconscious considerations. Aspects of theory that invite such treatment include the most pronounced moderator—growth needs strength. Similarly the treatment of social factors could be enhanced by exploring the extensive research that now exists in that area, including the evidence as to how transference operates to facilitate social relationships and the research on mimicry. In addition the original theory on the formulation of creative outcomes raises numerous questions that might be answered from an unconscious perspective.

CHAPTER 6

THEORIES BASED ON B. F. SKINNER AND ORGANIZATIONAL BEHAVIOR MODIFICATION

B.F. Skinner's heritage has extended out into two versions. First there was the classical conditioning theory (Skinner 1953). This was followed by social learning theory (Bandura 1977). In the same way organizational behavior has experienced these two generational effects (Luthans and Kreitner 1975, 1985) as it moved from conscious process as a meaningless by-product (OB Mod.) to consciousness as an important causal agent. Evaluations have characteristically focused on the most recent version, with the theory rated at the four-star level in terms of validity and at the same level in terms of importance (Miner 2005, Chapter 8)—specifically at 4.31. Meta-analyses and other comprehensive reviews have yielded similar support (see Miner 2005, 2007). In general Skinner and those who followed him have been viewed as opposed to personality considerations and to psychoanalysis in particular. A theory that gave conscious thought processes merely the status of a by-product did not seem very receptive to individual differences in such constructs as personality traits.

SETTING THE RECORD STRAIGHT: SKINNER AND PSYCHOANALYSIS

Skinner and Sigmund Freud (with the latter's dedication to unconscious processes) are often considered polar opposites. Overskeid (2007), however, has written a piece arguing that this view is fallacious. Let me outline his position and the points he makes.

Psychoanalysis and Behaviorism: Two Positivists

There is no evidence that Freud knew anything about Skinner, but Skinner knew Freud's work well; Skinner cited Freud more than any other author, and he was often influenced by Freud. Ferster, a particularly close collaborator of Skinner's, was psychoanalyzed himself and used behavioral theory to understand (and extend) psychodynamic concepts. Both Skinner and Freud had intellectual roots in the positivist tradition; they both believed that research should be empirically driven, although each in his own way strayed from this path as his career developed.

Consciousness and Civilization

Their careers were similar in that having made a name in a specialized area, they moved on to attack the broad problems of civilization in highly speculative ways—Freud (1930) in *Civilization and Its Discontents,* Skinner (1971) in *Beyond Freedom and Dignity.* Both attributed civilization's problems to the fact that people are controlled by forces of which they are not conscious. Both emphasized that the system operating outside awareness may have a powerful effect without the person understanding how and why. Freud discussed primary process and the reality principle; Skinner was concerned with contingency-shaped behavior and rule-governed behavior. Their concepts of the unconscious varied widely, but both made important distinctions between unconscious and conscious processes.

Skinner and the Freudian Dynamisms

Skinner expressed agreement with Freud on a number of matters—on rationalization, on dream symbolism, on defense mechanisms generally, and specifically on repression.

Skinner at one point undertook studies to see if he could measure whatever escaped the repressing forces, and he was in contact with Henry Murray (author of the TAT) in this regard. Ultimately all this led to his applying to the Boston Psychoanalytic Institute as a first step in undertaking a personal psychoanalysis. This application was not acted upon favorably, and so Skinner's effort to undergo psychoanalysis never did come to fruition. There is reason to believe from his subsequent interviews and writings that he may have been in search of a resolution to problems related to the death of a younger brother and the sibling rivalry involved. He discusses numerous defense mechanisms in this regard—reaction formation, displacement, projection, psychosomatic symptoms, and slips of the tongue, among them.

Skinner's Flexibility

In general Skinner did not accept introducing unobservable inner variables to explain behavior. Yet in dealing with specific instances he was more flexible. At such times he was prone to accepting Freud's conceptualizations, as well as Freud's terminology. Thus he wrote of the superego, the id, and the ego. He attributed to Freud the increased understanding that has occurred with regard to wishful thinking and similar departures from reality-based thought. Clearly he felt that unconscious considerations as articulated by Freud had a great deal of authenticity, or at least he felt this at certain points in time, when considering certain subject matters.

Overskeid's (2007) archival research presents a view of Skinner that is well documented and scholarly. However, it does not always match completely with others' views, or even with Skinner himself (see the interview reports by Evans 1968). For one thing Skinner was indeed flexible and never did completely resolve the conflict between his own theory and his admiration for Freud. In any event it is important to recognize that Skinner did, at least in certain contexts, leave the door open to interpretation in terms of unconscious processes.

CONDITIONING AND THE UNCONSCIOUS

A central theme in this presentation is that conditioning, and thus radical behaviorism, as well as the first version of organizational behavior modification (Luthans and Kreitner 1975), can have unconscious effects.

Evidence of Unconscious Involvement

As Ito and Cacioppo (2007, 129) indicate:

> Much research has focused on the role of the amygdala (located bilaterally in the median temporal lobe) in both explicit and implicit evaluative processes. Initial association between the amygdala and evaluative responses came from work on the acquisition of conditioned fear responses. . . . Studies using very brief presentations of stimuli show that the amygdala is . . . involved during implicit evaluative responses. . . . The involvement of the amygdala . . . is not limited to emotional expressions.
> Furthermore—
> Dissociations between implicit and explicit evaluative processes have been assessed with electrodermal activity in various contexts as well. In the domain of classical conditioning this has been done by presenting the conditioned stimulus below conscious awareness (Ito and Cacioppo 2007, 148);
> and again—"unconscious emotions can play a role in priming, conditioning, and preference formation" (Prinz 2005, 379).

Kruglanski and Duchesne (2006, 736) say in commenting on Gawronski and Bodenhausen's (2006) model of implicit and explicit attitudes: "Pavlovian conditioning may be propositional, whereas evaluative conditioning is not. They conclude that despite surface dissimilarities between implicit and explicit attitudes both may be mediated by the same underlying process."

The abstract to Olsson and Phelps (2004, 822) states the following:

> This study compared fear learning acquired through direct experience (Pavlovian conditioning) and fear learning acquired without direct experience via either observation or verbal instruction. We examined whether these three types of learning yielded differential responses to conditioned stimuli (CS+) that were presented unmasked (available to explicit awareness) or masked (not available to explicit awareness). In the Pavlovian group, the CS+ was paired with a mild shock, whereas the observational learning group learned through observing the emotional expression of a confederate receiving shocks paired with the CS+. The instructed-learning group was told that the CS+ predicted a shock. The three groups demonstrated similar levels of learning as measured by the skin conductance response to unmasked stimuli. As in previous studies, participants also displayed a significant response to masked stimuli following Pavlovian conditioning. However, whereas the observational learning group also showed this effect, the instructional-learning group did not.

Thus, with regard to the Kruglanski and Duchesne (2006) conclusion, it would seem that implicit and explicit attitudes may not be mediated by exactly the same underlying process. Yet the clear fact of both explicit and implicit conditioning is apparent in both cases.

Evidence from the Placebo Effect

In Chapter 1 of this volume data were presented indicating that placebo effects are mediated by conscious processes, including classical conditioning, and by similar unconscious processes. This provides additional evidence to the effect that conditioning can well occur on an unconscious basis. I cite various reports and reviews on research that support this conclusion (Stewart-Williams and Podd 2004a, 2004b; Kradin 2008; Price, Finniss, and Benedetti 2008).

ON THE "WHY" OF HUMAN CONSCIOUSNESS

Radical behaviorism contends that conscious thoughts do not really make any difference; that they are merely a by-product of processes in which the organism is already involved. This contention would appear to provide further evidence that conditioning leaves the door open to unconscious processes (because real consciousness is not anywhere to be found as a possible obstruction). What data do we have that this is true?

Dijksterhuis, Chartrand, and Aarts (2007, 113, 115) have the following to say on this issue: "No one has provided a convincing answer to the question of why we have consciousness, and neither will we.... We [do] not know whether consciousness indeed causes something or whether it is merely a correlate (i.e., a by-product) of some unconscious process that really did the job." One step toward answering this question seems to be involved in the discussion of training research in Chapter 4 of this volume. The research noted by Rule and Ambady (2008) may account for some of the physiological underpinnings of consciousness.

ON PRIMING AND CONDITIONING

Obvious parallels exist between hypnotic processes and consequences, and what happens when priming is applied (see Bargh 2005). In much the same way similar parallels exist between conditioning processes and consequences on the one hand and priming on the other (Ito and Cacioppo 2007). Thus insights into the unconscious processes activated in the presence of conditioning may be gained by studying what happens in the presence of priming and its derivatives:

- Findings from reverse priming suggest that unconscious accuracy motivation may be operative (Glaser and Kihlstrom 2005).
- Significant-other primes facilitate judgments about gender categories more than gender per se, or than nonsignificant-other primes (Andersen, Reznik, and Glassman 2005).
- On creative tasks, priming with a promotion focus served to produce better results than when a prevention focus was used (Higgins 2005).
- If a primed motive threatens the attainment of a long-term goal, counteractive control may serve to shield the long-term goal against the primed motive (Trope and Fishbach 2005).
- Individuals primed with cooperation become more cooperative and those primed with competition more competitive (Dijksterhuis, Chartrand, and Aarts 2007).
- Subliminal priming with positive words results in more positive affect than priming with negative words (Ferguson 2007).

- When two aspects of a single act of remembering—primed and self-report—are contrasted, memory operates very differently (Payne and Stewart 2007).
- Under successful priming, perceivers can make accurate unconscious inferences about faces that they do not even know they have seen (Hall and Andrzejewski 2008).
- Using abstract trait primes leads to assimilative first impressions, while using exemplar trait primes leads to contrasting first impressions (Weisbuch, Unkelbach, and Fiedler 2008).
- Displays that are degraded in some form (like projectives) yield stronger priming effects (Wittenbrink 2007).
- Priming measures possess predictive validity (Wittenbrink 2007).
- People are motivated by role models who highlight strategies congruent with their primed regulatory goals (Lockwood and Pinkus 2008).
- Primed subjects tend to be more flexible than control subjects (Ferguson, Hassin, and Bargh 2008).
- Goals may be primed by situational (contextual, environmental) cues (Aarts, Dijksterhuis, and Dik 2008).
- Only individuals primed with achievement goals indicated an implicit negative evaluation of alternative temptations (Fishbach and Trope 2008).
- Tests of amnesic patients indicate that priming may be fully intact even though recognition memory is not (Levy, Stark, and Squire 2004).
- Priming has been shown to be stable, unconscious, and remains in effect for up to 17 years (Mitchell 2006).
- Gender discrimination is increased when a person is primed with a sense of personal objectivity (Uhlmann and Cohen 2007).
- Priming facilitates testing cultural factors by clarifying what is salient and accessible to the participant (Oyserman and Lee 2008).

APPLICATIONS TO THE LUTHANS AND KREITNER THEORY

My intent here is not to replace social learning theory formulations; we clearly need consciousness as it is introduced in, for instance, the second version of Luthans and Kreitner (1985). But we also need to study unconscious formulations as they may apply in the context of the first version of Luthans and Kreitner (1975). This has not yet been done, but the procedures to facilitate it are now available. This first version of the theory has largely been abandoned (see Locke and Latham 2004), a consequence which would appear to be premature in the light of more recent findings on conditioning and its correlates, such as priming. In particular such phenomena as shaping, modeling, and self-management would benefit from further study in their unconscious ramifications. McClelland, Koestner, and Weinberger (1989) suggested as much in their now classic article (see Miner 2008, 14–15); it is time that we revived their applications.

CONCLUSIONS

Organizational behavior modification, as it emerged in relation to social learning theory, was given a four-star rating on validity; also noted previously was the 4.31 importance rating provided by scholars from organizational behavior. When these figures are divided (the second by the first), the result is a value of 1.08. Although there is the suggestion of some degree of overevaluation here by organizational behavior as a whole, this tendency is not marked. On balance the validity and importance evaluations appear to be largely in line with one another.

As I have noted there are two versions of behaviorism, and this variation extends to the field of organizational behavior and to organizational behavior modification. Luthans and Kreitner ultimately did propose the second, social learning version, but they did not at the same time reject the first. In fact Luthans at one point indicates a preference for the original theory; thus I am left with the conclusion that the two versions are offsetting. In any event, Skinner, as the original source of behaviorism, appears to have harbored many beliefs that mirrored Freud, and there is much in his conditioning research that suggests a proclivity for unconscious determination. Organizational behavior modification, in fact, might have been served better had it pursued its unconscious ramifications rather than social learning theory. But that did not happen.

CHAPTER 7

EQUITY THEORY AND DISTRIBUTIVE JUSTICE

Equity theory is much like expectancy theory in that it draws heavily on conscious processes in both its theoretical formulations and its research designs. There are some deficiencies regarding validity, largely because Adams (1965), the originator of the theory, was unable to solve all its intricacies, but nevertheless it receives a four-star rating (Miner 2005, Chapter 9; 2007, Chapter 9). The theory's importance rating at the hands of organizational behavior peers is 5.93, and it is among the few that have been labeled as institutionalized (Miner 2006b). Meta-analytic results, in line with the theory's validity rating, are uniformly positive, as are meta-analytic findings for various types of justice, including the distributive type. Further to the treatment of equity theory as predominantly rational, the following letter to the editor provides an example of what is involved.

LETTER TO PAUL SACKETT

Industrial and Organizational Psychology: Perspectives on Science and Practice is a new journal published by the Society for Industrial and Organizational Psychology (SIOP), which presents a focal article, followed by 9 or 10 commentaries, and then a response from author(s) by the author(s) of the focal article. My letter to the editor, Paul Sackett, follows—

Dear Paul:

The recent issue of *Industrial and Organizational Psychology* (1/3) for September 2008 contains an editorial by yourself which calls for an exchange of perspectives. Furthermore the article on which I wish to comment—Hough and Oswald's Personality Testing and Industrial-Organizational Psychology: Reflections, Progress, and Prospects—indicates "the hope that this will stimulate further discussion with our readership."

My comment is focused not on the actual content of the focal article and the commentaries, but on what is not said. Certainly this is a good and typical I/O psychology discussion of personality testing; yet there is very little treatment of projective techniques and the unconscious motives that they predominantly measure. Let me elaborate.

A check of the 339 citations in the 10-article set contains only 4 publications that I can clearly identify as dealing with projectives—3 by Jane Loevinger and 1 by John Miner; there may be more that I have missed, but I doubt that there are many. Both of these authors receive favorable mention in the text for their contributions, suggesting that projectives might warrant more attention.

No citations appear to have been made to David McClelland or Robert House, or to any of those who have worked with them in the area of projectives. Expanding the net a bit further, there are no citations to theorists who have been concerned with unconscious motives at all—Ed Locke, Gary Latham, Robert Lord, James March, Chris Argyris, for instance. No citations are made to the *Journal of Personality Assessment* which is the major source for contributions to the recent outburst in psychometric research on projectives. I have looked at 6 edited volumes dealing with recent research related to unconscious processes, and none of the names included as contributors are to be found in the citations. Quite possibly more such evidence could be cited, but hopefully I have made my point that I/O psychology is typically neglecting a very fruitful area of investigation; further to this conclusion I would suggest a perusal of my 2008 book *From Unconscious Motivation to Role-Motivated Leadership* (Armonk, NY: M.E. Sharpe).

I have put this comment in the form of a letter to you for lack of any guidelines as to a form that might be preferable; I would be glad to recast it if that is appropriate, but I do hope that you will see fit to giving my ideas the visibility of publication. There is a blind spot here in the I/O literature that does not appear to reflect what is going on in other areas of psychology.

As Ever,
Jack

The remaining citations within the 10-article set essentially deal with self-report measures and conscious considerations. It seems evident that projective techniques and unconscious features are underrepresented in the typical literature on personality measurement in Industrial/Organizational Psychology. Paul Sackett declined to publish my letter, and that is why it is reproduced here.

CONSCIOUSNESS IN EQUITY THEORY AND DISTRIBUTIVE JUSTICE

This same preference for conscious processes is inherent in equity theory and in the various justice types, including distributive justice. In the latter instance the identification of particular types is uniformly based on self-report questionnaire items (see Miner 2005). Although there may be some departures from the norm, perceived inequity would seem to be primarily a conscious process, whether overreward inequity, the type Adams studied in his research (Folger 2005), or underreward inequity is involved. Reference sources appear to be established on a primarily rational basis, with thought being given to what sources are selected. In most cases responses to perceived inequity are also a matter of choice. Training programs designed to produce a more ethical and moral climate rely upon conscious thought (see, for instance, Greenberg 2006, where the justice training consisted of describing the construct, reviewing case studies, presenting role-playing episodes, and involving the participant managers in group discussions). Explanations to restore a sense of justice are intended to produce further thought among those involved. The results from expectancy theory (see Chapter 1 in this volume) are often intertwined with equity theory, while still seeming to produce somewhat disparate findings: Yet expectancy theory also is a largely conscious theory—on this score the two do not seem to differ.

DOES UNCONSCIOUSNESS PRODUCE DISPARATE RESULTS?

What we have then is a theory, and set of research results, that for the most part are based on conscious underpinnings. Would this change if the theory were shifted to emphasize unconscious phenomena, or if research that focused on unconscious processes and measures were highlighted? The answer seems to be, Sometimes yes and sometimes no.

The No Change Answer

There is a view that the explicit findings that have been reported to date would change very little were a greater amount of research that dealt with implicit considerations entered into the mix. This view is predicated on the idea that the phenomena involved when conscious and unconscious processes are engaged are not that different, if they differ at all. John Bargh has championed such a view—that unconscious measures produce much the same results that one finds when conscious processes are activated. Others, besides Bargh, have set forth this position, but it is based primarily on Bargh's research, or it has come to be.

Much of this research deals with the goal-setting and goal-pursuit processes. Thus Ferguson, Hassin, and Bargh (2008, 151) contend:

> This work suggests that *flexibility*—one of the widely assumed hallmarks of conscious goal pursuit . . .—also characterizes nonconscious goal pursuit. These findings are thus in harmony with the notion that goal pursuit operates in the same way, regardless of whether the goal is activated with or without conscious intent. . . . Flexibility is not uniquely conscious.

These three authors note five different studies to this effect. The "results draw automatic and controlled goal pursuit a little closer" (Ferguson, Hassin, and Bargh 2008, 157). Bargh has repeatedly emphasized this similarity between conscious and unconscious (see Bargh, Gollwitzer, Lee-Chai, Barndollar, and Trötschel 2001). On occasion, however, he has added that unconscious self-regulation is more efficient and consistent (Fitzsimons and Bargh 2004).

In an address to a New York City meeting of the Association for Psychological Science, as reported by Nicholson (2006), Bargh stated that "pretty much everything can be primed. . . . Bargh likened priming to a hypnoidal state. . . . So it is possible that unconsciously directed behavior uses the same mental processes as consciously goal-directed behavior" (26).

Others have championed this same position (see, for example, Dijksterhuis, Aarts, and Smith 2005; Glaser and Kihlstrom 2005; Malle 2005; Chartrand, Dalton, and Cheng 2008). According to Chartrand, Dalton, and Cheng (2008), moods, both positive and negative, in response to success and failure were reported to be the same under both conscious and unconscious conditions. Hassin (2005, 211) notes "that the cognitive components of working memory can, at least under some circumstances, operate outside of conscious awareness. . . . The mental organ whose essence is cognitive control, can operate completely outside of conscious awareness." Characteristically, when there is any qualification of these endorsements, the fact that unconscious processes are more efficient is emphasized.

The Yes Answer—Disparate Results Occur

In Chapter 5 of this volume I noted correlational data, using the various Miner Sentence Completion Scale (MSCS) measures as well as Implicit Association Test (IAT) data, indicating that in both instances a wide range of correlations occurred extending from rather low negative values up through quite high positive ones. The implication from the correlations that are low and close to zero is that unconscious and conscious data do not produce the same results—that disparate findings do occur. These data are opposite from those cited in the previous section. However, the research favoring the no change answer is limited, dealing primarily with goal-related findings; thus, although Bargh and his coworkers do generalize, the extent to which this is warranted is problematic. One would like to have more research on this point.

One finding that indicates a difference is that although trait ratings were the same immediately after an encounter, being based both on implicit and explicit impressions, two days later only the effects of implicit impressions survived (Uleman, Blader, and Todorov 2005). Thus, time differences in retention as between conscious and unconscious do occur. Furthermore, according to Chartrand, Dalton, and Cheng, "Although nonconscious self-regulation consumes fewer resources than conscious regulation, it is still depleting" (2008, 353). Thus the extent of depletion under resource load differs between the two. Given that both implicit and explicit attitudes are influenced by contextual factors, it is still true that the two are not equivalently sensitive to the same set of factors (Ferguson 2007). Implicit attitudes on occasion do not reflect the same situational influences that are more easily incorporated within explicit attitudes. "Conscious thought is constrained by the low capacity of consciousness. Unconscious thought does not have this constraint because the unconscious has a much higher capacity" (Dijksterhuis and Nordgren 2006, 96).

Rudman (2004) endorses that implicit attitudes often differ from self-reports; this is not universally true but it is common. In this view implicit attitudes derive from past and typically forgotten experiences; explicit attitudes are associated with more recent and/or accessible experiences. Emotional phenomena appear to affect implicit attitudes more. These conclusions are not unlike those of McClelland, Koestner, and Weinberger (1989) derived from comparisons of projective and self-report measures. Furthermore, consciousness does not have the same neural correlates as unconsciousness (Sergent and Dehaene 2004).

Research using the IAT and comparing different age groups indicates that conscious and unconscious attitudes toward racial groups do not follow the same pattern (Baron and Banaji 2006). Implicit attitudes favoring the in-group develop early and then continue on the same track. Explicit attitudes become increasingly egalitarian; the two diverge somewhere in the vicinity of age 10.

Taking the evidence on balance there clearly are phenomena where the unconscious processes do map the conscious data, and thus where equity theory and its research findings can be extended into the implicit realm. However, this is by no means always true, and so in any given instance we need to entertain the possibility that unconscious processes may diverge from what is known from the largely self-reported data. More research is needed here, but we need more and better theory also.

ASPECTS OF EQUITY THEORY AND DISTRIBUTIVE JUSTICE VULNERABLE TO UNCONSCIOUS CONSIDERATION

Given that new findings may possibly emerge when unconscious factors are introduced into equity theory investigations, a question arises as to where and when within the theory this is most likely to happen.

When Stress Occurs

Under crisis conditions decision making tends to be conscious, but not always; it can be automatic and unconscious (Sweeny 2008). This same conclusion applies to the stress produced by inequity. Thus the creation of overreward, and underreward, inequity realistically can produce responses that are not perceived by the responder.

Transference responses that are unconscious are particularly likely under conditions of threat and subsequent stress. In this way the familiar social support reaction is accounted for (Andersen, Reznik, and Glassman 2005). Also Leary (2007) reports that implicit egotism is obtained easily, yet when conscious processes are introduced so that people think more deliberately these automatic effects tend to disappear. "But when people are placed under cognitive load, positive self-evaluations increase" (322). Thus with the introduction of stress, automatic response patterns are reintroduced in such a way as to reduce the load on cognitive processes. All in all there is much evidence that when stress is introduced, as it is when the typical inequity and distributive injustice occur, unconscious manifestations are very likely to dominate.

For example, this apparent need for measures that operate outside of awareness is particularly evident in the study of sleeplessness reported by Greenberg (2006). In this study stress was introduced when the pay of the nurses involved was reduced by roughly 10–12 percent and measured by evidence of insomnia. The pay cut was based on a shift from nonexempt status to exempt; this is presented as an instance of stress of an underreward nature occasioned by a distributive injustice. All variables were measured by self-reports; stress levels were determined by reports of anxiety and burnout, while episodes of insomnia were recorded in diary entries by the nurses themselves. No unconscious measures were in fact utilized.

When Organizational Culture Is Involved

The transmission of social norms from organizational cultures can well occur in the absence of awareness (Fitzsimons and Bargh 2004). Thus people may unconsciously act upon the characteristic norms of their group and organization without realizing what they are doing. Although organizational culture is not specifically noted as a variable of equity theory, there are many points where it can enter in, including reference group choice, differences in equity sensitivity, response predispositions under inequity, variations in distribution rules, and the like. Studies indicate that such effects of organizational culture do exist within the confines of equity theory and distributive justice (see, for example, Erdogan, Liden, and Kraimer 2006). These points of vulnerability to the influence of unconscious factors from the cultural domain represent particularly attractive features for expanding equity theory and solving some of its problems. However, doing this will require adopting methods and measures beyond the self-reports that have been used so frequently in the past.

When Distortion Is Possible

Distortions may occur in many ways within equity theory; they may apply to one's own inputs and outcomes, but they may as well apply to reference individuals and groups. The multiple ways in which this may occur are discussed at length in Miner (2005, see 137–138). These various distortions, from whatever source, can create a number of errors.

Furthermore, distortions can provide an opportunity for unconscious factors to enter into behavior. This occurs primarily due to the operation of heuristics, which in their attempt to reduce effort (Shah and Oppenheimer 2008) may serve to introduce a variety of errors and distortions. Heuristics involve a combination of the conscious and unconscious (Evans 2008), but the important consideration for present purposes is that in this mix much happens that is beyond the scope of an individual's awareness. Thus to truly understand heuristics, it is necessary to look into the operation of unconscious procedures, using projectives, priming techniques, or whatever. Because equity theory is often concerned with anger-producing situations, this may be an ideal context into which to introduce the James and Mazerolle (2002) conditional reasoning approach (see Chapter 3 of this volume) to the measurement of unconscious factors. In any event the evidence serves to recommend the points where distortion may intervene in equity situations as ideal for incorporating nonrational factors.

Thus an additional point of vulnerability to unconscious considerations is added. Strangely a theory that has relied upon conscious thought and self-report measures extensively seems particularly in need of further investigation by measuring the unconscious in many of its features.

CONCLUSIONS

As noted in the first paragraph of this chapter, equity theory and with it the theory of distributive justice is given a validity of four stars, and from organizational behavior as a whole an importance value of 5.93. These figures, when divided, yield a ratio of 1.48. Accordingly the importance rating appears to overestimate the estimated validity by a substantial amount; this is consistent with field's judgment that the theory has been institutionalized.

Equity theory is without question a conscious or rational theory. Does this translate into any change from what might be expected from unconscious theorizing? The answer is both yes and no, but one has to take into account that disparate results may occur. Unconscious factors are most likely to emerge when stress occurs, when organizational culture is involved, and when distortions within equity theory are most likely to be operative. At these three points unconscious considerations became a high probability matter; they should indeed be given special attention in future research and theorizing.

CHAPTER 8

ATTRIBUTION THEORY AS APPLIED TO MANAGERIAL PERCEPTIONS

Attribution theory has long been a part of social psychology. It has had many contributors and versions. The attribution theory as applied to managerial perceptions (Green and Mitchell 1979; Mitchell and Wood 1980) is more indigenous to organizational behavior than other attribution theories. This theory appears to be best classified as focused on unconscious considerations; although the road to this position has been somewhat long and winding, a number of points of interest have arisen along the way. Conscious considerations are often intertwined as well. This attribution theory rates four stars on estimated validity; its importance rating at the hands of organizational behavior specialists is 4.18 (see Miner 2005, Chapter 11). As far as practical usefulness is concerned, it has proved to be rather deficient, and the theory has not turned out to be particularly amenable to meta-analysis. Yet there have been a number of positive reviews, particularly by Martinko and his collaborators (see Martinko, Douglas, and Harvey 2006; Martinko, Harvey, and Douglas 2007). Power motivation, in particular, has not proved to operate as hypothesized by the extended theory (Ferrier, Smith, Rediker, and Mitchell 1995).

INDICATORS OF UNCONSCIOUS MOTIVATION IN THE THEORY'S ORIGINS

Because attribution theory is by nature perceptual it inherently involves conscious thought, but even at the beginning there were at least two sources of motivation that operated beyond awareness.

Achievement Motivation

The first of these, growing out of the social psychological work on attribution theory, was Bernard Weiner's combining of attributional factors with the need for achievement (Weiner and Sierad 1975; and later Weiner 1985). As noted in Chapter 4 of this volume mobilizing needs activates unconscious processes. "There seems to be general agreement that familiar situational features automatically activate representations of behavioral goals, plans, and intentions. . . . That goal and motive structures are used in understanding the behavior of others has been recognized by achievement motivation researchers for some time, as shown by the use of projective techniques" (Bargh 1990, 105). Thus by resorting to achievement motivation Weiner introduces unconscious processes, which are continued as well by the Weiner theory's serving as an origin for the Mitchell formulations. Further evidence for this unconscious basis derives from Aarts, Dijksterhuis, and Dik (2008, 272): "Results indicated that participants who were primed with the achievement goal outperformed those who were not primed with the goal."

The Management of Ineffective Performance

A second line of evidence as to the operation of unconscious factors in the development of the attribution theory as applied to managerial perceptions derives from my own views on performance failure and the factors that contribute to it. On page 322 of Miner (2005) I list a number of strategic factors that may contribute to ineffective performance (see Table 17.1). This schema was in fact adopted as a listing of what goes into managerial attributions regarding the reasons for individual and group performance failures. The listing contains much that is of an unconscious nature. In the following I have explained how this can occur, drawing upon those categories specifically designated in Felps, Mitchell, and Byington (2006)—emotional problems, motivational problems, and work-group problems. Also it should be noted that this presentation includes multiple references to unconscious processes as such that are now incorporated in the theory:

> When feeling emotionally negative, people often take action to improve their mood. *Mood maintenance* behaviors are efforts to improve one's affect and can be either consciously or unconsciously motivated (195).

> The transfer of affect is largely automatic and subconscious, occurring through mimicry and psychological feedback. . . . More conscious processes can occur as well (201).

> Plus there are numerous references to *The New Unconscious* research under such headings as Defensiveness and Negative Psychological States (189–195).

Let us return to the factors that may contribute to ineffective performance and their implications for unconscious processes. The Felps, Mitchell, and Byington (2006) discussion starts with motivational considerations which in my listing are:

- Strong motives frustrated at work: pleasure in success, fear of failure, avoidance motives, dominance, desire to be popular, social motivation, need for attention
- Unintegrated means used to satisfy strong motives
- Low personal work standards
- Generalized low work motivation

In this category evidence of unconscious factors includes much of what is said in Chapter 4 of this volume. In this vein "goals can be primed by situational cues. . . . Importantly goal-priming effects are more pronounced when there is a current need or desire making it more pertinent to attain a goal" (Aarts, Dijksterhuis, and Dik 2008, 271). Furthermore roles may serve this same purpose: "Goals relevant to a role that an individual occupies can be automatically activated by cues inherent to the role or its physical or social environment, without awareness or intention to pursue the goal" (Diekman and Eagly 2008, 438).

The Felps, Mitchell, and Byington (2006) treatment is devoted next to emotional factors including moods. This translates in my listing to:

- Frequent disruptive emotion: anxiety, depression, anger, excitement, shame, guilt, jealousy
- Neurosis: with anxiety, depression, anger predominating
- Psychosis: with anxiety, depression, anger predominating
- Alcohol and drug problems

Chapter 1 in this volume contains discussions of how emotional factors may operate without awareness; so too does Chapter 7 on inequity, which is also noted as a source of emotional problems by Mitchell and his collaborators. Certainly neuroses and psychoses, as well as alcohol and drug problems, are consistent with psychodynamic interpretations involving unconscious processes. To this view should be added the following:

A great deal of affective processing takes place on implicit levels (Koole and Kuhl 2008, 299).

One final moderator of nonconscious mimicry is mood state (Dijksterhuis, Chartrand, and Aarts 2007, 70).

Many other models similarly suggest that emotions can be generated by some combination of automatic and controlled processing (Barrett, Ochsner, and Gross 2007, 181).

Finally the Felps, Mitchell, and Byington (2006) article takes up a topic that in my listing is considered under work-group problems:

- Negative consequences of group cohesion
- Ineffective management
- Inappropriate managerial standards as criteria

The unconscious nature of much of what happens as a consequence of behavior in this category is attested to as follows:

A long-standing and sophisticated program of experimentation has shown that representations of significant others from one's past may affect one's inferences, recollections, evaluations, and feelings about a new acquaintance when the new acquaintance resembles the significant other (Reis and Collins 2004, 234).

This transference effect can occur without any knowledge or awareness of its occurrence (Skowronski, Carlston, and Hartnett 2008, 328; see also Andersen, Reznik, and Glassman 2005; Chen, Fitzsimons, and Andersen 2007). It is said to function as a "social glue" (Dijksterhuis, Chartrand, and Aarts 2007, 71), and thus its instrumentality for work-group relationships. A similar mechanism for unconsciously facilitating behavior in a work-group is described as follows:

> Ostracized individuals mimic more, but they especially mimic members of the group that excluded them in the first place, emphasizing the possibility that mimicry after exclusion is aimed at restoring bonds. . . . The *automaticity* of the mimicry process is crucial (Dijkster-huis, Chartrand, and Aarts 2007, 69, 71).

Other aspects of Table 17.1, such as Physical Problems—physical disorders of emotional origin—might be noted as sources of unconscious processes. However, the presentation to this point seems sufficient; the crucial consideration is that Mitchell and his collaborators did identify factors that research has shown operate beyond awareness.

BIASES INHERENT IN THE ATTRIBUTION MODEL

On page 190 of Miner (2005) Figure 11.2 sets forth an attributional model for the Mitchell theory. Biases may enter in this model at link #1 and, as indicated subsequently, at link #2. Such biases may have inherent in them both conscious and unconscious processes (see the discussion of heuristics in Chapter 7 of this volume). These biases and heuristics are treated at some length in various sources (Gilovich, Griffin, and Kahneman 2002; Certo, Connelly, and Tihanyi 2008; Evans 2008), but the important consideration for present purposes is that they tend to incorporate unconscious factors. The failure to support the hypotheses regarding power utilization of the Mitchell et al. attribution theory may well be a consequence of biases introduced in the performance of controlled (executive) tasks (see Smith, Jostmann, Galinsky, and van Dijk 2008). Hall, Ariss, and Todorov (2007) showed that additional knowledge may introduce "systematic bias in predictions" (288) in that basketball fans were led astray, and thus were less accurate in their predictions, when provided with more information on the teams involved; thus rationality was lost.

Specific Attribution Theory Biases

Certain biases have been labeled in terms of their ties to attribution theory. One such oper-ates as follows:

> People have a surprising tendency to downplay situational demands and evaluate the behavior of others in terms of enduring character despite logical expectations. . . . This tendency to downplay situational context has been termed the *"fundamental attribution bias"* (Aviezer, Hassin, Bentin, and Trope 2008, 265–266).

Again:

> One goal of the research was to examine the neural bases of one indication of self-enhancement—namely the *self-serving attribution bias*. This bias reflects the tendency to take credit for good actions and deny responsibility for bad ones. The results indicated that the self-serving bias was common and significant, and that it was associated with enhanced activation in the bilateral caudate nucleus, a subregion of the striatum (Taylor and Sherman 2008, 67).

Other attributional biases have been noted (see Martinko, Douglas, and Harvey 2006), but these are primary.

Conscious and Unconscious Mechanisms

Emotional processes appear to play an important role in the extent to which unconscious considerations influence attributions. Whenever positive affect is at a low level, there is a pronounced tendency to deliberate and thus utilize conscious processes; at such times behavior of any kind is less likely. Whenever positive affect is at a high level, intuitive action without deliberation, and thus without awareness, becomes much more likely. Accordingly regulation of positive affect serves to coordinate the balance between conscious and unconscious processes. Affect regulation may in turn be primed by situational factors (Koole and Kuhl 2008).

This significance of emotion, and emotional regulation for attribution theory as applied to managerial perceptions, is attested to by research on poor performers conducted by Taggar and Neubert (2004): "In terms of theoretical implications, our results suggest . . . the prominent role of emotions in influencing behavioral intentions" (963).

CRITICISMS AND ALTERNATIVES

Numerous criticisms, alternative theoretical perspectives, and deviant research findings vis-à-vis this theoretical perspective have been presented over the years (see Miner 2005, 196–200). These are diversified in nature but often point to the involvement of unconscious factors.

The Mitchell Criticisms

One of the most telling of these criticisms came from Mitchell (1982) himself, and this one was in fact independent of the conscious-unconscious nexus. The problem appeared to be that attributions, as the Mitchell theory presents them, seem to be rather *minor* in their causative effect; much more significant are personal, social, and particularly organizational policies that bypass attributions and relegate them to a rather weak role. This caution would seem to have served as a major wet blanket insofar as the development of the theory is concerned (Martinko, Douglas, and Harvey 2006).

The Unconscious Criticism

Much more significant in the long run, however, has been a major reemergence of the unconscious interpretation of attribution theory, as expressed by Cronshaw and Lord (1987) and later by Lord (1995) and also Lord and Maher (1991). These formulations operate in the same domain as the Mitchell et al. theory. They take the position that because of heavy demands on conscious processes, exceeding the load capabilities to be found there, deliberate information processing becomes impossible when attribution variables are mobilized and default implicit capabilities are activated instead. Thus the highly rational perceiver-as-scientist position espoused by Mitchell et al. is replaced by automatic, implicit activations that operate much more rapidly; awareness accordingly is lost on the part of the perceiver, but the potential for action is gained. The Lord and colleagues interpretation appears to project an either/or view here, presenting their position as a replacement for the attribution theory as applied to managerial perceptions characterization. Yet Martinko, Douglas, and Harvey (2006) in reviewing this position are somewhat more cautious in considering the data; they do not reject the Mitchell et al. theory out of hand.

Martinko et al. Reconsidered

As far as organizational behavior is concerned the Martinko, Harvey, and Douglas (2007) review represents a much more comprehensive effort than anything presented previously. Thus it is important to consider the opinions expressed as regards the Mitchell et al. theory, and how they match up with the Lord criticisms:

> Davis and Gardner (2004) propose that the distance between leaders and members determine whether or not the members engage in the effortful rational processing suggested by attribution theory or engage in the automatic processing suggested by Lord and his colleagues. . . . Automatic processing is more likely in distant leader-member relationships (572).
>
> When we look at this area as a whole, we are struck by the impression that the majority of the work in this area suggests automatic processing as suggested by Lord and his colleagues as opposed to the more traditional rational information processing (572).
>
> In contrast to much of the prior work on leadership, this body of work suggests that, as opposed to the effortful and rational process described by the Green and Mitchell model, the process by which attributions are generated in these contexts is more appropriately characterized as automatic and cybernetic. . . . These types of social perceptions are probably best explained by theories of categorization and template matching (i.e. automatic processing) as opposed to the more cognitively laborious processes (576).
>
> In routine everyday situations, people generally do not exert the cognitive effort required to make causal attributions. Consequently, perceptions of charisma or leadership qualities that are not particularly important to individuals are probably processed through peripheral (i.e. automatic) routes. . . . Social perceptions are probably better described by the more cybernetic models of information processing (577–578).

Thus, these reviewers do appear ultimately to come down on the side of unconscious, automatic approaches. They are particularly concerned that the Green and Mitchell (1979) model ignores the link between attributions and emotions.

The Role of the Capacity Principle

The Lord theory regarding attributions states that conscious thought processes fail when they are overloaded and that accordingly unconscious processes take over within the domain involved. Thus the capacity principle is violated and automaticity replaces the overloaded executive or controlled thought processes. Is this a tenable conclusion? Can it be used as a core concept on which to base the Lord proposals? The evidence on this score is quite convincing (see the discussions by Bargh and Williams 2006; Dijksterhuis and Nordgren 2006). Yes, such overloading processes do operate with a resulting resort to automaticity, as Lord describes. Furthermore there is substantial psychological evidence that, consonant with this process, glycogen is used up in the brain in a manner that might well account for what happens (Gailliot 2008).

The End of the Road?

This should be the end of the road for unconscious processes within the domain of attribution theory as applied to managerial perceptions: Martinko and his people, as the primary reviewers of the theory over the years, have indeed endorsed the theory in its unconscious version (the Lord version) and this type of endorsement appears entirely justified.

But a problem developed. More recently Martinko, Moss, Douglas, and Borkowski (2007) published a research article that completely ignores unconscious processes (and the Lord contributions on the subject as well). Is this an indication of ambivalence? Does it represent some kind of disclaimer? I do not know. However, situations of this kind are becoming far too common in organizational behavior, where conscious and unconscious versions of a theory are endorsed at one and the same time, without talking to one another (see in this connection Chapter 2, on goal-setting theory, in this volume).

In any event a need exists to present my version of the theory at this point. Quite simply I feel that as Mitchell et al. often imply the theory's domain may be handled on a conscious basis; managers can attempt to deal rationally with problems of poor performance. They may even exclude biases and do a reasonably good job on this score. However, the automatic version of the theory as proposed by Lord is also correct under certain circumstances, in accord with the Martinko, Harvey, and Douglas (2007) conclusions. I have offered some suggestions on when people are likely to use processes of which they are aware, and when they will tend to employ automatic processes of which they are not aware. Thus, in line with the thesis of this book as a whole, I continue to subscribe to the view that conscious and unconscious approaches may be mobilized as the individual's load capabilities permit. From what is known about the typical balance as between the two, unconscious activations tend to predominate, however.

CONCLUSIONS

Attribution theory as applied to managerial perceptions, as indicated earlier, has an estimated validity rating of four stars and an importance rating of 4.18. When the former is divided into the latter the result is a value of 1.05. This suggests that the organizational behavior scholars approximate the rated validity in their judgments; there is very little by way of an overevaluation of this theory.

Taking supportive data from several different sources, I conclude that the attribution theory as applied to managerial perceptions has the characteristics of an essentially unconscious theory, although on occasion it can operate on a conscious basis. The automatic processes articulated by Lord and his colleagues certainly are activated often. Evidence in line with this view is adduced from attribution theory, from formulations regarding the management of ineffective performance, and from biases inherent in the attribution model. Some uncertainty regarding Martinko et al.'s endorsement of the Lord views regarding automaticity occurs because of a subsequent failure to mention this position. Nevertheless my own conclusion is that, as is typically the case, both unconscious and conscious processes tend to operate when the attribution theory as applied to managerial perceptions is mobilized.

CHAPTER 9

EXISTENCE, RELATEDNESS, AND GROWTH THEORY

Existence, relatedness, and growth theory (Alderfer 1972) represents an attempt to refine Maslow's (1943, 1954) need hierarchy theory to produce more valid results. However, my judgment (Miner 2006b) based largely on Miner (2002) was that it only raised the estimated validity from two stars (Maslow) to three stars (Alderfer). In fact in the opinion of organizational behavior as a whole the importance rating given need hierarchy theory was 4.14 and existence, relatedness, and growth theory was 3.58 (thus, at a somewhat lower level). I am not aware of any meta-analyses on either theory although probably because it has lived longer, need hierarchy theory has had more discussion. Both theories produce rather mixed reviews. In recent years there appears to have been a resurgence of interest in Maslow's theory. This position is stated by Latham and Pinder (2005), as well as by Latham (2007). These authors adduce evidence generally supportive of the theory, but what they note appears to be rather tangential in nature. I would retain my view that a three-star rating represents the most favorable evaluation that can be given to this set of theories. In my judgment they are at best mixed in their validity.

REPRISE ON MINER (2002)

Although I retain the same rating, at least on the Alderfer (1972) theory, the considerations underlying this evaluation have changed.

Measurement Issues

The research in this area, including that of Alderfer (1972), has consistently utilized some type of self-report measure. There have been many different measures, but all have been of this type. Yet Maslow calls for measures that distinguish extreme groups on his needs, and he has indicated that, as with other need theories, unconscious motivation should be mobilized. In neither case have these aspects of need hierarchy theory been respected. Alderfer (1972) in continuing to draw upon the need designation follows Maslow, but his choice of measures and designs does not. In fact, to my knowledge, the characteristic of the need designation as involving unconscious motivation has never been mobilized in any research on either the Maslow or the Alderfer theory. This is clearly inappropriate.

Concerns about Self-reports

I am now convinced that the Alderfer and Maslow theories have not truly been tested, in spite of the long intervals that have transpired since these formulations. Earlier I was influenced to a degree by the studies that drew upon self-report measures; now I am of the opinion that this was not justified and that accordingly the size of the domain in which further research is needed is wider than I originally thought. I would refer the reader to Chapter 1 of Miner (2008) and in particular to pages 14 to 17 for the reasoning behind my rejection of the self-report data as relevant. Also consideration should be given to Schultheiss and Brunstein (2001) and Cogswell (2008), as well as to the discussion in Chapter 4 of this volume.

ALDERFER'S NEEDS

To what extent do Alderfer's three classifications of needs require unconscious confirmation in the research conduced on them?

Existence Needs

In most instances existence needs were adequately represented by the self-report measures. Thus, what was said on this score appears to have been mostly correct (see the conclusion reached in Miner 2002). As I indicated previously "the research seems to support a low-level cut. . . . It does seem useful to think of some among the physiological and safety needs as dominating" (141).

Relatedness Needs

Social and relatedness needs have been discussed previously in their ties to unconscious motivation. This was given major attention in Chapter 5 of this volume. In addition I would recommend a reading of Chapter 3 in John Bargh's (2007) *Social Psychology and the Unconscious: The Automaticity of Higher Mental Processes*. This chapter was written by Chen, Fitzsimons, and Andersen and provides considerable insight into the research on the unconscious basis of interpersonal relationships. It concludes with the following comment:

> At this point, a reader may be left with the impression that much of what happens in close relationships does so automatically: Automaticity underlies how people think and feel about their significant others and themselves, whether people expect to be accepted or rejected, how they regulate themselves as they strive to attain goals associated with significant others or to protect themselves and their relationships, and, finally, how they behave toward others. Moreover, we have emphasized that this wide range of automatic processes and phenomena is likely to be maintained over time, repeatedly re-surfacing in new interpersonal encounters.

Nonetheless we would strongly argue against the conclusion that relationship processes and phenomena are *always* automatic (Chen, Fitzsimons, and Andersen 2007, 163).

The point here is that relatedness needs are best measured by instruments that consider both processes and phenomena of which people are aware, and those of which they are not. In any event the measures have to take into account automatic, unconscious considerations; they cannot leave these entirely out of the mix, as self-report indexes do.

Further to the evidence on relatedness needs as they are influenced by first impressions, discussed in Chapter 5 of this volume, let me invoke the following: "The processes underlying impression formation occur extremely quickly and are often lasting and influential" (Harris and Garris 2008, 161). Accordingly early impressions may serve to have much to do with social relationships of a lasting nature; "the interpretation of cues to others' personality traits can occur without effort, intention, or awareness" (Choi, Gray, and Ambady 2005, 311).

Growth Needs

Also in Chapter 5 of this volume growth needs and their ties to self-actualization needs were discussed. Such needs were shown there to have the potential for unconscious mobilization. They are often activated by priming processes, which have been discussed frequently in previous chapters. Checks performed at the end of experiments indicate that participants in priming situations are unable to guess at any better than chance levels as to the content of the subliminal exposure (Andersen, Reznik, and Glassman 2005, 436). "People can strategically switch from conscious and effortful action initiation (guided by goal intentions) to having their goal-directed actions effortlessly elicited by the specific situational cues" (Gollwitzer, Bayer, and McCulloch 2005, 488). Accordingly, once again, the proximity in the activation of conscious and unconscious processes is demonstrated, and thus the need for the utilization of measures that tap both. Chapter 4 made the point that measures of self-actualization that consider factors of which the individual is unaware should be included, as well as the self-report indexes.

FURTHER ON SELF-ACTUALIZATION

Self-actualization is often considered to incorporate creativity (by Maslow 1987 for instance). This subject was treated in Chapter 5 of this volume, particularly as it relates to emotional considerations, but it requires further discussion here. Positive emotion was the focus of the previous treatment, and indeed it is often implicated in creativity discussions. Creativity can in fact be enhanced by priming and thus may be at least potentially an unconscious process. Furthermore, it has been found that primes for deviancy also enhance creativity (Dijksterhuis, Chartrand, and Aarts 2007).

I have also noted that emotions, and in particular positive emotions, tend to activate creativity. Yet positive emotions have numerous other unconscious effects; they tend to produce a higher level of stereotyping, for example (Gollwitzer, Parks-Stamm, Jaudas, and Sheeran 2008). In fact "there is evidence that extreme emotion, and efforts to regulate them, interfere with rational decision making and tax cognitive resources, thus increasing the likelihood of ill-considered behavior" (Cyders and Smith 2008, 821). Creativity and self-actualization can carry with them a number of consequences, thus improving performance or on occasion serving detrimental purposes. Creativity is a two-step process whereby unconscious processes appear to be more powerful in an incubation period, but as new insightful solutions emerge into consciousness the advantage may be lost (Zhong, Dijksterhuis, and Galinsky 2008). Different methods of introducing unconscious processes appear to produce somewhat differing results here. However it is clear that under appropriate circumstances creativity can be enhanced through the activation of unconscious mechanisms.

PREPOTENCY

The Alderfer (1972) formulations regarding prepotency, and thus the relation existing between needs, differ from Maslow's interpretation. Research in this area has produced inconsistent results and is confounded by the fact that needs have been measured with inappropriate indexes.

Unconscious Relationships between Needs

The work that has been done on motivation outside the realm of awareness in recent years has done little to improve this situation. Research on priming and goal contagion introduces understanding, but it makes the source of motivation much more difficult to attribute (Aarts, Dijksterhuis, and Dik 2008).

Furthermore priming a motivation source may not contribute to the performance of that particular need. To understand how the activation of a goal influences behavior, one has to consider as well how that goal relates to other more overriding concerns. "When a given goal (partying) interferes with the attainment of one's high-order interests (doing well on an exam), activating the interfering goal promotes the pursuit of these interests rather than the interfering goal" (Fishbach and Trope 2008, 290). At such times performance on the higher-order goal, and thus on the impending exam, actually improves. Interrelationships among needs consequently may be thoroughly confounded as unconscious factors are introduced. Given considerations of this kind it may in fact be almost impossible to establish prepotency relationships, as between relatedness and growth needs in the above example, for instance. Prepotency thus would appear to be a conundrum that will take a very long time to solve, if it ever is solved.

The Role of Projectives

In any event it is apparent that disentangling unconscious factors is essential to solving the prepotency problem, and projective measures do get at these unconscious considerations. Consequently it may be worthwhile to look into the viability of projectives for this purpose.

In fact, sparked by the success of projective methods such as the Rorschach Inkblot Technique (1942) in personality diagnosis, social psychologists first initiated their research efforts to identify indirect procedures for measuring attitudes (Payne, Jacoby, and Lambert 2005, 398). Out of these efforts came certain partially structured measures of attitudes (Vargas, Sekaquaptewa, and von Hippel 2007). Typically, partially structured projectives attempt to get at unconscious motives, such as needs, by focusing attention on desired characteristics while still retaining a degree of ambiguity in the stimulus and in the method of obtaining responses. Examples would be the Thematic Apperception Test (TAT) pictures used by McClelland and his collaborators (see Chapter 4) that focus on achievement themes. Similarly the Miner Sentence Completion Scales (MSCS; see Miner 2008) focus the stems on the particular subscales involved in the three versions of the test. The Picture Arrangement Test (PAT) is also partially structured in nature, directing attention to certain characteristics such as social needs, aggressive needs, dependence, emotions (both positive and negative), self-confidence, and super-ego strength. These are the projective measures that seem most amenable to use in organizational behavior.

I have not given attention to the Rorschach, not because it continues to lack psychometric soundness (such soundness has been well established now from data presented in Chapter 1 of Miner 2008), but because the test is not really partially structured. The inkblots involved are highly ambiguous, thus they are particularly suitable for eliciting unconscious material. However, they are not as suitable for focusing on specific characteristics or content that one may be particularly interested in investigating. The Rorschach has been used in organizational behavior research, but only rarely. Certain indexes, such as the use of color to designate emotion and of movement responses to indicate empathy or creativity, do appear promising. Yet I am forced to admit that my personal knowledge in this area is sufficiently lacking so that I am unable to map out potential organizational behavior applications, and certainly not applications to the prepotency dilemma.

CONCLUSIONS

Per the information provided early on in this chapter, existence, relatedness, and growth theory obtains an estimated validity of three stars, with an importance rating at the hands of organizational behavior overall of 3.58. The resulting ratio, when the appropriate division is made, is 1.19. That result leads to the conclusion that organizational behavior tends to overestimate the validity of existence, relatedness, and growth theory but not to the pronounced degree that occurs with some other theories.

This is essentially an unconscious theory given its dedication to needs that operate beyond the pale of awareness. All of these needs, except for those of an existence nature that would seem to operate often on conscious principles, clearly are characterized by their unconscious nature; thus they warrant measurement on unconscious terms rather than via self-reports. Approaches aimed at establishing some version of prepotency have not proved very successful. Various projective indexes including the TAT, sentence completion measures, and the PAT when applied in a focused manner offer some promise, but have not fulfilled that promise to date; the Rorschach appears to lack the necessary focus on specific needs to justify its use in studying prepotency, but this apparent deficiency may be a function of my personal lack of up-to-date familiarity in this area.

CHAPTER 10

PSYCHOANALYTIC THEORY AS APPLIED TO ORGANIZATIONS

Harry Levinson has applied psychoanalytic theory to organizational behavior. His work is based on the writings of Sigmund Freud (1938) and thus gives considerable attention to the unconscious, but it includes some original contributions as well. A good presentation of the current version of psychoanalytic theory is contained in Westen (1998); it is clear that the theory as set forth by Freud is somewhat outdated and needs to be brought up to date.

Much of the evidence regarding psychoanalytic theory does not qualify as entirely scientific, in that it is frequently of a clinical nature (see Westen and Weinberger 2004). Levinson himself did little research to support his theory; and others often have been remiss as well. There is research available on certain of the propositions of the theory, and I will concentrate on the results of this research here. However, it should be recognized that Levinson and his theory are deficient in this regard. For this reason I am able to give the theory only a rating of three stars on validity; its importance rating at the hands of organizational behavior scholars is somewhat lower, at 2.84 (see Miner 2007, Epilogue on Motivation 1). To the best of my knowledge Levinson's theory has been evaluated through meta-analysis on only one occasion (see Bornstein 2002), and because of the mixed research support (see Miner 2002) the theory's practical usefulness emerges as somewhat questionable as well. I will cite the publications that are particularly relevant from Levinson's rather extensive writings as I take up each topic.

NEEDS

Levinson (1973) devotes considerable attention to motivation and its consequences. His own preference is for a psychoanalytical informed view. In his 1981 book he gives particular attention to various types of needs with what he labels as ministration, maturation, and mastery needs receiving the most extensive treatment. On this score he has the following to say:

> Ministration needs require supportive and facilitative efforts that come from outside the person; maturation needs require conditions for the natural unfolding within the person. When both needs have been sufficiently met at each step of the person's development, the conditions are created for the next stage: the gratification of mastery needs. Each person must master enough of the world to survive in it (Levinson 1981, 236).

Consequently a need hierarchy involving a type of prepotency is espoused. Mastery needs are at the top, and they serve to integrate and consolidate the person around psychoanalytic principles.

Needs by their very nature have to some degree an unconscious component. How this component may enter into their activation and operation has been discussed at several points previously in this volume (see in particular the treatments in Chapters 4, 5, and 9). There an understanding of how unconscious factors are bound into various types of needs is provided. Levinson is one of these need theorists, and the needs he considers are not unlike those treated previously.

A good example of Levinson's approach to needs and how they relate to the psychological contract is contained in Meckler, Drake, and Levinson (2003). Unconscious needs are given special attention, and dependency needs (as in the ministration designation) are emphasized in particular. Unconscious considerations are also treated at some length in Pratch and Levinson (2002). This treatment includes a strong endorsement of the use of projective techniques to measure unconscious factors, including sentence completion indexes and the TAT, in evaluating executives.

NARCISSISM IN TOP MANAGEMENT

Levinson has devoted himself to assessing why top management has failed in its efforts to address challenges from changing economic circumstances. He has taken on this issue on several occasions.

The Position Established in Levinson (1994)

Consider the following quotes:

> The explanations are fundamentally psychological, significantly having to do with individual and organizational narcissism, unconscious recapitulation of family dynamics in the organization, exacerbating dependency, psychologically illogical organization structure and compensation schemes, inadequate management of change, and inability to manage cognitive complexity (428).

> Fundamental among the causes of their inability to adapt effectively . . . all became significantly narcissistic (429).

The narcissism of the chief executive often sets a similar tone for the corporation as a whole (432).

Another form of chief executive narcissism is the kind of behavior that assumes that all significant decisions eventually will rise to the CEO's level (432).

One useful way of breaking into the rigidly narcissistic hierarchy is to bring people systematically into the organization from other companies (434).

Levinson's (1998) Position

Subsequently Levinson has elaborated on his position:

The most pervasive problem among people who exercise power over others is that of narcissism in its many forms (237).

Workaholics are likely to combine both forms of narcissism to varying degrees. They not only drive themselves toward impossible ego ideal goals, for example, unconscious fantasized omnipotence, but also tend to demand the same intensity of commitment and level of perfectionist behavior of others (238).

Evidence and Conceptualizations

Although experimental evidence on unconscious narcissism as posited by Levinson is limited, the concept does receive support from a series of studies concerned with implicit egotism; implicit egotism is clearly unconscious, as reflected in the priming methods used to study it, and it appears to have much in common with narcissism as well (see Pelham, Carvallo, and Jones 2005). Thus this research would seem to provide proxy evidence for Levinson's (1994, 1998) contentions. However, it does not extend to top management subjects.

That Levinson's treatment is consonant with psychoanalysis leaves no doubt, however. Freud (1931) describes a narcissistic libidinal type in one of his collected papers; such individuals would appear to provide the essence of the type of person that Levinson describes. Further discussion on the topic is also to be found in Rosenthal and Pittinsky (2006), and here the focus is definitely on executive leadership. Narcissism is clearly tied to the need for power. "Implicit leadership theory suggests that we choose as our leaders those people who seem most leaderlike. . . . This is especially true of narcissistic leaders. Narcissistic leaders are not only likely to abuse their power, but . . . are more likely to convince their followers to buy into the abuse" (625).

TRANSFERENCE

Another area where Levinson's theoretical hypotheses jibe with the research evidence is that of transference.

Levinson's Hypotheses

Levinson (1968, 1981), as is characteristic of those who espouse psychoanalytic views, embraces the transference concept on various occasions. He sees transference as an unconscious process that brings past attitudes and goals, especially those involving powerful parental figures, into the present. To this he adds the hypothesis that transference may be applied to organizations and institutions as well as individuals. Such organizations are said to possess the same power that individuals had, and thus become transference objects in the same sense.

Experimental Evidence

I have already reviewed in previous chapters evidence of an experimental nature that indicates that transference may occur independent of awareness (see Andersen, Reznik, and Glassman 2005; Chen, Fitzsimons, and Andersen 2007). "Two types of significant-other goals have been explored—. . . goals that an individual normally has when with a significant other, and goals that the significant other has for the individual" (Chartrand, Dalton, and Cheng 2008, 349). "We are almost always encountering significant others or anthropomorphized objects or perceiving others who are pursuing their own goals, or being faced with temptations or social norms. . . . These are all environmental triggers of nonconscious goals" (354). I believe these quotes encompass the kind of extension to organizations that Levinson had in mind for the transference of which he wrote.

Other evidence that expands the transference phenomenon and attests further to its unconscious nature as subject to priming is contained in Shah (2005) and Kruglanski and Pierro (2008). There is little doubt that numerous research studies credit the correctness of Levinson's hypotheses as regards transference.

REPRESSION

Among the descriptions of the unconscious given in Chapter 1 of Miner (2008) are several that derive from a psychoanalytic orientation and that make specific reference to repression (see Carr 2002 and Gabriel 1999). Anna Freud (1946) also gives the construct considerable attention. Unconscious repression is at the heart of many psychoanalytic concepts and interpretations.

Levinson (1970, 1981) uses repression in his presentations, but perhaps not as frequently as some of his other constructs. Nevertheless, it is clearly apparent that repression as a defense is important to his expositions.

In Chapter 2 of Miner (2008) I presented a discussion of the experimental evidence on repression that existed as of the time that book was written. A goodly amount of this research emanated from Michael Anderson and his colleagues at the Memory Control Laboratory at the University of Oregon. Research from this source is quite extensive (see Anderson 2003, 2005; Anderson, Ochsner, Kuhl, Cooper, Robertson, Gabrieli, Glover, and Gabrieli 2004; Johnson and Anderson 2004; Levy and Anderson 2002; Levy, McVeigh, Marful, and Anderson 2007). I reproduce here what I had to say then on this subject (from Miner 2008, 27–28), with special reference to the implications for repression:

Memory and Forgetting

- Repression has remained controversial for nearly a century because of the lack of well-controlled evidence validating it. Here we argue that the conceptual and methodological tools now exist for a rigorous scientific examination of repression. . . . Repression is, in fact, a scientifically tractable problem. . . . Experimental psychology will no longer sweep repression under the rug (Anderson and Levy 2006, 512–513).

- What are the mechanisms by which human beings willfully control awareness of unwanted memories. . . . Although my colleagues and I view this question through the lens of cognitive psychology, the situation bears a strong resemblance to repression. . . . The resulting theory may not be identical to Freudian repression, but it clearly speaks to the situation characterized by Freud. . . . The end result may be impaired memory for the things that people avoid thinking about. This suggests that the think/no think paradigm of Anderson and Green (2001) may provide a useful laboratory model of the repression proposed by Freud. . . . It is now no longer possible to say that there is no mechanism that could possibly support repression. . . . If the proper experiments are conducted the current phenomena may have most of the core characteristics of repression envisioned by Freud (Anderson 2006, 328, 336, 340, 345).
- Our results establish a direct link between internal operations that control phenomenal awareness of a memory and its later accessibility. These findings thus support a suppression mechanism that pushes unwanted memories out of awareness, as posited by Freud (Anderson and Green 2001, 368).
- Our work does not demonstrate unconscious repression (Anderson and Levy 2002, 503).

Brain Mechanisms

Research indicates that neural systems in the brain are activated when unwanted memories are suppressed; once triggered, this network of neurons keeps the unwanted memories from awareness (Anderson, Ochsner, Kuhl, Cooper, Robertson, Gabrieli, Glover, and Gabrieli 2004; Anderson 2006). Functional magnetic resonance was used to study this process. As hypothesized, prefrontal cortical and right hippocampal activity combined to predict the extent of forgetting. Thus a neurobiological process underlying motivated forgetting was demonstrated: "People suppress consciousness of unwanted memories by recruiting lateral prefrontal cortex to disengage the hippocampal processing that supports recollection" (Anderson 2006, 337).

The Controversy

A major disagreement with the Anderson et al. findings (2004) and interpretations has been mounted by Kihlstrom (2002), who feels that the Oregon researchers claim too much. This dissent is important because Kihlstrom is one of the more influential advocates of the new unconscious position (Hassin, Uleman, and Bargh 2005). The controversy regarding evidence of repression is developed further by Winerman (2005), who describes research indicating that motivated forgetting works better when emotional content is involved than when it is absent. Winerman notes an instance of a failure to replicate the original results but also presents results from a meta-analysis supporting the motivated forgetting position. On balance, this report on the controversy achieves a level of objectivity that is to be applauded. Yet all parties are in agreement that to date unconscious repression has not actually been demonstrated. The mechanism to accomplish this has been identified, but not the fact of the matter, at least not as yet (as of 2010). A report on the state of this controversy subsequent to the article that appeared in *Science* is contained in O'Connor (2004), a *New York Times* piece entitled "Theory Given on Burying of Memories by People."

Subsequent Evidence

Since the writing of the above, evidence has continued to accumulate both from Oregon and elsewhere (Levy and Anderson 2008; MacLeod and Saunders 2008; Smith and Moynan 2008). This evidence supports and extends the arguments from Oregon.

Further endorsement of the repression interpretation derives from Edwin Locke (see Chapter 2 of this volume) and from B. F. Skinner (see Chapter 6). The term is used as well by others involved in the experimental research with unconscious processes (see Harmon-Jones and Harmon-Jones 2008; Koole and Kuhl 2008). Suppressed thoughts have been found to assert themselves in dreams with high frequency consistent with the psychoanalytic view (Wegner, Wenzlaff, and Kozak 2004). All in all the evidence supporting Levinson and others of a psychoanalytic persuasion regarding the significance of the repression construct is quite convincing.

DEPENDENCE

As indicated previously Levinson gives attention to dependence needs in connection with his ministration category of needs. In actual fact he introduces dependence processes frequently throughout his theorizing on organizational functioning (see, for example, Levinson 1998).

The Process Dissociation Approach

A particularly appropriate vehicle for studying interpersonal dependency is the process dissociation approach to unraveling the relationships between conscious and unconscious phenomena. This approach has been applied to multiple areas (see Payne and Stewart 2007) and was originally developed in the context of memory and learning. However, I will illustrate its use from an article by Bornstein (2002) as applied to the dependency construct. This approach draws upon the oral dependency score derived from the Rorschach to get at unconscious dependency. It has been shown that the Rorschach index involved is in fact projective in nature (Bornstein 2007).

I present the process dissociation approach in a series of steps:

Step 1. Converging Behavior Predictions

This first step, converging behavior predictions, requires that measures employed in assessing conscious and unconscious features of a construct do in fact predict what they are intended to assess, and they must do so reliably.

A wide range of measures of a self-reporting nature has been used to determine dependency. When evaluated against behavioral indicators of dependence these measures yield validities falling primarily in the .30 to .50 range. A meta-analysis puts the average at $r = .31$. Good reliability of both an internal consistency and a test-retest nature has been demonstrated.

Projective indexes used to get at unconscious dependency have been dominated by the oral dependency score from the Rorschach, although other projectives including sentence completion scales have been used. The projectives as a group had $r = .37$ validity against behavioral indexes in the meta-analysis; the two validity values in the .30s are not significantly different. Good reliabilities are reported, including scorer agreement in the .90s for the Rorschach measure.

Thus the assumptions required at Step 1 are indeed met for both explicit and implicit measures of dependency.

Step 2. Modest Positive Intercorrelations

The second step, modest positive intercorrelations, is designed to demonstrate that the measures of conscious and unconscious dependency are related to one another, but only moderately. Typically, this is assumed to be with r between .20 and .40. Based on twelve studies of the intercorrelations involved, the mean r between explicit and implicit dependency indexes was found to be .29; thus the correlation was within the bounds accepted as modestly positive and accordingly met the Step 2 criterion.

Step 3. Differential Effects of Moderating Variables

The third step, differential effects of moderating variables, is described by Bornstein (2002) as perhaps the most important. This requirement involves identifying moderators that influence the scores on one of the types of measures and not the other, or that influence the two types of tests in different ways; Step 3 creates evidence of a dissociation between the processes involved and consequently that the mechanisms operating differ. Variables serving to moderate results can be naturally occurring, as for instance mood variations, or they can represent experimental treatments, such as induced anxiety levels.

With regard to dependency, operative moderating variables have been established in three areas:

- Gender and gender role effects
- Mood effects
- Instructional manipulations

In the first instance and then using self-report indexes, meta-analytic results indicate that women scored significantly above men on dependency. The mean effect size was $d = .41$. With projective indexes, however, no significant gender differences are in evidence, although there is a slightly higher score among men than among women on the projectives. Though not as pronounced, these same conclusions hold using measures of gender role orientation.

Two studies looked into the effects of mood states. Participants in the negative mood treatment evidenced a significant increase in Rorschach indexes of dependency but no change in the self-report index. A naturalistic replication using hormone-shift measures from menstruation data for females confirmed this increase in the Rorschach index. Accordingly, once again a moderator was established between the two dependency measures, indicating that under projective (unconscious) conditions mood states had an elevating effect on dependence while under self-report (conscious) conditions no such effects from mood states were in evidence.

With regard to instructional manipulations, sets to respond to the two measures were established for responding as "very dependent" and "very independent" individuals. The former increased scores on the self-report index and the latter decreased these same scores; no change as a function of instructional set was observed on the Rorschach. Using a subtler instructional framing approach the results obtained were identical to those indicated above, thus once again establishing the existence of a particular moderating variable.

Making Predictions

In making predictions for an individual at least one of each type of measure should be administered. For the projective type this will typically include the Rorschach in order to obtain its oral dependency score; for the self-report type more latitude is available. The scores thus obtained may then be split into high and low groups using available normative data. With these dependency scores a fine tuning of the resulting data may be created as follows:

- High projective score and high self-report score is defined as *high dependency*
- High projective score and low self-report score is defined as *unacknowledged dependency*
- Low projective score and high self-report score is defined as *dependent self-presentation*
- Low projective score and low self-report score is defined as *low dependency*

Note that the high dependency and unacknowledged dependency categories call for unconscious dependence processes in accord with Levinson's formulations and consequently support his theorizing. These categorizations have been shown to be related differentially to diagnostic data using clinical populations (Bornstein 2002). Also categorizations of this type along with the data marshaled in support of the previously mentioned Steps 1 through 3 have been used to argue for the use of dependency as an integrating variable across both conscious and unconscious measures (see Cogswell 2008).

CONCLUSIONS

Psychoanalytic theory as applied to organizations (Levinson 1968, 1970, 1973, 1981, 1994, 1998) possesses an estimated validity of three stars and is given an importance rating by organizational behavior scholars of 2.84. Dividing this second value by the former, the resulting figure is .95. Accordingly the importance ratings tend to underestimate the presumed validity, although to a nonsignificant extent; consequently the two evaluations would appear to be essentially identical.

Consistent with its origins in psychoanalysis, this organizational theory is judged to be of a predominantly unconscious nature. Evidence to this effect is presented for needs, for narcissism, for transference, for repression, and for dependence. The process dissociation approach to integrating conscious and unconscious processes is presented with special reference to dependency relationships. This represents another procedure for separating out data of which the individual is unaware. As a result dependency relationships may be fine-tuned to yield greater information.

CHAPTER 11

SELF-DETERMINATION THEORY

Self-determination theory is an overarching theory developed by Edward Deci, and later with Richard Ryan, that has been the subject of considerable controversy. It has been around in some form for a number of years (Deci 1975, 1980; Deci and Ryan 1985; Ryan and Deci 2000). Discussions of the theory refer to it frequently as cognitive evaluation theory (see Miner 2005), although strictly speaking this designation is appropriate only for one of the subtheories within the self-determination framework (Ryan and Deci 2000). In Miner (2005) I devote only a few pages to theorizing of this kind, and then only as an addendum to the treatment of expectancy theory; it is not considered there as a major theory.

RELATIONS TO EXPECTANCY THEORY

Like expectancy theory (see Chapter 1 in this volume), self-determination theory is first and foremost a rational, conscious construction. This is not only my personal judgment, but it is supported by numerous others (see Bargh, Gollwitzer, Lee-Chai, Barndollar, and Trötschel 2001; Fitzsimons and Bargh 2004; Aarts, Dijksterjuis, and Dik 2008; Ferguson, Hassin, and Bargh 2008; Koole and Kuhl 2008).

Furthermore Deci worked with Vroom when both were at Carnegie-Mellon University, did research with him on expectancy theory, and published with him (Vroom and Deci 1971) on that subject. From this point on the two theories began to diverge, however. Let me return to what I said previously:

> Expectancy theory formulations have in general distinguished between extrinsic and intrinsic motivation, but they have viewed the two as additive, so that the distinction is of no special importance. There is, however, a line of reasoning and research that challenges this additive assumption. Statements of this position (see Deci and Ryan 1985) pose a clear threat to expectancy theory in this regard.

Intrinsic motivation is defined as based on the desire for competence and self-determination. Among those who challenge expectancy theory, it is measured almost exclusively by observing the amount of time spent on a task during a period when the subjects have a free choice as to what to do with their time. Intrinsic motivation is said to be facilitated by enhancing the subject's sense of self-determination, for instance by providing a choice of what to work on or what order to work on tasks, and by enhancing a sense of competence through the use of positive feedback. Extrinsic rewards, among which money is the most often cited, have a controlling aspect and an informational aspect. If the controlling aspect is salient, intrinsic motivation is decreased. If the informational or feedback aspect is salient and positive, intrinsic motivation is increased.

Many organizational behavior scholars have found it difficult to accept the view that extrinsic motivation often operates to reduce intrinsic motivation. The results of research testing expectancy theory do not seem to be consistent with such an interpretation. Furthermore, incentive pay systems repeatedly have been found to increase performance levels. It is hard to believe they should be abandoned because they control intrinsic motivation and reduce it. It seems unlikely that the phenomenon described by Deci and Ryan (1985) has practical relevance (Miner 2005, 119).

Yet there is reason to believe that intrinsic motivation can act as Deci and Ryan say, at least on occasion.

RELATIONS TO GOAL-SETTING THEORY

Self-determination theory has had equally controversial problems with goal-setting theory (see Chapter 2 of this volume). These problems are delineated in Bartol and Locke (2000) and in Latham (2007). Difficulties are cited with regard to construct validity issues and with the measurement of loss of control as a mediating factor. Insufficient attention is given to the role of self-efficacy and to how goals may operate. Confusion exists as to what intrinsic motivation really is. Once again the inability of self-determination theory to generalize appropriately to the practical situation is pointed up. The results posited for creativity are predicated largely on undermining studies conducted using children as subjects. The theory appears to suffer from being culture bound. Self-set goals do not yield results that are superior to those obtained when goals are set in some other matter. While some people clearly view the self-determination theory work of Deci and Ryan more favorably, Latham (2007) in the most recent formulation on the subject from a goal-setting perspective clearly does not share this view.

EVALUATIONS

Again let me draw from Miner (2005) regarding evaluations at the hands of meta-analysis:

More recent analyses unfortunately have not resolved this puzzle. At last count there were something like eight meta-analyses of the literature bearing in one way or another on the issue at hand. Furthermore, unlike what has been the case in most other literatures, the results obtained do not always coincide; in fact, a substantial controversy now exists as to what the literature really says, and whose approach to aggregating it is most valid (or least flawed). It is quite possible now to find a meta-analysis that supports almost any position one wishes to espouse (110).

On this meta-analytic front I would particularly recommend a reading of the following: Deci, Koestner, and Ryan (1999); Cameron and Pierce (2002); and Patall, Cooper, and Robinson (2008). The latter, dealing with choice, is most up-to-date and appears to be somewhat more authentic.

Certainly the results of the meta-analyses, the evaluations from the expectancy and goal-setting perspectives, and the damaging findings as to practical implications add up to some serious questions regarding self-determination theory. Taking on both of the most influential theories in the organizational behavior literature cannot possibly be considered a plus. Accordingly I have given the theory advanced by Deci and Ryan a mixed evaluation and a three-star rating on estimated validity (see Miner 2006b). The mean importance rating as established by the field of organizational behavior is 4.27, however. There is indeed something here, as the undermining research clearly demonstrates, but there are many questions as well.

NEEDS

Ryan and Deci (2000) have the following to say: "Using the empirical process, we have identified three needs—the needs for competence, relatedness, and autonomy—that appear to be essential for facilitating optimal functioning of the natural propensities for growth and integration, as well as for constructive social development, and personal well-being" (68). These sound much like the needs for achievement, affiliation, and power with shades of self-actualization, as discussed in Chapter 4 of this volume. Autonomy and competence are said to be involved primarily when cognitive evaluation theory, and thus intrinsic motivation, is activated.

I have considered various types of needs at several points in this volume; they tend to focus near to the McClelland triumvirate and invariably require that unconscious elements be incorporated in their measurements. Yet many of the needs theories, including self-determination theory, have failed in this regard.

That this depicts the reality of the situation for self-determination theory depends, however, on the motivation system invoked. McClelland, Koestner, and Weinberger (1989) indicate that Deci (and Ryan), in research that was not in a position to actually test the needs specification, used a similar motivational system to characterize the operation of intrinsic factors and their undermining effects. McAdams and Pals (2006) indicate that the needs of self-determination theory indeed have been used by Deci and Ryan (1991). Similar findings regarding the use of needs theorizing are reported by Linnenbrink-Garcia and Fredericks (2008) for Ryan and Deci (2000).

Thus, it appears that self-determination theory and its predecessors did indeed employ needs concepts to explicate the theory. However, an additional consideration must be taken into account; the treatments to date appear to deal with needs as if they were conscious constructs, and thus erroneously to measure them in self-report terms. Kehr (2004), however, in line with his own theorizing, interprets Deci and Ryan (2000) to the effect that unconscious motives are involved in the specification of needs. This interpretation is clearly more consistent with my own views, but it departs from previous statements. Yet Kehr (2004, 492) notes that these unconscious "links have not been explored systematically." Thus such approaches as projective techniques and related indexes of unconscious motives have not been brought to bear; Kehr (2004) does not invoke any original research in line with his views. In any event self-report measures remain inconsistent with the objective at hand.

THE TERROR MANAGEMENT CONTROVERSY

Another point, beyond needs, where unconscious considerations may enter into the evaluation of self-determination theory has to do with terror management.

Self-esteem as Anxiety-Buffering Terror Management: Plus and Minus

Pyszczynski, Greenberg, Solomon, Arndt, and Schimel (2004) argue, based on an extensive review of the literature, that self-esteem is largely generated to buffer people against anxiety created by the fear of death. Thus it is seen as a defensive process to assist in terror management.

In response to this argument Ryan and Deci (2004) offer "an alternative, yet complementary, perspective based on self-determination theory . . . that deals not only with defensive self-esteem but also with the intrinsic developmental propensities that lead people to pursue competence, connection, meaning, and significance" (473). They indicate further "that the healthy development of self is more about the unfolding of intrinsic growth tendencies than about flights from anxiety" (476). Accordingly the Ryan and Deci (2004) position follows that of self-determination theory as expressed in Ryan and Deci (2000).

Unconscious Concerns

Subsequently terror management theorists have returned to the subject of self-esteem (Greenberg 2008; Greenberg, Solomon, and Arndt 2008). The case they make appears quite convincing, and it includes the presentation of evidence that priming on terror management themes can serve to contribute not only to the operation of unconscious factors, but to bolstering their arguments. Clearly we are dealing with a subject matter that tends to elicit the intervention of unconscious considerations, and that can be influenced accordingly to a substantial degree. It is important to look into unconscious motivation here, as the terror management theorists have done; the Ryan and Deci conclusions do not include investigations of this type. Consequently one has to conclude on the side of those who have studied the impact of motives that occur without awareness and have taken these into account, versus those who have not considered these motives.

CREATIVITY, CULTURE, AND ROLES

Ryan and Deci (2000) indicate that self-determination theory is concerned with creativity, cultural differences, and life roles. All of these themes represent situations where unconscious processes have been shown to enter in. Do these phenomena represent a source of vulnerability for self-determination theory insofar as introducing unconscious considerations into the theory's operations? Let us look into the evidence.

The Creativity Enigma

I have considered creativity, and the research on it, previously in Chapters 5 and 9 of this volume. There it was established that creative endeavor can involve unconscious processes, as well as conscious, and that emotional factors, probably most extensively positive feelings, are likely to be activated. But how the mix of conscious and unconscious combine to produce creative output remains an enigma. Deci and Ryan (1985) have continued to maintain, however, that self-determination situations lead to the production of creative ideas (see Morling and Kitayama 2008), and they have done so over a number of years.

In this connection it is well to consider the following:

> The results of this meta-analysis suggest that choice can have a positive overall effect on intrinsic motivation, as well as on a number of related outcomes including effort, task performance, perceived competence, and preference for challenge. Results for measures of creativity and satisfaction were in the predicted direction but not statistically significant. . . . The positive effect of choice on motivation may be diminished, indeed reduced to zero, when rewards external to the choice are also provided (Patall, Cooper, and Robinson 2008, 294, 298).

Certainly major tenets of self-determination theory do receive support from this most recent meta-analysis, but not the creativity formulation. Consequently one is left with a further enigma regarding the true nature of creativity. Perhaps subsequent research on unconscious considerations will help to unravel this dilemma.

Culture and the Unconscious

Similarly cultural transmissions have been considered previously as well; Chapter 3 touched upon this issue, and Chapter 7 gave considerable attention to organizational culture. The tendency for North American culture to be distinctive with regard to motivational issues (see Morling and Kitayama 2008) has been noted repeatedly, and has been the subject of consideration by the self-determination theorists. Priming studies have been conducted using three groups of countries—the United States and Canada; Southeast Asia involving Hong Kong plus Nepal, the Philippines, and Singapore; and Western Europe with Germany and the Netherlands. The results show that the three groups are differentiated with regard to individualism and collectivism. "Once a particular cultural focus is cued, it is likely to carry with it relevant goals, motives, actions, ways of interpreting information, and processing strategies" (Oyserman and Lee 2008, 331). This type of study opens up the area of culture and its unconscious motivation aspects to investigation, although to the best of my knowledge the self-determination theorists have not used this bridge to study the unconscious features of culture. Yet this is another area where a vulnerability to study beyond awareness exists; that it might well make a useful contribution to the theory goes without saying.

Roles

Deci and Ryan have also considered that life roles represent an important area where investigation might yield valuable knowledge. This too is an aspect of their theory that could well identify significant contributions were unconscious processes included. That roles, like the cultures of which they are a part, are subject to the introjections of unconscious features is clearly evident from research. This research is contained in Miner (2008). It is epitomized by the exploratory factor analysis contained in Chapter 32 written by Jennifer Miner (2008). This analysis confirms that sixteen of the seventeen subscales from the three MSCS measures produce results of the predicted nature, and thus indicate that the role prescriptions hypothesized are supported. This support comes from measures, the MSCSs, that are projective in nature and that therefore include unconscious factors. Furthermore the one departure from expectations (see Table 32.2), which occurs in the case of Avoiding Risks, represents a shift from entrepreneurial motivation to hierarchic. Here hierarchic managers are demonstrated to involve more risk taking, consistent with other studies and with Miner and Raju (2004) as explicated in Chapter 27 of that same volume. All in all there is substantial evidence here that roles are of an unconscious nature and thus would benefit from studies using measures that tap motivation of this type.

CONCLUSIONS

Self-determination theory has an estimated validity of three stars and an importance rating of 4.27 at the hands of organizational behavior scholars, as indicated earlier in this chapter. Dividing the second value by the first yields a figure of 1.42, indicating that the importance rating represents a substantial overestimate of the theory in terms of its presumed validity.

Given the controversy that exists between both the expectancy and goal-setting theories (with their marked popularity among organizational behavior scholars) and self-determination theory, this overestimation is surprising. It appears to result from the highly rational nature of the self-determination concepts. Yet there are many points in the theory and its research support that are vulnerable to reinterpretation from an unconscious perspective. This is true in particular of the use of need theorizing. Closely related is the controversy with the terror management theorists as to the interpretation of self-esteem and its relation to anxiety. Other areas that appear amenable to investigation and perhaps reinterpretation in terms of unconscious considerations are creativity, culture, and the development of role prescriptions. On all of these grounds self-determination theory and its subtheory cognitive evaluation theory would benefit from further study using motivational processes that do not involve conscious awareness. This, however, would require a major departure from the existing theory and from its predominantly conscious orientation.

CHAPTER 12

THEORY OF BEHAVIOR IN ORGANIZATIONS

The theory of behavior in organizations is outlined in Figure 23.1 on page 670 of Miner (2002). This is a complex theory, and the schematic involved in the figure invokes numerous variables. Many of these are considered at various points in this part of Book 6 (on motivation), and I will refer to these treatments subsequently. The theory of behavior in organizations is one that comes closest to the expectancy theory among those considered here, and like expectancy theory it represents a highly rational, conscious formulation.

To a large extent the theory of behavior in organizations is contained in a single book (Naylor, Pritchard, and Ilgen 1980). The theory is more concerned with behavior than with organizations; in fact one reviewer indicates that the 'in organizations' part of the title "represents a weak main effect" (Cummings 1981, 663). I can find no evidence of any meta-analyses having been conducted in relation to the theory, and although the theory has been reviewed, both the output of relevant research and the number of reviews are somewhat limited in nature. Very little discussion is devoted to practice and practical applications. "Heuristics, degraded judgments, satisficing, and the like play an important role in organizational motivation. The theory's authors recognize this, but they prefer to pursue an optimizing type of theoretical statement. The alternative would be to develop a theory of what human beings actually do, rather than a theory of ideal processes" (Miner 2002, 678). On all of these grounds I have been loath to award an estimated validity rating above three stars; organizational behavior as a whole gives an importance rating of 3.94 to the theory of behavior in organizations (Miner 2006b).

PRIOR TREATMENTS OF THEORETICAL VARIABLES

I list each of the chapters of this part below, along with the specific topics from the theory of behavior in organizations considered in each; this is by way of a recapitulation of what has been said previously on each topic and where these statements may be found. In many of these instances the statement is concerned with how the research on unconscious motivation enters in, and thus with how an understanding of the workings of unconscious factors might serve to amplify the effectiveness of the particular theory.

Chapter 1 on Expectancy Theories

Valence, emotions, and expectancies: Valence and emotions (affect) are components of the Figure 23.1 model. Expectancies and expectancy theories are discussed at several points in the book, often with the objective of differentiating the authors' theory from alternative formulations.

Chapter 2 on Goal-Setting Theory

Goals and intentions: Although the Naylor, Pritchard, and Ilgen (1980) book contains relatively little on goals and goal setting per se, this subject is amplified at some length subsequently (Naylor and Ilgen 1984). This latter essay represents one of the few instances where the authors have returned to their theoretical task after the publication of their book.

Chapter 3 on Kurt Lewin's Social Psychology

Goals and intentions, group norms, and climates: The authors' contributions on goals and intentions were noted earlier; group norms and their enforcement are considered part of a chapter on leadership; climates, and in particular organizational climates, are given chapter-length billing.

Chapter 4 on Achievement Motivation Theory

Needs: This is the first of several chapters within this volume that deals with needs and their motivational properties. The authors' handle needs and also temporary need states within Figure 23.1. Needs and need categories are differentiated and exemplified, but all such designations are said to be arbitrary and often circular. Thus there is no commitment to a specific list of needs.

Chapter 5 on Job Characteristics Theory

Needs (see commentary on Chapter 4).

Chapter 6 on Organizational Behavior Modification

Learning: Learning is invoked as it enters into the theory in terms of how it permits change in individual abilities, and in the perceptions of expectancies, valences, outcomes, and roles; learning is a means to change. Conditioning is one method of learning.

Chapter 7 on Equity Theory and Distributive Justice

Stress, heuristics: Role conflict is presented as the primary source of stress in a chapter concerned with roles and role behaviors. Heuristics is given much wider consideration. Heuristic techniques are simplifying mechanisms that enhance one's coping abilities. They introduce shortcuts to eliminate some of the individual process stages required for individual choice. Heuristics invokes alternatives to the more idealized theory and the one proffered, which is distinctly rational. Heuristic techniques are important, but as long as they produce results similar to rational processes, they can be ignored. Nevertheless, it is recognized that heuristics, as degraded products, can yield unconscious contributions (Tversky and Kahneman 1974).

Chapter 8 on Attribution Theory

Needs, heuristics, and emotions: Needs are considered in the commentary on Chapter 4 and heuristics in the commentary on Chapter 7. Emotions (affect) are noted in Chapter 1 and are positioned theoretically in Figure 23.1.

Chapter 9 on Existence, Relatedness, and Growth Theory

Needs (see commentary on Chapter 4).

Chapter 10 on Psychoanalytic Theory

Needs (see commentary on Chapter 4).

Chapter 11 on Self-Determination Theory

Needs and roles: Needs are treated here (with a commentary in Chapter 4). Roles are a component of Figure 23.1 and are given chapter-length treatment as well by the authors.

Mention should also be made of how the theory of behavior in organization deals with individual differences. A note to Figure 23.1 indicates, "Individual differences are assumed to be operating at each internal process stage in the theory." Elsewhere it is indicated that no theory of behavior can be complete without recognizing the various ways in which individual differences exert an influence; and indeed the authors' theory does provide such recognition (as with abilities, personality, and needs). Yet the conceptual problems invoked are said to be considerable and in fact "beyond the scope of the present theory" (15). As with need states, no categorization or classification system is provided to deal with individual differences. Even so, individual differences do enter in as some type of moderator at points A through I in Figure 23.1; there are no specifications as to how and what variables are involved.

ON SPECIFIC PROCESSES WITHIN THE THEORY OF BEHAVIOR IN ORGANIZATIONS

Several of the processes described in the previous listing call for further discussion. In particular I want to show how unconscious processes may be involved, and thus to note points at which vulnerability to interpretation going beyond human awareness may be operative.

This has been done in many of the citations within this volume specified in the previous section, but I want to use additional data to make the points here. Although my treatments will be selective, this discussion should add up to a clear indication that the theory of behavior in organization requires further research as to its unconscious implications.

On Heuristics

Heuristics require conscious processes, but there is ample evidence that an unconscious component exists as well (see Gilovich, Griffin, and Kahneman 2002; Dane and Pratt 2007; Keys and Schwartz 2007; Evans 2008; Gigerenzer 2008). There is much misunderstanding with regard to the nature of heuristics, and accordingly it may prove helpful to review some common misconceptions or erroneous beliefs about the subject:

1. Heuristics produce second-best results; optimization is always better.
2. Our minds rely on heuristics only because of our cognitive limitations.
3. People rely on heuristics only in routine decisions of little importance.
4. People with higher cognitive capacities employ complex weighting and integration of information; those with lesser capacities use simple heuristics.
5. Affect, availability, causality, and representativeness are models of heuristics.
6. More information and computation is always better (Gigerenzer 2008, 21).

None of these assumed characteristics of heuristics are in fact true, although they are often believed to be. Yet it is true that unconscious operations are involved.

That Naylor, Pritchard, and Ilgen (1980) eschewed direct engagement with heuristics is in part a function of what was known on the subject at the time their book was written; in fact empirical knowledge of unconscious factors at that time was very much in its infancy. Indeed for organizational behavior the subject has remained in a rather clouded status. Consider the following statement from an award-winning paper: "We were informed by a growing body of literature in psychology that has shown how a large portion of cognitive thought occurs outside of consciousness. . . . Yet despite burgeoning interest in nonconscious and automatic processes among psychologists, organizational scholars have yet to focus extensively on these mechanisms and how they may influence behavior in organizations. For this reason, we hope that our treatment . . . may help to put the 'nonconscious' into organizational studies" (Dane and Pratt 2007, 50). In fact even within psychology much remains to be learned (see Krizan and Windschitl 2007, 116).

My point simply is that heuristics presented, and still present, real obstacles to the formulation of precise specifications to those who are concerned with their study. Naylor, Pritchard, and Ilgen were not alone in this regard.

On Goals and Intentions

Goals and intentions are handled by Naylor and Ilgen (1984) primarily within a separate essay that gives no attention to unconscious considerations. However, such considerations have been given a great deal of attention within psychology. That goals of an unconscious nature are important and multifaceted is abundantly evident from a reading of the literature (see Ambady and Skowronski 2008; Moskowitz and Grant 2009; numerous chapters on goal processes in Shah and Gardner 2008). Much of the research in this area utilizes priming approaches (Shah 2005), and indeed this was the approach utilized as goal setting without awareness was brought into organizational behavior (Stajkovic, Locke, and Blair 2006). Yet it remains true that approaches of this kind are having spotty acceptance in the study of organizations (see for instance the fact that unconscious goal setting is not integrated into the recent research by Kozlowski and Bell 2006).

On Emotions, Affect, and Valence

Research on emotions (affect) yields substantial evidence that unconscious processes can be involved. A number of different procedures have been utilized; evidence of fear in the face independent of awareness has been a robust finding (see deGelder 2005). Compelling evidence exists that affective guidance of attention occurs unconsciously (Clore, Storbeck, Robinson, and Centerbar 2005). Age effects tend to be less pronounced in unconscious than in conscious processing (Peters, Hess, Västfjäll, and Auman 2007). Priming is an important source of unconscious activation of affect (Winkielman, Halberstadt, Fazendeiro, and Catty 2006).

Studies of unconscious valence serve to reflect not only that affect occurs without awareness, but that the same is true of valence itself. A number of accounts of this type of research exist (see Winkielman and Berridge 2004; Crano and Prislin 2006; DeWall and Baumeister 2007; Kensinger 2007; Cunningham, Van Bavel, and Johnsen 2008; Ruys and Stapel 2008). All in all the evidence for unconscious operations insofar as emotions (affect) and valence are concerned add substantially to the potential of the theory of behavior in organizations for investigation on this score.

On Individual Differences

I have noted that the theory's authors tend to avoid hypotheses regarding individual differences. Does this open up opportunities for the study of how unconscious factors may operate? I believe it does.

One way in which this may happen is with regard to the use of moderator designs. For instance it has been shown that priming may serve to activate unconscious aggression. However, this occurs only among individuals who are lacking in agreeableness. A potential for agreeableness serves to short-circuit the aggression-related cues involved, probably by recruiting prosocial thoughts in reaction to the aggression-related primes (Meier, Robinson, and Wilkowski 2006). In any event an individual difference variable operates to moderate the activation outside of awareness. Similarly people who are more dominant tended to respond automatically with a greater responsiveness to probes along the vertical dimension of space. Individuals who are less dominant, and thus characterized by a weaker orientation to power, were less likely to react unconsciously; they were not predisposed to favor top-down metaphors (accordingly they exhibited little by way of such a bias). Again an individual difference variable was clearly mobilized in the extent to which an unconscious bias operated (Moeller, Robinson, and Zabelina 2008). Additional examples can be cited. There is evidence, for instance, that individual differences in the capacity to control attention represent a major contributor to differences in working memory. In such studies behavior is found to be determined by the interplay of automatic and controlled processes (Barrett, Tugade, and Engle 2004).

Other instances where individual differences are activated in support of the viability of unconscious processes are contained in Miner (2008). Here the use of projectives is predicated on the soundness of these techniques. Evidence to this effect is contained in Chapter 1 of Miner (2008), and there in contradistinction to the deficiencies of self-reports (Dunning, Heath, and Suls 2004). Other evidence on this score is contained in Vargas, Sekaquaptewa, and von Hippel (2007) on the predictive power of projectives in general and in McGrath (2008) on approaches to improve the soundness of Rorschach interpretation by tying it to indexes of unconscious process such as the Implicit Association Test (IAT).

To make the point on the important role of unconscious factors in individual differences that is demonstrated in Miner (2008), I would point to Chapter 9 on Academy of Management members who completed both Form P of the MSCS (which did predict success indexes) and Form H of the MSCS (which did not make such predictions). Similarly in Chapter 22 dealing with the class of 1948 at Princeton University, where the predominant occupation of the respondents and the MSCS version were congruent (as hypothesized), prediction did occur, and when they were not congruent, prediction was lacking in most instances. Overall the data were consistently supportive of projective measures—specifically when those measures were based on individual difference indexes that admitted unconscious processes into the measurement procedure.

CONCLUSIONS

The theory of behavior in organizations—like its exemplar expectancy theory—has a ratio of estimated validity to its importance rating that suggests an overestimation of presumed validity. The actual figures are three stars for validity and 3.94 for the importance rating bestowed by organizational behavior, as noted earlier. Thus the ratio is 1.31, even above the overestimation inherent in expectancy theory.

Both theories are predominantly of a conscious nature. Both would benefit from the introjection of unconscious processes, but it would appear that this is particularly true of the theory of behavior in organizations, in large part because the theory incorporated a greater number of variables that have a propensity for translation into operation beyond awareness. This is true of heuristics, of goals and intentions, and of emotions, affect, and valence. Beyond these, the theory's take on individual differences lends itself in particular to a vulnerability to interpretation in terms of unconscious considerations.

PART II

THEORIES OF LEADERSHIP

CHAPTER 13

NORMATIVE DECISION PROCESS THEORY

The Basically Conscious Proclivity of the Theory
  Brain Mechanisms
  Dysfunctions of This Conscious Proclivity
Data That Are Lost Because of a Concentration on Conscious Processes
  Conflict Situations
  Environmental Priming
  Additional Instances
Heuristics
On Conflict between Subordinates
Conclusions

Normative decision process theory comes in two versions (Vroom and Yetton 1973; Vroom and Jago 1988). The second book represents an attempt to further perfect the theory presented in the first book. Both books deal with decision making in terms of the degree to which a manager should share decisions with subordinates vis-à-vis making decisions himself or herself. This is the Victor Vroom of expectancy theory fame, but other than a strong reliance on conscious processes, the two theories have little in common.

The normative theory is clearly a leadership theory, not an essentially motivational formulation. Its estimated validity is rated at five stars, and in the eyes of organizational behavior as a whole its average importance evaluation in 4.44 (see Miner 2005 and 2007). Because the authors have devoted considerable effort to developing appropriate training programs to go with their theories, the rating on practical value is high, too. Meta-analyses dealing with the theories themselves in their diversity of conceptualization appear to be nonexistent. However, application of the approaches advocated would almost certainly tend to promote participation or power sharing in some form, even though the authors oppose resorting to participation across-the-board. Meta-analytic results reported previously did little to foster power sharing in any form. However, more recent findings (Stewart 2006) are more encouraging; not only are the newer studies more consistent with a higher performance correlation, but moderator findings indicate that "empowering leadership . . . is more beneficial in some settings than others" (Stewart 2006, 44). This puts the results in substantial alignment with the Vroom and Yelton (1973) and Vroom and Jago (1988) hypotheses.

THE BASICALLY CONSCIOUS PROCLIVITY OF THE THEORY

Normative decision process theory, no matter what its version, is essentially about decision-making, and these decisions should be stated explicitly. Thus this is very much a conscious approach to theorizing. The training program used to teach the theory reinforces this explicit emphasis. The questions that feed into the decision trees and mathematical equations are consistently of a self-report nature. In fact, to the extent that the theory becomes mathematical—

83

and this is considerable in the second version of the theory—it virtually precludes other than conscious processes (Hassin 2005). In speaking about expectancy theory, Vroom (2005)—the theory's author—deplores his frequent use of mathematical formulations. However, this has not dissuaded him from extensive and complex uses of that same approach as he developed normative decision process theory.

Brain Mechanisms

"The ACC (anterior cingulate cortex) has primarily been implicated in decision making and the integration of more rational cognitive processes" (Rule and Ambady 2008, 45). "The ACC is where thought and consciousness begin to occur" (46). Thus much of what is the focus of normative decision process theory can be identified as localized within a specific region of the brain.

Dysfunctions of This Conscious Proclivity

Reliance primarily on conscious processes carries with it certain dysfunctions, at least for particular people. This is especially manifest in older people. Because of changes in the cortex with age, declines in the deliberative mode consisting of conscious, analytical, reason-based, verbal, and relatively slow thought processes occur—exactly the kind required by normative decision theory. Thus poorer decisions are likely to occur among older people with declines in explicit memory (Peters, Hess, Västfjäll, and Auman 2007). Other instances of changes with age are also attributable to frontal lobe atrophy. Planning functions and the control of thought may be disrupted; increased prejudice, depression, and problem gambling may be fostered (von Hippel 2007). Such declines are not likely to influence the thinking of most managers, but they may effect some, given the variability in age of onset known to occur.

Furthermore, there are some forms of emotional regulation that are cognitively costly (Richards 2004). Not as much is known in this area as might be desired, but the research indicates that certain types of regulation become habituated in some people, leading to unintended consequences for cognitive functioning. The cognitive consequences of emotional control vary, but they may be detrimental to the decision making of normative theory. In this connection, research indicates that "mental suppression to regulate memory for traumatic events in distressed survivors appears to be counterproductive in at least three ways: It paradoxically increases the probability that those events will be remembered, it enhances access to other negative personal material, and it compromises the ability to access specific aspects of the broader personal past beyond the memory of the trauma itself" (Dalgleish, Hauer, and Kuyken 2008, 262). There are sizable individual differences in these regards.

Another source of dysfunction in cognitive functioning is powerlessness (Smith, Jostmann, Galinsky, and van Dijk 2008). A number of experiments serve to indicate that when people have little power they find it difficult to distinguish between what is goal relevant and what is not. Accordingly, "empowering employees may reduce costly organizational errors" (441). People functioning in low-power roles clearly suffer deficiencies in cognitive processes of a conscious, rational nature; their reduced functioning is not motivational. Again the implications for normative decision process theory are substantial.

With regard to the use of self-report data, Dunning, Heath, and Suls (2004, 78) comment on the dysfunctions involved: "A wealth of evidence suggests that people make substantial errors when they evaluate their abilities, attributes, and future behavior. Several psychological mechanisms conspire to produce these faulty self-assessments, but many of them can be sorted into two general classes:

1. Erroneous self-assessments arise because people often do not have all the information necessary to provide accurate assessments, and they do not take into account what they do not know.
2. Erroneous self-assessments arise because people neglect relevant and useful information that they do have in hand. . . . Our review of the processes underlying flawed self-judgment is not exhaustive. . . . There are other classes of psychological mechanisms that are also responsible. . . . To name just one example, people are often motivated to reach flattering conclusions about themselves."

This particular type of dysfunction involving flawed self-reports operates more generally across people; it is therefore widely applicable to normative decision process theorizing.

DATA THAT ARE LOST BECAUSE OF A CONCENTRATION ON CONSCIOUS PROCESSES

Not only do thought processes fail to function effectively because of dysfunctions of conscious processes, but other consequences occur because a theory's proclivity for the conscious may exclude any measurement of the unconscious. "Research has shown that . . . behavior may contain automatic, habitual aspects not accounted for in models of reasoned action" (Ajzen 2001, 48). Under such circumstances, predictors may need to be added to a theory because deficiencies in the focus of measurement may result in data simply being lost to inductive endeavor.

Conflict Situations

"Evidence that human preferences, beliefs, and behavior are influenced by sources that are outside the reach of conscious awareness, control, intention, and self-reflection is incontrovertible" (Stanley, Phelps, and Banaji 2008, 164). But what about those situations where these unconscious processes come into direct conflict with conscious thoughts? This happens in cases where dual processes are operative (see, for example, Crano and Prislin 2006; De Neys 2006; Nosek 2007; Eitam, Hassin, and Schul 2008; Ranganath and Nosek 2008). In the absence of unconscious measurement, the dynamics of such conflict situations will surely be lost, and when awareness is lacking (as is indeed the case on occasion), the whole motivational basis of behavior may be lost as well. Only in the ideal case where conscious phenomena are able to achieve an overriding status will theories such as that of normative decision process prove effective; thus there are real threats to theory inherent in such conflict situations.

Environmental Priming

Most processes that are sufficiently complex are comprised of automatic as well as controlled features (Bargh 2007). Some suggest, indeed, that the vast majority of activities of the mind occur outside of consciousness (Rule and Ambady 2008). This often happens as a consequence of priming by aspects of the physical environment so that these features serve to spark reactions and behaviors that are outside of awareness (Bargh 1990, 2005; Kay, Wheeler, Bargh, and Ross 2004; Dijksterhuis, Chartrand, and Aarts 2007). The environmental situations involved tend to be characterized by a degree of ambiguousness. "For some, the dismissal of introspection as relevant to the assessment . . . is difficult" (Nosek, Greenwald, and Banaji 2007, 266).

Additional Instances

Other instances where the failure to measure unconscious processes because of a concentration on the conscious exclusively, or simply because of a neglect of the unconscious, can be cited. Numerous examples exist: "The evidence suggests that self-regulation is central in transference, in that activation of a significant other representation has important self-regulatory consequences that may be triggered outside of awareness. The role of the unconscious in the relational self is thus quite clear" (Andersen, Reznick, and Glassman 2005, 467). "The findings are consistent with the notion that lie detection is, for the most part, an unconscious process" (Choi, Gray, and Ambady 2005, 317). "People can have subliminally triggered emotional reactions that drive judgment and behavior, even in the absence of any conscious feelings accompanying these reactions" (Winkielman and Berridge 2004, 121). "Implicit attitudes stem from past (and largely forgotten) experiences, whereas explicit attitudes reflect more recent or accessible events" (Rudman 2004, 79). "It appears that people do not like to admit that physical attractiveness factors into their impression formation process, suggesting that it is a largely unconscious process" (Harris and Garris 2008, 154). "Participants who were asked to deliberate carefully produced less valid assessments than did those who were allowed to use their 'gut reactions.' . . . relying on cognitive strategies that are not consciously mediated may facilitate accuracy" (Gray 2008, 111). Instances of these kinds demonstrate what is lost when there is a failure to measure unconscious considerations.

HEURISTICS

Vroom (2005) indicated that a resort to heuristics seemed needed were any revision of expectancy theory carried out; the same would seem to apply to normative decision theory, although Vroom does not apply the recommended heuristic revision specifically to that theory. In any event heuristics has been discussed and examples given in previous chapters of this volume—particularly Chapters 7, 8, and 12. In this regard it is worthy of note that "researchers in the areas of management and psychology have explained intuition through a wide range of phenomena, including heuristics, . . . expertise, . . . and nonconscious information process" (Dane and Pratt 2007, 34). Certainly heuristics represent an important consideration when conscious explanations are given more than their share of attention.

ON CONFLICT BETWEEN SUBORDINATES

Previous research on the handling of conflict among subordinates as considered by normative decision process theory raised questions about the theory's validity in this particular area (see Miner 2005). Recent research tends to support the theory in this regard and thus indicates that training in the theory should prove beneficial. Conflict-handling style did not emerge as a fruitful individual difference variable (Cogliser and Schriesheim 2006), contrary to expectations. These results may suffer from certain departures from typicality in the sample used, however. In any event the theory's recommendation that participation be fostered where conflict is anticipated continues to hold true.

CONCLUSIONS

As indicated previously, normative decision process theory has a validity of five stars and an importance evaluation (as given by organizational behavior) of 4.44. Dividing yields a value of .89, with an appropriate conclusion being that the organizational behavior scholars slightly underestimate the effectiveness of the theory; this finding is out of line with the indication previously that theories with a conscious focus tend to be overestimated with respect to their validity.

Certainly normative decision process theory in its essential nature is a conscious formulation. Perhaps the difficulty is that research on the theory has been limited in recent years, and when it does occur it tends to be at the hands of the authors. Due to dysfunctions of the conscious processes so frequently invoked, along with the loss of evidence from unconscious measures, a need for tapping what happens beyond awareness has developed. This is true of conflict situations, of environmental priming contexts, and in other instances. How and when heuristics may operate as regards normative decision process theory represents a major area for future investigation.

CHAPTER 14

LEADER-MEMBER EXCHANGE THEORY

The Conscious Theory
The Unconscious Theory
   Eliteness Motivation
   What Is Eliteness Motivation?
   Eliteness Motivation and Creativity
   Enter in Growth Need Strength (and Self-Actualization)
Similarities
Roles
A Reconsideration of LMX Measurement
Conclusions

Leader-member exchange (LMX) theory was originally known as vertical dyad linkage (VDL) theory but its name was changed to make it more relevant in human and social terms. Whatever its name, the theory is the product of George Graen, whose earliest contributions to organizational behavior were to expectancy theory. There, as in the present instance, he championed the operation of roles and role making.

Predicated on a number of meta-analyses dealing with aspects of the theory (see Miner 2005), of which the one conducted by Gerstner and Day (1997) has proved to be most influential, I originally gave a rating of five stars to the theory's validity (Miner 2005, Chapter 14). A problem even then, however, was that evaluations of the dyadic relationship tended to vary between leaders and subordinates. More recently this differentiation has been shown to be a consequence of the different relational schemas applied by each (Huang, Wright, Chiu, and Wang 2008). Leaders' LMX schemas focus more on work-related role-expectations, while members' schemas are more related to social and developmental needs; thus the constructs involved are not the same. Nevertheless the theory is rated as to importance by organizational behavior scholars at 4.69.

THE CONSCIOUS THEORY

Graen's ties to the highly conscious expectancy theory are perpetuated in leader-member exchange theory. The dyads involved are described in terms of conscious thought processes, and the questions used to measure them are of an entirely self-report nature. The various sets of guidelines for achieving fast-track status set forth by Graen (1989, 2003) are consistently of a conscious type (see Miner 2006b, Chapter 13). Training to induce high-LMX formation in all dyads consisted of entirely rational teaching on how to apply the model (Graen, Novak, and Sommerkamp 1982). All in all, from a managerial viewpoint, the theory appears to be largely conscious.

88

THE UNCONSCIOUS THEORY

However, this devotion to rationality is not maintained from the other side of the dyad. Subordinates often experience a degree of eliteness with their status as the chosen few at the hands of their leader; this is not always a conscious process.

Eliteness Motivation

The training to produce high-quality exchanges across the board does indeed have the intended effect, but the duration of the influence produced tends to be short-lived. It appears that the training "serves to eliminate any elitist motivations that may have driven the behavior of high LMX people previously. These individuals may have considered themselves winners before, but with the intervention this status is taken away from them" (Miner 2006b, 161). Now everyone is a winner, and there is nothing about their status that might be considered elite; the nature of their relationship with the leader has changed.

What Is Eliteness Motivation?

"Within the sociological literature, the distinction between administrative elites and rank-and-file practitioners within a profession is discussed. It is these elites that the professional theory considers its leaders" (Miner 2008, 288). This elite status is what eliteness motivation is about.

The original research on the topic occurred among consultants from McKinsey and Company (see Miner 2008, Chapter 5; also Miner and Miner 1978, Chapters 9–13). Here, eliteness derives from association with groups of people who are viewed as elite or prestigious by oneself or by others. Certainly being employed by McKinsey and Company meets this criterion as a prestige association. However, we found that this was characteristic of the successful McKinsey consultants, those most likely to be retained by the firm. "There appears to be a consistent pattern of prior identification with membership in prestige organizations and groups among the more successful consultants—private prep schools, small private colleges, prestige business schools, the Navy and Air Force rather than the Army, the commissioned officer group in service, and the management group in business. Coupled with this is the evidence of upward mobility relative to their fathers, which suggests a positive striving to achieve these elite associations. All these variables combine to define the eliteness motivation construct" (Miner 1971, 375–376).

Eliteness motivation as thus defined represents a type of need. Needs have already been considered in Chapter 4 and 5 of this volume and will be revisited in later chapters as well. Elliott and Fryer (2008, 246):

> think it is best to restrict the term *goal* to commitments that have their origin in conscious acts of volition. Once in place in the cognitive system, goals may be activated and may operate in a thoroughly automatic, nonconscious fashion as compellingly demonstrated by Bargh and colleagues. . . . Goals are to be differentiated from needs and motives, in that needs and motives have their origin in inherent tendencies or nonconscious affective learning processes. . . . Needs and motives may at times affect behavior without goal mediation.

As we have seen Huang, Wright, Chiu, and Wang (2008) found that the schemas of members of dyadic relationships were characterized by social and developmental needs and accordingly were largely of an unconscious nature.

Eliteness Motivation and Creativity

Achieving elite status, as with in-group or high LMX people, often yields a feeling of elation for those who have strong needs or motives of this kind. At the same time it can also yield a sense of guilt as a result of the violation of the democratic values involved. Thus two emotions—one positive and one negative—tend to be aroused in concert when eliteness needs are activated. This same pattern was noted in Chapter 5 of this volume as being associated with creative endeavor (see George and Zhou 2007), or it may emerge as emotional ambivalence (Fong 2006). In addition we know that emotion is often unconscious (Winkielman and Berridge 2004). Creativity may be a source of guilt (Greenberg, Solomon, and Arndt 2008; Leung, Maddux, Galinsky, and Chiu 2008), but it too may emerge out of the unconscious (Zhong, Dijksterhuis, and Galinsky 2008). In this connection consider the following: "A good case can be made for viewing interest as an emotion. . . . Interest is thus a counterweight to feelings of uncertainty and anxiety. . . . Interest won't—and shouldn't—win the tug-of-war between approach and avoidance, but, over the long haul, interest will motivate people to encounter new things" (Silva 2008, 57–58). Thus a composite emotion such as elation-guilt is seen to produce the conditions for creative activity.

All this is interrelated, and of significance, but does it have any meaning for the interpretation of high LMX situations? The answer appears to be yes, in that relationships of this type, with their tendency to bring eliteness motivation into the picture, tend as well to produce innovation and creative endeavors (see Tierney, Farmer, and Graen 1999; Elkins and Keller 2003). In short the same emotional amalgam operates in the high LMX situation to yield creativity, and it does so under conditions conducive to the activation of unconscious processes. Thus the creativity enigma set forth in Chapters 5, 9, and 11 previously continues to unfold.

Enter in Growth Need Strength (and Self-Actualization)

We turn now to another type of need intervention, and consequently to another way in which unconscious considerations enter into leader-member exchange theory—"needs or goals that are concerned with growth and advancement versus safety and security" (Molden, Lee, and Higgins 2008, 169). Needs once again are shown to be of an unconscious nature. Initially growth need strength was introduced into the leader-member exchange research program through a misadventure; it was subsequently aborted, as the job design effort (see Chapter 5) with which it was connected was not made part of the theory. Nevertheless growth need strength was indeed integrated into the research agenda as a moderator contributing to high LMX status (see Miner 2005, 266). Graen, Scandura, and Graen (1986) deal with this situation. Subsequently Graen (2005, 208) acknowledged this finding as follows:

> Leaders may offer role making leading to HQ LMX relationships, but not all followers are interested in building such a relationship. It seems that the willingness to take advantage of the opportunity to engage in role making to develop a new role and a high quality relationship with a supervisor is dependent on the strength of the follower's growth need (Graen, Novak, and Sommerkamp 1982; Graen, Scandura, and Graen 1986; Hackman and Oldham 1976). Only the top third of the subjects in each field experience accepted new role making and augmented their hard performance. It appears that subjects must really have strong growth needs.

Note that here again we are concerned with the needs of the follower, not the leader. The importance of growth needs has been reiterated over the years (Fried, Levi, and Laurence 2007; Graen 2007a), and as a result growth need strength is formally and firmly integrated into leader-member exchange theory. However, the original research is not always described in the same terms. The circumstances surrounding the original research involving growth needs may not be elaborated fully. Furthermore, additional moderators beyond growth need strength are proposed; these moderators include, but are not limited to, having a clear self-concept, being optimistic, being a risk taker, being a romantic, and having a Type A personality. In a sense, then, the impact of the original moderator is diluted by the addition of others.

Further research by Martin, Thomas, Charles, Epitropaki, and McNamara (2005) brings locus of control into the mix as well. "It was predicted that people with an internal locus of control develop better quality relations with their managers and this, in turn, results in more favorable work-related reactions. Results from two different samples supported this prediction, and also showed that LMX either fully, or partially, mediated the relationship between locus of control and all the work-related reactions" (141). One could imagine that additional needs or variables may mediate or moderate LMX relationships.

SIMILARITIES

The matter of similarity as involved in dyadic relationships is important because research has not always found the expected in this area, and because there are data indicating that unconscious considerations tend to operate here. The demographic similarity findings with regard to relationships within the dyad are particularly conflicted; sometimes leader-member data match up well and sometimes they do not (Miner 2005).

One has to wonder whether findings on unconscious relationships might add insight in this regard. Chapter 5 of this volume discusses the operation of similarities in the absence of awareness. Markman and Gentner (2005, 107) consider the role of similarity in the cognitive architecture and how similarity relates to automatic processing. They say that "some types of similarity are determined automatically. When the cognitive system recognizes similarities, they influence cognitive processing, even when the person does not intend processing to be affected by similarities." Thus there is reason to believe that research in this area might yield new data. In particular mimicry may be activated and thus involved. "Research extends previous work by demonstrating that participants who have recently been excluded exhibit increased nonconscious behavioral mimicry. . . . Moreover, mimicking others' behaviors does not simply create rapport; it may also directly address threatened belongingness needs" (Lakin, Chartrand, and Arkin 2008, 821). This is most likely when exclusion has occurred in relation to an in-group member, as when a high LMX leader is involved.

A related body of research has to do with sociometer theory (see Leary 2007) and the development of a technology to measure social response at the unconscious level (Pentland 2008; Pentland and Heibeck 2008). This computerized technology would appear to have considerable relevance for leader-member exchange theory; it involves wearing a badge that measures:

- face-to-face interactions using an infrared sensor
- speech features to assess nonlinguistic social signals and identify social context
- body movement
- indoor tracking and user localization

- information from different users
- the physical proximity to other people (Pentland and Heibeck 2008, 72)

The full implications of this technology have not yet been demonstrated, however.

ROLES

As I have indicated previously the utilization of role theory and of role-making processes is also a matter that can involve unconscious considerations. Leader-member exchange theory invokes role making frequently (see Figure 14.1 on page 261 in Miner 2005). With regard to the unconscious implications of such situations Andersen, Reznik, and Glassman (2005, 444) note, "The evidence shows spread of activation from significant-other representations to normative self-aspects such as roles and standards." Furthermore, other researchers state: "Affective reactions, even those that are presumed to be automatic and to reflect unconscious content, are contingent on the cognitive context active at the time of measurement. The results suggest that humans are remarkably inferential creatures, and that affective consequences depend on sophisticated unconscious inferential processes" (Clore, Storbeck, Robinson, and Centerbar 2005, 399). Clearly this is another respect in which activations beyond awareness take on significance for leader-member exchange theory.

A RECONSIDERATION OF LMX MEASUREMENT

Given the considerations I have indicated, it appears that any measurement procedure applied to leader-member exchanges should deal with unconscious processes; this becomes particularly relevant in the case of the experiences of members or subordinates within the dyad. Heretofore these measurements have always been of a self-report nature, using questions such as "How would you characterize your working relationship with your leader (your member)?" Various facets of this rational measurement process are discussed in Sanchez and Byrne (2004); Maslyn and Uhl-Bien (2005); Schyns and Paul (2005) and Greguras and Ford (2006; see also Ng, Koh, and Goh 2008). These sources include the results of factor analyses.

Real evidence had been found to confirm the existence of unconscious measures, should they be necessary. "Research on latency decomposition, projective tests, and miscellaneous other procedures indicate that indirect measurement of individual differences in implicit social cognition is possible" (Lane, Banaji, Nosek, and Greenwald 2007, 61). "Many contemporary implicit measures are based on response time, or the speed with which respondents can perform some task; others severely constrain the amount of time in which respondents are permitted to respond and are based on the number of errors respondents make. These measures are designed to tap respondent's automatic responses by minimizing the extent to which respondents carefully and deliberately process information. At the other extreme are partially structured implicit measures like the Thematic Apperception Test" (Vargas, Sekaquaptewa, and von Hippel 2007, 107).

CONCLUSIONS

As rated previously in this chapter, leader-member exchange theory received a five-star evaluation against an organizational behavior importance rating of 4.69 for a ratio of .94. Events since, however, have served to qualify this situation. Some five years have transpired since that conclusion was reached, and they have been very active years for the theory. Graen (individually and more recently with his wife, Joni) has published a number of new volumes in the Information Age series, each with roughly ten or more contributions (in 2004 *New Frontiers of Leadership,* in 2005 *Global Organizing Designs,* in 2006 *Sharing Network Leadership,* in 2007 *New Multinational Network Sharing,* and in 2008 *Knowledge-Driven Corporation: Complex Creative Destruction*). Furthermore in the interval since the prior rating a large number of journal articles on the theory have appeared, many of them using some type of moderator design, for example Piccolo and Colquitt (2006); Sparrowe and Liden (2005); and Lapierre and Hackett (2007). Finally there is the exchange between Graen (2006, 2007b) and House, Javidan, Dorfman, and de Luque (2006). This extends a long-standing controversy that goes back at least to House and Aditya (1997). It encompasses an extensive review of leader-member exchange theory, beyond the critique of the GLOBE (an international comparative analysis), and in the process it raises many questions with regard to that theory. Overall, taking into account these more recent contributions, I am left with the judgment that the rating of leader-member exchange theory needs to be decreased from the original value of five stars to at most four stars. This creates a ratio against the organizational behavior finding of 4.69 to 1.17 rather than .94. It is consistent with what House, Javidan, Dorfman, and de Luque (2006) say.

This value of 1.17 reflects more consistently the judgment that leader-member exchange theory is a balanced formulation of conscious and unconscious aspects; it represents a minimal overestimation on the part of the organizational behavior scholars of the theory's validity. The theory in its resort to self-report data is clearly conscious in nature, but this focus is contradicted by the resort to various need features that emphasize unconscious considerations.

CHAPTER 15

INFORMATION PROCESSING THEORY OF LEADERSHIP

Automatic Processes and Automaticity
    Specifics on Automatic Processes
    Specific Automatic Processes Extending beyond Bargh
Implicit Processes and Implicit Leadership Theories
    Implicit as the Coequal of Automatic
    Implicit in the Information Processing Literature
    Moving to Research Involving Priming
Prototypes and Prototype Matching
Conclusions

Information processing theory is presented in two books—Lord and Maher (1991) and Lord and Brown (2004)—plus a large number of journal articles. We have interfaced with the theory previously in Chapter 8 of this volume, where an unconscious interpretation of attribution theory is presented using information processing concepts (see Cronshaw and Lord [1987] and Lord [1995]). This view takes the position that in attribution situations, conscious and deliberative demands tend to become overloaded, and automatic processes are activated instead to replace them. Thus the perceiver-as-scientist interpretation of attribution theory gives way to an information theory interpretation and an unconscious version of the attribution process comes to the fore.

I have evaluated this theory at the four-star level; organizational behavior in general gives it a 3.84 importance rating (see Miner 2005, Chapter 15). Nevertheless, the usefulness of the theory is limited primarily because a technology to put the ideas into practice has not evolved. In the early period (the mid-1980s) a meta-analysis played an important role in generating information processing theory (see Lord, DeVader, and Alliger 1986). However, applications of this kind have been few in number since these early days. In general, information processing theory as a whole has not proved to be very amenable to meta-analysis. Nevertheless there have been meta-analyses devoted to aspects of the theory. A case in point involves a variant of control theory developed by Lord and Levy (1994) that incorporates information processing principles (see Johnson, Chang, and Lord 2006). Here the propositions of the theory received substantial support, even though the meta-analytic studies utilized were not conducted with a primary intent to test the theory. Foti notes several positive meta-analytic studies, presented as posters at meetings, in connection with our exchange of letters (see Foti and Miner 2003). Overall, similar support for information processing theory has been characteristic of the nonqualitative reviews as well. In general the evidence provides nothing that would lead to a questioning of the rating within the four-star range.

Furthermore there is evidence for classifying information processing theory as dealing largely with unconscious considerations, although conscious features become more salient in certain aspects of the theory. What I have in mind here is shown in Table 15.1 on page 284 of

Miner (2005). In that table, *controlled* is understood to incorporate conscious deliberation and *automatic* to include unconscious considerations. Certainly research on the theory deals with both modes in some mix. As a dual process type of theory, however, it does explicitly incorporate unconscious features and accordingly justifies its classification as moving well beyond the level of human awareness. These matters will concern us at some length as we move on.

AUTOMATIC PROCESSES AND AUTOMATICITY

In the section on Terminology and Features of the Introduction to this volume I discuss the term "automatic" as reflective of unconscious features (see Bargh 1994; Lillard and Skibbe 2005; Moors and De Houwer 2006, 2007; Scherer 2005). The Moors and De Houwer references serve to document the confusion that on occasion has permeated this area. In any event various references to automaticity and to automatic processes of one kind or another occur frequently in the literature on information processing theory, in particular the literature concerned with theoretical presentations. These terms, in that literature, serve to emphasize that unconscious features are involved. However, there is more that needs to be said on the subject: What does the evidence indicate are included under this umbrella?

Specifics on Automatic Processes

Because of the limitation of conscious processing . . . , to shift the regulation of goal pursuit from conscious control to *automatic* control can be an adaptive way of ensuring effective goal pursuit even under new, complex, or difficult circumstances (Bargh, Gollwitzer, Lee-Chai, Barndollar, and Trötschel 2001, 1025).

A burgeoning set of social-cognitive research has found evidence for an increasing role for *automaticity* in self-regulation. Goals can be activated nonconsciously by situation cues and go on to guide cognition, emotion, and behavior, all without need for conscious intervention or guidance (Fitzsimons and Bargh 2004, 159).

The *automaticity* of the association between situational features and goals could . . . be assessed with any of the variety of standard methods . . . (priming, memory load, speeded response). . . . After a subject's chronic goal within a situation has been identified, it might be possible to activate that goal by presenting the triggering feature outside of the subject's awareness (Bargh 1990, 115).

Automatic attitudes may be especially reflective of contextual factors as compared with more deliberate attitudes (Ferguson and Bargh 2007, 218).

Much of social life is experienced through mental processes that are not intended. . . . These processes are *automatically* triggered by features of the immediate social environment . . . Recent research has shown these nonconscious influences to extend beyond the perception and interpretation of the social world to the actual guidance . . . of one's important goal pursuits and social interactions (Bargh and Williams 2006, 1).

Automatic evaluation is an important addition to the emerging model of goal development, representation, and operation (Ferguson, Hassin, and Bargh 2008, 161).

These are all statements of automatic processes that are based on research involving John A. Bargh. But there is more to be indicated.

Specific Automatic Processes Extending beyond Bargh

There are two lines of research showing that features of social groups are capable of *automatically* activating goals and subsequent goal-directed activity relevant to the situation at hand (see Moskowitz, Solomon, and Taylor 2000, and Aarts, Chartrand, Custers, Danner, Dik and Jefferis 2005) (Dijksterhuis, Chartrand, and Aarts 2007, 102).

A process is considered to be *automatic* if it meets at least one of four basic criteria. These criteria are the perceiver's lack of awareness, the perceiver's absence of intention, the efficiency of the process (i.e., its minimal use of cognitive resources), and the perceiver's lack of control (Bargh 1989, 1994). Thus, a process may be considered automatic in varying senses and to varying degrees (Chen, Fitzsimons, and Andersen 2007, 135).

Even though *automatic* evaluative acts last only a fraction of a second and occur without the person's intention or awareness, they have a host of downstream outcomes (Ferguson 2007, 237).

Fazio, Sanbonmatsu, Powell, and Kardes (1986) found *automatic* evaluative priming effects only for primes for which participants had strong attitudes. . . . [But] when the accessibility task was separated from the priming measure by a 2-day delay, the moderation effect went away and weak attitude primes also showed *automatic* priming (Wittenbrink 2007, 38–39).

If the reverse priming effects do represent an *automatic* correction, they provide evidence for a complex, sophisticated, and even volitional unconscious (Glaser and Kihlstrom 2005, 182).

Most phenomena of interest to social psychologists are governed by a combination of *automatic* and controlled processes (Uleman, Blader, and Todorov 2005, 373).

Our evidence supports four main conclusions. First, *automatic* activation of significant-other representations in transference occurs in the form of subliminal triggering of significant-other representations. Second, the affect linked to the significant other can be *automatically* activated in transference. . . . Third, there is an *automatic* spread of activation from the significant-other representation to the self in transference. . . . Fourth, self-regulation may arise in transference to protect the self (Andersen, Reznik, and Glassman 2005, 454).

The flexibility and goal directedness of counteractive control strategies does not necessarily mean that the use of these strategies is always based on conscious deliberation. Like any knowledge, counteractive control strategies may be *automatized* (Trope and Fishbach 2005, 561).

Researchers have identified biologically programmed systems that govern the *automatic* and effortless recognition of emotional displays (Gray 2008, 114).

IMPLICIT PROCESSES AND IMPLICIT LEADERSHIP THEORIES

In the Introduction to this volume the term "implicit" was considered as essentially identical to "automatic." That is the usage that prevails in most literatures. I will take up this meaning first.

Implicit as the Coequal of Automatic

The origins of the implicit terminology may be traced back to the Thematic Apperception Test (TAT) and thus to somewhat before the article by McClelland, Koestner, and Weinberger (1989) as discussed in Chapter 1 of Miner (2008). McClelland (1980) "summarized evidence that *implicit* motives predict spontaneous behavioral trends over time, whereas self-attributed motives predict immediate specific responses to specific situations as choice behaviors" (McClelland, Koestner, and Weinberger 1989, 691).

> *Implicit* motives have generally been found to predict operant behaviors, and self-attributed motives have been found to predict respondent behaviors (695). However, there is much more that needs to be said on the subject.

> Response latency measures have yielded an explosion of interest in *implicit* attitudes. Less forthcoming have been theoretical explanations for why they often differ from explicit (self-reported) attitudes (Rudman 2004, 79).

> People gravitate toward people, places, and things that resemble the self. We refer to this tendency as *implicit* egotism, and we suggest that it reflects an unconscious process that is grounded in people's favorable self-associations (Pelham, Carvallo, and Jones 2005, 106).

> Results for explicit stem-cued recall replicated better performance for each age group at its peak time. In stark contrast, *implicit* performance was better at off-peak than at peak times of day, . . . highlighting the need to consider individual differences (May, Hasher, and Foong 2005, 96).

> These data are the first to show an asymmetry in the development of *implicit* and explicit race attitudes, with explicit attitudes becoming more egalitarian and *implicit* attitudes remaining stable and favoring the in-group across development. . . . Mean levels of *implicit* and explicit attitudes diverge around age 10 (Baron and Banaji 2006, 53).

> Experiments provide evidence for *implicit* insights. . . . That the *implicit* insights formed in this paradigm are nonconscious is shown both by evidence from past experimental probing at debriefing . . . and by evidence from immediate probing and reconstruction. . . . [Other experimentation] demonstrated the implicitness of *implicit* insights through a direct manipulation of intent and awareness (Hassin 2005, 210).

> We want to make several points. . . . First, *implicit* impressions exist, and there is good experimental support for them. . . . Second, *implicit* impressions affect trait judgments of others. . . . Third, *implicit* and explicit impressions of the same person can be held simultaneously and their effects can be empirically distinguished (Uleman, Blader, and Todorov 2005, 363).

Sometimes it pays to rely on more *implicit* gut-level intuition. . . . The benzodiazepine midazolam, which inactivates the hippocampus, causes profound explicit memory deficits in healthy participants, but enhances their ability in making *implicit* transitive inferences. . . . Disengaging the hippocampal memory system can be advantageous for this more implicit form of learning (Frank, O'Reilly, and Curren 2006, 700).

New *implicit* measures of attitudes . . . promise to assess attitudes that respondents may not be willing to report directly or may not even be aware of themselves (Wittenbrink and Schwarz 2007, 1).

The brain imaging methods . . . with their emphasis on either the spatial distribution or timing of brain activity, are well suited for examining the *implicit* underlying mechanisms for attitudes (Ito and Cacioppo 2007, 150).

Besides the interpretation of the term *implicit* as unconscious, *implicit* attitude measures are sometimes assumed to reflect automatic attitudes (Gawronski and Bodenhausen 2007, 268).

From this research, a model with three identified neural components related to the automatic activation and regulation of *implicit* attitudes is beginning to emerge. The amygdala is implicated in the automatic evaluation of socially relevant stimuli, while the anterior cingulate and dorsolateral prefrontal cortices are involved in the detection and regulation, respectively, of *implicit* attitudes (Stanley, Phelps, and Banaji 2008, 164).

Research on *implicit* learning has established that humans can learn and use complex patterns of information without intending to learn them and without being aware of the patterns. . . . Humans' ability to learn relations *implicitly* seems to exceed their ability to process this type of information consciously (Eitam, Hassin, and Schul 2008, 262).

Methodological advances of the past quarter century enable us now to go beyond self-report of attitudes on questionnaires and surveys, to *implicit* measures of those attitudes that the individual is unable to manage strategically for self-presentational purposes. There are now a variety of methods to get at these *implicit* attitudes (Bargh 2007, 7).

The term *implicit* has become widely applied to measurement methods for which subjects may be unaware of what is being measured, unaware of how it is being measured, or unable to control their performance on the measure (Nosek, Greenwald, and Banaji 2007, 277).

Clearly these authors are using the term "implicit" in the same sense that "automatic" has been applied.

Implicit in the Information Processing Literature

Yet disparities occur in the information processing literature. There are instances where "implicit" is used in a sense where it would not appear to apply to unconscious processes at all, and where it is operationalized in self-report terms (see Lord, Foti, and DeVader 1984; Lord and Maher 1991). I broached this issue in the exchange of letters with Roseanne Foti (Foti and Miner 2003, 91), but we never did get to a resolution. The Epitropaki and Martin

(2004, 2005) research represents one of the major investigations using the information processing approach and it consistently uses the implicit terminology (even in its titles). Yet a close reading reveals no clear commitment to the unconscious, although at points the authors come very close. Self-report type measurement is invoked in these studies and the LMX scales developed by Graen (see Chapter 14 of this volume), which are entirely conscious in nature, are used as a criterion.

However, changes are occurring in this regard. In the preface to a book titled *Implicit Leadership Theories,* Lord (2005) states:

> People only know reality in terms of the internal representations they construct. What is particularly intriguing about this perspective is that the meaning construction process occurs primarily at the preconscious, *implicit* level, and consequently people have little insight into this process. Further, because the internal representations people construct correspond in fundamental ways to social and physical realities, they provide effective guidance to actions, thereby subjectively affirming the correctness of one's internal representations.
>
> Several factors make the term *implicit* theories appropriate for describing the systems perceivers use to construct meaning with regard to leadership processes.
>
> 1. These systems may operate automatically or *implicitly,* producing effects that are outside of perceiver's conscious awareness. . . .
> 2. They are an inherent, *implicit* part of the sense making process. . . .
> 3. Because *implicit* theories are rich cognitive structures that not only provide conceptual units, but also specify the connections of such units to other constructs, they can be the mechanisms for empirical effects that are *implicit* and hard to recognize (x).

This statement should establish the theoretical position of unconscious processes, and implicit considerations, within the information processing theory of leadership. Yet in the book in which Lord's preface appears (Schyns and Meindl 2005a), "implicit" is not always used as Lord indicates, and measures based in a conscious, rational perspectives are used to operationalize study variables; some are clearly of a self-report nature, and projective measurement is not invoked.

Subsequently, however, in Medvedeff and Lord (2007, 20) one finds statements such as: "Schemas are important cognitive structures that guide social perceptions, often operating *implicitly* outside of a perceiver's awareness." Often repeated statements, confirming that unconscious considerations are involved, are needed to make the point.

Moving to Research Involving Priming

A study by Johnson, Selenta, and Lord (2006) provides a validation of the working self-concept theory proposed by Lord and Brown (2004) and represents the first clear use of an unconscious measure in a study involving Lord. This study primed various self-concepts using written vignettes. The findings yielded support for the proposition that the self-concept is a significant self-regulatory mechanism influencing both attitudes and behavioral outcomes.

Another study by Scott and Brown (2006) served to support the Lord and Maher (1991) hypothesis and, although not intended to assess the Lord and Brown (2004) propositions, proved to be consistent with them. This study dealt with the speed involved in categorizing leaders as leader and as either males or females. Agentic (male) leadership traits were less available than communal (female) when the leader was female. The more strongly that a behavior has been encoded into its unconscious, underlying trait, the faster the reaction time to the trait should occur, following the logic of the Implicit Association Test (IAT—see Blair and Banaji 1996). The extent to which the trait has been encoded may be assessed by the degree to which the behavior primes the trait. Thus again unconscious priming was brought to bear. Later a follow up on the Scott and Brown (2006) study was carried out providing greater detail on the male-female leadership differential (see Johnson, Murphy, Zewdie, and Reichard 2008). To be perceived as effective, female leaders needed to demonstrate both sensitivity and strength; male leaders needed only to demonstrate strength.

The use of priming in an information processing theory study is further exemplified by Ritter and Lord (2007). Primed representations of significant others were found in a transference study to elicit classifications of novel individuals. Individuals exposed to a leader not reminiscent of a previous leader typically used a general leader prototype to form leader expectations. Individuals exposed to a leader similar to a previous leader activated a significant-other representation to make judgments. Thus, through priming, an alternative to the prototype matching procedure used in prior information processing research was identified; introducing these unconscious processes made a difference. Evidence to this effect has recently been adduced from a meta-analysis of relevant studies (Van den Bussche, Van den Noortgate, and Reynvoet 2009).

PROTOTYPES AND PROTOTYPE MATCHING

I need to elaborate somewhat more on the subject of prototypes. These are "amalgams of features that have been abstracted from individual exemplars previously encountered" (Maddox and Dukes 2008, 207). They are not a single exemplar, but abstractions created from multiple exposures. "People classify prototypical patterns faster than distorted patterns and recruit fewer neural responses to perceive prototypical patterns. . . . Manipulations that enhance fluency (e.g., priming, clarity, increased stimulus duration, multiple prior exposures) yield more favorable judgments of stimuli" (Winkielman, Halberstadt, Fazendeiro, and Catty 2006, 799), as do prototypes.

Protype matching occurs when a given perception (say of a leader) is matched against such an abstracted prototype. Such matching has been compared to the use of role prescriptions in Miner's role motivation theory (Hunt, Boal, and Sorenson 1990, 5; see also Foti and Miner 2003, 109), but that is really a matter for consideration in the next chapter.

CONCLUSIONS

As noted at the beginning of this chapter, the information processing theory of leadership has a validity of four stars and an importance rating in terms of the judgments of organizational behavior scholars of 3.84. When the second figure is divided by the initial one, the consequence is a value of .96; thus the importance value is essentially identical to the validity value.

Information processing theory of leadership qualifies as essentially unconscious in nature, given its stand on automatic processes and its proximity to other interpretations of implicit processes. In this latter regard the use of priming research designs recently, as well as statements by the theory's primary author, have moved it much closer to the prevailing specification in terms of an unconscious perspective. Consideration is also given to prototypes and prototype matching as they interact with evidence on the conscious-unconscious trajectory of the theory.

ROLE MOTIVATION THEORY OF LEADERSHIP

The major sources for role motivation theory are Miner (1993b) and Miner (2008). One would anticipate that this theory has been fully explicated, since its source is the author, but there are additional points that need to be made. The theory is evaluated as to validity (by the author) at four stars (Miner 2005, Chapter 17; Miner 2007, Chapter 15), and its practical usefulness is at the same level; organizational behavior scholars agree with an average importance rating of 4.05.

Meta-analysis has been applied rather extensively to the hierarchic theory (see Chapters 25 and 26 of Miner 2008; also Chapter 30 for a related analysis). Work by Certo, Lester, Dalton, and Dalton (2006) is relevant as well. Task theory has been put to a similar test (see Chapters 27 and 29 of Miner 2008, and Collins, Hanges, and Locke 2004). Spangler (1992) and Zhao and Seibert (2006) are also relevant. Research by Rauch and Frese (2000) represents a start in the direction of a meta-analysis, but it is incomplete in this regard for lack of appropriate studies. Group theory is treated to a degree in the Stewart (2006) meta-analysis. The professional role motivation theory has not been the subject of any meta-analytic studies, although Miner (2006c) does contain relevant references on the subject. Similar references regarding the other three theories are contained in this source as well. Chapter 31 of Miner (2008) also bears upon the professional theory. All of these sources are consistent with a four-star evaluation of role motivation theory generally.

Given that much of the evidence favoring the theory derives from the Miner Sentence Completion Scale (MSCS) in one of its versions (all of which are projective in nature), it seems warranted to conclude that unconscious motivation is permitted to enter into these results and thus into the evaluation of the theory.

ROLE MOTIVATION THEORY IN BRIEF

In addition to what has been said previously, certain concepts may be introduced in new ways.

The Telescoping Phenomenon

Role motivation theory starts at the macro level with the various organizational forms involved, of which there are currently four. Below this, at a more micro level, are sets or patterns of roles consisting at the hierarchic level of favorable attitudes to superiors, desire to compete, desire to exercise power, desire to be distinct and different, and a desire to perform routine duties responsibly. These role prescriptions or prototypes (see Hunt, Boal, and Sorenson 1990) are represented at the professional level by the desire to learn and to acquire knowledge, the desire to exhibit independence, the desire to acquire status, the desire to help others, and a value-based identification with the profession. At the task level the roles become a desire to achieve through one's own efforts, a desire to avoid risk, a desire for feedback on performance, a desire to introduce innovative solutions, and a desire to plan and establish goals. Finally, at the group level the roles are a desire to interact socially and affiliate with others, a desire for continuing belongingness in a group, a favorable attitude toward peers, a desire to have cooperative/collaborative relationships, and a desire to participate in democratic processes (Miner 2005).

These two levels telescope in turn down to an emotional or affective base represented by the lead in for all of the versions of the MSCS:

> Please complete these sentences to express your real feelings.
>   Try to do every one. Be sure you make a complete sentence.

Thus the operational index at the individual level is a measure of feeling. This is the base to which the various levels—forms, roles, and unconscious emotions—telescope down. Thus for all its complexity, role motivation theory boils down to an emotional phenomenon.

Levels of Abstraction among Needs

The humanistic psychologist Abraham Maslow (1955) differentiates various levels of abstraction within his hierarchy of needs, such as his specification of growth and deficiency needs (see Miner 2002; Molden, Lee, and Higgins 2008). Given that the motives activated by role prescriptions are similar to needs, including the fact that both operate in an unconscious manner, it seems appropriate to apply this level of abstraction concept to them as well. Accordingly I have attempted to label the patterns of motives operating in each of the four organizational forms at a higher level of abstraction than the specific roles (5 or 6 in specific cases) possess. These higher-level designations, like all such, are invariably less precise, but they do carry a general sense of the essence of the motives involved.

- Hierarchic (managerial) form: need for power
- Professional (specialized) form: need for self-actualization
- Task (entrepreneurial) form: need for achievement
- Group (team) form: need for affiliation

Chapter 4 of this volume dealing with McClelland's theory presents evidence regarding these four needs. Also Smith, Dijksterhuis, and Wigboldus (2008) add experimental data regarding the effectiveness of need for power, whether or not decisions are made consciously. With regard to the need for self-actualization and its unconscious activation, see Sui and Han (2007), and Andersen, Reznik, and Glassman (2005). Beyond McClelland's work the need for achievement requires further treatment to be accomplished later in this chapter. The need for affiliation is considered in relation to unconscious factors in Andersen, Reznik, and Glassman (2005). All of these needs operate at the unconscious level, as appropriate to their being measured at this level using projective techniques.

The Role of Followers

The theoretical formulations presented here emerged during my reading of the book dedicated to the memory of Jim Meindl edited by Shamir, Pillai, Bligh, and Uhl-Bien (2007). This book is in keeping with Meindl's romance of leadership theory (see Chapter 21 of this volume) and serves to emphasize the roles of followers in interpreting leadership.

My take from role motivation theory of leadership is that input from followers is an important consideration, but it alone is insufficient. Observers are best used to describe all participants (followers plus leaders and any other people involved) who serve to create the pattern of role prescriptions (prototypes) operating in a given situation. Then, those particular individuals involved who match most closely these social constructions (as identified by the observers based on MSCS scores) are classified as leaders.

Components of this process involve various participants including leaders; it is leader centric, but also observer centric. Certain quotes may help illustrate this point:

> Chronic regulatory orientation appears to play a role in determining the kinds of role models that individuals seize upon to harness their motivation. . . . Individuals use role models who match their regulatory strategies (Lockwood and Pinkus 2008, 255).

> The stronger the affect, the more likely it is that the goal it stems from will rise in priority until it comes fully to awareness (Carver and Scheier 2008, 317); this is with reference to MSCS responding.

> The different roles that individuals occupy may automatically activate role-congruent behavior and cognition (Diekman and Eagly 2008, 439).

> The neurobiological evidence provides a possible reason for the consistent emergence of the approach-avoidance distinction in motivation (Gable and Strachman 2008, 564), as with the positive and negative response on the MSCS.

> Our analysis suggests that volitional action control is particularly served by *intuitive affect regulation* . . . , a form of affect regulation that combines both automatic and controlled processes (Koole and Kuhl 2008, 295).

Clearly roles are subject to unconscious activation, and emotions (as exhibited in the MSCS responses) play an important part in this process. It appears that introducing the MSCS stems with an emphasis on feeling serves in large part to prime the production of unconscious responses involving emotion.

USE OF THE FOUR FORMS

The Mumford Theory

The idea of categorizing leaders in some manner (in terms of charismatic, ideological, and pragmatic types) using autobiographical data has much appeal (historiometric methods). It uses a classification procedure that is essentially conscious in nature, but this is true as well of the role motivation theory of leadership, which establishes the four forms in terms of responses to the Oliver Organization Description Questionnaire. Beyond this, however, difficulties arise because the three leadership types do not fit well into the four forms. The problem is that the theory is largely developmental and thus does not establish stable relationships of any kind; in hierarchic bureaucracies, pragmatic leadership appears to be the dominant type, but this is not always the case, as is evidenced by the move from Mumford (2006) to Mumford, Antes, Caughron, and Friedrich (2008) to Ligon, Hunter, and Mumford (2008). Thus I am unable to establish any stable ties between the role motivation and Mumford formulations beyond the fact of categorization.

The Sims Theory

In the case of a second theory there is not only categorization but also something that matches well with the role motivation forms. I draw upon the Liu, Lepak, Takeuchi, and Sims (2003) article to make my point. The similarities are as follows:

Sims	Miner
Directive leadership as with contract workers	Hierarchic forms and the need for power
Transactional leadership as with job-based employees	Task form and the need for achievement
Transformational leadership as with alliances	Group form and the need for affiliation
Empowering leadership as with knowledge-based employees	Professional form and the need for self-actualization

A subsequent article deals only with directive and empowering leadership (Pearce, Manz, and Sims 2008) among these four, offering hypotheses regarding how corruption may occur in each instance, as well as how it may be ameliorated by shared leadership. But see as well Sims, Faraj, and Yun (2009), which returns to the previous categorization.

Structuring the *Handbook of Motivation Science*

Part II of the influential *Handbook of Motivation Science* (Shah and Gardner 2008) contains chapters that serve to structure the rest of the book, which consists of 39 chapters. Here one finds the following:

- Chapter 2 on belongingness motivation deals with the group form and the need for affiliation (Leary and Cox 2008).
- Chapter 3 on control motivation deals with the hierarchic form and the need for power (Thompson and Schlehofer 2008).
- Chapter 4 on self-enhancement motivation and self-affirmation deals with the professional form and the need for self-actualization (Taylor and Sherman 2008).

• Chapter 7 on achievement motivation deals with the task form and the need for achievement (Senko, Durik, and Harackiewicz 2008).

It is evident that the four forms and their characteristic motivations are given advance billing by the handbook's authors.

TASK FORMS AND ENTREPRENEURSHIP

The task form has been somewhat more problematic than the other three forms insofar as leadership is concerned. At the same time its involvement in research on unconscious considerations has been considerable (Hisrich, Langan-Fox, and Grant 2007).

The Baron Findings

"Several measures and methods developed by the field of cognitive science may prove useful to researchers investigating various aspects of entrepreneurial cognition. These techniques include . . . reaction time, priming, measures of working memory, and measures of creative cognition" (Baron and Ward 2004, 553). Many forms of errors may be noted, including overconfidence, the illusion of control, and the law of small numbers (i.e., the tendency to use a small sample of information as a basis for firm conclusions). Other cognitive biases are manifest, especially in the initial decision to become an entrepreneur. Baron (2004) notes that entrepreneurs are excessively confident about their own chances of success (the strong optimistic bias). "Given the impressive success of a cognitive approach in other fields (e.g. psychology, education) there are grounds for predicting that it may also yield positive results when applied in the field of entrepreneurship" (237). Information that occurs below the level of conscious awareness is particularly important. So too is affect (Baron 2007a). Risk propensities may vary at different phases of the entrepreneurial process (Baron 2007b), although this remains uncertain due to the nature of meta-analysis on which this hypothesis is based.

The Busenitz Research

Busenitz and Barney (1997), reporting on differences between entrepreneurs and managers, indicate that two biases and heuristics characterize the former—overconfidence and representativeness (the tendency to make decisions based on insufficient sample sizes). As a consequence they tend to perceive less risk in a given decision situation (Busenitz 1999). Heuristic-logic produces innovative ideas that are not always factually based or very linear. Examples are representativeness errors, affect infusion into decision processes, planning fallacy, and the illusion of control. The results are not always negative, such as those produced by the avoidance of sunk costs, but they often are (Mitchell, Busenitz, Bird, Gaglio, McMullen, Morse, and Smith (2007). The use of heuristics can produce the development of blind spots and unintended escalation (Busenitz and Arthurs 2007).

Other Evidence on Unconscious Factors in Entrepreneurship

Research by Forbes (2005) also indicates that cognitive biases are particularly characteristic of entrepreneurs—in particular the tendency to be overconfident. White, Thornhill, and Hampson (2006) report that "individual differences in testosterone are associated with entrepreneurial behavior. Increasingly, it is evident that the heuristics and biases used by entrepreneurs differ from those found in the non-entrepreneurial population" (30). Franke, Gruber, Harhoff, and Henkel (2006) found that venture capitalists were infected by a similarity bias; they "tend to favor teams that are similar to themselves in type of training and professional experience" (802). This process is consistent with the research on unconscious similarity biases (Markman and Gentner 2005).

REACTIONS TO ALTERNATIVE VIEWS

What follows are various unrelated statements on issues with which I have disagreed, and expressing my current position from a role motivation theory perspective.

On Risk Taking

Rauch and Frese (2007), consistent with their own research, reject what they believe are the Miner and Raju (see Chapter 27 of Miner 2008) findings on risk taking. However, it appears that Rauch and Frese used self-report measures of risk, as did Stewart and Roth (2001), and for such self-report analyses, I would agree with their findings. There is no apparent need to reject the Miner and Raju data. However, Rauch and Frese do take this position, and incorrectly so, based on misinformation regarding the Miner and Raju meta-analyses (from Stewart and Roth 2004). I remain convinced that unconscious motivation as measured by projective techniques produces more risk taking on the part of managers and more risk avoidance on the part of entrepreneurs. To support this conclusion I refer to more recent data not mentioned by Rauch and Frese (see Miner 2008, Chapter 32, 432; also Xu and Ruef 2004; Gianotti, Knoch, Faber, Lehmann, Pascual-Marqui, Diezi, Schoch, Eisenegger, and Fehr 2009).

On Scoring the MSCS

Vecchio (2003, 322) says, "Miner's theory of person-system fit (perhaps one of the more promising avenues of research, in terms of theory and strength of findings) has not received much attention in recent years. This neglect may partially stem from reliance on measures (role sentence completions) that involve more elaborate scoring procedures in comparison to other paper-and-pencil measures." I believe this judgment to be correct; there has been a consistent effort to recast the Miner Sentence Completion Scales into self-report measures and thus to reduce their projective (unconscious) nature (see Miner 2008, Chapter 24; also Chan, Rounds, and Drasgow 2000; Chan and Drasgow 2001). To give in to this proclivity represents a move in the wrong direction; it should be resisted. Scoring the MSCSs may be difficult, but difficulty is sometimes required to get things right; the MSCSs are intended to measure unconscious motivation, and they should not be deprived of that strength.

On Business School Professors as Managers?

Jiang and Murphy (2007) contend that business school professors make good executive managers, yet this flies in the face of Miner (2008, see Chapter 9). Who is to be believed? The Jiang and Murphy sample consists mostly of professors who appear to have held previous positions as managers in business organizations; they are not representative of professors in general. Thus, the two studies are not comparable; they deal with a sample not predisposed to managerial talent (Miner) versus a sample so predisposed (Jiang and Murphy).

On Whether the Correlation between Implicit and Explicit Measures Equals Zero

McClelland, Koestner, and Weinberger (1989) reported a zero correlation between implicit and explicit measures when needs were used. I have reported a more positive relationship in Chapter 4 of this volume, with correlations in the .14 to .15 range and up. However, there is reason to believe that the explicit measures have not been suitably matched with those of an implicit nature in these analyses. When this is done (Schultheiss, Yankova, Dirlikov, and Schad 2009) the results for needs appear more appropriately to approximate zero. "The statistical independence between implicit and explicit motives appears to be genuine and to reflect a true dissociation between the types of motivation preferences individuals spontaneously express when writing imaginative stories and what they declare their motivational needs to be when asked directly. Our findings therefore are consistent with McClelland et al.'s (1989) argument that implicit and explicit motives do not correlate" (79). Given these data, I defer to this evidence, as specifically identified with the measurement of needs. "Schultheiss . . . has argued that implicit and explicit motives are mediated by different brain systems" (79).

CONCLUSIONS

Role motivation theory of leadership possesses a validity estimated at four stars and organizational behavior scholars give it an importance rating of 4.05. Dividing the latter value by the former yields a ratio of 1.01, indicative of the fact that the two are closely aligned.

The theory is shown to telescope the four organizational forms into its role prescriptions, and then finally into the emotions involved in the question posed by the MSCSs. Levels of abstraction are used to establish primary needs, and observers are recommended—as opposed to followers—to establish unconscious role prescriptions. The use of the four forms is supported by their involvement in the Mumford theory, the Sims theory, and in the structuring of a major handbook. The task theory is given special attention as it implicates unconscious processes. Finally this chapter takes up various alternative views to those of role motivation theory considering the matter of risk taking, the scoring of the MSCSs, business school professors as managers, and the correlation between implicit and explicit measures of needs.

CHAPTER 17

CHARISMATIC LEADERSHIP THEORY

Charismatic leadership theory has several different authors. Among them, the theories of Robert House (1977) and Bernard Bass (1985) stand out. Both are predicated on prior contributions, by Max Weber and James M. Burns respectively. Of the two, Bass's transformational theory appears to have spanned the largest amount of subsequent research; on the other hand, however, House's theory came first, and his eight propositions on charisma are in fact incorporated in the Bass formulations, above and beyond Bass's own propositions.

Given this situation and other relevant considerations I am inclined to give equal billing to both theories here. This represents a break with past practice. However, both theories have an estimated validity of four stars, which normally would be the dominant consideration in this type of situation. The Bass theory has the higher importance rating at 5.06, presumably because it is more widely researched and cited; it has a higher practical usefulness as well. The House theory has a very similar importance rating at 4.76. In further justification of the equal treatment for both theories, both are considered to be primarily of an unconscious nature; this evaluation needs further substantiation, however. The sources for these ratings are Miner (2005), Chapters 18 and 19, and Miner (2007), Chapter 16.

With regard to his theory, Bass (1985, 20) says:

> We see the transformational leader as one who motivates us to do more than we originally expected to do. . . . Such a transformation can be achieved in any one of three interrelated ways: . . .
>
> 3. By altering our own need level on Maslow's (or Alderfer's) hierarchy or expanding on our portfolio of needs and wants.

Bass (1985) devotes considerable space to the need hierarchy, and thus to the unconscious processes involved, including those addressed by Freud (see Chapter 5 of this volume, as well as Chapter 9).

House (1977, and other citations) brings additional evidence regarding unconscious motivation to bear on his version of charisma theory, albeit of a different nature. In this case it was achievement motivation theory and its needs that predominated. House was strongly influenced by David McClelland and his theorizing; he was affected in particular by David Berlew, a former student of McClelland's, who interpreted achievement motivation theory for House. As a result a series of propositions were stated—and tested—dealing with the charisma of U.S. presidents (see House, Woycke, and Fodor 1988; House, Spangler, and Woycke 1991). These hypotheses are in fact referred to as the integrated House-McClelland model (House and Howell 1992). The introduction of McClelland's theory, along with his scoring system for needs, clearly brings the arousal of unconscious factors into House's theory of charisma (see Chapter 4 of this volume and House 1995). Thus House and Bass become aligned in this regard, even though the two utilize different routes to achieve this unconscious end.

THE META-ANALYTIC LITERATURE

A broad array of research studies on aspects of the charisma perspective has been published, and suitably a number of meta-analyses reviewing them have appeared as well. In particular I would note Lowe, Kroeck, and Sivasubramaniam (1996), Dumdum, Lowe, and Avolio (2002), and Judge and Piccolo (2004), all of which are of relatively recent vintage and appear to maintain their validity over any effects of common-method bias. To these, I would add findings reported from the Stewart (2006) meta-analysis. Avolio (2004) discusses these meta-analytic efforts and concludes that transformational leadership in particular has a high level of validity.

Organization Size as a Moderator

To these initial very positive findings, I need to add one disclaimer. When CEO charisma is measured using data from top management team members, "perceptions of CEO charisma were not associated with subsequent organizational performance, even after we incorporated the potential moderating effect of environmental uncertainty" (Agle, Nagarajan, Sonnenfeld, and Srinivasan 2006). This null effect holds for charisma as it operates at the very top of large U.S. corporations, but it does not apply to smaller firms where the charisma has less room to dissipate (Ling, Simsek, Lubatkin, and Veiga 2008; Peterson, Walumbwa, Byron, and Myrowitz 2009). In these smaller firms CEO charisma operates with the same force and validity as found in previous meta-analyses.

More Problematic Meta-analytic Findings

Mumford (2006, 5) contends, "Historiometric methods may be viewed as a form of meta-analysis, admittedly a specialized form, where general conclusions are obtained by cumulating results across studies—specifically historic cases or biographies." Be that as it may, it is worthwhile to look at the results obtained by charismatic leadership—one of the three types of outstanding leadership described by Mumford. On this score the central finding to emerge "is that charismatic, ideological, and pragmatic leadership are not associated with marked differences in performance when appropriate controls are applied in contrasting these leaders with regard to performance differences. This finding, or more correctly nonfinding, holds across a range of measures" (Mumford 2006, 93). Remember, however, that all three types of leaders are of an outstanding nature; thus the failure to find charismatic leaders superior is not too surprising (see Bedell-Avers, Hunter, and Mumford 2008).

Another research program with problematic findings insofar as their quantitative contribution across studies is concerned involves the GLOBE (Global Leadership and Organizational Behavior Effectiveness) analyses. Here charismatic/value-based leadership is defined as reflecting the ability to inspire, to motivate, and to expect high performance outcomes from others based on firmly held core values. This includes six leadership subscales labeled as visionary, inspirational, self-sacrifice, integrity, decisive, and performance oriented (House and Javidan 2004, 14). Leadership of this kind stresses goal setting and performance improvement of the types represented by charismatic and transformational leadership theories (Javidan 2004, 277). The GLOBE studies extend across 62 societies and thus as a whole approximate a meta-analysis. Charismatic/value-based leadership was hypothesized to "be universally perceived as leading to effective leadership," and respondents in societies report that [such] behaviors contribute to effective leadership: It is universally perceived as important, yet there is variability among cultures" (Dorfman, Hanges, and Brodbeck 2004, 673, 677, and 703). Thus the GLOBE research gives a strong endorsement to charismatic leadership of both the House and Bass types. Unfortunately, however, both House and Bass implicate unconscious features in their theories, while the GLOBE program is much more problematic in this regard.

THE GLOBE RESEARCH AND THE UNCONSCIOUS

Let us look at what we can know as to the involvement of the unconscious in the GLOBE analyses. House and Javidan (2004) state:

> The theory that guides the GLOBE research program is an integration of implicit leadership theory (Lord and Maher 1991), value-belief theory of culture (Hofstede 1980; Triandis 1995), implicit motivation theory (McClelland 1985), and structural contingency theory of organizational form and effectiveness (Donaldson 2001; Hickson, Hinings, McMillan, and Schwitter 1974). . . . The core GLOBE cultural dimensions . . . reflect not only the dimensions of Hofstede's and Triandis's theories, but also McClelland's theory of human motivation and economic development (McClelland 1985). The humane, power distance, and performance orientation of cultures are conceptually analogous to the affiliative, power, and achievement motives in McClelland's theory of human motivation. Implicit motivation theory is a theory of nonconscious motives originally advanced by McClelland, Atkinson, Clark, and Lowell (1953). . . . We will test the assumption that middle manager reports of explicit motives, if aggregated to the societal or organizational level, function in the same way that McClelland asserts implicit motives function. Whereas McClelland's theory is an individual theory of both nonconscious and conscious motivation, the GLOBE theory is a theory of motivation resulting from cultural forces (16–17).

Elsewhere reference is made to "the set of self-report scales" (Hanges and Dickson 2004, 122) used to test the hypotheses. In addition, the following statement occurs: "A second limitation of the research presented here is that it is monomethod: All scale data presented were collected using questionnaires" (Hanges and Dickson 2004, 145). Thus it would appear that, in spite of the mixture with McClelland's statements and with references to unconscious processes, no claim is made that other than conscious operations actually occurred in the GLOBE studies. None of the research used projective techniques, priming, thin-slice methodology, or any other procedures to tap unconscious features.

On the Use of the Term "Implicit"

In Chapter 15 of this volume (on information processing theory of leadership) I made the point that the term "implicit" may be misused; it also may be misused by the GLOBE researchers, where it is invoked repeatedly without carrying the meaning of "unconscious." I cite some examples:

> We used both implicit and explicit concept analysis in our research. . . . Making implicit concepts explicit and then quantifying these concepts is important because it results in the construction of a translation rule (Gupta, deLuque, and House 2004, 156).

> These naïve or idiosyncratic individualized leadership theories have been studied under the rubrics implicit leadership theory, leader categorization theory (Lord, Foti, and DeVader 1984) or, more generally social cognition theory applied to leadership. . . . Implicit leadership theory in general is widely regarded as a valid perspective (Dorfman, Hanges, and Brodbeck 2004, 670).

> We broadened the concept of individualized implicit leadership theories (ILT) into a cultural-level theory labeled culturally endorsed implicit leadership theory (CLT) (Dorfman, Hanges, and Brodbeck 2004, 711).

On Peterson's (2004) Review of the GLOBE Book

> GLOBE takes a step toward assessing whether the forms of leadership that have been found most useful in nations like the United States, in which leadership has been frequently studied, are useful elsewhere. It does so by using the idea of "implicit leadership theory" in a way that needs to be read with care. As the authors accurately indicate, research about people's implicit leadership reflects applications of theories about nonconscious cognitive structures like scripts and schemas to conscious thought and behavior. Like all conscious thought, explicit answers to survey questions about leadership are affected by nonconscious structures that are shaped by culture. But only when the inaccuracies of bias in such explicit reports are being considered have studies that used the means of survey items been thought of as implicit leadership theory research. As I read the leadership material, I found it helpful to think "explicit leadership perceptions and ideas" in place of what the authors called implicit leadership theory (Peterson 2004, 644).

Thus both Peterson and I have considerable doubt as to whether the GLOBE approach deals with anything other than conscious processes. I refer the reader to the discussion and studies on implicit theories in Chapter 15 of this volume; also to the fact that the GLOBE researchers make no mention anywhere in their book to the seminal article on implicit-explicit differences by McClelland, Koestner, and Weinberger (1989); this is a major shortcoming.

CHARISMA AND RESEARCH ON UNCONSCIOUS PROCESSES

Indeed there is evidence that charismatic leadership is associated with unconscious factors.

The Mortality Salience Studies

Cohen, Solomon, Maxfield, Pyszczynski, and Greenberg (2004) conducted a study to find out if charismatic leadership is influenced by the activation of terror management priming.

When mortality salience was introduced with regard to political candidates, people showed an increased preference for a charismatic candidate and a reduced preference for a relationship-oriented candidate. The primes used were mixed in with other questionnaire items and were as follows:

- Please briefly describe the emotions that the thought of your own death arouses in you.
- Jot down, as specifically as you can, what you think will happen to you as you physically die and once you are physically dead.

The activation of mortality salience in this way produced more positive evaluations for the charismatic candidate and more votes. Similar results were shown to be involved in the ratings of President George W. Bush after the events of 9/11 (Landau, Solomon, Greenberg, Cohen, Pyszczynski, Arndt et al. 2004). In other studies mortality salience has been induced by ten outside-of-awareness exposures to the word *dead* (Greenberg, Solomon, and Arndt 2008, 122). It is apparent that exposure to primes of this nature does activate responsiveness to charismatic leadership.

Promotion and Prevention Focus

When people are in a promotion focus, whether from a chronic disposition or experimentally induced, they are not aware of trade-offs of their strategic eagerness in decision making or problem solving. The same is true for the strategic vigilance of people in a prevention focus ... but they are unlikely to intend or be aware of the costs of the strategy they use.... I have presented evidence for the conclusion that unintended thought is also a product of the rational use of basic self-regulatory strategies (Higgins 2005, 532–533; see also Higgins 2008).

When such statements are combined with data on leadership styles, they become indicative of the unconscious nature of a charismatic approach—"leaders' ability to prime their followers' promotion focus helps us understand why transformational and charismatic leadership has been found, in prior works, to be positively related to followers' affective commitment and to organizational innovation" (Kark and VanDijk 2007, 521). "Higgins (2000) introduces the concept of regulatory fit to explain the subconscious process of adaptation in which people adjust their thinking to become more congruent with the demands of their environment" (Neubert, Kacmar, Carlson, Chonko, and Roberts 2008, 1221).

Additional Evidence

A further extension of Higgins's theorizing occurs with regard to regulatory mode (see Higgins, Kruglanski, and Pierro 2003) where a typology involving locomotion and assessment is introduced via a priming manipulation. Here a locomotion mode applies to moving before action. As Benjamin and Flynn (2006) found, "Followers with more of a locomotion mode reported higher levels of motivation when working for transformational leaders than did followers with more of an assessment mode" (221). "We found that people with a stronger locomotion mode responded more favorably to transformational leadership" (299).

Furthermore Erez, Misangyi, Johnson, LePine, and Halverson (2008) found in a field study that firefighters commanded by charismatic officers were happier than under a noncharismatic officer and that these relationships were mediated by the charismatic leader's positive affect. "Arousal is also slow to decay, people are often unaware that they are aroused, and it easily transfers from situation to situation" (613). Thus counterproductive results may be involved when charismatic arousal is invoked.

In reviewing literature on leadership, Gupta, MacMillan, and Surie (2004, 245) conclude that "the neocharismatic leadership perspective focuses on how leaders evoke superordinate performance from followers through a transcendence of self-interested behavior by appealing to higher needs for self-actualization, deeply held personal values, and implicit motivations of followers." All in all the evidence appears to provide convincing evidence that charismatic leadership can occur outside of awareness.

POINTS AT WHICH UNCONSCIOUS MOTIVATION MIGHT BE INVOKED

There are a number of points at which these findings on unconscious processes might well be brought to bear to amplify our understanding of charismatic leadership. The evidence on these matters does not indicate the level of involvement of unconscious considerations, but these are aspects where further research in this regard might bear fruit.

CEO Involvement

One such source involves the research on CEO involvement. A study of this type by Zhu, Chew, and Spangler (2005) finds that "human-capital-enhancing human resource management fully mediates the relationship between CEO transformational leadership and subjective assessment of organizational outcomes and partially mediates the relationship between CEO transformational leadership and absenteeism. . . . Transformational CEOs are more likely to adopt human-capital-enhancing human resource management" (39, 48). With regard to compensation, CEO charisma among Fortune 500 executives was directly related to CEO pay, but not to any firm performance measures. CEO charisma also was related to shareholder value under conditions of uncertainty (Tosi, Misangyi, Fanelli, Waldman, and Yammarino 2004). This latter finding has been confirmed as a result of research by Flynn and Staw (2004), again using U.S. charismatic CEOs. Data from Taiwanese CEOs links transformational leadership to organizational innovation, as would be expected from theory (Jung, Wu, and Chow 2008).

Theoretical Relevance

In addition to the aforementioned findings on innovation, other evidence exists that ties charismatic leadership to its theoretical roots. Various measures of both transformational and charismatic leadership have been found to converge on a common validity (Rowold and Heinitz 2007); the two are indeed very similar. Charismatic leaders express more positive emotion, and these emotional states are linked to follower mood, suggesting a type of mood contagion (Bono and Ilies 2006). Leader self-sacrifice was found to be characteristic and effective as well for charismatics (van Knippenberg and van Knippenberg 2005). Charismatic leadership is expected to create a consensus, a similar mindset, among followers in that they perceive the leader in similar ways—and indeed they do (Feinberg, Ostroff, and Burke 2005). Team creativity is fostered by the diversity of educational specializations found within a team when charismatic leadership is present; charismatic leadership enables the teams to use the cognitive resources inherent in their heterogeneity (Shin and Zhou 2007).

It seems to me that introducing unconscious measures into the situations described in this section might well yield major benefits and greater understanding. Certainly charisma, when present, acts to invoke unconscious processes; it would appear to be a good place to look for new research findings.

CONCLUSIONS

This chapter draws upon two perspectives on charismatic leadership—that of Robert House and that of Bernard Bass. The former (House) presents a theory that has a validity rated at four stars and an importance evaluation from organizational behavior of 4.76; the ratio resulting is 1.19, indicating that the importance rating appears to overstate the estimated validity of the theory to some degree. The Bass theory also possesses a four-star validity, but its importance rating is 5.06. When the validity is divided into the importance bestowed by organizational behavior scholars, a value of 1.27 results. Again organizational behavior overestimates the validity of the theory, and to a somewhat greater degree.

Both theories implicate unconscious processes—Bass through ties to Maslow's (and Alderfer's) need hierarchy theory and House through ties to McClelland's need achievement theory. Meta-analytic studies support the validity of these theories, although not for all firms and with all analytic procedures. In particular the GLOBE program must become problematic on this score due to its failure to include unconscious factors in its measurement processes; only self-report procedures are clearly in evidence. No indexes of unconscious processes are described in the 818-page GLOBE volume, the term implicit is clearly misused, and this factor is noted by a major reviewer, as well as this author.

Distinct experimental evidence is reported to the effect that charisma necessarily invokes processes that extend beyond awareness; this becomes apparent from the mortality salience literature, from studies on a promotion and prevention focus, and from additional evidence on unconscious considerations. A number of studies on charisma are cited that might invoke the unconscious aspects of charisma and would thus warrant further research in this regard.

CHAPTER 18

CONTINGENCY THEORY OF LEADERSHIP

Fred Fiedler's contingency theory of leadership has developed in an incremental fashion following the course of its research trajectory. In the end it has answered many questions, while leaving a substantial number unanswered as well. The theory is best stated in two volumes—Fiedler (1967) and Fiedler and Chemers (1974), but there are many variations in between and in the years since their introduction. I have given it a three-star evaluation, and organizational behavior in general has bestowed upon it a 4.33 importance rating (see Miner 2005, 2007). Its practical usefulness is in line with its validity, based on the Leader Match applications (Fiedler and Chemers 1984). An extension of the basic theoretical position, in the form of cognitive resource theory (Fiedler and Garcia 1987), is not the major focus of this treatment. It too is given a rating of three stars, with an importance rating of 4.46.

Contingency theory of leadership has had an expanding exposure to meta-analysis as the research has increased (Strube and Garcia 1981; Peters, Hartke, and Pohlman 1985; Schriesheim, Tepper, and Tetrault 1994). The upshot of these evaluations is in line with the three-star rating; the octants, especially octant two, do not always operate as hypothesized, and there are other needs for adjustment, but in general there is good reason to believe that the theory warrants further investigation and exploration, and certainly not abandonment.

The Leader Match application also has received a favorable evaluation at the hands of meta-analysis (Burke and Day 1986). Although intended to utilize and in fact be based on contingency theory, there is serious doubt whether this is the case; it seems apparent that differences do occur between the content of contingency theory and what Leader Match teaches (Jago and Ragan 1986).

WHAT DOES LPC MEASURE?

It is important at the outset to establish what the Least Preferred Coworker (LPC) component of contingency theory measures. This is not done easily. Fiedler has offered different interpretations at different times, and on occasion at the same time (see Foa, Mitchell, and Fiedler 1971; Fiedler 1972, 1973, 1978; Fiedler and Chemers 1974; Ayman, Chemers, and Fiedler 1995). To my knowledge he has never entertained the possibility that LPC might represent a projective technique.

The Roya Ayman Interpretation

Yet Ayman (2002), who has published with Fiedler as a coauthor, on occasion has done just that:

> One key issue of misunderstanding regarding the LPC scale is the researchers' assumption that it is a self-report measure. The LPC scale is not a self-report measure of behaviors or personal values of a respondent. It is an indirect measure of the leader's inner needs or orientation, similar to a projective test like the Thematic Apperception Test (McClelland 1965). This characteristic has been a double-edged sword for the LPC scale. Its strength is that it is not a direct measure of an individual's characteristics. Therefore, the naïve respondent has little ability to influence the responses or know about the results (Kennedy and Gallo 1986). This strength is also its weakness as it contributes to the scale's low face validity (200–201).

> For those with low LPC scores, when someone interferes with their goal accomplishment, they become bitter and thus describe the individual very negatively. This may be due to the fact their self-worth flows from task accomplishment. However, individuals with high LPC scores are more relationship oriented, and do not perceive the lack of task completion as a significant threat to their self-worth (202).

> In general the LPC scale has not shown any empirical evidence of convergence with other trait measures. A potential reason for this could be based on what was mentioned earlier, that the LPC measure is an indirect, quasi-projective test (204).

> It seems clear that the LPC scale does not directly measure behavior and that it has an acceptable level of stability and reliability. Its lack of relationship with most other measures of similar constructs may be due to its quasi-projective nature (205).

LPC as a Projective: Pros and Cons

Since we have no proof that the LPC measure is projective in nature, or perhaps better a quasi-projective, what is the probability of the truth of this hypothesis? Really the key factor is to determine whether LPC truly gets at some type of unconscious factor.

One way of considering these issues is to look at Fiedler's background. He was trained as a clinical psychologist (at the University of Chicago) and also underwent a personal psychoanalysis; thus there is both a background in projectives and in exposure to unconscious considerations. His early publications were on therapeutic relationships, but intermingled with these were studies of projective measures (Fiedler and Siegel 1949—*The Free Drawing Test as a Predictor of Nonimprovement in Psychotherapy*) and of unconscious processes (Fiedler and Senior 1952—*An Exploratory Study of Unconscious Feeling Reactions in Fifteen Patient-Therapist Pairs*). Fiedler wrote predominantly in the clinical psychology literature for some six years before transitioning gradually into leadership.

This does not demonstrate anything about the clinical, projective, and unconscious orientations of LPC, but it does make the point that Fiedler had the qualifications to create a measure of this kind. On the other hand there can be no certainty that Ayman's hypothesis is true. It is researchable, but no such research has been conducted. We simply do not know.

LPC might be compared with various other projective techniques; more specifically, studies using the TAT could be instituted to check the hypothesis that low LPC = achievement motivation and that high LPC = affiliation motivation. Priming studies could be invoked to determine whether unconscious motivation is activated by LPC scales. Currently we do not have these answers, and until research is done to confirm them we will not know either way. Sentence completion measures à la Miner (2008) could be used. There is much to support the projective perspective on LPC, but not enough to fully confirm such a view.

What Becomes Available if the Unconscious Is Broached?

What if the LPC scale is a projective and brings material that is beyond awareness to the fore? My objective here is to indicate the kind of material that might emerge as a result. Let us look at the data.

Pencil-and-paper-based deliberative implicit measures have a lot to offer. They have the potential to add predictive power beyond what can be achieved with explicit measures or spontaneous implicit measures . . . a number of spontaneous measures have also been adapted for use with paper and pencil (Vargas, Sekaquaptewa, and von Hippel 2007, 109). *The LPC scale has these potentials* (see also Vargas, Sekaquaptewa, and von Hippel 2007, 112).

Behavior may contain automatic, habitual aspects not accounted for in models of reasoned action (Ajzen 2001, 48). *Thus the LPC scale may go beyond whatever in contingency theory is documented at a conscious level.*

The various studies . . . suggest that subjective biases in interpreting the attributes and behaviors of others are capable of running off in an automatic and implicit fashion. Projection, then, being an egocentric bias in person perception, should also have the capacity to be an automatic process (Kawada, Oettingen, Gollwitzer, and Bargh 2004, 547). *Accordingly projection could operate with regard to the LPC scale to elicit unconscious material.*

Material primes are most likely to affect behavioral choices when normative demands are least explicit (or conversely, most ambiguous) (Kay, Wheeler, Bargh, and Ross 2004, 85). *The LPC situation does possess the characteristic that it is ambiguous.*

The findings presented by Winkielman, Berridge, and Wilbarger (2005) are compelling in that they suggest that we can have emotions in the absence of awareness. The perceptual theory of emotion predicts this possibility. After all, unconscious perception is possible in other modalities (Prinz 2005, 375). *Consequently, the LPC scale would appear to have this potential.*

In the literature of cognitive psychology, automatic processes are held to be inevitably evoked by the presence of a relevant environmental stimulus; once triggered, their execution proceeds rapidly, effortlessly, and incorrigibly to completion, leaving no traces accessible to conscious recollection (Glaser and Kihlstrom 2005, 171). *LPC, too, would seem to possess this characteristic.*

Perceivers demonstrate a striking ability to detect the type and quality of others' social relationships. This ability seems to derive from a largely effortless process of detection, a process of which people are not consciously aware. This remarkable ability may be rooted in a basic need (Choi, Gray, and Ambady 2005, 322). *Such a feature would seem to relate to the need for affiliation as hypothesized to be manifest in the LPC score.*

There may be some forms of self-regulation in transference that transpire relatively automatically, and that offer evidence that relationship-protective self-regulation can sometimes proceed automatically (Andersen, Reznik, and Glassman 2005, 453). *Again affiliation is in evidence.*

Broaching the Unconscious with Regard to Goals

The matter of goal setting has been a consistent concern of those who have studied unconscious processes. Ayman, however, has also introduced this factor into LPC interpretation, especially with regard to the low-end aspects of task motivation. What, then, does the research say here?

Goal-dependent processes are thus not necessarily intentional or controlled. . . . Recent research has convincingly demonstrated that unconsciously activated *goals* to engage in a process can also be causally effective (De Houwer and Moors 2007, 186–187).

Automatic attitudes vary depending on current *goals,* task instructions, recently encountered attitude objects and attitude-relevant contexts, and even mood (Ferguson and Bargh 2007, 237).

Goals activated outside of awareness should affect perception and behavior just as it is true for trait constructs that are activated outside of awareness. . . . Our findings suggest that positive as well as negative *goals* are projected. This implies that goal projection may potentially serve self-defensive as well as self-enhancing purposes (Kawada, Oettingen, Gollwitzer, and Bargh 2004, 547, 554).

Two experiments, using markedly different implicit-learning paradigms, demonstrated facilitation of implicit learning when the *goal* of achievement was primed. . . . Nonconscious *goal* pursuit can increase the likelihood of learning *goal*-relevant structures in the environment. . . . [and] can help people achieve their goals even in novel environments. . . . The current results lend further support to the emerging view that implicit learning is a motivated process (Eitam, Hassin, and Schul 2008, 261–262, 266).

Recent research has shown these nonconscious influences to extend beyond the perception and interpretation of the social world to the actual guidance, over extended time periods, of one's important *goal* pursuits and social interactions (Bargh and Williams 2006, 1).

The mere activation of a *goal* representation suffices to motivate people to work on the primed *goal* without conscious thought and intent (Dijksterhuis, Chartrand, and Aarts 2007, 99).

Automaticity underlies how people think and feel about their significant others and themselves, whether people expect to be accepted or rejected, how they regulate themselves as they strive to attain *goals* associated with significant others or to protect themselves and their relationships, and, finally, how they behave toward others (Chen, Fitzsimons, and Andersen 2007, 163).

This literature on goals beyond awareness is consistent with Ayman's (2002) interpretation of the LPC score at the low end, but it also provides some support for what happens at the high end as well.

CONSCIOUS PROCESSES WITHIN CONTINGENCY THEORY

In contrast to LPC the other components of contingency theory of leadership appear to be primarily conscious. Self-report measures tend to be used in these instances—in the measurement of aspects of situational control and influence, for instance. However, the possibility that unconscious processes may intrude upon the conscious on occasion should not be overlooked (see Gawronski and Bodenhausen 2007, 272). Thus with regard to the components of situational control and influence, leader-member relations is a matter of group systems (see Uhl-Bien 2003; Michael Maccoby 2004; Stewart 2006), while both task structure and position power are aspects of hierarchic systems (see Moeller, Robinson, and Zabelina 2008). Although these different organizational forms would seem to invoke similar conscious or deliberate processes, primarily because they are measured by self-reports, each tends to recruit some unconscious activity as well.

Leader Match, as a programmed learning exercise, would appear to be intended as a highly conscious management development effort, although it may well not achieve that intention. Cognitive resource theory, like contingency theory of leadership as a whole, is somewhat of a mixture, but it does contain consciously measured constructs involving self-report indexes.

STRESS AND COGNITIVE RESOURCE THEORY

Cognitive resource theory brings intelligence, stress, and experience (see Figure 13.3 on page 249 of Miner 2005) into the purview of contingency theory of leadership; it is really an addendum to the latter. Stress in particular is of interest. Fiedler has dabbled with this construct previously, but it becomes particularly manifest in the context of cognitive resource theory (Fiedler 2002). Although "we know very little about the operation and consequences of counteractive control when individuals are stressed, fatigued or emotionally aroused" (Fishbach and Trope 2008, 292), and of many other related phenomena, some things have been learned. To some extent these are indicated in Chapter 7 of this volume. The fact that unconscious activation tends to occur under stress (see DeWall and Baumeister 2007; Porcelli and Delgado 2009) is well established. Yet Fiedler utilizes a self-report index to measure stress. Nevertheless, stress does represent a major source warranting the investigation of phenomena beyond awareness. Cognitive resource theory—and contingency theory as a whole—would benefit from a more sophisticated (unconscious) approach to this area.

IS CONTINGENCY THEORY REALLY AN UNCONSCIOUS OR CONSCIOUS FORMULATION?

Let us look at the merits on this issue. Locke and Latham (2004, 395) recommend that we "study subconscious as well as conscious motivation and the relationship between them." In the latter connection Locke (2007, 869) claims, "There can be a rational use of intuition based on previously gained knowledge stored in the subconscious, but the subconscious must contain material based on reality for it to be potentially useful." This contention might be questioned. Previously stored material may have even negative relevance for current reality. Thus negative stereotypes toward the elderly held by the young may contribute to cardiovascular events much later (Levy, Zonderman, Slade, and Ferrucci 2009). Further on this matter Rudman (2004, 81) indicates, "The argument that implicit and explicit attitudes are conceptually distinct can help to explain why the two types of attitudes are often dissociated, and why response latency measures (sometimes) predict behavior better than self-reports." DeNeys (2006, 433) adds that research "provides clear evidence that all reasoners have access to both an automatic, heuristic reasoning system and an executive, analytic reasoning system." And finally, "contrary to popular belief, decisions about simple issues can be better tackled by conscious thought, whereas decisions about complex matters can be better approached with unconscious thought" (Dijksterhuis and Nordgren 2006, 95).

Fiedler's theory is without doubt a complex formulation, and accordingly I would much prefer to recommend pursuing its study on an unconscious basis. However, that is not possible given the uncertain status of the LPC score. We have nothing to clearly establish that LPC is inherently unconscious, even though explicit operations are distinctly in evidence. Consequently I am forced to consider the contingency theory of leadership an essentially balanced position; there is too much going on here to do otherwise. On the other hand, I do believe that a number of aspects of the theory, including the LPC score, warrant investigation that moves beyond awareness.

CONCLUSIONS

Contingency theory of leadership has a validity of three stars and an importance rating at the behest of organizational behavior of 4.33. Dividing as appropriate yields a ratio of 1.44, indicating that the theory is indeed overestimated as to its validity by organizational behavior scholars.

The Ayman interpretation of the LPC score presents a strong case for the score's being viewed as projective in nature, and thus for its unconscious underpinnings. However, Fiedler does not say this, and no research to *prove* this interpretation has been forthcoming. Conscious processes are to be found at many points in contingency theory, as are the prospect of unconscious processes. Stress, as envisioned by cognitive resource theory and at various points in relation to contingency theory, represents a good candidate for investigation beyond awareness. Given the potential for positing both implicit and explicit features operating within contingency theory, I am inclined to interpret the theory as being essentially balanced in terms of its implicit-explicit status.

CHAPTER 19

SUBSTITUTES FOR LEADERSHIP THEORY

Steven Kerr's substitutes for leadership theory started in the late 1970s (Kerr 1977; Kerr and Jermier 1978) and spanned some twenty years (Kerr and Slocum 1981; Howell, Dorfman, and Kerr 1986; Kerr, Hill, and Broedling 1986; Howell, Bowen, Dorfman, Kerr, and Podsakoff 1990; Frost 1997; Jermier and Kerr 1997). His work consisted entirely of journal articles (and an interview); there never has been a presentation in book form. Kerr is not saying that leadership in hierarchic organizations will be replaced completely by other factors; he merely is indicating that other factors in addition to leadership play an important role in controlling and influencing followers—and leaders, too. He wants to make the point that leadership is not the be-all and end-all of organizational functioning, that there are other sources of control within organizations. The evidence accumulated over many years points to the need for a theory of organizational control and influence processes that includes direct leader behavior as one factor among many. This is the point Kerr wishes to make. As Lord and Smith (1999) note, many of the substitutes are indirect products of managerial action, but not direct effects; an example would be an organizational control system originated by top management.

A meta-analysis conducted by Podsakoff, MacKenzie, and Bommer (1996) clearly established that there is a main effect running from substitutes to performance-related criterion variables. However, the evidence on moderator relationships is overwhelmingly negative. Furthermore there is reason to believe that in many respects substitutes for leadership theory represent merely a reincarnation of House's path-goal theory (see Chapter 20). Remember that House was Kerr's mentor at the City University of New York during the latter's doctoral studies. This position has been emphasized by Schriesheim (1997), who was at Ohio State University with Kerr in the same time period. Thus on balance the pluses and minuses for the substitutes for leadership add to a three-star validity similar to the practical usefulness of the theory, but well below the 4.46 value awarded by organizational behavior (Miner 2005, 2007). This latter value clashes severely with an up-to-date assessment by Avolio, Walumbwa, and Weber (2009).

A CONSCIOUS THEORY

The evidence favoring a conscious or rational view of substitutes for leadership theory is quite convincing.

The Links to Expectancy Theory

As noted in Chapter 1 of this volume expectancy theory is without doubt a conscious theory. Vroom never did do anything about expanding his theory beyond the rational realm; as a result this characterization as rational serves best to define the theory at present.

Building on this base, House developed his version of the theory—the path-goal theory of leadership (see Chapter 20 of this volume). Path-goal theory is in fact an expansion of expectancy theory into the leadership domain, and it retains the same rational designation. As we have seen, Kerr built his substitutes theory on that of his mentor, House, thus perpetuating the same rational focus. The lineage of substitutes for leadership theory may be traced directly back to Vroom's expectancy theory, thereby retaining the conscious cognitive emphasis of the original.

The Use of Self-report Questionnaires

The research reported in the Kerr and Jermier (1978) article at the inception of the substitutes for leadership way of thinking was of a self-report nature. There have been other questionnaires of a similar genre developed and applied, but all have been in the same vein. The measurement procedures associated with the theory have remained consistently of a conscious type, thus reinforcing the ties to expectancy theory.

ON THE USE OF UNCONSCIOUS CHARACTERIZATIONS

The fact that a theory such as that of substitutes for leadership does not employ unconscious constructs should not be construed as meaning that the unconscious will never figure in the theory's function. Thus as Bargh (2005) indicates, "A person cannot possibly think about and be consciously aware of all of the individual muscle actions in compound and sequential movements—there are too many of them and they are too fast" (45). Among tennis players it is well recognized that many shots occur well before a decision is made to undertake them. In the same vein Gawronski and Bodenhausen (2007) make the point that "whereas indirectly assessed attitudes seem to be conscious in the sense that they are introspectively accessible to self-report, they still seem to involve an unconscious component, such that they can influence other mental processes outside of conscious awareness" (272–273). Put somewhat differently, it seems "there is true unconscious behavior and there is unconscious behavior that is mediated by instances of conscious awareness" (Dijksterhuis, Chartrand, and Aarts 2007, 55).

With regard to the Implicit Association Test (IAT), Nosek, Greenwald, and Banaji (2007) make the point "that the IAT and self-report both have spheres of . . . predictive validity indicates that the IAT is not properly interpreted as a lie-detector or as revealing something more *true* or more *real* than self-report" (285). This conclusion applies to what has been said previously, that "actions of an unconscious mind precede the arrival of a conscious mind—that action precedes reflection. . . . In broad-brush terms the cognitive and social psychological evidence does support Freud as to the existence of unconscious mentation and its potential to impact judgments and behavior. . . . Freud's historic importance in championing the power of the unconscious mind is beyond any doubt" (Bargh and Morsella 2008, 73).

My point here is that a theory must actually utilize constructs of a given type to characterize the theory as being of that type; it is not sufficient that those constructs are represented somewhere within the theoretical domain of the theory. That the unconscious appears within the domain of substitutes for leadership is not relevant; what matters is that unconscious constructs actually appear within the formulation of the theory. Even where rationality dominates, there are bound to be some vestiges of unconscious material in evidence, and often a considerable amount.

THE SUBSTITUTES FOR LEADERSHIP THAT HAVE IMPLICATIONS FOR THE UNCONSCIOUS

It seems evident that ties to the unconscious are most likely to be found in various substitutes for leadership, including aspects of the leadership phenomena itself. To identify these features I used the data provided in Table 16.2 on pages 305–306 of Miner (2005); this table is titled "Effects of Various Organizational Characteristics on Members' Task-relevant Information and Motivation in Mechanistic and Organic Organizations." Six such effects stand out as being particularly vulnerable to incorporating aspects of the unconscious and thus moving beyond the rational, conscious orientation of substitutes for leadership theory.

Goal Setting

Chapter 2 of this volume contains an extensive examination of the implications for identifying features extending beyond awareness associated with goal setting. Glaser and Kihlstrom (2005) indicate that "goals and behaviors can also be activated automatically and will be pursued nonconsciously" (173). Dijksterhuis, Chartrand, and Aarts (2007) state, "Priming or the mere perception of goal-related stimuli can influence explicit goal-setting in several ways. . . . A goal that is primed in the course of perceiving goal-relevant stimuli should automatically direct as well as energize activity that is instrumental in attaining the goal" (98–99). And again, "Nonconsciously triggered goals remain accessible and responsible for goal-directed action until the goal loses its incentive value" (109).

Charismatic Leadership

A second effect that warrants attention is charismatic leadership, as treated at length in Chapter 17 of this volume. Numerous instances where unconscious processes might be invoked are described. As Kark and Van Dijk (2007) note, "Leaders' ability to prime their followers' promotion focus helps us understand why transformational and charismatic leadership has been found, in prior works, to be positively related to followers' affective commitment and to organizational innovation. . . . Moreover, leaders' abilities to prime both prevention and promotion foci among their followers at different points in time, or among different subgroups of followers, are likely to explain the array of different outcomes that leaders can promote" (521, 522). See also Kearney and Gebert (2009).

Tasks

This and the following effects are approached most completely in Chapter 16 of this volume, and to a degree in an earlier work by Miner (2008). Entrepreneurship is a function of the demands that the task presents. These demands and how entrepreneurs handle them are given special attention in Chapter 16. Included are the various ways in which the unconscious factors into what happens.

Professional Orientation

This, too, is a means by which substitutes may use unconscious processes to promote organizational effectiveness; it is in fact the fourth effect by which the listing in Table 16.2 may best achieve results. Professional norms may well come to govern behavior, and they can easily control the behavior of professionals even when they are not supposed to do so, or when these professionals are not aware that this is happening.

Work Group

The fifth effect in Table 16.2 consists of peer group social influences and the operation of teams, especially other team members. At the unconscious level, significant other, and generalizations from them, as well as transference, play an important role, as does the concept of affiliation motivation. Chapter 5 in this volume on job characteristics theory represents a primary source, as do several other chapters that focus on affiliation or social needs. "Research shows that social stimuli can automatically access this brain system [a neural system centered on the amygdala], even in the absence of the perceiving individual's conscious awareness of their presence" (Olsson and Phelps 2007, 162). And again, "Research suggests the adaptive benefit of being able to negotiate the social environment according to important objectives in a relatively automatic fashion, without the necessity of conscious deliberation at every turn" (Ferguson, Hassin, and Bargh 2008, 153). "Most significant-other relationships are probably neither entirely negative nor entirely positive, and we suspect most, if not all, significant-other relationships begin positively and may become negative or most likely ambivalent while emotional relevance remains high" (Andersen, Reznik, and Glassman 2005, 457). Den Hartog, DeHoogh, and Keegan (2007) note, "The literature on substitutes for leadership suggests that leader charisma and belongingness may have an interactive effect on helping and compliance" (1133). In the same vein see Keller (2006) and Wilkowski, Robinson, and Friesen (2009).

Organizational Development and Training

This final effect appears to be parceled out among the other organizational forms. It tends to rely the most on work group systems, and thus the unconscious processes indicated there would seem most likely to bear fruit, although task and professional considerations are relevant as well.

CONCLUSIONS

As noted previously substitutes for leadership theory has a validity rated at three stars and an importance rating from organizational behavior of 4.46. The disparity here is considerable; when the latter figure is divided by the former, a value of 1.49 results, indicating a substantial over-evaluation on behalf of people from organizational behavior relative to my assessment.

Because of its clear links to expectancy theory and its extensive use of self-report measurement procedures, substitute for leadership theory emerges as a predominantly conscious formulation. Unconscious processes inevitably appear within the domain of the theory, but they are not to be found within the construct structure that the authors offer; thus this is a theory that as written is devoid of mention of processes that go beyond human awareness. There are, however, points among the substitutes that offer some prospect of revealing unconscious phenomena. Among these are goal setting, the effects of charismatic leadership, and the various organizational forms—task, professional, and work group—that extend beyond the managerial systems of hierarchies.

CHAPTER 20

PATH-GOAL THEORY

This is another instance among the various theories of a path-goal nature where alternative views are in evidence. The version proposed by Martin Evans, a product of his dissertation at Yale, was the first to emerge, and shortly thereafter came a second version from Robert House.

Evans set forth his ideas in two articles (Evans 1970a, 1970b), and he has written (but sparingly) on the subject since; his most comprehensive and recent coverage is in a book chapter (Evans 2002). Much of his writing in recent years has involved the belief that path-goal theory has neither been adequately measured by its constructs nor adequately tested.

House has written equally sporadically on the subject, but his major article on path-goal theory was "A Path-Goal Theory of Leader Effectiveness" (1971); this was followed shortly by a later report (House and Mitchell 1974), which offered considerable promise. However, House has more recently concerned himself with charismatic leadership and then with the GLOBE research (see Chapter 17). His efforts regarding path-goal theory have been limited to "Path-Goal Theory of Leadership: Lessons, Legacy, and a Reformulated Theory" (House 1996), and appear at present to have come to an end.

These two versions—one by Evans and the other by House—are very similar. There is little to distinguish between them, and neither one has initiated a long-term research commitment. Perhaps because its author has become better known, the House version is generally considered the more important; clearly his influence on substitutes for leadership theory has been the more pronounced (see Chapter 19). Both versions are rated at three stars in terms of validity, and the importance rating from organizational behavior for the House theory is 4.58, with the Evans theory rated somewhat lower (see Miner 2006b).

FURTHER TO THE EVANS AND HOUSE CONTRIBUTIONS

Sources for this review of path-goal theory are Miner (2002) and Evans (2002), plus various articles published since.

Meta-analytic and Other Reviews

The first meta-analysis (Indvik 1986) was plagued by a small number of cases, in part because of the sparsity of the research at that time but also because the large number of propositions involved in the theory tends to spread studies out, making it difficult to accumulate many instances on any one proposition. The conclusion at that point was that continued testing of the theory was warranted but that the moderator analyses provided grounds for caution. Subsequent meta-analyses with larger numbers of studies (Wofford and Liska 1993) continued to raise questions regarding the moderators; this concern has also been expressed by others (Podsakoff, Todor, Grover, and Huber 1984) and is consistent with what was found regarding the related spin-off dealing with substitutes for leadership (see Chapter 19 of this volume).

Summarizing these data Evans (2002, 132) says, "These results are disappointing for proponents of the theory because past research has merely scratched the surface of the theory." He also indicates that the leader needs to be a diagnostician to use the theory effectively, a conclusion on which I wholeheartedly agree. Nevertheless the theory's authors have not done the needed research themselves to make up for the "shortcomings" of others; thus my three-star rating of path-goal theory.

The Theory as a Conscious Phenomenon

Path-goal theory is variously described as having a "rationality bias," or "concerned with a rational, conscious model of human behavior," and the like. It derives from expectancy theory (see Chapter 1 in this volume) and is intended to apply that theory to the leadership domain. Measurement, to the extent the theory is operationalized, tends to be largely of a self-report nature. Measures are consistently referred to as "questionnaires" or "scales." Evans (2002) frequently notes the need for new measures, but these, too, are described as scales.

The Extent to Which Unconscious Processes Are Activated

Both Evans and, in particular, House make reference to various needs and to charisma in their theoretical formulations; one would think that these references might elicit some consideration of unconscious process. Unfortunately, however, such references are few. Evans (2002, 134), for instance, in his most recent summary on the theory limits himself to the following: "There are unconscious motives," and then he moves on to other matters. The problem is that tests of the theory either have not been carried out with regard to the various needs specified or their implications for the unconscious have been ignored; this has been particularly true of House's (1996) reformulated propositions, which seemed to offer great hope for a revival of path-goal theory (Hunt 1996).

The Fate of Unconscious Processes

One of the few tests of a need-based hypothesis from path-goal theory is a study by Fulk and Wendler (1982) that looked into achievement-oriented leadership. This research, although generally supportive of theory, used a scale previously developed by House that is of a self-report nature; thus there is no contribution to an understanding of how motives that extend beyond awareness might fit into path-goal theory. Furthermore, no mention at all is made to McClelland and his work on achievement motivation.

A second relevant study is that of Schriesheim, Castro, Zhou, and DeChurch (2006) on transformational leadership. This study, too, used measures of a self-report nature and thus is unable to contribute to an understanding regarding the role that unconscious considerations may play. The research attempted to test House's reformulated proposition regarding charismatic leadership. Support for this hypothesis was not obtained.

Not only did the research carried out by Evans and House fail to address the constructs of an unconscious type that the theory's authors on occasion introduced, but those who followed have fallen into the same trap. This represents a characteristic problem for organizational behavior; once an approach to operationalization and measurement is introduced, usually by a theory's author, it tends to become perpetualized from then on in the subsequent research.

A WAY INTO THE UNCONSCIOUS: VALENCE RESEARCH

Previously in connection with expectancy theory I proposed that one aspect of the theory that was vulnerable to unconscious intrusions was the valence construct. The same would appear to be true of path-goal theory. Both Evans and House incorporated valence into their versions of the theory.

Some Previous Statements Extrapolated

A treatment previously (in Chapter 1) noted the work of Barrett, Ochsner, and Gross (2007). It is relevant to elaborate here on this contribution:

> Three kinds of behavioral evidence support the idea that people can automatically evaluate stimuli or events for affective value or valence.
>
> 1. Many behavioral studies have found that the subliminal or nonconscious presentation of a valenced stimulus can generate autonomic responses . . . , changes in the activity of facial musculature . . . and behavior . . . , can bias perception of subsequently presented stimuli in a valence-congruent fashion . . . , and can generate "mystery moods" that are misattributed to other causes. . . .
> 2. Brief supraliminal presentations of a valence stimulus facilitates access to valence congruent behavioral responses that seem affective in nature. . . .
> 3. Behavioral and autonomic indices of affective response may implicitly reveal changes in the evaluation of the stimulus not reflected explicitly in conscious experience. . . .
>
> Taken together . . . these findings indicate that stimulus valence may be computed rapidly, and can influence subsequent behavior and experience (191).

Thus valence responses can be identified through procedures that bring them to the surface, where otherwise they would not be consciously in evidence. Path-goal theory has previously lacked evidence that these valence responses exist, and accordingly has been devoid with regard to one of its major constructs.

Furthermore, Peters, Hess, Västfjäll, and Auman (2007, 5) indicate that "automatic information-processing abilities such as implicit memory and learning appear to be largely spared by age. . . . In general older adults appear to perform less well than do younger adults on tasks demanding greater deliberation (explicit tasks), but there appear to be few, if any, age differences in tasks thought to tap into more implicit processes." One is forced to wonder how often science has been led astray by the characteristic process of basing research on samples drawn from student populations.

Finally previous research findings by Ruys and Stapel (2008) should be expanded as follows:

> When exposure to the priming stimuli was super-quick, global mood, rather than a specific emotion, was evoked. These findings are the first to empirically demonstrate
>
> 1. that specific emotions can be evoked without conscious awareness of their cause,
> 2. that unconscious exposure to emotion-eliciting pictures can evoke the specific corresponding emotion and does not evoke other emotions of similar valence, and
> 3. that unconscious emotion induction develops from global affect to elicitation of specific emotions (390).

Thus prior conclusions that unconscious emotion is limited to global affect, and does not reflect specific emotions, are seen to be incorrect.

New Contributions

Prior treatments emphasized the role of face processing in unconscious emotion recognition. Pascalis and Kelly (2009) conclude as follows in this regard:

> There has been much debate regarding the "special" nature of face processing. Researchers have put forth numerous developmental models that attempt to account for this early preference. . . . We review these models and their supporting evidence drawing on literature from developmental, evolutionary, and comparative psychology. We conclude that converging data from these fields strongly suggests that face processing is conducted by a dedicated and complex neural system, is not human specific, and is unlikely to have emerged recently in evolutionary history (200).

Three areas within the cortex become more activated in humans when viewing human faces using fMRI studies. In this way unconscious emotions can be identified, or at least their identification can be aided.

In contradistinction to the preceding discussion of unconscious emotions and valences, I want to call attention to a meta-analysis of emotional reactions drawn from normal industrial/ organizational psychology (see Kaplan, Bradley, Luchman, and Haynes 2009). This analysis dealt only with conscious dispositional affect; the authors recommend looking further into more ephemeral affective states. "People who tend to experience positive emotional states perform better at work, whereas those who experience a preponderance of negative states tend not to perform as well" (171). But what would be the effects of incorporating unconscious affectivity within this conclusion?

CONCLUSIONS

Consistent with previous indications House's version of path-goal theory carries a three-star estimated validity and an importance evaluation from organizational behavior of 4.58. Dividing the importance rating by three yields a value of 1.53, indicating that the field in general tends to overestimate the House theory's validity. This is also true of the Evans version, but to a lesser extent, with a ratio of 1.37. Neither theory has a high rating on practical usefulness.

Meta-analyses and other reviews do not give a particularly strong endorsement to path-goal theory in any form; the theory appears to be especially deficient in its handling of moderator relationships. As a derivative of expectancy theory, path-goal theory presents a rational, conscious formulation; it has been tested only using self-report measures, although the theorists make reference to needs and to charisma, which would appear to implicate motivational states that extend beyond awareness. At such points the theory is clearly vulnerable to the intrusion of unconscious factors into its essentially conscious domain. Furthermore, as a derivative from expectancy theory, path-goal theory has the potential to activate unconscious processes in its pursuit of valence-related constructs. Methods of identifying emotional phenomena that thus may be unearthed are given consideration and discussed in some detail.

CHAPTER 21

THE ROMANCE OF LEADERSHIP

The romance of leadership is a theory, largely concerned with charismatic considerations, that focuses on followers. Its primary sponsor has been James Meindl, often writing with various graduate students or former graduate students. The estimated validity for the theory is at three stars; applications have not been developed. Importance ratings by organizational behavior scholars average 3.46 (see Miner 2006b).

I am aware of the existence of only one meta-analysis dealing with the romance of leadership, although as noted in Chapter 17 of this volume meta-analyses focused on charismatic leadership theory do exist as well. This one (dealing with the romance) is the product of Schyns, Felfe, and Blank (2007). Initial findings indicated that the results were mixed. As a consequence of the addition of new studies it was possible to calculate the effects of a number of moderators. The authors conclude, based on the use of this expanded sample of studies, that "the results indicate a positive relationship between Romance of Leadership and the perception of transformational leadership. Only the moderating effect of region of origin was significant. In line with social constructivism and information processing approaches of leadership, our results indicate that the perception of leadership comprises more than merely the actual behavior the leader exhibits" (505).

However, in discussing these results, Avolio, Walumbwa, and Weber (2009, 435) say "Schyns et al. (2007) conducted a meta-analysis to determine whether they could tease out the effects controlling for such things as measurement error and sampling bias while focusing on whether followers had a tendency to romanticize their perceptions of transformational/charismatic leadership. Their results revealed a modest relationship between the romance of leadership and perceptions of transformational/charismatic leadership, accounting for approximately 5% of the variance in leadership ratings."

To this evaluation should be added the conclusion reached by Waldman, Javidan, and Varella (2004, 374): "Despite the claims of Meindl and Ehrlich (1987), the present findings point toward actual effects associated with charisma, as opposed to attributional or illusory phenomena." Yet at the same time Meindl's own research gives reason to believe that there is considerable validity to the romance of leadership position. In this regard, I have previously noted that the Meindl findings are clearly antithetical to Bass's theory, and House's too (Miner 2005, 378):

> If charismatic leadership is a mirage, it needs to be studied at the level of follower perceptions; much of the current theory and research would seem to miss the point. From the evidence the romance of leadership is a real enough phenomenon on occasion. However, we do not know how often it occurs, and when it does, how much variance it accounts for. There is good evidence that leadership effects do occur . . . and that the romance of leadership may not always operate. . . . Probably certain followers in certain states are more susceptible to romance of leadership effects.

THE ROMANCE AS OF THE MID-1980S

To give an idea of what the romance of leadership involved close to the time of its inception, I draw upon Meindl, Ehrlich, and Dukerich (1985). Here are some quotes from these authors.

> It appears that the concept of leadership is a permanently entrenched part of the socially constructed reality that we bring to bear on our analysis of organizations. . . . The concept has thereby gained a brilliance that exceeds the limits of normal scientific inquiry. The imagery and mythology typically associated with the concept is evidence of the mystery and near mysticism with which it has been imbued (78).

> A bias in the interpretation and explanation of events is a subjective tendency to prefer one interpretation over another; such an interpretation may or may not be an error according to some objective criterion for assessing the event. . . . (80).

> A bias toward leadership could be systematically related to performance levels in a positive or negative way. These ideas were tested (81).

> The tendency to ascribe high levels of control and influence to leaders arises from private needs to find causes among human actors. Accordingly, the exacerbation of those needs would tend to foster the development of a romantic conception. . . . (97).

> To the extent that observers are psychologically invested in a romanticized view . . . we might expect selective perception, confirmatory biases, and other processes to be present. . . . (99).

Based on these expressions, I submit that romanticization extends beyond rationality, and in fact engages the unconscious. I should also note that I joined Jim Meindl on the business school faculty at SUNY/Buffalo shortly after this article was written.

THE ROMANCE AS OF THE EARLY 1990S

For a view of the romance from the early 1990s, I quote from Meindl (1990):

> The significance of implicit theories of leadership has been defined in terms of their implications for systematically biasing indices of leader behavior. . . . (162–163).

> The development of what we label the romance of leadership scale or RLS . . . was not intended to tap romanticizing directly, but focused instead on the extent to which leadership is likely to be prominent in actors' implicit theories of organizations (168).

> Transformational leadership, with its emphasis on charisma and vision, is in part a matter of perception and attribution, myth and symbol, that is likely to have a romanticized component to it (182).

> A bias toward the leader as a prominent force in the development of leader relationships is predictably strongest in areas when the romanticization is heaviest . . . (186).

> Behavioral contagion is signaled when observers possess some latent motivation to act in a certain way . . .

> Hysterical contagion is focused on the spreading of affective and cognitive experiences and their manifestation in a set of symptoms that are typically psychosomatic in nature. . . . The pervasive spread of charismatic experiences is likely to involve elements of both behavioral and hysterical contagion (190–191).

> The contagion of charisma may have a hysterical component to it. . . . The syndrome becomes a symptomatic expression (192).

These quotes mobilize a number of considerations that require comment.

On the Term "Implicit"

Meindl (1990) uses the term "implicit" repeatedly in referring to the romance of leadership. It is not always apparent what sense (conscious or unconscious) he has in mind, but on the evidence it appears that he tends to follow the Lord interpretation. In Chapter 15 (on information processing theory) of this volume, the ins and outs of implicit usage are presented; it appears that Lord first used "implicit" to mean "unconscious" in the preface of Schyns and Meindl (2005a). However, Jim Meindl died in 2004, and his book with Schyns clearly had implicit featured in its title. One assumes that he died aware that Lord was now using the term to mean "unconscious"; probably he was alert to this meaning long before. In any event as of the year 2005 the unconscious interpretation became manifest, and, as I have indicated in Chapter 15, this view became increasingly manifest thereafter. My guess is that Meindl's use of "implicit" in 1990 had that same intent. However, I left SUNY/Buffalo in 1994, and I was never able to verify his interpretation of "implicit" directly.

On the Nature of the Romance of Leadership Scale

A copy of the romance of leadership scale is contained in Meindl (1990) on page 169; it clearly is a self-report measure. This raises some question regarding the unconscious intent of the exposition there, although as we have seen using conscious measures where unconscious applications would have been more appropriate has been rather common in organizational behavior. In any event, Meindl does present a conscious measure, and he does not present any unconscious measure (such as one involving priming or some projective technique). I would encourage the use of the latter by future investigators.

On Attribution Error

Meindl (1990) makes frequent mention of biases and errors associated with the process of attributions to leadership. I have treated this issue previously in connection with my discussion of attribution theory applied to managerial perceptions (see Chapter 8 in this volume). He refers in this regard to the use of heuristics, which by their nature involve an unconscious element. Meindl's treatment of attributions and their operation appear to be entirely consistent with past practice in this area.

On Charisma

Chapter 17 in this volume makes it clear that charisma, when present, acts to invoke unconscious processes. Thus again the romance of leadership concept is shown to involve processes that extend beyond awareness. This is evident from the mortality salience literature, from studies on a promotion and prevention focus, and from other evidence. Meindl appears to be correct in positing that charisma serves to invoke unconscious processes and otherwise has the potential to act in accord with his theory. Chapter 17 presents a view that charismatic leadership has positive effects, but still leaves room for processes beyond awareness.

On Mimicry

Meindl (1990) describes a mimicry process that serves to support the behavioral contagion involved when charisma is activated. This mimicry is described in Chapter 5 of this volume, and is shown there often to be unconscious in nature. There is more on this subject in Chapter 14 of this volume, again with the clear indication that mimicry can well occur automatically. A particularly lucid portrayal of the mimicry phenomenon is provided by Iacoboni (2009), who notes, "Social psychological studies have demonstrated that imitation and mimicry are pervasive, automatic, and facilitate empathy. Neuroscience investigations have demonstrated physiological mechanisms of mirroring at single-cell and neural-system levels that support the cognitive and social psychology constructs" (653). Further, "Mirror neurons . . . provide a prereflective, automatic mechanism of mirroring what is going on in the brain of other people that seems more compatible with our ability to understand others effortlessly and with our tendency to imitate others automatically" (666).

On Psychopathology

Finally Meindl (1990) invokes various emotional pathological conditions—including psychosomatic symptoms and hysteria—to characterize his concept of charisma. Hysteria, in particular, is activated when contagion is involved. This tendency to refer to psychopathological conditions and states carries with it the implication that unconscious factors are involved. (See Volume 1 of Sigmund Freud's *Collected Papers* (1950), specifically Paper II, "On the Psychical Mechanisms of Hysterical Phenomena," and Paper X, "The Ætiology of Hysteria," both in Volume I). Thus Meindl continues to bring unconscious phenomena to bear.

THE ROMANCE AS OF THE MID-1990S

For a view of the romance of leadership from the mid-1990s, I refer to Meindl (1995):

> Followers react to, and are more influenced by, their construction of the leader's personality than they are by the true personality of the leader. It is the personalities of leaders as imagined or constructed by followers that become the object of study, not the actual or clinical personalities per se (330–331).

> Affect intensity—This is an individual difference variable that refers to the tendency of some people to generally over- or underreact, affectively or emotionally, to potentially arousing events in their environment. These group-level processes function to cause the constructions of individual members to become a collaborative, negotiated, intersubjectively shared system of leadership concepts that link and unify followers within the group (336).

> Those who have aspirations for an objective theory of leadership will find great difficulty with the inherently subjectivistic, social constructionist view being advanced here (339).

This is the construction of leadership that Meindl put forward as of the mid-1990s. He continued to advocate much the same position until his death in 2004 (see Bligh, Kohles, and Meindl 2004; Meindl 2004).

IMPLICIT LEADERSHIP THEORIES
(SCHYNS AND MEINDL 2005A, 2005B)

Schyns and Meindl collaborated on the introduction to their 2005a anthology *Implicit Leadership Theories: Essays and Explorations,* which was published shortly after Meindl's death, was planned by the two authors, and both authors collaborated on the introduction (see Schyns and Meindl 2005b). However, the work of managing and editing the volume fell to Schyns. Thus the final product was influenced only to a degree by Meindl. I will selectively quote from particular authors to convey their perceptions of Meindl's ideas.

> Individuals characterize a leader similar to self as ideal. . . . [They] may view themselves as potential leaders and thus project their own traits into idealized images. . . . Idealized images mirror descriptions of parental traits (Hansbrough 2005, 64). *Thus a degree of unconscious transference seems to be involved.*

> Person-based, as well as inferential-based, modes are carried out by means of automatic or controlled processes. . . . Automatic processes. These processes only require a minimum amount of cognitive resources. . . . Controlled processes. . . . The occurrence of automatic processes is more likely in situations in which insufficient information is available (Müller

and Schyns 2005, 85–86). *Following Lord and Maher (1991), implicit leadership theories were accordingly operationalized as* "person-based automatic processes which have been aggregated on a group-level" (89).

People tend to overestimate leaders' responsibilities and neglect external circumstances. . . . Little is known as to how far followers' personality influences the tendency to develop a romantic view of leaders. . . . In this study the influence of followers' personal characteristics on the tendency to overestimate leaders is examined (Felfe 2005, 199, 203).

"People who rated themselves as more dominant and achievement oriented were found to show more romance of leadership" (217), *but this study used a self-report measure.*

Recognition-based processes are grounded in automatic categorization processes, while in-ferential processes are grounded in controlled attribution processes. . . . Need for leadership is the extent to which an employee wishes the leader to facilitate the paths toward individual, group, or organizational goals. . . . The relation between leadership and need for leadership is strong, with observers inferring high need for leadership and high leader dependency whenever a charismatic leader is around. . . . Social modeling . . . of the followers thus plays an important part in the spread of the charismatic affect (deVries and vanGelder 2005, 279, 281, 296, 299). *Thus the research supports both the role of needs and the role of mimicry.*

An implicit theory is a cognitive schema: an organized configuration of knowledge, derived from past experience, which is used to interpret experiences. . . . These individual schemas are unconscious memory processing structures, applied to encode and retrieve information. . . . Our minds make up for the missing information. . . . When an event has a high degree of familiarity, almost automatically the prototypical schema is activated (Kroon 2005, 336). *The author here applies these ideas to the start-up phase of new entrepreneurial firms; he goes on to say that* "in more atypical situations, the cognitive structure of information becomes more conscious" (338).

FOLLOWER-CENTERED PERSPECTIVES ON LEADERSHIP (SHAMIR, PILLAI, BLIGH, AND UHL-BIEN 2007)

This book, subtitled *A Tribute to the Memory of James R. Meindl,* does not present anything written by Meindl himself. However, it does contain numerous treatments by his students. The book begins with a chapter from Shamir (2007), which largely encapsulates Meindl's contri-butions as noted previously. Subsequently a chapter by Lipman-Blumen (2007, 10) notes:

Driven by existential anxiety, we find leaders garbed as omnipotent saviors quite irresistible. When such leaders temporarily fulfill our needs, we easily succumb, as Meindl (1995) noted, to the romance of leadership. This writer, too, invokes unconscious considerations.

Others do, as well:

Categorization and characterization were relatively automatic processes. . . . Such reasoning is very consistent with Meindl's (1990) argument that perceivers have romanticized views of leadership (Medvedeff and Lord 2007, 23).

Even subliminal affective stimuli presented for very brief periods (30 ms) can influence affect and associated ratings of charismatic leadership (30).

There is also evidence related to heroism:

One of Jim Meindl's major contributions to the field of leadership has been his assertion that many people view leaders as heroic figures and overattribute desirable performance effects to them (Offerman and Scuderi 2007, 72). There is indeed evidence consistent with this view (Wansink, Payne, and van Ittersum 2008).

In Memory of Jim Meindl (as Leader) from His Students (as Followers)

One of the chapters dedicated to Meindl from his students was written by Mayo and Pastor (2007). In it, they focus on charismatic leadership, building on social contagion theory to provide a network-based model (110). A second such chapter spearheaded by Chao C. Chen proposed the impact of "change strategy on charisma attributions is mainly due to different emotions aroused" (Chen, Belkin, and Kurtzberg 2007, 129).

Another chapter was written by three former students of Meindl at various points in time, with a combined experience in this capacity of over fifteen years. They conclude:

Ironically this tribute volume to Meindl is in some ways a social construction of *his leadership*, his lasting impact on us (his followers), and his overall influence on the field. We think he would have appreciated this irony, as well as our humble attempts to ultimately romanticize him and his leadership (Pillai, Kohles, and Bligh 2007, 161). No doubt this romanticization was indeed fostered by Jim's death at a relatively young age (see Allison, Eylon, Beggan, and Bachelder 2009), but on the other hand who knows what status he might have achieved had he been allowed to complete the development of his theory.

Two additional chapters involving Meindl's students tend to emphasize and extend his views on followership (Carsten and Bligh 2007; Uhl-Bien and Pillai 2007).

Karl Weick's (2007) Concluding Chapter

The concluding chapter in the follower-centered perspectives book was written by Karl Weick, who as editor of the *Administrative Science Quarterly* accepted and published Meindl's article on the romance of leadership (see Meindl, Ehrlich, and Dukerich 1985). Weick is an extremely propitious choice for this role, in that he championed constructs very similar to those put forth by Meindl. I have described Weick's theorizing in a prior book (Miner 2006a, 90–108); thus the reader may get a sense of the similarities here. Elsewhere Weick gives more attention to intuition and meditation, as well as to the unconscious processes with which Meindl dealt (see Weick and Putnam 2006).

MORE FROM MEINDL'S STUDENTS

Since the book on follower-centered perspectives, Meindl's students have continued to perpetuate his views, and in some cases to extend them. Thus Pastor, Mayo, and Shamir (2007) present research that states:

Our findings contribute to the refinement of Meindl's . . . social contagion model of charismatic leadership. Meindl explicitly posited arousal as an antecedent of charisma and asserted that a shared sense of arousal provides the necessary basis for the beginning of the spread of charisma effects among followers. . . . The results of the present studies indicate that, indeed, high levels of arousal can increase ratings of charisma, but only for leaders with some charismatic appeal. . . . a refinement of Meindl's theory (1593).

A study on presidential rhetoric by Seyranian and Bligh (2008) indicates that:

Our results collaborate the theory that charismatic leaders use specific rhetorical devices (negation, inclusion, stressing similarity to followers, imagery, using less inspiration, and conceptual language) . . . to achieve their ends. . . . The current research and our proposition concerning social identity framing contribute to the sparse literature on how charismatic leaders affect social change (71).

Williams, Pillai, Lowe, Jung, and Herst (2009) report:

Overall, our findings suggest that situational and contextual elements play an important role in follower perceptions of charismatic leadership and effectiveness. . . . The findings show that both leadership ratings and party identification are related to voting preference and choice, and that, in combination, these variables can predict the vote for a particular candidate (80).

These quotes would seem to indicate that Meindl's views are being perpetuated; furthermore they give an indication of the direction they are likely to take. A case in point is the Bligh and Kohles (2009) analysis of Barack Obama's recent presidential victory and his prospects for future success.

CONCLUSIONS

I noted when this chapter began that the romance of leadership carried an estimated validity of three stars and an importance rating of 3.46. Dividing this importance rating from organizational behavior by three yields a value of 1.15; thus the judges have overestimated the validity, but not by a large amount.

The romance of leadership would appear to be a predominantly unconscious theory. Evidence to this effect is derived from Meindl's writings in 1985, 1990, and in 1995, supplemented by data from two edited books published subsequently dealing with the romance of leadership. Special attention is given to the unconscious implications of the term "implicit," the nature of measurement processes, attribution errors, charisma, mimicry, and the mobilization of psychopathology. The book, presented as a tribute to Jim Meindl, is particularly important because in a sense it represents the romancing of Meindl as a leader by his followers; this feature is in fact noted by several of his students. The last chapter of this book by Karl Weick is shown to be especially appropriate. Finally several quotes from research articles written by Meindl's students in the period 2007–2009 are presented to provide an idea of the direction in which the romance of leadership may now be headed subsequent to Meindl's death.

PART III

ORGANIZATIONAL DECISION MAKING

ADMINISTRATIVE BEHAVIOR AND ORGANIZATIONS

With this chapter I start over, emphasizing now the macro aspects of organizational behavior, rather than the micro concerns of motivation and leadership. This first such chapter is devoted appropriately to two books and the issues they tackle—*Administrative Behavior: A Study of Decision-Making Processes in Administrative Organizations* (Simon 1947, 1957, 1976, 1997), which was issued in four editions, although I will focus primarily on the first and fourth versions, and *Organizations* (March and Simon 1958).

This so-called Carnegie School of thought on decision making receives a rating on estimated validity of five stars and an equally high importance rating from organizational behavior scholars; it has been institutionalized (see Miner 2006a, Chapter 3). However, its estimated usefulness is rather low, and it has not proved capable of generating meta-analyses to support its high validity.

ESTABLISHING THE CONDITIONS FOR UNCONSCIOUS ACTIVATION

The concepts of bounded rationality and satisficing are predicated on some type of overloading of the conscious system such that decision making is forced into unconscious processing. Simon (1997) believes that these concepts have been proven correct, and he has much to say on the various consequences that may result.

Simon's Views on the Prerequisites for Unconscious Processing

Various views on constraints operating to restrict the use of conscious processing, and what may be done to deal with them, are expressed in March and Simon (1958) and in a number of articles written by Simon (1955, 1962, 1967, 1978, 1987, 1991). These constraints are variously expressed as limits on attention, limits on information and its storage, and as restrictions imposed by the emotions aroused in the process of decision making.

The Views of Others on Bounded Rationality and Satisficing

Others have confirmed this proclivity associated with bounded rationality to set up the later activation of unconscious processes. Thus Weber and Johnson (2009) note that conscious attention is a scarce resource for decision makers and may elicit automatic processes. Carver and Scheier (2008) indicate that strong emotions can rearrange goal priorities among processes beyond awareness and even extend to making certain goals conscious that were not previously. Nickerson and Zenger (2004, 621) say that as Simon specified "human minds are limited in the rate at which knowledge can be assimilated, accumulated, and applied." Schwab and Miner (2008, 1122) note that "individual outcome-based learning has . . . received substantial empirical support in studies that have also shown how the limits of human rationality constrain it." McMullen, Shepherd, and Patzelt (2009) point to the fact that top managers have limited attention and that there are numerous calls on their attention; attention is therefore a limited resource. Delmar and Shane (2004, 386) show that "firm founders lack the cognitive capacity to undertake all firm organizing actions simultaneously." Michel (2007) contrasts two banks in the ways in which they managed cognitive uncertainty and the overload associated with bounded rationality.

Miller (2008), in discussing Simon's views, explains: "Simon retained the notion of rationality as maximizing as a benchmark for developing a contrasting empirically based characterization of bounded rationality. Simon assumed that decision makers would exhibit generalizable decision patterns despite their deviation from normative rationality; yet Simon recognized that conscious attention was scarce" (936, 942). Thus Simon retains some commitment to rationality in spite of his evident attacks on it. Medvedeff and Lord (2007) note "that emotions may alter the dynamics underlying leadership perceptions. The idea that emotions can serve as a reorienting mechanism has been recognized for many years (Simon 1967). . . . Positive affect induces a reliance more on heuristics and preexisting scripts and schemas" (42, 44).

CHESTER BARNARD'S INFLUENCE AND THE CONCEPT OF INTUITION

In Chapter 7 of Miner (2006b) I note that Barnard had a strong influence on Simon and his thinking (see Simon 1947). In particular Barnard's concept of intuition was significant, which brings us from the prerequisites of unconscious processing to the actual activation of unconscious factors in Simon's theoretical thought (and March's, as well).

Simon on Intuition

There can be no doubt that Simon (1987) ultimately came to endorse intuition and the unconscious processes involved. He states:

> The intuition of the emotion-driven manager is very different from the intuition of the expert. . . . The latter's behavior is the product of learning and experience, and is largely adaptive; the former's behavior is a response to more primitive urges, and is more often than not inappropriate. We must not confuse the "nonrational" decisions of the experts—the decisions that derive from expert intuition and judgment—with the irrational decisions that stressful emotions may produce (Simon 1987, 62).

Simon thus indicates that logical processes equal conscious thinking expressed in words or by other symbols—that is, by reasoning—while nonlogical processes equal those not capable of being expressed in words or as reasoning, which are manifest in judgment, decision, or action; he draws heavily on Barnard.

Yet it is worthwhile to look at how Simon's views evolved in this regard. In his small book, *The Shape of Automation for Men and Management,* he reports initially:

> In the psychological laboratory we give a subject a problem . . . and ask him to think aloud while he solves it. We have no illusion that all his thought processes will rise to the level of consciousness or be verbalized, but we hope to get some clues about the course his thoughts take. . . . We are seeing only the superficial parts of the process. . . . There is a vast iceberg underneath, concealed from view and from the consciousness of the subject. . . . Perhaps the subconscious parts of the process are no different in kind from the parts we observe. . . . We can explain these human processes *without* postulating mechanisms at subconscious levels that are different from those that are partly conscious and partly verbalized. . . . Much of the iceberg is, indeed, below the surface, but its concealed bulk is made of the same kind of ice as the part we can see. . . . The secret of problem solving is that there is no secret (Simon 1965, 78–79, 82).

This initial report was later replaced by a view more consistent with what we now know. Thus the following statement appears in the commentaries to the fourth edition of *Administrative Behavior* (Simon 1997):

> Wholly persuaded . . . that a theory of decision-making had to give an account of both conscious and subconscious processes, I finessed the issue by assuming that both these processes were essentially the same. . . . Many . . . have concluded that the theory . . . applies to "logical" decision-making and not to decisions that involve intuition and judgment. That was certainly not my intent. . . . We have acquired a solid understanding of what the judgmental and intuitive processes are. . . . Rational and intuitive processes are so different that they are carried out in distinctive parts of the brain. . . . Some people, when confronted with a particular problem, make major use of intuitive processes in solving it, while other people make relatively more use of analytical processes (Simon 1997, 131–132).

Comments on the Carnegie School Views

At this point it may be helpful to note certain conclusions from Miner (2006a).

> A central thesis in Simon's thinking was that rational decision making is limited or bounded by (1) a person's skills, habits and reflexes; (2) the values and concepts of purpose that influence the decision; and (3) the person's knowledge, particularly of the consequences of alternatives (43).

> While economic man maximizes—selects the best alternative from among all those available to him, his cousin, whom we shall call administrative man—satisfices—looks for a course of action that is satisfactory or "good enough" (44).

The book *Organizations* (March and Simon 1958) has much in common with Thompson's *Organizations in Action* (1967). . . . However March and Simon's inventory of propositions is largely induced from empirical research, while Thompson's derives from conceptual premises (45).

A separation in view points . . . took Simon and March in different directions after their collaboration on *Organizations* in 1958 (49).

Personal motives become much less important in organizational decisions than programmed organizational roles (49).

Hierarchy is the adaptive form for finite intelligence to assume in the face of complexity (Simon 1977, 114). Thus adding computers to the decision process should not change the essentially hierarchical nature of organizations (49).

Intuition is really not much different from other problem solving, but it is problem solving embedded in years of experience so that it has become automatic and not easily accessible to consciousness. . . . This kind of intuition yields competent decisions because of its origins in lengthy learning. It should be contrasted with intuition embedded in stress and emotion, which is much more likely to yield irrationality (51).

Depending on what factors . . . enter, . . . this process can produce quite variant versions of satisficing. . . . Overconfidence may enter as a substitute for an adequate search for alternatives, with the result that overly risky decisions may be made (54). Thus, heuristic problem solving.

ON THE CONCEPT OF INTUITION

What do others have to say on the concept of intuition and how it works? Let us see how this unravels.

Views on Intuition

Extension memory seems ideally suited to support flexible and efficient affect regulation processes. To denote affect regulation processes that are under the control of extension memory, we use the term *intuitive affect regulation* (Koole and Kuhl 2008, 298).

Insights from blindsight patients regarding nonconscious visual information processing have important implications for *intuitive* judgments (Rule and Ambady 2008, 40).

In cases in which *intuition* is based on extensive unconscious thought it should not be distrusted. . . . People tend to engage in a great deal of conscious thought when they deal with complex problems, whereas they should engage more in unconscious thought (Dijksterhuis and Nordgren 2006, 106, 108).

Our findings suggest that it may be useful to rely on *intuition* to guide decisions, particularly when explicit memory fails (Frank, O'Reilly, and Curran 2006, 706).

Researchers in the areas of management and psychology have explained *intuition* through a wide range of phenomena, including heuristics . . . , expertise, . . . and nonconscious information processing (Dane and Pratt 2007, 34).

Findings support the idea that moral judgment can be driven by *intuitive* processes, rather than deliberative reasoning. One of these *intuitions* appears to be physical purity, because it has a strong connection to moral purity (Schnall, Benton, and Harvey 2008, 1219).

Most of the action in moral judgment is in the automatic, affectively laden *intuitions*, not in conscious verbal reasoning (Haidt 2008, 70).

Research in psychology posits important boundaries to individual's cognitive capacities (Simon 1955), and business ethics scholars make related claims about individuals' "bounded moral rationality." . . . Individuals engaged in mental processes outside their conscious awareness . . . first use *intuitions* and then post hoc (moral) reasoning (Sonenshein 2007, 1025, 1027).

For many complex decisions, all the data in the world can't trump the lifetime's worth of experience that informs one's gut feelings, instinct, or *intuition* (Matzler, Bailom, and Mooradian 2007, 13).

Emotions . . . constitute the "extra" in the extrarationality of *intuitive* decision-making using tacit knowledge (Sayegh, Anthony, and Perrewé 2004, 196–197).

Heuristics, Biases, and Intuition

Surely intuition is closely tied to bounded rationality, but so are numerous biases and heuristics (Kahneman, Slovic, and Tversky 1982; Tversky and Kahneman 1984; Gilovich, Griffin, and Kahneman 2002). Simon started this work, and he is often recognized as the father of heuristics research with his views on bounded rationality and satisficing (see Fiedler 2008). Still, satisficing by itself does not engage the unconscious, although it does qualify as a heuristic. Managers make an entirely conscious choice to satisfice, to choose to seek a solution that is good enough, but not to seek maximization. However, numerous other biases or heuristics do engage the unconscious to varying degrees, as indicated previously (see Krizan and Windschitl 2007; Certo, Connelly, and Tihanyi 2008; Shah and Oppenheimer 2008). Intuition is closely involved here in many instances.

On the Involvement of Meditation States

"Calm contemplation and mental relaxation are one means by which the rational analytical mind may be quieted in order that intuition may have its voice" (Burke and Sadler-Smith 2006, 175). Thus meditation is suggested as a means to engage intuition. Furthermore meditation is advocated in views that call for a degree of mindfulness to hang on to current objects by bringing wondering (wobbling) attention back to the intended object (Weick and Putnam 2006). Yet meditation would seem to have the objective of concentrating forcefully on certain conscious concepts. What does the process imply?

Kozhevnikov, Louchakova, Josipovic, and Motes (2009, 645) report that Buddhist "Deity Yoga practitioners demonstrated a dramatic increase in performance on imagery tasks compared with . . . other groups. The results suggest that Deity meditation specifically trains one's capacity to access heightened visuospatial imagery abilities." How long these states can last is not known; the authors do not claim any unconscious involvement and in fact note their conscious activation. However, reviews of the evidence on meditation states indicate that hypnagogic conditions may be elicited, brain changes may occur, and a state that borders on sleep may develop (Vaitl, Birbaumer, Gruzelier, Jamieson, Kotchoubey, Kübler, Lehmann, Miltner, Ott, Pütz, Sammer, Strauch, Strehl, Wackermen, and Weiss 2005; Cahn and Polich 2006). Certainly there is much here that looks like hypnosis and could accordingly involve intuition and unconscious processes. As Bargh (2005, 49) says, "There are obvious parallels between hypnotic and priming phenomena, and the neuropsychological research . . . supports the notion of dissociated will or control in hypnosis as well as in priming effects. In both cases, the will is apparently controlled from outside, by external forces." Thus, the possibility that meditation states may activate unconscious processes does exist.

CONCLUSIONS

As indicated in the beginning of this chapter, the Carnegie School views as expressed in *Administrative Behavior, Organizations,* and their related publications have an estimated validity of five stars and an importance rating at the hands of organizational behavior in the five-star range, as well (5.81). Dividing the latter figure by the first yields a value of 1.16, suggesting that the importance rating tends to overestimate the presumed validity, but not by a great deal.

These Carnegie School views are shown to respect considerable application of unconscious processes, although Simon is inclined to favor rationality to the extent it is attainable, and the satisficing heuristic appears to operate primarily on a conscious basis. Following in Barnard's (1938) footsteps, Simon endorses the use of intuition. Originally Simon considered intuition to produce the same results as rational processes, but later he replaced this view with a more differentiated position. After a review of the ideas concerning the Carnegie School views from Miner (2006a), I set forth the research findings on intuition, including those on bounded moral rationality. The role that biases and heuristics play in the formulations of Simon is addressed, and its ties to intuition are considered. Research on meditation states is given special attention with reason to believe that unconscious factors and intuition may be introduced in this regard via the medium of parallels to hypnosis.

IMAGE THEORY

Image theory has much in common with the theory of bounded rationality espoused in the previous chapter (see Chapter 22 in this volume). It has been considered in some ways comparable to Lord's theory of leadership (Chapter 15 in this volume) and to Weick's theorizing (Chapter 6 in Miner 2006a); both of these positions invoke unconscious processes to a considerable degree.

Beach (1990) discusses image theory and the research on it at considerable length, providing perhaps the most comprehensive statement of the theory. Although Terence Mitchell has collaborated on the theory on occasion, he gives a large part of the credit involved to Beach. A treatment of the unconscious processes invoked is presented in Mitchell and Beach (1990); this is a major consideration, especially for the compatibility test. When intuition conflicts with rational analysis, the theory predicts that intuition can be expected to win out. Beach's *Leadership and the Art of Change: A Practical Guide to Organizational Transformation* (2006) is a small book dealing with organizational culture, but such matters are considered as well in numerous other publications. Recently a statement of how image theory emerged and developed has been presented by Beach and Mitchell (2005). This position represents an alternative to previous statements, but it is nevertheless worthy of consideration.

I have rated the theoretical validity of image theory at four stars (see Miner 2006a, Chapter 7; 2007, Chapter 17), largely because it is based on a substantial body of research conducted primarily by Beach and his collaborators. There are no meta-analyses available. In the same places I report an importance rating of 3.65 from the 71 organizational behavior scholars. This figure may well have been decreased by the relatively recent origin of the theory as compared with other theories contained in this volume; quite possibly many of the evaluators were not very familiar with image theory, although there have been numerous publications on the subject. Estimated usefulness receives a three-star rating.

FRAMING DECISIONS

Positive framing produces more automatic processes, while negative framing brings more controlled and thorough processes into play. Although compatibility remains in evidence, negative framing acts to reduce the fit between current and trajectory images. Thus organizations tend to be best served by framing information negatively in order to induce deliberation; it pays to depict the glass as half empty rather than half full. This reported finding is consistent with the effects of positive emotions (Bono and Ilies 2006), but it shows even stronger support for the impact of negative affect (Wong, Yik, and Kwong 2006). And so the research on image theory appears to receive justification from alternative sources. The conscious processes thus invoked by negative emotions do tend to take precedence.

INTUITION

As an addendum to what was said on the subject in Chapter 22 of this volume, image theory, too, engages intuitive processes, and through this medium handles unconscious considerations; the compatibility test, as previously indicated, is primarily involved.

It is possible to understand intuition "as a composite phenomenon invoking interplay between knowing (intuition-as-expertise) and sensing (intuition-as-feeling). . . . Intuition and rational analysis are better conceived of as two parallel systems of knowing" (Sadler-Smith and Shefy 2004, 76). Thus the position adopted by Simon is endorsed. Indeed intuitive processes are advocated for executive decision making. While screening for violations does not utilize probability information, choice decisions clearly do incorporate probability considerations. Accordingly research on image theory provides strong support for the compatibility-profitability differentiation.

Research involving a variation in significance, irreversibility, and accountability indicates that when all three are high, the strategy for choice selected tends to be the most analytic (conscious) available; when all three are low, the least analytic strategy is utilized. This position from image theory receives support from other research as well (see Mitchell, Friga, and Mitchell 2005). Additionally it appears that people carry out the profitability test using a wide repertoire of approaches, although how this might be integrated into the theory is not readily apparent.

THE ROLE OF ORGANIZATIONAL CULTURE

Beach gives considerable attention to the matter of organizational culture (see, in particular, Beach 2006). As such culture serves in the role of principles to establish images guiding decision making.

Principles Established

These principles indicate how culture acts on organizational participants:

1. It specifies what is of primary importance to the organization, the standards against which its successes and failures should be measured.
2. It dictates how the organization's resources are to be used, and to what ends.
3. It establishes what the organization and its members can expect from each other.
4. It makes some methods of controlling behavior within the organization legitimate and makes other illegitimate—that is, it defines where power lies within the organization and how it is to be used.
5. It selects the behaviors in which members should or should not engage and prescribes how these are to be rewarded and punished.

6. It sets the tone for how members should treat each other and how they should treat nonmembers—competitively, collaboratively, honestly, distantly, or hostilely.
7. It instructs members about how to deal with the external environment—aggressively, exploitatively, responsibly, or proactively (Beach 1993, 12).

Cultures of this kind provide a value image for members of an organization. Accordingly members tend to favor certain decision options and avoid others. Topics such as cultural norms (Fitzsimons and Bargh 2004) and national cultures (Oyserman and Lee 2008) often offer useful insights in this regard. However, although "people in all cultures have shared perceptions about the personality characteristics of the typical member of their own culture and of typical members of other cultures, recent collaborative work has provided validated assessments of the personality profiles of over 50 cultures, and judged by these criteria, perceptions of national character are unfounded stereotypes" (McCrae and Terracciano 2006, 156). Thus not all conclusions regarding national cultures are worthy of generalization to the organizational context.

Unconscious Considerations

Writing in the introduction to *The New Unconscious,* James Uleman says of the perspective provided by the new unconscious: "Perhaps the drama it seems to lack at the moment, compared to the psychoanalytic unconscious, will be found in how it impacts our culture and institutions in the future. But that is a different book and set of concerns" (2005, 15).

Thus it would seem that unconscious processes are likely to provide considerable fodder for future publication activity regarding culture. No such volume had appeared at the time this book went to press, but the potential is still there. Certainly unconscious considerations regarding culture are worthy of being highlighted.

ON CULTURES AND MULTICULTURES

Cultures influence human behavior and human experience consciously to some extent, but to a large extent their impact occurs unconsciously; people often are not aware of how they are influenced by culture. Some support for this view derives from evidence that cultures and cultural transmission do in fact occur within monkey groups (Huffman, Nahallage, and Leca 2008); social learning is clearly in evidence in these groups.

But even more to the point, multiculture exposure has been shown to foster creative endeavor, with ties to unconscious considerations (Leung, Maddux, Galinsky, and Chiu 2008; Maddux, Leung, Chiu, and Galinsky 2009). What seems to be crucial here is

a) whether the experience allows for juxtaposition and integration of cultural differences,
b) whether the individual is open to new ideas, and
c) whether the multicultural context encourages learning and minimizes the need for firm answers and existential anxiety.

> . . . In this context, exposure to foreign cultures is expected to have both an immediate and potentially sustainable effect on creative performance (Leung, Maddux, Galinsky, and Chiu 2008, 179).

Indeed creative performance itself does involve much that is of an unconscious nature (see George 2008, 445–450), as has been indicated previously. Interestingly "individuals assigned goals on all tasks (both creative tasks and the intervening task) exhibited a higher overall level of creative performance than those in the other conditions (Madjar and Shalley 2008, 800). Thus a particular type of multitasking in addition to exposure to multiple cultures serves to promote creativity; there clearly is something about multiple sources of stimulation involved here that is determining.

On Affect and Culture

This multiple stimulation hypothesis may well extend to emotional processes (see Chapters 11 and 14 in this volume). However, one should consider the following:

> We present a novel role of affect in the expression of culture. Four experiments tested whether individuals' affective states moderate the expression of culturally normative cognitions and behaviors. We consistently found that value expressions, self-constructs, and behaviors were less consistent with cultural norms when individuals were experiencing positive rather than negative affect. Positive affect allowed individuals to explore novel thoughts and behaviors that departed from cultural constraints, whereas negative affect bound people to cultural norms. As a result, when Westerners experienced positive rather than negative affect, they valued self-expression less, showed a greater preference for objects that reflected conformity, viewed the self in more interdependent terms, and sat closer to other people. East Asians showed the reverse pattern for each of these measures, valuing and expressing individuality and independence more when experiencing positive than when experiencing negative affect. The results suggest that affect serves an important functional purpose of attuning individuals more or less closely to their cultural heritage (Ashton-James, Maddux, Galinsky, and Chartrand 2009, 340).

On the Use of Power

Point 4 in the list of cultural specifics under the subhead "Principles Established" given previously points to the role of power. Here too unconscious considerations have been shown to occur. Thus Sivanathan, Pillutla, and Murnighan 2008, 135) find that "people over-react to an increase in power, but they react appropriately to a loss in power." Fast, Gruenfeld, Sivanathan, and Galinsky (2009, 502) report: "Three experiments demonstrated that the experience of power leads to an illusion of personal control. Regardless of whether power was experientially primed (Experiments 1 and 3) or manipulated through roles (manager vs. subordinates; Experiment 2), it led to perceived control over outcomes that were beyond the reach of the power holder." Priming to assure the activation of unconscious processes clearly contributes to this effect. Thus, once again, factors that extend beyond participants' awareness are implicated in culture.

CONCLUSIONS

Image theory has much in common with the concept of bounded rationality; thus many of the findings of Chapter 22 are also in evidence here. Image theory has a validity of four stars and an importance rating of 3.65 at the hands of organizational behavior. Dividing as appropriate yields a ratio of .91; consequently the importance data seem to provide somewhat of an underestimate of rated validity, although not by much.

Along with other similar models, image theory appears to operate in large part in the unconscious domain. Framing decisions positively produces more frequent responses of an automatic nature and thus contributes to activation beyond awareness. This is also true when intuition is mobilized, as it tends to be in the case of compatibility tests. Thus compatibility and profitability are shown to engage quite different processes.

Beach theorizes that organizational cultures serve to operate in the role of principles to establish images that guide decision making; thus cultural factors exert a major influence on decision processes, and they often do so unconsciously. This is true with regard to exposure to multiple cultures and to emotional responses in varied cultural contexts, as well as to the ways that cultures mobilize the use of power.

CHAPTER 24

BEHAVIORAL THEORY OF THE FIRM, ORGANIZATIONAL LEARNING, AND THE GARBAGE CAN MODEL: THEORIES INVOLVING JAMES MARCH

The three models considered here all involve work by the noted organizational theorist James March in some way. They include (1) *A Behavioral Theory of the Firm* (Cyert and March 1963, 1992), (2) a set of contributions dealing with organizational learning (March 1991; Levinthal and March 1993), and (3) the garbage can model (Cohen, March, and Olsen 1972; March and Olsen 1976). These theoretical contributions have been evaluated at 5.43, 5.20, and 4.38 respectively by the 71 organizational behavior scholars; all are rated at three stars as to their estimated validity (see Miner 2006b). The validity figures are substantially lower because much of the "research" reported represents case studies or computer simulations that are really more about theory development and less about theory testing. The behavioral theory of the firm has been found to be institutionalized, but none of the three theories has a practical usefulness above two stars. March characteristically has opposed applications and any normative formulations of his theories. These theories have not been found conducive to meta-analysis, largely because the research on them is not cumulative; in fact much of it is not really research in the normal sense of the term. March was primarily a theorist, and in this regard he has continued to excel over many years. However, this theorizing has been the major thrust of his work analyzing data, constructing computer models, and describing decisions (see Miner 2006a, Chapters 4 and 5).

In this connection it may be helpful to indicate that March often wrote poetry, which typically involves some play on words. This same feature is to be found in much of his theorizing; consequently the images he attempts to invoke may take precedence over the clarity of his theories. March writes very well, but not always in a way that benefits the consistent presentation of his ideas and the clear conveyance of his thought.

CORRECTING ANY ERROR IN MINER (2006A)

With an eye to this same clarity of presentation on my part, let me introduce here a correction to what I have said previously. In Miner (2006a) I said on page 74 that "foolishness appears to be strongly aligned with Barnard's appeal to intuition, which Simon rejected." Barnard and Simon did not see completely eye-to-eye on this matter, but I did *not* mean to indicate that Simon rejected the concept of intuition; in fact he came to accept intuition quite fully, consistent with what I have said in Chapter 22 of this volume. Perhaps this correction will help to make my discussion of March's theorizing subsequently more understandable. Both March and Simon viewed intuition as "real," although Simon favored the use of more rational approaches to decision making whenever possible.

DEALING WITH UNCONSCIOUS CONSIDERATIONS IN KEY PUBLICATIONS

With this effort at clarification let me take up what March had to say with regard to unconscious factors, first quoting from his key publications as noted previously, and later incorporating some of his other publications as well.

A Behavioral Theory of the Firm

The theory outlined in this volume characterizes the firm as an *adaptively rational* system rather than an *omnisciently rational* system (Cyert and March 1963, 99).

We assume three different kinds of such bias: (1) bias reflecting special training or experience of various parts of the organization, (2) bias reflecting the interaction of hopes and expectations, and (3) communication biases reflecting unresolved conflict within the organization (122).

This book [*A Behavioral Theory of the Firm*] is built around three . . . ideas. The first is *bounded rationality,* the observation that rational actors are significantly constrained by limitations of information and calculation. . . . They follow rules-of-thumb. The second idea is *imperfect environmental matching* . . . not uniquely determined by the demands of the environmental setting in which they arise. . . . The third idea is *unresolved conflict* (Cyert and March 1992, 214–215).

Thus the concepts of bounded rationality to set up the influence of unconscious considerations and of biases and heuristics to consummate these considerations are introduced (see Chapter 22 in this volume).

Organizational Learning

> Adaptive systems that engage in exploration to the exclusion of exploitation are likely to find that they suffer the costs of experimentation without gaining many of its benefits. . . . Conversely, systems that engage in exploitation to the exclusion of exploration are likely to find themselves trapped in suboptimal stable equilibria (March 1991, 71).

> *Little Models and Old Wisdom . . .* it may be instructive to reconfirm some elements of folk wisdom asserting that the returns to fast learning are not all positive (85–86).

> 1. Temporal *myopia.* Learning tends to sacrifice the long run to the short run. 2. *Spatial myopia.* Learning tends to favor effects that occur near to the learner. 3. *Failure myopia.* Organizational learning oversamples success and undersamples failures (Levinthal and March 1993, 110).

Once again, in the area of learning, biases and heuristics are shown to operate to place limits on the effectiveness of organizational processes.

The Garbage Can

> Measured against a conventional normative model of rational choice, the garbage can does appear pathological, but such standards are not really appropriate. The process occurs precisely when the preconditions of more normal rational models are not met (Cohen, March, and Olsen 1972, 16).

> Organized anarchies . . . can be viewed for some purposes as collections of choices looking for problems, issues and feelings looking for decision situations in which they might be aired, solutions looking for issues to which they might be an answer, and decision makers looking for work. These ideas are translated into an explicit computer simulation model of a garbage can decision process (1).

> We can treat *intuition as real. . . .* Intuition permits us to see some possible actions that are outside our present schema for justifying behavior (March and Olsen 1976, 78).

Accordingly the garbage can model as well is seen to involve unconscious processes.

DEALING WITH UNCONSCIOUS CONSIDERATIONS ELSEWHERE

March did not limit his allusions to matters beyond rationality to these key publications; there were other such allusions as well.

On the Resort to Foolishness

> A . . . requirement for a technology of foolishness is some strategy for suspending rational imperatives toward consistency (March 1999, 319).

> A technology of rationality has to be balanced by other technologies that free action from the constraints of conventional knowledge and procedures and introduce elements of foolishness into action (March 2006, 203).

Survival may . . . be served by the heroism of fools and the blindness of true believers. Their imperviousness to feedback is both the despair of adaptive intelligence and, conceivably, its salvation (201).

For a knight errant to make himself crazy for a reason merits neither credit nor thanks—the point is to be foolish without justification (March as quoted with regard to Don Quixote by Augier 2004, 171).

March advocates a technology of foolishness and advises us to engineer choice in such a way as to strike a balance between exploration and exploitation (Augier 2004, 171).

Organizations will learn to use technologies of rationality for simple problems, but not for complex ones (March 2006, 209).

Those who have worked with March add further elaborations to his theorizing:

Technologies of foolishness are manifestly nonrational behaviors at the individual level, but they are at the same time processes that facilitate broader organizational adaptation and learning over time. The [Carnegie] school does not claim that organizations identify some idealized amount of foolishness, but is instead sensitive to how organizational slack and other apparent nonoptimizing behavior may serve a constructive purpose (Gavetti, Levinthal, and Ocasio 2007, 533).

Further on Bounded Rationality, Intuition, and Heuristics

Certain other references on the topics that concerned us initially require mention. Among these are March (1994) and March, Sproull, and Tamuz (1991), as well as statements by others who have had long involvement with this work (Miller and Chen 2004; Argote and Greve 2007; Moore, Oesch, and Zietsma 2007). All attest to the activation of various unconscious mechanisms within the theories presented by James March. To this ensemble should be added a report on a seminar that included the participation of March himself (Augier and Teece 2005).

MINDFULNESS IN THE INTERPRETATION OF ORGANIZATIONAL LEARNING

A perspective on organizational learning that features the unconscious processes involved has been presented by Linda Argote with various coauthors (see in particular Argote and Todorova 2007). This perspective deals with learning processes for creating knowledge and establishes a fourfold table between the degree of mindfulness and the source of experience (own-direct vs. others-indirect). In the upper left quadrant dealing with less mindful and one's own source of experience are listed "Automatic Processes" grouped with "Trial and Error" and "Stimulus-Response" learning"; these, in contrast to the very mindful considered to be inferential, deliberate, and controlled. Thus once again learning processes are designated as being automatic (unconscious) on occasion (see Chapter 6 in this volume). "Controlled processing is primarily under the individual's control and requires attention; automatic processing occurs without the active control of individuals" (Argote and Todorova 2007,

197). The role of mindless work in creative processes (i.e., foolishness) is given particular attention in Elsbach and Hargadon (2006) and in Levinthal and Rerup (2006). Maitlis and Ozcelik (2004) discuss how decision processes of the kind considered may operate under the influence of emotions.

EVIDENCE FROM THE NEW UNCONSCIOUS PERSPECTIVE

This section contains research evidence on March's theories as adduced from the perspective of the new unconscious (see Miner 2008, Chapter 2; Hassin, Uleman, and Bargh 2005).

Foolishness and Incubation

Sternberg (2005) argues convincingly against the very bouts of foolishness that March seems to extol; it is not clear that the two are talking about the same thing, but there would seem to be some degree of overlap. However, a meta-analysis that focuses on creative tasks is more supportive of the March hypothesis:

> The meta-analysis supports the existence of incubation effects and also identifies some potential moderators. . . . Individuals solving creative problems were more likely to benefit from an incubation period. . . . The positive incubation effects found with creative problems are a direct reflection of their multi-solution nature. . . . Another finding of the meta-analysis was the beneficial effect of an incubation period filled with low demand tasks. . . . One possible explanation is that performing low cognitive demand incubation tasks allows the occurrence of some unconscious problem-solving processes. . . . The reasonably large effect sizes found with creative problems indicates that, with this class of problem at any rate, incubation is a potentially valuable mechanism for fostering creative thought (Sio and Ormerod 2009, 107, 109–110).

This is quite strong evidence in favor of March's argument for foolishness, but it does not prove unconscious involvement. There is research to indicate that effects of this kind might be primarily of a conscious nature (Lassiter, Lindberg, González-Vallejo, Bellezza, and Phillips 2009). Unfortunately, however, this research could not rule out unconscious effects beyond those specifically studied. Another study indicates that "these findings confirm and extend unconscious-thought theory by demonstrating that processes that increase the mental activation of correct solutions do not necessarily lead them into consciousness" (Zhong, Dijksterhuis, and Galinsky 2008, 912).

Consistent with the March (2006) formulations, "conscious thought is constrained by the low capacity of consciousness. Unconscious thought does not have this constraint" (Dijksterhuis and Nordgren 2006, 96). Thus decisions with regard to complex issues are best approached via unconscious processes (see the research reported in Frank, O'Reilly, and Curran 2006) in particular.

Overall on these matters I am inclined to agree with March, while recognizing that there are a number of unresolved issues. I am particularly influenced by the incubation meta-analysis, the only such meta-analysis that I have been able to unearth dealing with some aspect of the March theorizing.

Risk Taking and Poor Decisions

March tended to view risk taking in organizational terms rather than from an individual perspective. Thus his views tended to be controverted by findings such as: "This . . . confirms the hypothesis that the variability among individuals with regard to monetary risk-taking behavior corresponds to different levels of activity in the right lateral prefrontal cortex," and "This research provides a cognitive neuroscience approach to investigating individual differences in complex forms of decision making, such as risk-taking behavior" (Gianotti, Knoch, Faber, Lehmann, Pascual-Marqui, Diezi, Schoch, Eisenegger, and Fehr 2009, 36–37). Examples of how such individual differences may intervene in organizational behavior to produce bad managerial decisions are contained in Campbell, Whitehead, and Finkelstein (2009).

ON WISDOM

Wisdom typically has been lumped with intuition in much of the literature. Thus "wisdom is associated with cognitive, affective, and reflective characteristics and . . . wise persons are knowledgeable, mature, tolerant, emphatic, experienced, and *intuitive*. . . . Our specific definition of wisdom as an expertise . . . was not intelligence in the usual sense, but a substantially more complex system of knowledge, procedural strategies, and *intuition*" (Baltes and Smith 2008, 57–58).

March's Views on Wisdom

March is anything but consistent in his views on wisdom; there are minuses and pluses.

On the minus side is the following: "I learned early to be skeptical about the words of aged scholars. Now that I have become one of them, I am even more skeptical. Age generates self-indulgence more reliably than it generates wisdom" (March 2007a, 9). This appears to be primarily a personal view. However, there are more positive references (March 1991, as quoted previously; March and Olsen 1976, 59; March 2007b, 1279). Also Augier (2004), quoting March from an interview: "I leave wisdom to others" (172).

Yet elsewhere March is described as a "deep source of wisdom" (March and Coutu 2006, 84). Furthermore in the aforementioned interview he is quoted as follows:

> Aspirations for importance or significance are the illusions of the ignorant. All our hopes are minor, except to us; but some things matter because we choose to make them matter. What might make a difference to us, I think, is whether in our tiny roles, in our brief time, we inhabit life gently and add more beauty than ugliness (89).

This does, indeed, sound like an espousal of wisdom, although perhaps unknowingly. All in all, I would conclude that March is favorably disposed toward wisdom, as he is toward intuition.

Age Effects

Definitions of wisdom's effects "all seem to include a blending of intellect, emotional sensitivity, empathy and practical knowledge" (Cozolino 2008, 111). However, there are differences between the Eastern and Western worlds. In the former, "wisdom . . . refers to a process of direct understanding without overt intellectualization and with a great deal of emotional involvement. . . . The Western tradition is relatively narrow in its limitation of wisdom to mainly cognitive features" (Takahashi and Overton 2005, 36–37). Yoga and meditation are often involved in the Eastern tradition, and equal weight is given to cognitive, affective, intuitive, and interpersonal domains. A discussion of how intuition enters in here is contained in Osbeck and Robinson (2005).

"Under ideal cognitive and physical health conditions, older adults will demonstrate an advantage due to greater life experience (practice). . . . Wisdom has been found to maintain itself across the lifespan, neither increasing nor decreasing with age. Unlike the physical body and the mechanisms of the mind, which both decline with age, wisdom fights to exist. . . . And as far as psychology can tell it is winning" (Jordan 2005, 167, 186). What this means is that wisdom becomes increasingly rare (Baltes and Smith 2008) as physical and cognitive declines serve to reduce the supply on which it draws (but see Hertzog, Kramer, Wilson, and Lindenberger 2008 for procedures that may well act to delay these declines). Maslow (see Chapter 9 of this volume) saw self-actualization, like wisdom, as inherently rare, suggesting that the two may have much in common.

Five Propositions for Wise Leadership

To elucidate the wisdom phenomenon further, let me quote certain propositions from the leadership literature:

1. Wise leaders use reason and careful observation.
2. Wise leaders allow for nonrational and subjective elements when making decisions.
3. Wise leaders value humane and virtuous outcomes.
4. Wise leaders and their actions are practical and oriented toward everyday life, including work.
5. Wise leaders are articulate, understand the aesthetic dimension of their work, and seek the intrinsic personal and social rewards of contributing to the good life. Wisdom is an ability that minimizes . . . cognitive limitations for leaders and others (McKenna, Rooney, and Boal 2009, 178–180, 184).

With age the first of these propositions tends to be threatened in particular, as atrophy occurs in the frontal lobes of the brain, thus limiting executive functions such as planning and controlling conscious thought (von Hippel 2007).

Conscious and Unconscious

Thus conscious processes tend to lose out with ageing, and controlled processing associated with deliberation declines. "This deliberative decline may lead to the relative enhancement of more implicit and automatic forms of knowledge" (Peters, Hess, Vätsfjäll, and Auman 2007, 2). Thus as the cognitive capacity of conscious factors fails, the unconscious once again takes over. The evidence indicates that unlike the decrease in conscious reasoning, implicit learning and memory are largely spared by the effects of ageing. Accordingly intuitive considerations become increasingly engaged as wisdom is involved more completely.

Emotions and the Development of Wisdom

> We focus on two brain regions, the amygdala and the orbitomedial prefrontal cortex. . . . The amygdala is capable of processing aspects of our environment of which we are totally unaware, making us automatically react to avoid people, places, and things that have previously had a negative effect on us. . . . A highly developed and well-regulated orbitomedial prefrontal cortex-amygdala network may well be a prerequisite for psychological maturity and the attainment of wisdom. . . . The taming of the amygdala may be one of the primary gifts of ageing and an important component of becoming a wise elder (Cozolino 2008, 149–151, 154).

> Research suggests that ageing is associated with a greater focus on emotional content and on positive over negative information. . . . Affect is involved in age-related improvements in wisdom. . . . Older adults may rely more on affective and intuitive processes in their everyday decisions (a general affective bias) and to actively deliberate less in those decisions due to cognitive limitations (Peters, Hess, Västfjäll, and Auman 2007, 7–8, 10, 14).

Clearly emotional considerations are major aspects of wisdom effects.

Wisdom as Learned

Csikszentmihalya and Nakamura (2005, 239) indicate that "wisdom can be learned" and is "to some extent teachable." This brings it well within the domain of March's theories. There is indeed evidence supporting this conclusion. Thus my earlier conclusion regarding the applicability of wisdom within this chapter is provided with further evidence to confirm it.

CONCLUSIONS

In accordance with information presented earlier in this chapter, the evaluation data provided look as follows:

for a Behavioral Theory of the Firm	5.43/3 = 1.81
for Organizational Learning	5.20/3 = 1.73
for the Garbage Can Model	4.38/3 = 1.46

The mean ratio here is 1.67; all values of the importance ratings tend to overestimate the presumed validities of the three theories. This is a substantial overestimation, given that all of the theories are considered to be of an unconscious nature. However, the fact that research carried out by the authors is largely conducted for theory-forming purposes, and not for theory-testing, tends to depress the estimated validities assigned.

Specific instances of the authors' use of unconscious constructs—including foolishness, bounded rationality, intuition, heuristics, and wisdom—are noted. Particular attention is given to March's views on wisdom. Then the results of research on the wisdom construct are considered in some detail as they relate to age effects, propositions on wise leadership, unconscious and conscious emphases, emotional involvement, and the extent to which learning is activated.

PART IV

SYSTEMS CONCEPTS
OF ORGANIZATIONS

CONTROL THEORY (USING THE CONTROL GRAPH)

Arnold Tannenbaum's control theory is an outgrowth of Rensis Likert's theory of systems 1–4 and 4T (see Likert and Likert 1976); both are closely tied to the University of Michigan and to the Survey Research Center there. Tannenbaum's theory should be distinguished from various other theories with the same or similar names. In particular it is not the cybernetics control theory (see Vancouver, Thompson, Tischner, and Putka 2002).

I have classified this theory as a systems theory on several grounds, one of which is the overlap with the systems theorizing of Likert. Another consideration is that systems theorizing by its nature tends to be wide ranging in its constructs, with variables so interrelated that everything seems to be related to everything else; this phenomenon characterizes control theory as well. Thus control theory extends its purview across the organization's boundary into the operative environment. In this respect it is clearly an open systems view. The most important contribution of control theory is the hypothesis, grounded soundly in research data, that a greater amount of control overall contributes to a more effective organization. Such control may well encompass many aspects of the external environment. Furthermore the parallel between the findings on the total amount of control and the stocks of learning across levels of an organization (Bontis, Crossan, and Hulland 2002) would seem to extend the applicability of the theory into additional domains.

Tannenbaum's theory is set forth in a number of articles and books, including most prominently the collection of articles in Tannenbaum (1968), the union research in Tannenbaum and Kahn (1957), and the international research in Tannenbaum, Kavčič, Rosner, Vianello, and Wieser (1974). Control theory and the control graph method have an estimated validity of four stars, reflecting the extensive research conducted and the effectiveness in predicting organizational performance. The importance rating, however, is only at 3.58; organizational behavior scholars as a group do not appear to recognize the theory as particularly effective (see Miner 2006a, Chapter 8). Furthermore control theory does not make any substantial contribution to practical usefulness, nor has it been the subject of meta-analyses. On the former score the problem is that little is said about how control might be increased were a company, or any organization, inclined to do so; on the latter score, although an extensive review is contained in Tannenbaum and Cooke (1979), these efforts have not been the subject of any quantitative presentations.

CONTROL AND PSYCHOLOGICAL NEEDS

In a number of publications Tannenbaum defines control as "the capacity to manipulate available means for the satisfaction of needs." Needs are also invoked in connection with discussions of the "organizational power syndrome," which also is reflected in various control processes. Thus needs are a major aspect of control theorizing, but they are not used with reference to specific needs (other than perhaps the need for power), and they are not given specific operational definitions.

The Measurement of Needs

Conscious needs are often measured using self-report indexes. This approach, however, leaves much to be desired; in fact procedures that tap unconscious processes, such as projective techniques, get at more of the essence of need measurement. This tying of needs to an approach that is characterized by tapping unconscious considerations is employed in previous chapters of this volume; it prevails in the McClelland, Koestner, and Weinberger (1989) research. The use of need theorizing has come to be synonymous with some measure, often involving projectives, that deals with the unconscious. That measures of this kind exist, and can be effectively scored is widely documented (see McClelland 1965; Kirkpatrick, Winter 2002; Wofford, and Baum 2002; Miner 2008; Sivanathan, Pillutla, and Murnighan 2008; Fast, Gruenfeld, Sivanathan, and Galinsky 2009). Such measures deal with all kinds of needs, and in particular they extend to the organizational power syndrome.

Tannenbaum's research does not use any of the self-report measures; nor does it apply priming or the projective indexes such as the TAT or some sentence completion index. However, it could well apply techniques such as the latter, and might well benefit from doing so. In actual fact Tannenbaum relies entirely on various measures related to the control graph method; thus it does not deal with needs in other than a generic sense.

Needs and Too Much Control

In Miner (2006a) on page 137, the following quote from Tannenbaum (1968, 58) appears:

> Too much control may be as dysfunctional as too little, and a hypothesis more general than that offered above would specify an optimum level of control above or below which the organization would function below its potential. We are not yet in a position to specify the optimum for specific organizations. We can safely assume, however, that many . . . organizations are operating at a level considerably below it.

Thus an organization may suffer from too much control. This hypothesis has not been tested in the Tannenbaum research, and consequently it remains open. However, research on needs does indicate a possible source of information. This research by Spreier, Fontaine, and Malloy (2006) indicates that a need may be overactivated and cause a leader to run amok; consequently the person can exhibit certain destructive potentials of overachievers. The same phenomenon may occur when achievement training is overextended.

The parallel here to the hypothesized dysfunctional effects of overcontrol is significant. Perhaps the study of unconscious needs would yield a solution to this unanswered question from control theory. There is, indeed, a good chance that it might, and that consequently the relationship of control to effectiveness might well be shown to be curvilinear.

HIERARCHY AND CONTROL

Another area in which further research on unconscious factors may prove fruitful has to do with hierarchy. Studies of industrial firms consistently indicate that hierarchical systems of control tend to predominate even in socialized societies (Tannenbaum, Kavčič, Rosner, Vianello, and Wieser 1974; Tannenbaum and Rozgonyi 1986); this is not true of all types of organizations, but it does occur often.

This preference for hierarchical structures should be considered in relation to certain findings reported by Moeller, Robinson, and Zabelina (2008):

> An association between dominance and facilitation of perception along the vertical dimension on this task would be due to relatively automatic perceptual processes (356).

> Study 2 replicated the systematic relation between personality dominance and biases favoring vertical, relative to horizontal, spatial locations in a paradigm in which the location of spatial probes varied randomly (359).

> We predicted a general bias in which high dominance would be associated with facilitated processing along the vertical dimension of space relative to the horizontal dimension of space. This prediction was systematically confirmed (359).

> Findings such as these will be useful to social-personality perspectives emphasizing the unconditional nature of automatic processing (360).

> Our data support this top-down perspective on spatial attention. . . . A metaphor-related theory led us to predict that individuals high in dominance would favor vertical locations in visual space. Two studies involving three replications support this prediction (360).

Whether or not unconscious biases such as this operate within control theory would be important to investigate; they may produce additional insights into how control is exercised.

ON CONSCIOUS PROCESSES WITHIN CONTROL THEORY

The control graph and the various measures derived from it utilize highly conscious perceptual processes; in many respects, then, this is a rational theory.

Subjective and Objective Control

A question arises as to the comparability between these perceptual, subjective control processes and the objective reality. Tannenbaum's theory holds that the two are basically the same. The best available evidence comes from research reported by Wall, Michie, Patterson, Wood, Sheehan, Clegg, and West (2004). This latter analysis compares subjective and objective performance measures and concludes that the two yield essentially comparable results. Thus it seems reasonable to assume that the control theory measures reflect much the same processes as are found in objective measures. Evidence from other sources is consistent with this view.

Laissez-Faire and Related Structures

Another source of substantiation comes from evidence where very little control is exerted at any level. Let me refer to Figure 8.2 on page 139 of Miner (2006a). Line 3 of the figure reflects an essentially laissez-faire structure, with very little control exerted at any level. Such a control graph is entirely consistent with what one finds based on research conducted on other situations of this kind (Hinkin and Schriesheim 2008). Once again the control graph evidence, using perceptual and rational measurements, matches up well with findings from other sources.

THE CONSCIOUS/UNCONSCIOUS BALANCE

All in all there is evidence from needs theory and from other sources of an unconscious nature that support a view of control theory as extending beyond the purely conscious. There is also evidence from the perceptual and deliberative nature of responses to the control graph that places the theory squarely in the rational or conscious realm. Taking the two lines of evidence together, it appears best to consider control theory as essentially balanced in nature; that is indeed my overall judgment.

CONCLUSIONS

Consistent with what was said earlier in this chapter, control theory (using the control graph) has an estimated validity of four stars and an importance rating, based on the judgments from organizational behavior as a whole, of 3.58. When the second value is divided by the first the resulting value is .90. This ratio appears to indicate that to some minimal extent organizational behavior underestimates the presumed validity of control theory as set forth by Arnold Tannenbaum.

This theory has been shown to be a balanced approach as between unconscious and conscious influences. Psychological needs are given a prominent position in the theory, and the power syndrome appears to invoke the need for power in defining control. Also control theory findings lead to an emphasis on hierarchic structures, which are characterized as well by unconscious activation. Evidence to the effect that the perceptual processes involved in the control graph are comparable to objective reality is presented. Similar validity information is given for laissez-faire situations and the like.

CHAPTER 26

KATZ AND KAHN'S SOCIAL PSYCHOLOGY OF ORGANIZATIONS

Katz and Kahn's (1966, 1978) open systems theory appears in two editions of their book *The Social Psychology of Organizations*. An organization is defined as an open system of roles, and consequently the theory emphasizes a view of organizations as contrived in nature and consisting of a structure of acts and events. This role-related aspect of the theory was first proposed and defined in an earlier publication (Kahn, Wolfe, Quinn, Snoek, and Rosenthal 1964). The defining characteristics of such an open-system are (1) *energic inputs* from the social environment; (2) *throughput* so that work is done within the system; (3) *output* into the environment; (4) a *cycle of events* such that the product exported provides the energy to repeat the cycle; (5) *negative entropy,* whereby more energy is imported from the environment than is expanded in work; (6) *information inputs* about how the environment and the system are functioning; *negative feedback,* which provides information to correct deviations; and a *coding* process that simplifies energic and information inputs and permits their selective reception; (7) a *steady state* marked by a stable ratio of energy exchanges; (8) movement to increasing *differentiation* (or elaboration or specialization); (9) the operation of the *equifinality* principle, whereby the system can achieve the same final state from multiple paths and conditions; and (10) (in the 1978 edition) *integration* and *coordination* to counter the differentiation.

Roles are created from certain recurrent activities within the pattern that yields the organizational output. Individuals are surrounded by others who operate as role senders. This process of role sending and receiving is described in Figure 26.1. *Role conflict* occurs when an individual experiences role sendings from one source that would make it difficult or impossible to comply with role sendings from another source. *Role ambiguity* occurs when there is a lack of role-related information or there are inadequacies in the communication of such information.

The Katz and Kahn theory has an estimated validity of three stars and an importance rating of five stars (5.33 to be exact) (see Miner 2006a). As far as meta-analyses are concerned, they appear to be restricted to the role-related aspects of the theory. Here the most up-to-date analyses do appear to provide support for the Katz and Kahn position (Thoresen, Kaplan, Barsky, Warren, and de Chermont 2003; Halbesleben 2006). However, a quote from the Conclusions section of Miner (2006a, 167) still seems to apply to the theory overall:

Figure 26.1 **Model of a Role Episode**

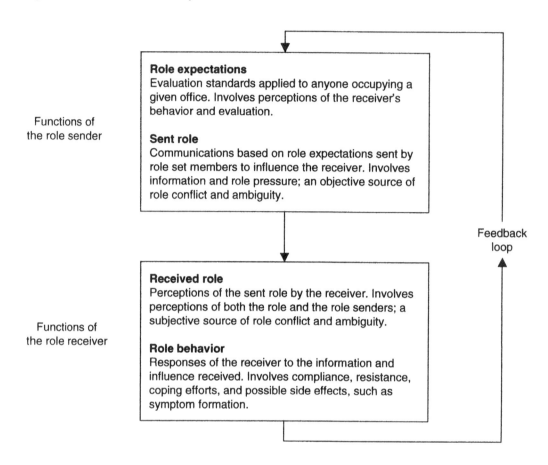

Functions of
the role sender

Role expectations
Evaluation standards applied to anyone occupying a
given office. Involves perceptions of the receiver's
behavior and evaluation.

Sent role
Communications based on role expectations sent by
role set members to influence the receiver. Involves
information and role pressure; an objective source of
role conflict and ambiguity.

Feedback
loop

Functions of
the role receiver

Received role
Perceptions of the sent role by the receiver. Involves
perceptions of both the role and the role senders; a
subjective source of role conflict and ambiguity.

Role behavior
Responses of the receiver to the information and
influence received. Involves compliance, resistance,
coping efforts, and possible side effects, such as
symptom formation.

Source: Adapted from Kahn, Wolfe, Quinn, Snoek, and Rosenthal (1964, 26) and Katz and Kahn (1966, 182).

The theory's validity is somewhat suspect, not so much because the theory has been shown to be wrong as because hypotheses derived from it have not been tested with sufficient frequency; thus the three stars. The problem appears to be inherent in the reliance on systems theorizing, which, by its very nature, tends to thwart hypothesis formulation and thus the research that would provide for validation. Because the Katz and Kahn theory is so segmented, it requires considerable research to provide support within each sector. Some supportive research has emerged, especially in the area of role relationships, but not enough to meet the requirements of such a multifaceted theory.

ON ROLE THEORY

Role theory considerations are consistently measured within the Katz and Kahn framework in terms of self-report indexes; thus they are assumed to be of a conscious or rational nature.

Unconscious Manifestations

Yet there is reason to believe that role theory considerations might well be approached from an unconscious perspective with sizable benefits to understanding. In Chapter 11 of this volume I noted that a factor analysis of the roles set forth in the various Miner Sentence Completion Scale (MSCS) measures produced support for the roles proposed there, and thus contributed to the construct validity of these sentence completion measures (see Jennifer Miner 2008, Chapter 32). I indicated further that roles can well operate in an unconscious manner, if appropriately measured, and thus would benefit from research that used measures tapping motivation of this type.

In support of such a characterization of roles let me offer several quotes from the literature of role theory:

> There is evidence that extreme emotions, and efforts to regular them, interfere with rational decision making and tax cognitive resources. . . . There are individual differences in the propensity to engage in ill-considered behaviors when experiencing intense emotions (Cyders and Smith 2008, 821). *Intense emotions of this kind are activated by role conflict and role ambiguity.*

> General consensus decreased as . . . judgments become more abstract, [and] job holders are less likely to agree on the importance of the work role requirement. . . . Overall, our findings strongly demonstrate the substantial role that the discrete occupational context plays in amplifying or attenuating consensus. . . . These results provide empirical evidence for the proposition put forth by Katz and Kahn (1978). . . . Our research shows that aspects of discrete occupational context influence not only the range of actions consensually deemed appropriate (tasks and responsibilities) but also the personal capabilities underlying such actions (traits) (Dierdorff and Morgeson 2007, 1237). *Thus unconscious considerations are shown to have an opportunity to enter in.*

> It was assumed that individuals' role models were essentially indistinguishable from significant others, such as parents, mentors, and leaders. . . . Role model constructs did not disappear in later stages, but rather become more complex and differentiated as individuals become more selective in the attributes they observed (Gibson 2003, 605–606). *Accordingly role models possess the unconscious processes of transference as treated in Chapter 5 of this volume.*

> Participants were most motivated by role models who matched their primed regulatory focus. . . . To the extent that cultures differ in their emphasis on promotion or prevention, we might expect to find corresponding cross-cultural differences in response to positive and negative role models (Lockwood and Pinkus 2008, 254–256).

Measurement Issues

The role-related constructs incorporated in the Katz and Kahn theory are repeatedly measured using self-report scales; they never bring priming or projective techniques or any other process that might involve unconscious considerations to bear. Thus role conflict and ambiguity typically are measured using existing scales (see Rizzo, House, and Lirtzman 1970; House and Rizzo 1972). Burnout, a construct that is very much role-related, is usually tapped with some version of the Maslach Burnout Inventory (Maslach and Jackson 1986), which is also of a self-report nature. This index is based on a three-factor structure (see Schutte, Toppinen, Kalimo, and Schaufeli 2000; Richardson and Martinussen 2004). Other burnout measures exist, but they appear to be used less often, and they too are all of the self-report type. In fact the burnout literature is dominated by measures that are typically characterized by their use of self-report procedures.

Role Theory and Burnout—Empirical Research

A number of empirical studies have linked role stress as a consequence of role conflict and/ or role ambiguity with one or more aspects of burnout. I consider this literature here. A new and improved index of role stress and it components, although still of a self-report nature, was developed using as a sample of employees of an electronics/software firm (Siegall 2000). A study of entrepreneurs showed that "cognitive style moderates the relationship between the structure of the work environment and burnout; for more structured work environments, more intuitive entrepreneurs will experience higher burnout than those who are more analytic" (Brigham and DeCastro 2003, 53). In a study using a number of professors from a French-Canadian university, role stressors were found to relate significantly to various dimensions of burnout (Fernet, Guay, and Senécal 2004). All measures were self-reported. Another study of employees from three Brazilian oil companies supported the moderating effects of political skill; greater political skill reduced the negative effects of role conflict. A key component of political skill is the development and leveraging of social capital (Perrewé, Zellars, Ferris, Rossi, Kacmar, and Ralston 2004).

In a qualitative study of role conflict within a board of directors, Golden-Biddle and Rao (2004) demonstrated both conflicts of interest and conflicts of commitment. In a larger study of university alumni, results showed that both role conflict and role ambiguity completely mediated the relationships between psychological support and role modeling with job attitudes among mentors and protégés. In addition, there was support for role conflict as a partial mediator of the relationship between vocational support and job attitudes. All measures were derived from self-reports of respondents (Lankau, Carlson, and Nielson 2006). In a study including LMX (leader-member exchange) relationships (see Chapter 14 in this volume), employees in a health care setting were analyzed. In such a setting, role stress had a particularly strong positive relationship to burnout; accordingly role stress was treated as the most proximally linked to burnout. Again mentoring had a direct negative effect on role stress, and self-reports were used extensively to measure the relevant variables (Thomas and Lankau 2009).

Role Theory and Burnout—Reviews

In addition to the previous empirical studies, there are also several reviews that deal with the relationship between role concepts and burnout. One of these reviews is of a meta-analytic nature (Thoresen, Kaplan, Barsky, Warren, and de Chermont 2003, 917). There it is said "that those high in negative affect as a trait are more likely than those lower in negative affect as a trait to encounter stressors (e.g., role ambiguity, role conflict, daily hassles) predictive of exhaustion," one of the components of burnout.

Similar statements occur in other reviews of the burnout literature (see Maslach, Schaufeli, and Leiter 2001; Maslach 2003; Halbesleben and Buckley 2004; Shirom, Melamed, Toker, Berliner, and Shapira 2005; Melamed, Shirom, Toker, Berliner, and Shapira 2006).

ADDING IN ROLE MOTIVATION THEORY

Role motivation theory was discussed in Chapter 16 of this volume. It envisions a role conflict that occurs when a person with one motivational pattern is thrust into an incongruent organizational form that rewards a disparate type of motivational pattern. This might happen if a person characterized by professional motivation is confronted with the role prescriptions of a hierarchic (managerial) organization. Such appears to be the case in the instances cited by Currie and Proctor (2005). Incongruence of this kind is illustrated with Chapters 29 through 31 of Miner (2008), specifically in Table 29.2 on page 389 for task motivation, in Table 30.2 on page 404 for hierarchic motivation, and in Table 31.2 on page 414 for professional motivation. Note that the correlations presented in these tables tend to be quite low, in contrast with the much higher correlations from the congruent analyses presented in the tables that precede those cited.

Misfits of this kind, if they involve prolonged role conflict, can produce burnout. A quote at this point seems relevant: Muchinsky says, "I believe burnout is the end result of incongruity, a forced fit between two things that no longer go together" (as given in Roch 2007).

Furthermore Hall (2002, 200) states, "Burnout happens when a person experiences frustration of his or her work goals over a prolonged period of time—in other words, when the conditions for psychological failure exist." Role motivation theory becomes particularly relevant here because (1) it draws upon projective measurement, as opposed to the self-report indexes that have been characteristic previously in this context, and (2) it defines roles in institutionalized terms (see Ashforth 2001, 164–165). Thus it utilizes the unconscious processes that would appear to be most appropriate.

ON THE NATURE OF BURNOUT

Burnout has been the subject of extensive research and theorizing beyond what has been discussed here to date. Some of these findings are worthy of further discussion. One such conclusion is that burnout is influenced by abusive supervision; emotional exhaustion, as a component of burnout, is particularly evident in these cases. Thus abusive supervision is added to the other sources that contribute to burnout (Wu and Hu 2009). Another source that can act to affect burnout is role conflict involving the home and work. A study of volunteer Australian ambulance drivers makes this point quite vividly (Lewig, Xanthopoulou, Bakker, Dollard, and Metzer 2007). It is also emphasized in a study of general medical practitioners. Here also work-family conflict was in evidence as a cause of burnout, as was a tendency toward perfectionism; this was true of general practitioners of both sexes (Houkes, Winants, and Twellaar 2008).

A final point must be made regarding strategies and procedures for reducing burnout. The evaluation of such programs has had mixed results, and as yet no procedure of this kind has established itself as preeminent. However, work with an action research program in a federal fire service has shown promise. In this instance stress was particularly evident as a result of a perception of politics in the handling of human resource decisions. Using collaborative research techniques in such cases, as with action research, can provide an effective opportunity for organization development as well as considerable insight into locally operating causes of burnout (Halbesleben, Osburn, and Mumford 2006).

CONCLUSIONS

As noted earlier the Katz and Kahn social psychology of organizations is an open systems theory that has a rated validity of three stars with an importance evaluation given by organizational behavior scholars of 5.33. The resulting ratio when the first figure is divided into the latter is 1.78. Thus it appears that organizational behavior as a whole tends to overestimate the validity of the Katz and Kahn open systems theory by a substantial degree. This theory is indeed a rational or conscious formulation, as shown by its measurement processes. Accordingly the overestimation appears to reflect a predilection for processes used to measure this type of theoretical variable.

As a systems theory the Katz and Kahn version is somewhat deficient in testable hypotheses. There are meta-analyses of research studies, but only in the area of role theorizing. These role theory formulations have characteristically been measured using self-reports, although there is good reason to believe that in such cases measures of an unconscious nature would more appropriately tap the underlying constructs. Quotes indicative of this predisposition are used to show how roles may come to operate outside of awareness. Examples from role theory are cited to show how such phenomena as role conflict, role ambiguity, and burnout are measured in self-report terms. It was shown that role stresses do in fact serve to instigate burnout. This is evident from a sizable body of research, both as documented in empirical publications and as incorporated in numerous reviews.

Furthermore role motivation theory was shown to have a capability to induce role stress by exposing individuals to organizational forms and their allied role prescriptions which are incongruent (represent misfits) vis-à-vis the characteristics of the individual (their role predispositions). Stress of this kind can, after repeated exposure, serve to provoke burnout. Adding role motivation theory to the evidence for a role theory-burnout link permits the use of unconscious measurement and institutionalized roles.

Examples of the wide-ranging scope of the burnout research are cited. These include studies of the impact of abusive supervision on burnout, of the importance of stress induced by work-family conflict in burnout, and of the effectiveness of programs aimed at preventing or limiting the extent of burnout.

CHAPTER 27

SOCIOTECHNICAL SYSTEMS THEORY

Sociotechnical systems theory is a by-product of the collaboration of Eric Trist and Fred Emery, combined with a network of other contributors. The theory began with work in the British coal mines (see Trist and Bamforth 1951; Trist, Higgin, Murray, and Pollack 1963) putting together a former miner (Bamforth) and a psychologist with training in psychoanalysis (Trist). It spread to Australia (with the addition of the theoretical contributions of Emery), to the United States, to the Nordic countries, to India, and to various other locations. The theory is presented in several books and some articles too, but I would recommend Emery and Trist (1973), Trist and Murray (1993), and Trist, Emery, and Murray (1997), which together cover the theory as a whole.

It is apparent that this is a systems type of theory, with an estimated validity of three stars and an importance rating from organizational behavior of 5.09 (see Miner 2006a, Chapter 10; Miner 2007, Chapter 18). The major contribution appears to be in the area of practical usefulness with special emphasis on autonomous work groups.

Several meta-analyses have been carried out recently dealing with team performance. One of these, by Stewart (2006), indicates a limited tendency for autonomous groups to perform better, "but additional research is needed to understand the environmental conditions that influence the extent to which autonomy improves performance" (46). Burke, Stagl, Klein, Goodwin, Salas, and Halpin (2006) conducted a meta-analysis on team performance focused on leadership and learning; this meta-analysis did not deal specifically with autonomous groups. Finally Hülsheger, Anderson, and Salgado (2009) included studies of teams conducted with primary emphasis on innovative work. Here the major method of measuring innovation was by self-report, an approach judged to be insufficient in and of itself. This meta-analysis, too, did not take up autonomous groups as a separate entity.

THE ROMANCE OF TEAMS

Allen and Hecht (2004) state: "We review evidence regarding the actual effectiveness of teams, in order to show that teams are not as effective as many believe them to be" (439) and "current beliefs in the effectiveness of teams are out of proportion to the evidence regarding their effectiveness" (454). The romance of the teams concept has reference to James Meindl's

(1990) romance of leadership (see Chapter 21 in this volume). Meindl (1990) himself had doubts as to the long-term consequence regarding the applicability of the romance view to teams.

The Overestimation of Team Performance

It is apparent that teams tend to be credited with more than is justified. See for instance the bold extrapolations of Day, Gronn, and Salas (2006) and the promotion of team performance proposed by Lipman-Blumen and Leavitt (2009). There is reason to believe that what teams can accomplish is often exaggerated.

The Limitations of Teams

Evidence to the effect that teams have less than the expected impact is widely available (see Troyer 2004; Zárraga and Bonache 2005; Minssen 2006). The benefits of teamwork are not always supported, nor are the benefits of autonomous teams.

THE HACKMAN CRITICISMS

Richard Hackman, widely recognized as an expert on groups and teams, has commented on the team approach. One such commentary is in a recent interview (Coutu and Hackman 2009). See also Wageman, Fisher, and Hackman (2009). With regard to sociotechnical systems theory Hackman (1978) feels that the coverage is incomplete:

1. The theory does not specify the attributes of group tasks that are required for effective and autonomous work groups. . . . Because key task attributes are not specified, it is not possible to devise measures of these attributes for use in theory-guided diagnoses of work systems prior to change, in evaluations of the effects of changes on the work, or in tests of the conceptual adequacy of the theory itself.
2. Individual differences among people are not explicitly dealt with in the sociotechnical approach. . . . The theory does not deal with the fact that social needs vary in strength among people. Such differences may affect whether individuals seek to participate in an autonomous group.
3. The theory does not address the internal dynamics that occur among members of work groups. . . . The assumption apparently is that members of autonomous work groups will develop on their own satisfactory ways of working together. . . . Given the substantial evidence about ways that groups can go "sour," the validity of that assumption must be considered questionable (64).

MIXED SUPPORT FOR THE SOCIOTECHNICAL APPROACH

A theory such as the Trist and Emery approach that yields mixed results when put to empirical tests is very likely to be vulnerable to unconscious interpretations. Certainly the fact that these theorists do not utilize their psychoanalytic knowledge to construct their theory is consistent with such a view. Individual differences are given short shrift, even though there are numerous points where introducing them would seem warranted. This is a rational and conscious theory, emphasizing the processes consistent with theorizing of this type, such as planning and the idea that hope is a human right (Ketchum and Trist 1992). This latter concept fits with the views of Luthans, Youssef, and Avolio (2007) and is part of the positive emphasis in organizational behavior (see Cameron 2008). In this latter regard it actually antedated the formal creation of this emphasis. In any event the mixed nature of the results obtained when relying exclusively on conscious considerations raises the possibility that the inclusion of unconscious considerations might serve to produce a more consistent level of validity, and thus an estimated validity above the three-star level.

Negative Effects of High Trust in Autonomous Teams

"A high level of trust can make the members of self-managed work teams reluctant to monitor one another. If low monitoring combines with high individual autonomy, team performance can suffer. . . . High trust was associated with higher team performance when individual autonomy was low, but with low performance when individual autonomy was high. . . . Under some conditions too much trust in a self-managing team can be harmful" (Langfred 2004, 385, 390). This can represent a deterrent to the institution of autonomous work groups under certain conditions.

Discipline in Autonomous Work Groups

"The severity of disciplinary actions made by formal managers is equivalent to actions taken by large groups through consensus decision-making. Selecting one member of the group, however, to handle a poorly performing member resulted in relatively lenient disciplinary actions. . . . Individual group members are reluctant to assume responsibility for disciplining a poorly performing group member. . . . Granting responsibility for making disciplinary judgments to individual members of the group *may* result in excessively lenient decisions" (Liden, Wayne, and Kraimer 2001, 63, 69). Thus the mixed results from research can result from the various ways in which autonomous groups are operationalized; unconscious considerations can be unexpectedly activated.

CONCLUSIONS

Interpretations of the research on sociotechnical applications vary widely—from "an amazing success story" (Katz and Kahn 1978, 709) to expressions of major concerns (Roy 1969). These are just as variable as the findings themselves (see Miner 2006a, 2007). However, the sociotechnical approach does appear to reduce human resource needs. Due to multiskilling, the flexibility of the work organization, and the assumption of managerial tasks by the group, fewer people are needed. Individual labor costs may be higher, but typically total costs overall are not excessive.

As indicated at the beginning of this chapter, sociotechnical systems theory has a rated validity of three stars and an importance rating from organizational behavior of 5.09. Dividing the second value by the first value yields a figure of 1.70. Thus the field of organizational behavior in general tends to overestimate the presumed validity of the theory by a substantial degree. Sociotechnical theory is shown to be a predominantly conscious theory. Yet, as with most such theories, it is vulnerable at several points to unconscious processes.

Using the romance of teams concept, the team approach is shown to be overestimated and to some degree deficient. The evidence in support of teams is decidedly mixed, again suggesting that unconscious factors may well be involved. Teams simply do not perform as well as might be hoped, and this holds as well for autonomous teams. Hackman provides evidence that sociotechnical theory is lacking in its specification of three things: (1) what constitutes autonomous teams, (2) what is meant by individual differences, and (3) the implication of internal dynamics within groups. Sociotechnical theory antedates the positive emphasis in organizational behavior, but historically it has given support to theorizing of this type. Yet there are other findings that raise questions as to the effectiveness of autonomous teams as operationalized in promoting the performance of teams that utilize this approach. Such concerns involve the extent to which trust is involved, and the conduct of disciplinary procedures.

Evidence on the operation of unconscious factors in social relationships is contained in Chapters 5, 9, and 10 of this volume; further evidence will be presented in Chapter 30.

CHAPTER 28

SOCIOLOGICAL OPEN SYSTEMS THEORY

James Thompson's work is an open systems theory dealing with organization-environment relations and their effects. This work is presented primarily in a single volume (Thompson 1967), although it is amplified by editorial selections prepared by others after Thompson's death (Rushing and Zald 1976). In many respects the theory thus presented is comparable to the March and Simon (1958) volume *Organizations*. However, while the latter introduces its propositions based on the empirical research available at the time (see Chapter 22 in this volume), Thompson's propositions are of a conceptual nature. They were developed to deal with various major areas of concern in the study of organizations; there are fifty-nine numbered and thirty-four subsidiary propositions spread across nine topic areas.

This is a widely dispersed theory that is not susceptible to meta-analysis. Furthermore it is not of a kind that is easily subjected to empirical testing. Thompson was aware of that fact; he knew that his concepts were overly abstract and that they lacked operational definitions. He himself did not conduct research on his propositions. As a result the estimated validity of this sociological open systems theory is set at three stars; organizational behaviorists overall establish an importance rating of 5.60, and the theory has met the criteria for institutionalization (see Miner 2006a, Chapter 11). As Thompson recognized, the theory has not generated an abundance of research, and when it has, this research has often been off the mark, testing researchers' hypotheses more than Thompson's hypotheses. Although Thompson's propositions have often proved correct (to the extent that his abstractions allowed for judging them), there have been instances where they proved clearly wrong. Had Thompson applied his concepts, he might have found that the differences that appeared obvious to him at a high level of abstraction were not nearly as clear at an operational level (as a researcher or consultant).

MINER ON THOMPSON'S THEORY

I have had the following to say on this subject:

> Due to its high level of abstraction and the lack of operationalized constructs, Thompson's
> theory has inspired little research, and in those studies that have been done it is difficult to

determine whether they are true tests of the theory or not. Furthermore, because the theory lacks logical interconnectedness, the verification of one theoretical proposition often does not increase confidence in the truth of other propositions not yet tested. . . . For many [the theory] has provided a whole host of valuable concepts and a framework for the rational understanding of organizations and their actions, even if the hypothesized relationships remain untested or in some cases appear untenable.

There can be no question that Thompson's theoretical work is widely respected. Conceptually, it represented a major leap forward. Thompson used the deductive approach far more than any previous theorist to develop new constructs and new relationships. His work was, and remains, a tremendous creative accomplishment (Miner 2006a, 208).

THE RATIONALITY OF THE THEORY

Perhaps the conscious emphasis of Thompson's sociological open systems theory is best portrayed by the fact that propositions are typically qualified by the phrase "under norms of rationality." Treatments are consistently said to be subject to the criteria of rationality and to rationality norms. This is a theory that is presented as unabashedly rational, and accordingly it leaves little room for unconscious interpretations.

ON HOW OTHERS CONSIDER THOMPSON'S THEORY

Criticisms of this theory are few and far between, but they are to be found. I have discussed some of these:

Perrow's Views

As cited in Miner (2006a), Perrow, a well-known sociologist, argues that Thompson is:

> too uncritically accepting of current organizations and current organizational forms. He fails to deal with such problems as socially irresponsible behavior and illegal acts, the frustration of needs of lower-level employees by management, and the quality of work life (Perrow 1976). Perrow contends that Thompson was wrong in being so uncritical and that his contribution would have been much richer had he been less detached (rational?). Perrow's criticism is in many ways more philosophical than scientific; in his writings Thompson was not the humanist others might have wished him to be. From a scientific viewpoint a theorist has a right to define his domain, and as long as the domain is not trivial (and Thompson's clearly was not) he cannot be faulted on that score (2006a, 209).

Pondy and Mitroff's Views

A paper by Pondy and Mitroff (1979) takes Thompson's theory to task for not being open enough. In fact the authors view the theory as essentially closed and controlled because it utilizes such concepts as standardization, buffering, and smoothing, which are attempts to introduce high degrees of certainty and stability into the organization. Pondy and Mitroff maintain that organizations need variety in their environments, and without it they experience the equivalent of sensory deprivation (Miner 2006a, 209).

Argyris's Views (see Chapter 34)

Argyris maintains "that one must deal with the irrational as well as the rational, the informal as well as the formal, the psychological as well as the sociological, if one is to understand organizations. Furthermore, Argyris (1972, 26) views sociological open systems theory as 'an explication of scientific management and engineering economics.'" He further explains in *The Applicability of Organizational Sociology:*

> Although Thompson aspires to present a realistic integration of the formal and natural system, the integration actually made favors the closed system, traditional management, economically oriented model which he rejects as incomplete. The "variable human" seems to be minimally variable and minimally human. . . . Man turns out to be the closed system Thompson so cogently describes as ineffective for existing living systems. Group dynamics and interpersonal relations are not included (Argyris 1972, 33–34).

ROOM FOR POSSIBLE UNCONSCIOUS ELABORATIONS

Given the strong and comprehensive commitment to conscious theory that Thompson exhibits, one is loath to propose alternatives that extend beyond this domain. Yet were such alternatives to be adopted, there are certain points that recommend themselves, and indeed such an approach is supported by the views that have been cited in opposition to Thompson.

Power Dynamics

Thompson often mentions power processes, as in the inducement-contributions bargain, or in the discretion exercised by top management, or in the power exercised by the dominant coalition. Yet these are always sociological concepts of power inherent in structural relationships; they never involve the psychological need for power as addressed, for instance, by McClelland and his compatriots (see Chapter 4 in this volume). Perhaps the inclusion of the *need* for power could embellish on an understanding of what is involved. Such an approach seems warranted.

Uncertainty

The concept of uncertainty in macro theory is used by Thompson to include generalized uncertainty, contingency, and internal interdependence of components. Uncertainties come both from inside the organization and from outside (environmental processes). Quite frankly this construct represents a quagmire (see Miner 2006a, 242–248). It would seem that uncertainty is inherently something that resides in human decision-making processes. Uncertainty may be caused by environmental sources, but it may be influenced by many different forces as well. It would appear to be a characteristic that could invade a dominant coalition—a top management team, an influential group of professionals, an entrepreneurial coalition, an autonomous group, perhaps an individual decision maker in any one of these roles. Clearly, then, decisions involving uncertainty can be potentially influenced by unconscious considerations no matter where they came from. This aspect of their determination needs to be given consideration.

CONCLUSIONS

As indicated previously, sociological open systems theory (the Thompson version) has an estimated validity of three stars and an importance rating of 5.60 as specified by organizational behavior scholars. Dividing this latter figure by the three stars yields a ratio of 1.87, thus indicating a sizable overestimate of this theory's validity on the part of organizational behavior. Using this gauge Thompson's views emerge as one of the most pronounced in this respect, and clearly his formulations are predominantly rational; they are institutionalized, but they lack practical usefulness.

My own criticisms of this sociological open systems theory are based on the insufficiency of the research and on occasion on the fact that the research tends to refute the propositions set forth; thus they are of a scientific nature. However, others such as Perrow (1976), Pondy and Mitroff (1979), and Argyris (1972) take the theory to task on conceptual grounds. Although the theory is unabashedly rational and conscious, it seems to me that there are points at which it could benefit from research that utilizes unconscious methods—projective techniques, priming procedures, and the like. In particular I would add in investigations of power *needs* and research that considers unconscious influences in the making of decisions that involved uncertainty.

CHAPTER 29

CONTINGENCY THEORY OF ORGANIZATIONS: DIFFERENTIATION AND INTEGRATION

Informal Organization and the Failure of Differentiation
Integration and Coordination Neglect
Ambidexterity and the Differentiation-Integration Trade-Off
Consciousness and Rationality in Contingency Theory
Uncertainty
Applications
   Organization Development
   Matrix
Conclusions

The primary presentation of contingency theory in the field of macro organizational behavior is Lawrence and Lorsch (1967a). This was followed by several other volumes on this or related topics—Lorsch and Allen (1973), Lorsch and Morse (1974), and Lawrence and Dyer (1983). This chapter also includes the constructs of differentiation and integration, defined as follows:

> *Differentiation* . . . the difference in cognitive and emotions orientation among managers in different functional departments and the differences in formal structure among these departments.

> *Integration* . . . the quality of the state of collaboration that exists among departments that are required to achieve unity of effort by the demands of the environment (Lawrence and Lorsch 1967a, 11).

Differentiation among functional specialists almost invariably creates a potential for conflict. Integration is the means by which conflicts are resolved. At the very simplest level, integration is achieved through adjudication within the management hierarchy. However, sizable demands created by the environment, which are typically mediated through the degree of differentiation, require the use of more extensive integration devices at lower levels. Among these integrative positions are product manager, program coordinator, project leader, planning director, and systems designer, all of which cut across and link major subsystems (Lawrence and Lorsch 1967b).

The environment includes not only forces external to the organization, but also "the physical machinery, the nonhuman aspect of production" (Lawrence and Lorsch 1967a, 27). The authors maintain that uncertainty may reside in equipment, as well as factors outside the firm's boundaries. Uncertainty is a product of unclear information, uncertain causal relationships, and long feedback spans from the environment. Accordingly, uncertainty would be greater for the research components of an organization than for the production subsystem. Highly uncertain environments require high degrees of differentiation and integration for effective performance (a state of unstable equilibrium). More certain environments typically require neither.

There are three major variables here—differentiation, integration, and environmental uncertainty. Of these, differentiation and uncertainty remain somewhat suspect under the research microscope, while integration is more secure. There are no meaningful meta-analyses available. Thus the estimated validity is set at three stars, the importance rating derived from organizational behavior is at 5.39, the theory is institutionalized, and the practical usefulness based on organization development applications and the matrix structure carries a four-star rating (see Miner 2006a, 2007).

INFORMAL ORGANIZATION AND THE FAILURE
OF DIFFERENTIATION

I have noted that the differentiation concept fails to hold up well at the hands of research—in particular the research done by the Harvard people. This appears to be because informal institutions often intervene in the differentiation process.

> We define informal institutions, in turn, as rules based on implicit understandings, being in most part socially derived and therefore not accessible through written documents or necessarily sanctioned through formal position. Thus, informal institutions include social norms, routines, and political processes. . . . For the most part, formal institutions have been analyzed and evaluated quite independently of informal institutions. . . . Informal institutions strongly influence the functionality of organizational forms. . . . Formal and informal institutions differ in the pace with which they change. Informal institutions possess inertia that slows the pace of change (Zenger, Lazzarini, and Poppo 2002, 278, 281, 284).

Zenger, Lazzarini, and Poppo add: "Formal and informal institutions are not merely alternative ways to govern exchanges. In most cases they are employed simultaneously and interact in complex ways" (2002, 290). Thus informal processes may intervene in the formal role-making processes of differentiation and as a result lead them astray. This issue is also considered in Nickerson and Zenger (2002), with results that depart "significantly from contingent-fit theories of organization" (548) such as that of Lawrence and Lorsch (1967a).

INTEGRATION AND COORDINATION NEGLECT

I have also noted that integration has tended to hold up well as a construct when applied by the Harvard group and by other researchers. Yet there is reason to believe that integration has been largely ignored by the organizational behavior literature, and by others as well. Thus Heath and Staudenmayer (2000, 156) state:

> We analyze coordination neglect as a cognitive problem that is rooted in the lay theories people use to think about organizing and coordinating with others. People have intuitive, lay theories about many things—social interactions, statistical causality, economic markets (Kahneman, Slovic, and Tversky 1982; Furnham 1988)—and we suggest they also have lay theories about organization. All theories are incomplete, particularly lay theories, and we are interested in understanding the psychological blind spots in these theories that may cause people to neglect to coordinate their actions with others.

As Heath and Staudenmayer (2000, 171) put it, "People focus on the division of labor rather than on the equally important process of integration." This latter is influenced primarily by communication—or the lack thereof. Thus integration failure is caused primarily by inadequate communication, or what amounts to the same things, failures of translation.

AMBIDEXTERITY AND THE DIFFERENTIATION-INTEGRATION TRADE-OFF

In Chapter 24 we considered the need to create a balance between exploratory and exploitative units, and thus to utilize ambidexterity as explicated by James March. The differentiation-integration situation is essentially of the same nature.

> Our analysis of these linkages extends previous work on organizational ambidexterity. . . . In dynamic contexts, individuals often must make on-going, flexible trade-offs between existing aligned activities and new adaptive activities. . . . Ambidexterity may benefit from targeted integration involving co-specialized assets (Taylor and Helfat 2009, 735–736).

> Managers face both high differentiation as well as high interdependency, requiring frequent adjustments and more informal means of integration. . . . Our study presents a first step toward uncovering the interrelationship between differentiation, integration, and achieving ambidexterity. . . . Future longitudinal research is necessary to investigate how structural differentiation and integration are developed and impacted over time (Jansen, Tempelaar, van den Bosch, and Volberda 2009, 808).

My position would be that in such situations future research should focus on unconscious considerations, perhaps involving the use of priming, in an effort to tease out what is involved. In any event I would refer the reader to Kreschmer and Puranam (2008) for a formal model of the differentiation-integration context.

CONSCIOUSNESS AND RATIONALITY IN CONTINGENCY THEORY

Contingency theory is basically a conscious theory. Measures employed are primarily of the questionnaire type and tend to use interviews, occasionally extending to clinical insights. Planning is noted and information is conveyed through training programs involving skill training, experiential learning, and team building. Lorsch and Allen (1973) point to "the cognitive limitation imposed by individual information processing capabilities" (229). Elsewhere in connection with the matrix (Davis and Lawrence 1977) the sizable information-processing load imposed by that structure is noted. However, this approach to bounded rationality is not extended to processes that move beyond awareness; this remains primarily a conscious, cognitive theory.

The application of the theory to micro-organizational behavior is addressed in Table 29.1, and here too conscious processes appear to dominate. For a number of variables psychological tests were administered, but these would seem to be mostly of a self-report nature; the only use of projective measures reported is in measuring competence. Here several projectives are employed, including the Thematic Apperception Test (TAT). Cognitive complexity, tolerance for ambiguity, dependency in authority relationships, and preference for group interaction

Table 29.1

Examples of High Environment-Organization-Individual Fit in Production and Research and Development Units

	Manufacturing plant	Research laboratory
Nature of environment	Certain	Uncertain
Organizational structures and processes	Short time orientation	Long time orientation
	Strong techno-economic goals	Strong scientific goals
	High formality of structure	Low formality of structure
	Influence concentrated at the top— directive	Influence diffused through many levels— participative
	High coordination	Low coordination
	Confrontation to resolve conflicts	Confrontation to resolve conflicts
Individual characteristics	Low cognitive complexity	High cognitive complexity
	Low tolerance for ambiguity	High tolerance for ambiguity
	Dependency in authority relationships	Independence in authority relationships
	Preference for group interaction	Preference for working alone
	High feeling of competence	High feeling of competence
Performance outcome	Effective	Effective

Source: Adapted from Lorsch and Morse (1974, 52, 112).

seem to be subject to influence by unconscious considerations, but they are not measured in such a way as to permit this; they should be.

Overall the results obtained with the various measures do match the differentiation-integration hypothesis in a number of instances. However, these findings can be explained without recourse to the environmental level, and thus to the dimension of certainty and uncertainty.

UNCERTAINTY

We have met the environmental uncertainty moderator previously in dealing with Thompson's theory (Chapter 28 of this volume) and found it wanting. Nothing that is said here in this chapter leads to a more favorable impression. The data provided do not support this factor as a moderator. Uncertainty is utilized in these theories because it incorporates the environment beyond the boundaries of the organization and thus creates an open systems perspective. However, it is not clear to me that including such an open systems perspective is warranted. Consider the following:

> One criticism that has been levied against coping theories is that they are excessively cognitive and rational. . . . Crisis decision theory leaves ample room for motivational and goal-oriented processes. . . . Processing at each stage of crisis decision theory may be more or less automatic. Much of human experience is nonconscious (Bargh 1994; Bargh and Chartrand 1999) and conscious processing is often disadvantageous due to the depletion of mental and

energy resources (Baumeister 2002). In the case of responding to negative events, engaging in relatively automatic processing at each stage benefits people by reserving their resources. . . . People rarely know with certainty or precision the outcomes their behaviors will produce, so they must choose responses without this knowledge. A great deal of research has examined judgments in uncertainty conditions (e.g. Kahneman, Slovic, and Tversky 1982) but future research can specifically address the degree of certainty people require before choosing a response to a negative event. Likewise, future research can also examine the amount of information people need for assessing severity and evaluating response options before they are willing to select a response. Availability of cognitive resources, potential for the negative event to worsen, and accountability may affect the degree of uncertainty people are willing to tolerate (Sweeny 2008, 70, 73). Thus, invoking uncertainty (of any kind) invariably introduces the potential for unconscious intervention, and this unconscious intervention needs to be measured and studied.

APPLICATIONS

Contingency theory is included in the theories that generate applications for two reasons—an organization development procedure and a matrix structure (see Miner 2006a). Both applications have produced new contributions to the literature recently.

Organization Development

A major contribution to the organization development literature of recent origins is the Cummings-edited *Handbook of Organization Development* (2008). This volume contains a chapter by Chris Argyris, whose theoretical work is discussed in Chapter 34 of this volume.

Matrix

The recent work on the matrix structure is reviewed by Galbraith (2009). Here roughly 25 percent of firms that have adopted matrix-like structures are reported to have been successful, a finding that continues to emphasize the difficulties inherent in this approach. Much of the communication in successful matrix organizations is of an informal nature and thus uses a largely voluntary type of coordination or integration.

CONCLUSIONS

Contingency theory in its macro-organizational behavior version, as indicated at the beginning of this chapter, possesses a validity of three stars and a rating on importance from organization behavior scholars of 5.39. Dividing as appropriate (the second value by the first) gives a ratio of 1.80. Consequently the importance rating appears to represent a sizable overestimate on the part of organizational behavior.

The theory uses the constructs of differentiation, integration, and—to make it an open systems theory—environmental uncertainty. Of these differentiation is often compromised by the interjection of informal institutions. Integration does quite well at the hands of research investigation but suffers in the literature from coordination neglect. The ambidexterity phenomenon involving exploration and exploitation is quite similar to the differentiation-integration situation in that both instances require a balance.

Contingency theory is primarily a conscious theory, although the cognitive limitations of bounded rationality are noted, and certain projective measures are used on occasion to supplement the more frequently employed self-report indexes. Environmental uncertainty, like differentiation, leaves something to be desired as a construct. Furthermore, it does not appear to be needed to explain what findings do emerge from the research. Unconscious considerations need to be studied more fully as they interact with the uncertainty of the decision process.

Further work has been done on applications of contingency theory, including organization development and the matrix structure. These extend what was said in Miner (2007).

CHAPTER 30

RALPH STOGDILL'S GROUP-FOCUSED SYSTEMS THEORY

Ralph Stogdill's theory is a systems theory with the usual emphasis on inputs, mediating variables, and outputs. As originally presented it represented on attempt to model its organizational behavior theory on work in psychology, and more specifically on group dynamics (Stogdill 1959). This version deals at length with group processes; there is relatively little that involves the organization as a whole and its exchange with the environment. The definitions and discussion are largely behavioral and are concerned primarily with actions. Thus the focus is on conscious processes and not with the unconscious. In Stogdill (1962) environmental processes are given some attention, but there is also further development of the group model. Later work by Stogdill (1966) recognized the fact that the theory lacked a truly organizational underpinning and a more fully developed open systems perspective; thus such considerations as mores, norms, intuitions, and cultures were added, marking the theory's trend toward including factors of an unconscious nature.

Treatment of the Stogdill theory is contained in Miner (2002, Chapter 13) and the rating data are given in Miner (2006b, Chapter 17). There the estimated validity is at three stars and the importance rating from organizational behavior has a mean value of 3.44. Practical usefulness is minimal. Although Stogdill did conduct considerable research using various versions of his theory, the results appear to have been quite mixed (see Stogdill 1965, 1972). There are no meta-analyses that can be brought to bear, and the 1966 version was not tested.

PRIOR TREATMENTS OF GROUP PROCESSES

There are several treatments of group and social processes that need to be brought to bear here using references cited in this volume. The reader is asked to refer to the following list of sources.

Chapter 5 on Social and Affiliation Motivation

- Markman and Gentner 2005
- Dijksterhuis, Chartrand, and Aarts 2007
- Chartrand, Maddux, and Lakin 2005
- van Baaren, Holland, Kawakami, and van Knippenberg 2004
- Miner 2008, Chapter 2
- Andersen, Reznik, and Glassman 2005
- Reis and Collins 2004
- Shah 2005
- Chen, Fitzsimons, and Andersen 2007
- Smith and Conrey 2007
- Kruglanski and Pierro 2008
- Maccoby 2004
- Uleman, Blader, and Todorov 2005
- Hall and Andrzejewski 2008
- Huang and Bargh 2008
- Allen and Hecht 2004

Collectively these references make the point that research on unconscious processes frequently intervenes to influence social and affiliation motivation.

Chapter 9 on Relatedness Needs

Beyond the references noted above, this chapter includes:

- Harris and Garris 2008
- Choi, Gray, and Ambady 2005

This chapter adds further evidence as to the unconscious nature of relatedness needs.

Chapter 10 on Transference

New references included here are taken from:

- Chartrand, Dalton, and Cheng 2008

This reference extends the previous references to how transference operates.

FURTHER POINTS ON THE GROUP-FOCUSED THEORY THAT MIGHT REQUIRE ATTENTION

In addition to the references from prior chapters, there are several findings from the current literature that should be given consideration.

Where the Findings Indicate Research on Unconscious Processes Might Be Invoked

> Greater group identification and higher levels of procedural justice typically work together to encourage group members to engage in group-serving cooperative behavior. However, when people who already identify with a group receive information indicating that the group is procedurally unjust, their motivation to engage in group-serving behavior may increase. This article reports two studies. . . . The findings of both studies support the hypothesis that among people who are highly identified with a group, learning about the group's injustice leads to short-term increases in group-serving behavior (Barry and Tyler 2009, 1026).

> In this article, we describe a new intervention strategy for improving intergroup relations: imagined intergroup contact. Preliminary empirical research has shown that the approach is deceptively simple but remarkable effective. Encouraging people to mentally simulate a positive encounter with someone from an outgroup promotes more positive attitudes toward that group. Imagined contact provides a firmly grounded intervention strategy (Crisp and Turner 2009, 238).

> The current investigation tested whether low belongingness increases a particular form of social monitoring that has recently been documented in the cognitive literature: gaze-triggered orienting. Low belongingness was operationalized either in terms of low trait self-esteem . . . or in terms of the priming of rejection-related thoughts. . . . Across the studies the normal tendency to orient attention in accordance with another individual's eye gaze was augmented under conditions of low belongingness. However, belongingness had no influence on a nonsocial form of orienting (Wilkowski, Robinson, and Friesen 2009, 495).

> This experiment examined the ability of pride to serve as an adaptive emotion within the context of social interaction. After an in vivo induction of pride or a neutral state, participants engaged in a group problem-solving task. In contrast to a conventional view that pride is often associated with negative interpersonal outcomes, results confirmed that proud individuals not only took on a dominant role within the group problem-solving task, but also were perceived as the most likeable interaction partners. . . . Pride . . . constitutes a functional social emotion with important implications (Williams and DeSteno 2009, 284).

> Recent findings from the masked priming paradigm have revealed a surprising influence of higher-lever cognitive systems (i.e., attention) on nonconscious cognitive processes. . . . Here we present evidence for a middle position by showing that the dependence of nonconscious processes on attention varies with the type of information to be processed. . . . These qualitatively different patterns suggest two distinct processing routes: one that is modulated by visual attention and one that is not (Finkbeiner and Palermo 2009, 42).

Metaphors and Unconscious Processes

> Metaphors such as icy stare depict social exclusion using cold-related concepts. . . . Two experiments . . . revealed that social exclusion literally feels cold. Experiment 1 found that participants who recalled a social exclusion experience gave lower estimates of room temperature than did participants who recalled an inclusion experience. In Experiment 2, social exclusion was directly induced through an on-line virtual interaction, and participants who were excluded reported greater desire for warm food and drink than did participants who were included (Zhong and Leonardelli 2008, 838).

Although such effects of metaphorical representations on the unconscious may seem strange, there is in fact evidence of this kind in the organizational behavior literature (see Andriessen and Gubbins 2009; Pablo and Hardy 2009).

Social Engagement and Cognition in Old Age

It may also be helpful to provide some relevant quotes regarding the relation between social engagement and cognitive decline with advancing age (see Hertzog, Kramer, Wilson, and Lindenberger 2008, 32–34).

> There is also longitudinal evidence supporting the hypothesis that social engagement has beneficial effects on cognition in old age. . . . Those persons with higher engagement experienced less cognitive decline. . . . Studies focusing exclusively on measuring social activity and participation have yielded positive results . . . whereas analyses of social-network size have had mixed results. . . . Overall, these studies suggest that persons who are more socially active and who do not feel socially disconnected experience less cognitive decline than do their less-active and more-disconnected counterparts. Studies of social engagement and dementia have yielded similar results. . . . Taken together, these data support the idea that a higher level of social engagement is related to a reduced risk of cognitive decline and dementia in old age. The basis of the association is not well understood, however.

STOGDILL ON NORMS AND CULTURES

As Stogdill moved toward true organizations (rather than extrapolations from small groups) and to an open systems perspective, he introduced a number of aspects of the social environment that went beyond the group-focused systems theory with which he originally started. In this aspect of the theory he had the following to say:

> The social environment must be regarded as a far more potent force than the physical environment in determining the purpose and form of organization. Religious belief has played a major part in the development of large, complex, stable societies.
>
> In recent centuries, particularly in Western cultures, religious doctrine has yielded considerably as the ultimate source of organization and governmental authority. Common law and political philosophy have been utilized increasingly as bases or criteria for the legitimation of organization. . . .

The economic philosophy, norms, and institutions of a society determine in part the purpose, form, and structure of the organizations it will develop. . . . Most societies develop professional specialists who have influence and often authority by virtue of their specialized knowledge and skills. If the specialists are numerous enough to form a professional society, the society is likely to formulate norms and standards. . . .

The norms of the fraternal and philanthropic organization of a society may permeate and influence the conduct of all organizations in the society. Family norms and local norms may also influence the practices of the organizations . . . (Stogdill 1966, 41–44).

This clearly is a very different type of theory than the group-focused theory with which Stogdill began.

PRIOR TREATMENTS ON NORMS AND CULTURES

Accordingly this formulation carries with it a much stronger commitment to unconscious processes rather than the conscious emphasis of the group-focused theory. References cited previously are noted below.

Chapter 3 on Group Norms

- Bamberger and Biron 2007
- Fitzsimons and Bargh 2004

Chapter 7 on Organizational Culture

- Erdogan, Liden, and Kraimer 2006

Chapter 11 on Creativity, Cultures, and Roles

- Ryan and Deci 2000
- Deci and Ryan 1985
- Morling and Kitayama 2008
- Patall, Cooper, and Robinson 2008
- Oyserman and Lee 2008
- Jennifer Miner in Miner 2008, Chapter 32
- Miner and Raju in Miner 2008, Chapter 27

Chapter 23 on the Role of Organizational Culture

- Beach 2006
- Beach 1993
- McCrae and Terracciano 2006
- Uleman 2005
- Huffman, Nahallage, and Leca 2008
- Leung, Maddux, Galinsky, and Chiu 2008
- Maddux, Leung, Chiu, and Galinsky 2009

- George 2008
- Madjar and Shalley 2008
- Sivanathan, Pillutla, and Murnighan 2008
- Fast, Gruenfeld, Sivanathan, and Galinsky 2009

On Professional Norms

Picking up on another type of norm to which Stogdill had reference, I would recommend Miner 2008, Chapters 9, 12, 19, 22, and 31, which consider various aspects of the professional process.

All of these prior treatments regarding Stogdill's endorsements of norms and cultures bring out a common point: this version leads to a theory that seems to operate from an unconscious perspective, in contrast to the earlier conscious orientation. Thus in the end—given the diametrically opposed nature of Stogdill's theories—I conclude that his is a balanced formulation overall.

CONCLUSIONS

As noted at the beginning of this presentation, Stogdill's theory overall has an estimated validity of three stars and an importance rating of 3.44. When the latter is divided by the former, the result is a factor of 1.15. As a consequence there is a slight overestimate of the presumed validity of the theory by the organizational behavior sample.

Given the balanced nature of Stogdill's theorizing overall, this is clearly aligned with expectations. From prior treatments it is apparent that the group-focused theory originally proposed has an essentially conscious or rational orientation, although there are numerous points at which unconscious processes might well intervene to interject a very different approach. The emphasis on norms and cultures proposed in Stogdill's later theory introduces a whole new type of conceptualization: a theoretical view that invokes much more of an unconscious perspective. Since the two theories ultimately come to stand side by side, they are best considered to be balanced.

PART V

BUREAUCRACY-RELATED CONCEPTS

WEBER'S THEORY OF BUREAUCRACY

Max Weber's theories were initially introduced in the German; he was known best for his thesis that the rise of Protestantism in previously Catholic Europe provoked the development of capitalism (Weber 1930). In this view, the Protestant ethic said that God intended profitability, and blessed it also; that waste and failure to devote time to profitable labor was contrary to God's will; that division of labor was to be desired since it contributed to the amount and quality of production; and that hard work was to be a large extent a duty to God, thus contributing to the accumulation of wealth. This tendency to rewrite history was perpetuated in Weber's later writings on bureaucracy, which were introduced to the English-speaking world through a series of translations (Weber 1946, 1947, 1968). However, there was considerable delay before this occurred.

A number of meta-analyses of Weber's theorizing on bureaucracy have appeared, with the most recent and complete being Walton (2005). This analysis provides "substantial support for the model of bureaucratic control" (1481). Accordingly I have given the theory a four-star rating; the 71 participants from organizational behavior provide a performance rating of 5.90 and indicate that the theory is institutionalized (see Miner 2006a, Chapter 14; also reproduced in Miner 2006b as Chapter 10; see also Miner 2007, Chapter 20). Judging the practical usefulness of the theory of bureaucracy is a difficult matter, since it is hard to differentiate what preceded Weber from what followed upon his descriptions and thus may have been caused by them.

ON CONSCIOUSNESS AND RATIONALITY IN WEBER'S THEORY

Weber's theorizing on bureaucracy is widely recognized as presenting a rational theory. Frequent references occur along these lines—to rationally established rules, rationally organized action, rational norms, rationalized bureaucracy, rational conditioning, rationally operationing staff and rational legal authority. This latter has been set equal to value rationality as it occurs in professional work (Satow 1975), although there has been some quarrel with this particular designation recently (see Adler, Kwon, and Heckscher 2008). In any event it seems apparent that conscious (rational) processes are extensively associated with and used to describe this particular version of bureaucracy. Weber continually notes that his theory is predicated on the use of rational-legal authority, and he attributes hierarchy to this source.

The categories of rational-legal authority are described as follows:

1. A continuous rule-bound conduct of official business.
2. A specified sphere of competence (jurisdiction). This involves:
   a. A sphere of obligations to perform functions which have been marked off as part of a systematic division of labor.
   b. The provision of the incumbent with the necessary powers.
   c. That the necessary means of compulsion are clearly defined and their use is subject to definite conditions. . . .
3. The organization of offices follows the principle of *hierarchy;* that is, each lower office is under the control and supervision of a higher one. . . .
4. The rules which regulate the conduct of an office may be technical rules or norms.
5. It is a matter of principle that the members of the administrative staff should be completely separated from ownership of the means of production. . . . There exists, furthermore, in principle complete separation of the organization's property (respectively capital), and the personal property (household) of the official.
6. There is also a complete absence of appropriation of his official position by the incumbent. . . .
7. Administrative acts, decisions, and rules are formulated and recorded in writing.
8. Legal authority can be exercised in a wide variety of different forms (Weber 1968, 218–219).

ON CHARISMA AND IRRATIONALITY IN WEBER'S THEORY

With all this emphasis on conscious processes and rational considerations, Weber also incorporated an irrational or unconscious factor into his theory—this had to do with charisma. Charismatic authority is personal: The leader's personality interacts with followers so that they attribute supernatural, superhuman, or at least exceptional powers to the leader. Charismatic authority rests on recognition by others and results in complete devotion to the leader. The hierarchical powers on which charisma is based must be demonstrated frequently and serve to benefit the followers, or authority will disappear. Typically, a charismatic community emerges over which the leader often exercises arbitrary control. *Irrationality* and emotional ties are characteristic. Economic considerations are downplayed. Free of ties to rules, whether rationally or traditionally derived, this kind of authority can be a major force for change and revolution. Weber tends to attribute Godlike features to charismatic leaders of this kind; charismatic changes often have religious inspiration. An example of charisma-based change of this kind taken from the Chinese experience is provided by Andreas (2007).

> Historically, many organizations have developed from a structure of charismatic authority, to rational-legal, to traditional, and then as traditional authority has failed, they have returned to the revolutionary charismatic form. Charismatic authority alone is highly unstable. The charismatic community that maintains itself over time must become rationalized or traditionalized to some degree. This *routinization of charisma* is particularly important to any succession that may occur.

Evidence of Unconscious Determination from Terror Management

In Chapter 17 of this volume dealing with the Bass (1985) and House (1977) theories, evidence is presented that charismatic leadership is indeed associated with unconscious factors. This evidence derives from the terror management research (see Cohen, Solomon, Maxfield, Pyszczynski, and Greenberg 2004) involving mortality salience primes (Landau, Solomon, Greenberg, Cohen, Pyszczynski, Arndt et al. 2004). (See as well Higgins, Kruglanski, and Pierro 2003; Benjamin and Flynn 2006.)

A recent article on the interpretation of death awareness research modifies this position (Grant and Wade-Benzoni 2009). It recognizes the difficulty of measuring the phenomena involved via self-reports and suggests another approach that appears to replicate the use of projective techniques to get at unconscious activation. Furthermore, it does not cite DeWall and Baumeister (2007), which appears relevant, and particularly emphasizes the role of unconscious motivations in mortality salience studies. Thus I continue to support what was said in Chapter 17, taking the position that Weber's treatment of charisma amounts to an endorsement of unconscious processes as reflected most prominently in his discussions of irrationality.

Further Evidence on the Unconscious Nature of Charisma

Shariff and Norenzayan (2007) present studies intended to resolve whether religion increases prosocial behavior in a business game. They note:

> Subjects allocated more money to anonymous strangers when God concepts were implicitly activated than when neutral or no concepts were activated. This effect was at least as large as that obtained when concepts associated with secular moral institutions were primed. A trait measure of self-reported religiosity did not seem to be associated with prosocial behavior (803).

EVIDENCE ON THE UNCONSCIOUS NATURE OF POWER AND AUTHORITY IN BUREAUCRACY

There is also evidence that the power and authority envisioned by bureaucracy can be enhanced on an unconscious basis:

> Across three experiments, and using two different instantiations of power, we found that power led to perceived control over outcomes that were uncontrollable or unrelated to the power. Power predicted perceived control over a chance event (Experiment 1), over outcomes in domains that were unrelated to the source of power (Experiment 2), and over future outcomes that were virtually impossible for any one individual to control . . . (Experiment 3). Furthermore, this inflated sense of control mediated power's positive effects on optimism (Experiment 2), self-esteem (Experiment 3), and action orientation (Experiment 3). A final experiment ruled out positive mood as an alternative explanation for the observed effects of power (Experiment 4). . . . Our experiments also help to shed light on why the powerful often seem to exhibit hubristic overconfidence (Fast, Gruenfeld, Sivanathan, and Galinsky 2009, 506–507).

In this same vein—"people over-react to an increase in power, but . . . they react appropriately to a loss in power" (Sivanathan, Pillutla, and Murnighan 2008, 135).

CONCLUSIONS

As I mentioned earlier in this chapter, Weber's bureaucracy theory possesses an estimated validity of four stars and an importance rating at the very highest level of 5.90. Calculating the ratio of 5.90 divided by 4.00 yields 1.48—a figure that should be evaluated in the context of a theory that by its very nature possesses both a rational element and an irrational component (charisma), and thus is basically *balanced.* The charisma estimation is consistent with that applied in Chapter 17 to other theories that utilize charismatic leadership. The rational element is extensively apparent in Weber's writings and in evaluations of this theoretical position. It is also apparent in the emphasis on hierarchy.

Yet Weber contrasts this rational emphasis with the charismatic leadership that also informs his theory. Here religion is part of the leadership inspiration, and subsequent routinization of charisma tends to mitigate Weber's emphasis on unconscious considerations. Also the evidence from terror management on charisma is blunted to a degree by other interpretations. Overall, however, there can be no question that unconscious factors do operate in charismatic leadership, and thus do contribute to what happens in bureaucratic theory. God concepts as they may occur in charisma do have an unconscious nature.

Furthermore, the emphasis on power and authority in bureaucratic theory as enunciated by Weber clearly serves to expand the scope of this variable from an unconscious perspective. Power is extended to hubristic overconfidence by those who hold it, and it operates beyond awareness to exaggerate its impact.

CHAPTER 32

THE THEORY UNDERGIRDING
THE ASTON STUDIES

Macro Results
    The Nature of Centralization
    The Taxonomy of Bureaucratic Structures
Micro Results
On Technology
Performance Relationships
Conclusions

The Aston studies were designed primarily to test Max Weber's theory as well as classical management theory (see Chapter 11 of Miner 2006b) and the technological aspects of Joan Woodward's (1958) formulations. Initially they were conceived by Derek Pugh, David Hickson, and C.R. (Bob) Hinings, but other later contributors include Diane Pheysey, Kerr Inkson, Roy Payne, Lex Donaldson, John Child, and Charles McMillan (Greenwood and Devine 1997). The studies themselves are contained in a four-volume set (Pugh and Hickson 1976; Pugh and Hinings 1976; Pugh and Payne 1977; Hickson and McMillan 1981). The original work was done at the Birmingham College of Technology, which later became the University of Aston in Birmingham. Nowhere is this Aston theory formally stated, although it is interspersed throughout the four volumes and a number of additional articles; basically it is based on Weber's theory of bureaucracy.

The major structural variables involved include:

- *Specialization*—the degree to which activities are divided into specialized roles, the number of different specialist roles established.
- *Standardization of workflow activities*—the degree to which standard rules and procedures for processing and controlling work exist.
- *Standardization of employment practices*—the degree to which standardized employment practices in, for example, recruiting, promoting, and disciplining employees exist.
- *Formalization*—the degree to which instructions, procedures, and the like are written down and documented, then filed.
- *Centralization*—the degree to which authority to make decisions is located at the top of the management hierarchy.
- *Configuration*—a blanket concept used to cover factors derived from the organization chart: (1) the length of the chain of command, (2) the size of spans of control, (3) the percentage of specialized or support personnel (Pugh 1976, 65).

These are the constructs entered into the macroanalyses, although additional microvariables were studied as well. Certain dimensions were established for the context within which this structure operated:

- *Origin and history*—whether the organization was privately founded and if changes were made in such factors as ownership and location.
- *Ownership and control*—type of ownership, whether private or public, and the degree of concentration of ownership.
- *Size*—the number of employees, net assets held, extent of market position, and the like.
- *Charter*—the nature and range of goods and services.
- *Technology*—the degree of integration in the organization's work process.
- *Location*—the number of geographically dispersed operating sites.
- *Dependence*—the extent of dependence on customers, suppliers, trade unions, owning groups, and the like (Pugh 1976, 71).

These are the constructs entered into the macroanalyses, which are the source of the most important contributions from the Aston research. Additional microvariables will be considered shortly.

Based on factor analysis, groupings of the basic variables were established as follows:

- *Structuring of activities*—combining specialization, standardization, and formalization into one construct.
- *Centralization of decisions (concentration of authority)*—combining centralization with the existence of considerable decision-making power in a higher-level chief executive, board, or council (in the case of a subsidiary). Standardization of employment activities loads on this factor.
- *Line control of workflow*—combining aspects of configuration (high percentage of line subordinates, low ratio of subordinates to superiors), with impersonal control through formalization of role performance (a component of formalization). Operational (but not personnel) control resides in the line hierarchy.

"These basic dimensions . . . are very much the stuff of which bureaucracy is made. Conceptually they stand in the Weberian tradition" (Pugh and Hickson 1976, 4). And again, "We must first of all isolate the conceptually distinct elements that go into Weber's formulation of bureaucracy. . . . The insights of Weber can then be translated into a set of empirically testable hypotheses" (28). That is what the Aston researchers attempted to do.

Certain other constructs beyond those noted previously are utilized on occasion:

- *Flexibility*—a structural variable involving the determination of changes over a period of time—the amount, the speed, the acceleration, and so on.
- *Charter*—a contextual variable describing the purpose and ideology of the organization.
- *Resources*—a contextual variable dealing with the human, ideational, financial, and material resources at an organization's disposal.

Performance is said to be represented by an organization's success in reaching its stated goals in various areas. Little use is made of performance variables in the research, however. There is also some variation in the specific constructs designated and the nature of their operationalization.

A number of meta-analyses are available. These include Miller (1987), Damanpour (1991), and Camisón-Zornoza, Lapiedra-Alcamí, Segarra-Ciprés, and Boronat-Novarro (2004).

Table 32.1

Correlations among Structural Measures and Involving Contextual Variables from the Original Aston Study

Structural measures	Specialization		Standardization		Formalization	
	Functional	Overall	Personnel procedures	Overall	Performance recording	Overall
Specialization						
Functional						
Overall	0.87*					
Standardization						
Personnel procedures	−0.15	0.09				
Overall	0.76*	0.80*	0.23			
Formalization						
Performance recording	0.66*	0.54*	−0.12	0.72*		
Overall	0.57*	0.68*	0.38*	0.83*	0.75*	
Centralization	−0.64*	−0.53*	0.30*	−0.27	−0.27	−0.20

Contextual variables	Structuring of activities	Concentration of authority (centralization)	Line control of workflow
Size of organization (employees)	0.69*	−0.10	0.15
Workflow integration (technology)	0.34*	−0.30*	−0.46*
Dependence	−0.05	0.66*	0.13

Source: Adapted from Pugh and Hickson (1976, 57, 100, 103, 141).
*Correlations statistically significant.

MACRO RESULTS

Results from the original Aston study and from later replications are contained in Tables 32.1 and 32.2. Table 32.1 is a reproduction of Table 15.1 of Miner 2006a and Table 32.2 is a reproduction of Table 15.2 in the same source.

The Nature of Centralization

Note that the centralization findings do not meet expectations, nor do they replicate completely. With regard to these data Pugh and Hinings (1976) explain the pervasive support for decentralization as follows:

> Discussion of centralization using the Aston schedule needs to be handled with care. The Aston measure had low reliability in the initial study. . . . Centralization is a more complex concept than standardization (and formalization). . . . In the case of centralization, the original measure has clear weaknesses, and subsequent findings based on it are confusing (172).

In fact, although the Aston studies do support Weber in general, Weber's position on centralization is not really clear; thus Weber and Aston appear equally uncertain.

Table 32.2

Significant Correlations among Structural Variables: National and Southeast England Studies

	Functional specialization	Formalization	Proportion of managers	Levels of hierarchy
Formalization				
National	0.69			
Southeast	0.70			
Proportion of managers				
National	—	—		
Southeast	0.31	0.28		
Levels of hierarchy				
National	0.51	0.48	—	
Southeast	0.63	0.56	—	
Centralization—overall				
National	−0.28	−0.53	—	−0.41
Southeast	−0.63	−0.43	—	−0.46
By decision type (all Southeast)				
Production	−0.63	−0.46	—	−0.52
Marketing	−0.30	—	—	—
Budget change	—	—	—	—
Personnel and buying	−0.58	−0.48	—	−0.63
Organizational change	−0.42	−0.34	—	—

Source: Adapted from Child (1972a, 169) and Grinyer and Yasai-Ardekani (1980, 412–413).

The Taxonomy of Bureaucratic Structures

One place where the Aston studies did deviate from Weber is in proposing a number of subtypes of bureaucracy based on factor analysis. This proposal, however, failed to receive empirical support. Mansfield (1973) goes so far as to suggest that the Weberian concept of a single bureaucratic type not be abandoned in favor of the empirical taxonomy. This interpretation has met with general approval.

MICRO RESULTS

Another instance where hypotheses advanced by the Aston researchers have deviated from Weber is with regard to what they call the administrative reduction of variance thesis. In this case, too, Weber has turned out to be more right than wrong (see the Damanpour ([991] meta-analysis). Thus Pugh and Payne (1977) summarize this excursion into microanalysis:

> The negative psychological consequences of bureaucracy predicted by many writers on organizations do not appear in any strong and consistent way. . . . The administrative reduction of variance thesis does not apply in any simple way at the lower levels of management and supervision. . . . Bureaucratic structures can provide satisfying work environments. . . . The climate studies show no evidence that less attractive climates consistently occur in bureaucratic structures (160–162).

All in all the Aston studies yield much greater support for Weber's theory of bureaucracy than for the variations on that theme that the researchers themselves have introduced.

ON TECHNOLOGY

But what about the hypothesis regarding technology transported from Woodward (1958)? The Aston researchers argue on the basis of their data that size—not technology—is the governing variable, thus tending to ally themselves more with Weber. Hickson, Pugh, and Pheysey conclude:

> Structural variables will be associated with operations technology only where they are centered on the workflow. The smaller the organization, the more its structure will be pervaded by such technological effects; the larger the organization, the more these effects will be confined to variables such as job counts of employees on activities linked with the workflow itself, and will not be detectable in variables of the more remote administrative and hierarchical nature (Hickson, Pugh, and Pheysey 1969, 394–395).

PERFORMANCE RELATIONSHIPS

The results from all of the attempts to link performance with study variables appears to have failed; thus Donaldson (1976) reports that analyses of the relationships involving organization structures show little association with performance, and nothing to support Woodward.

CONCLUSIONS

The Aston studies as reported by Derek Pugh, David Hickson, Robert Hinings, and various others were intended to provide a test of Weber's theory of bureaucracy. The beginning of this chapter contains evaluation data for this theory—an estimated validity of four stars and an importance rating of 4.28, for a ratio of 1.07. This figure indicates a balanced evaluation of the theory undergirding the Aston studies.

As a test of Weber's theory, the Aston theory performs well on structural considerations such as specialization, standardization, and formalization, but the results on centralization are inconsistent with expectations and confirm Weber's uncertainties on this score. In general the macro expectations of Weber's theory are supported, but the diversified concepts of bureaucracy's subtypes are not. Nor is there support for the Aston studies in their interpretation of the microanalyses. Contrary to the Woodward concept of the role of technology, the Aston researchers found size to be the more operative variable, in line with Weber. However, the results obtained using performance as a criterion did not contribute to the effectiveness of the Weber theory.

Overall Weber's theory of bureaucracy holds up well against the Aston conclusions, but the innovations those researchers introduced as modifications to Weber do not do as well. In these analyses it is assumed that the Weber theory of bureaucracy remains a balanced theory, as posited in Chapter 31; it is after all the thesis against which the Aston propositions are tested.

PETER BLAU'S THEORY
OF DIFFERENTIATION

Peter Blau's theory of structural differentiation in organizations was developed at much the same time as the Aston formulations (see Chapter 32 of this volume). Both used Weber as their base, and both serve to test Weber's theory of bureaucracy (but in somewhat different ways). Blau does depart from Weber in certain respects, but he also recognizes that bureaucratic structures are essential to the utilization of complex technologies and to the support of arrangements involving division of labor, both of which yield major benefits. On Weber himself, Blau notes: "Perhaps the most difficult task for a scholar is to develop a new approach to the study of reality. . . . It is no exaggeration to say that Weber was one of the rare men who have done just this" (Blau 1974, 57).

Blau wrote about and did research on bureaucracy as well as a number of other topics of a sociological nature. He is especially well known for his contributions to social exchange theory (Blau 1964, 1977; see also Phillips, Rothbard, and Dumas 2009). However, our major concern is with his work on bureaucracy. In this area the validity of his theorizing is set at four stars and receives an importance rating of 4.31 from organizational behavior experts (see Miner 2006a, Chapter 16; 2007, Chapter 22). The validity evaluation is based in part on a meta-analysis conducted by Donaldson (1996), which is heavily weighted with Blau's own studies (see Blau and Schoenherr 1971; Blau, Falbe, McKinley, and Tracy 1976).

DIFFERENTIATION IN ORGANIZATIONS

Building on the results of a study of governmental employment security units, Blau developed a largely deductive theory of differentiation in organizations that primarily extends Weber's position rather than opposes it. Differentiation occurs when the number of geographical branches, occupational positions, hierarchical levels, and divisions (or units within branches or divisions) increases. The hypotheses are the following:

The Original Statement

1. Increasing size generates structural differentiation in organizations along various dimensions at decelerating rates.

1A. Large size promotes structural differentiation.
1B. Large size promotes differentiation along several different lines.
1C. The rate of differentiation declines with expanding size.
1.1. As the size of organizations increases, its marginal influence on differentiation decreases.
1.2. The larger an organization is, the larger is the average size of its structural components of all kinds.
1.3. The proportionate size of the average structural component, as distinguished from the absolute size, decreases with increases in organizational size.
1.4. The larger the organization is, the wider the supervisory span of control.
1.5. Organizations exhibit an economy of scale in management.
1.6. The economy of scale in administrative overhead itself declines with increasing organization size.
2. Structural differentiation in organizations enlarges the administrative component.
2.1. The large size of an organization indirectly raises the ratio of administrative personnel through the structural differentiation it generates.
2.2. The direct effects of large organizational size lowering the administrative ratio exceed its indirect effects raising it owing to the structural differentiation it generates.
2.3. The differentiation of large organizations into subunits stems the decline in the economy of scale in management with increasing size (Blau 1974, 302–317).

The Recent Restatement

These propositions have been restated more recently as follows:

First, the large size of organizations increases their differentiation in various dimensions at decelerating rates. This is the case whether the division of labor, vertical levels, horizontal subdivisions, or other forms of differentiation are examined. For every form of differentiation, in other words, the size of an organization is positively related to the extent of differentiation, but all these correlations are most pronounced for smaller organizations and become increasingly attenuated for those in the larger size range. In mathematical terms, the influence of size on differentiation is indicated by a polynomial with a positive main and a negative squared term.

Second, large size reduces administrative overhead (the proportion of administrative personnel), which implies an administrative economy of scale. Third, degree of differentiation, which entails greater structural complexity, is positively related to administrative overhead. Finally, large size directly reduces yet indirectly (mediated by its influence on differentiation) increases administrative overhead, but the direct negative exceeds the indirect positive effect on administrative cost; this produces the net negative effect that finds expression in the administrative economy of scale.

The theory seeks to explain why the rate of differentiation with the increasing size of organizations declines for larger organizations. . . . (Blau 1995, 12).

BLAU'S DYSFUNCTIONS OF BUREAUCRACY

At various points Blau takes up dysfunctions of bureaucracy that Weber did not recognize. He notes, for example, the tendency for impersonal government agencies to provide inappropriate or insensitive treatment of clients (Blau 1955); the nonresponsiveness to membership interests characterizing certain oligarchies (Blau 1956); the ways in which corporate structures mobilize power in support of purposes that may be inimical to human welfare, as well as that threaten individual liberties and democratic institutions (Blau and Schoenherr 1971); and the fact that overly centralized bureaucracies may have deleterious consequences for the exercise of professional discretion (Blau 1973).

In addition, Blau has given particular attention to operationalizing the constructs of bureaucratic theory—size, complexity, specialization, expertness, administrative staff, hierarchy, rules, impersonality, and career stability. This is not done in the same manner as the Aston researchers, but it is done effectively nevertheless.

Blau was clearly a humanist who wrote about humanistic endeavors. This produced elaborations on Weber that went well beyond bureaucratic theory itself. However, he was also a scientist, and he conducted very effective research studies to that end.

BLAU'S RESEARCH

The theory of organizational differentiation evolved from a study of employment security units, so that study cannot be used to test the theory. However, subsequent research on samples drawn from government finance departments, department stores, universities and colleges, teaching hospitals (Blau 1974), and manufacturing plants (Blau, Falbe, McKinley, and Tracy 1976) consistently supports the theoretical hypotheses across all types of differentiation. The role of size in organizational structure appears to be important, and correlations with differentiation are substantial, rising as high as the 0.80s in certain instances. This is consistent with the Aston findings.

Clearly, Weber viewed size as a major correlate of bureaucracy, though he did not rule out bureaucratization of small organizations. Weber's predominant position on centralization appears to be that it occurs in conjunction with bureaucracy; yet, some of Weber's statements may be and have been interpreted differently on occasion. This makes the relationship between centralization and other indexes of bureaucratization, such as formalization and control, particularly important. Blau and Schoenherr's (1971) research has addressed this issue.

The data from state employment agencies indicate a predominantly negative relationship between formalization and centralization, but there are exceptions. Thus as with the Aston results, uncertainty prevails in this area, as it does regarding Weber's position itself.

CRITIQUES OF BLAU'S THEORY

In reviewing the evidence on differentiation theory, Bluedorn (1993) concludes that the major challenges to the theory come from longitudinal studies. These studies raise questions that move well beyond the content of the original theory (either Blau's or Weber's), and in fact indicate that a more comprehensive formulation dealing with change processes as well as scale is now needed.

Donaldson (1996, 2001) interprets Blau's theory and research as consistent with structural contingency theory and consequently gives the theory of differentiation a strong endorsement.

Argyris (1972), in contrast to Donaldson, takes a negative position on Blau's theory and research. He emphasizes Blau's failure to consider the informal organization (although Blau [1955] had done this in his dissertation). He also takes issue with the way in which variables were operationalized in the research (using official descriptions of organizational structure) on the grounds that these may well be invalid. To some extent Blau has answered Argyris's arguments with his research outside the civil service context. On one point, however, this is clearly not the case. Blau's theory of differentiation specifies causal influences from size to the structural variables. However, his tests of the theory are cross-sectional rather than longitudinal, and thus do not bear directly on the causal hypotheses. Clearly, additional research is needed that considers what organizations do as they increase in size and what temporal relationships are involved. This early criticism has been answered by more recent longitudinal tests of the theory, but not entirely to the satisfaction of the theory's advocates.

Turner (1977) takes Blau to task on philosophical grounds, questioning the role of explanation and Blau's claim to deductive rigor. This critique is aimed as much at all the theoretical approaches of modern sociology as at Blau's theory specifically.

A final point has been raised by Scott (1990a). His view is that structures are often determined not by size but by cultural forces such as belief systems, laws, and regulatory frameworks, as well as professional norms and pressures to conform to existing modal models. Thus size arguments must compete with a variety of alternative explanations. This takes us well beyond either of the theories considered in this chapter (Blau or Weber).

CONCLUSIONS

Early in this chapter I indicated that the validity of Blau's theory of differentiation is given a four-star rating and the importance rating from organizational behavior is at 4.31. When the second value is divided by the first, the resulting figure is 1.08, essentially the same as for the Aston research; thus both theories appear to be well balanced between conscious and unconscious emphases.

Given that Blau was providing a test of Weber's theory of bureaucracy, as was the case with the Aston researchers, the results obtained are clearly supportive, but there are certain departures as well. A comprehensive statement of the original theory of differentiation is presented, along with more recent restatements. Blau did note various dysfunctions of bureaucratic theory as presented by Weber, but these are often colored by Blau's humanist predilections. Research conducted by Blau and his coworkers indicates considerable support for the theory of differentiation including sizable correlations between size and differentiation. Thus Blau's research gives credence to Weber's theory of bureaucracy as well. The uncertainty regarding the status of centralization remains a source of concern.

Critiques of the Blau theory range from the positive reactions of Donaldson to the questions raised by Bluedorn, Argyris, and Scott. In general they call for more research, particularly of the longitudinal type.

CHAPTER 34

GOAL CONGRUENCE THEORY AND ORGANIZATION DEVELOPMENT

Next we turn to a set of theories that place their primary emphasis not on the positive features of bureaucracy, but on the dysfunctions. These dysfunctions are viewed as so overriding in some cases that a recommendation is made to destroy bureaucracy as an organizational form. This position holds in particular for Chris Argyris's goal congruence theory and for his version of organization development.

Evaluations of Argyris's theories are contained in Miner (2006a), Chapter 17, and Miner (2007), Chapter 23. There the estimated validity is at three stars and the performance rating is established by organization behavior scholars variously at 4.23 and 4.38, depending on whether the early theorizing involving goal congruence or the later work dealing with organizational learning is the focus of attention. As far as meta-analysis is concerned, I am not aware of any such analyses that have been conducted that deal directly with Argyris's work. However, his ideas have been subjected to criticism sufficiently often to justify the three-star rating (see Miner 2006a, 2007).

THE GOAL CONGRUENCE PHASE

Argyris presented his goal congruence theory several times in somewhat different versions (Argyris 1957, 1964, 1973).

Employees as Infants

A central feature of these presentations is the idea that employees in bureaucratic systems become much the same as infants; they are characterized by the following (see Argyris 1957, 50):

A state of passivity
A state of dependence on others
Being capable of behaving in only a few ways
Having erratic, casual, shallow, quickly dropped interests
Having a short time perspective (primarily in the present)
A lack of awareness of self (as adapted in Miner 2006a, p. 307).

Thus, states Argyris, "healthy employees often become passive, dependent, and submissive over time. . . . Employees may . . . adapt by resorting to emotional defense mechanisms such as escape from reality and psychosomatic illness, or become apathetic and uninvolved" (1957).

There is some support for this view:

> These potential functions and children's responses are in many ways similar to the functions leaders fulfill toward their subordinates and the way subordinates react to their functions. . . . There is a strong correspondence between parenthood and leadership (deVries and van Gelder 2005, 283).

> The organizational side received its impetus from the writings of Chris Argyris (1957) who focused on what organizations could do to liberate individuals with higher-order needs (Greiner and Cummings 2004, 376).

Higher-Order Needs and Self-Actualization

Another concept to which Argyris gave special attention is that of higher-order needs, and in particular self-actualization. Needs of this kind are inhibited and blocked by bureaucracy. We have considered how such needs may operate at the unconscious level previously (see Chapters 4, 5, 9, and 10 in this volume). The unconscious processes involved are especially emphasized in Pelham, Carvallo, and Jones (2005), Leary (2007), and Greenberg (2008).

On Causality

There is evidence that bureaucratic organizations tend to attract certain emotionally disturbed individuals at the lower levels, presumably because these people can function effectively in such positions. But this does not mean the organization *caused* the pathology. It seems probable that Argyris, observing organization members within a limited time span and noting the contiguity of pathology and formal structure, incorrectly attributed direct causation to the structure, when in fact it was often the ambiguity and anxiety-reducing structure itself that permitted particular individuals to function in an organizational setting at all. (See Miner and Anderson 1958; Diamond 1986.)

REFERENCES BY ARGYRIS TO UNCONSCIOUS ACTIVATION

As Argyris has moved on more recently to organizational learning phenomena, references that seem commensurate with an unconscious interpretation become more frequent. In this connection, Bargh and Williams (2006) write, "Nonconscious processes appear to serve a default, background regulatory function, freeing the conscious mind from the concerns of the immediate environment" (1), and again, "The automatic influences on social life are many and diverse. Other people, their characteristic features, the groups they belong to, the social roles they fill, and whether or not one has a close relationship with them have all been found to be automatic triggers of important psychological and behavioral processes" (3).

On Skilled Unawareness

Thus Argyris (2004) often writes of such phenomena as "organizational anti-learning practices, skilled *unawareness,* and organizational defensive routines" (5). In the same source he notes: "If *unawareness* is skillful then it must be produced by some design-in-use" (11); "They were skillfully incompetent (producing programs that were counterproductive to their intentions) and skillfully *unaware* of their incompetence" (21); "The existence of skilled incompetence means *unawareness* of the inability, and *unawareness* is also connected to a theory-in-use—hence it is skilled *unawareness*" (41); "Their *unawareness* is supported by managerial practices that suppress the evidence of the *unawareness*" (50); "The students were *unaware* of their defensiveness" (79); "The model is presented as not having the gaps. The authors appear *unaware* of the gaps and unaware that they are *unaware*" (88); "One hypothesis is that the deconstructionists may also exhibit incompetence and skilled *unawareness*" (101); and similar quotes continue through to the end of the 222-page book.

In the same vein Argyris uses this *unawareness* wording in several recent book chapters. Thus Argyris (2005) may be quoted to the effect that "if *unawareness* is behavior then it too must be designed. Hence skilled incompetence is combined with skilled *unawareness*" (263); "A self-protective mind-set generates skills that produce consequences that are counterproductive to valid learning and systematic denial that this is the case. The incompetence and *unawareness* or denial are skilled" (263); "Although writers typically exhibit skilled incompetence and skilled *unawareness,* the same individuals are more accurate in diagnosing the others' cases" (271); and "On double-loop issues they too are likely to be skillfully incompetent and skillfully *unaware* of their incompetence" (275).

Argyris (2008) uses similar wording—"the HR professionals used defensive reasoning to craft their interventions . . . being skillfully *unaware* that they were producing these consequences while doing so" (63); "If the OD and change professionals had been skillful . . . they would have recognized that they adhered to a theory of organizational change that was ineffective and that when used made them skillfully *unaware*" (65).

These statements may be compared with the following in describing automatic processes: "The interpretation of cues to others' personality traits can occur without effort, intention, or *awareness*" (Choi, Gray, and Ambady 2005, 311) from *The New Unconscious* (Hassin, Uleman, and Bargh 2005).

On an Underground Organization

Another apparent source of unconscious activation deals with references to an underground. Thus Argyris (2004) writes, "Conditions such as these [being undiscussable] make the world of defensive reasoning primarily an *underground* organization" (2). There are other references to an *underground* on pages 3 and 4, and elsewhere in the book as well. Also, in Argyris (2005) the author states, "In all organizations there are managerial components that are above ground and *underground*. The above ground in organizations is managed by productive reasoning . . . The *underground* organization is dominated by defensive reasoning" (277). Furthermore in Argyris (2008) he uses the following terminology: "Under these conditions [the undiscussability of the undiscussable] much important dialogue goes *underground*" (55); and, as well, "These consequences [defensive routines] create an *underground* world that competes with the above ground world in organizations. . . . It [is] unlikely that the *underground* world will be dealt with" (58); and "Once the *underground* features are surfaced the strategies tend to be to create new controls. . . . We must include a thorough analysis of the *underground* organization" (66).

Defenses, Defensive Routines, and Defensive Reasoning

At various points in the previous material, there have been references to defensiveness and defensive routines. "Defensive reasoning is omnipresent and powerful. It inhibits learning. . . . Human beings become so attached to defensive reasoning that many see it as natural, realistic, and necessary" (Argyris 2004, 212–213). In actual fact Argyris has often made such matters a centerpiece of his presentations (see his books *Strategy, Change, and Defensive Routines* [1985] and *Overcoming Organizational Defenses: Facilitating Organizational Learning* [1990].

In Chapter 10 of this volume I discussed defensiveness and in particular the use of repression by Harry Levinson—"Unconscious regression is at the heart of many psychoanalytic concepts and interpretations"; "it is clearly apparent that repression as a defense is important to his [Levinson's] expositions." Chapter 10 then goes on to note the evidence that exists as to the way repression operates as a defense mechanism. This line of research continues up to the present with emphasis on the effects of actions to induce forgetting (see Cue, Koppel, and Hirst 2007; Anderson and Levy 2009; Román, Soriano, Gómez-Ariza, and Bajo 2009).

Double-Loop Learning and the Bringing-to-Consciousness Phenomenon

Figure 34.1 describes Argyris's concept of the learning process. This is taken from page 314 of Miner (2006a). Clearly double-loop learning is the desired outcome (see Argyris and Schön 1996). A number of techniques are described with the objective of moving people to double-loop learning. "In order to implement the Model II versions of the caring, concern, honesty, courage, and trust . . . human being(s) will have to learn new double-loop learning skills" (Argyris 2004, 94). This is done by utilizing various case analysis and role-playing procedures. As Argyris (2004) says, "The case served as a projective technique" (57). Argyris indicates it is necessary to move learning from an unconscious process to a conscious process. This is what the educational experience attempts to do in achieving double-loop learning.

What is involved here is the bringing-to-consciousness phenomenon as described in Chapter 4 of this volume. By bringing unconscious material to the conscious level it is possible to get the unconscious under control. This is what psychotherapists attempt to do as they use interpretations to help patients gain insight. Argyris appears to have used this model in developing his approach to gaining conscious recognition in the double-loop learning process. Thus his learning seminars are said to:

1. Describe the defensive patterns that underlie the learning paradox.
2. Design, jointly with the participants, ways to interrupt the circular, self-reinforcing processes that inhibit double-loop learning.

Figure 34.1 **The Distinction between Single-Loop and Double-Loop Learning**

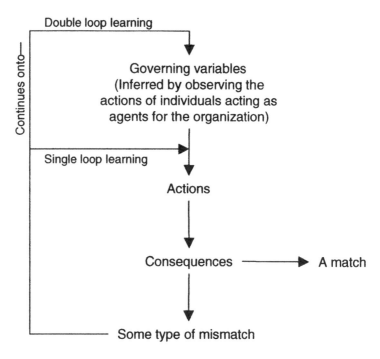

Source: Adapted from Chris Argyris, *On Organizational Learning* (1992). Cambridge, MA: Blackwell, p. 8. and other sources by the same author.

3. Help the participants assess the degree to which their action strategies are likely to limit the implementation of the solutions they have designed.
4. Help the participants realize how they have participated in creating and maintaining a behavioral world where the strategies they redesign to correct the situation are unlikely to be effective.
5. Involve the participants in sessions . . . where they can develop the concepts and skills they need in order to escape from this bind.
6. Reduce the use of defensive reasoning and increase the use of productive reason.
7. Reduce . . . organizational defensive routines, and replace them with high-quality inquiry, good dialect, and double-loop learning (Argyris and Schön 1996, 282–284).

On Changing the Status Quo

Argyris makes much of the need to eliminate the status quo. In Argyris (2004), he states: "They [use a defensive mind-set to] sanction all sorts of programs on leadership, learning, change, and commitment, that espouse changing the *status quo* but actually maintain it" (7); "We may be encouraging scholars and practitioners to believe that the *status quo*, and its errors and defensive routines, is unalterable" (83); and "Our theory permits robust predictions, because tests can be conducted in changing the *status quo*, and because changing the *status quo* is such a rare event" (113). And in Argyris (2005): "It is important that scholars take more initiatives in building theories and in conducting empirical research that questions the *status quo*" (272); "One of my mentors told me that I was compounding the felony of seeking changes in the *status quo* by using intervention as my preferred method for empirical research" (275).

Defending the status quo may be interpreted as a type of system justification. "People are motivated to defend, justify, and rationalize the *status quo*" (Jost, Pietrzak, Liviatan, Mandisodza, and Napier 2008, 592). Furthermore, "System justification processes can operate nonconsciously, leading people to implicitly accept and defend current social arrangements. . . . Studies have documented the nonconscious operation of system-justifying biases. . . . System justification goals seem to guide thoughts, feelings, and behaviors through mechanisms that are outside of conscious awareness" (596).

Argyris emphasizes that in eliminating the status quo by installing double-loop learning, culture change may be involved as well (see Walsh 2004; Carmeli and Sheaffer 2008). This, too, can act to produce unconscious processes (see Oyserman and Lee 2008).

On the Role of Unconscious Processes in Organizational Behavior

Without question Argyris drew upon unconscious considerations in developing his theories; the result may well be that he has identified certain problems inherent in practitioner-academic interactions. Consider the following: Rynes, Bartunek, and Daft (2001, 350) write, "As Argyris (1996) . . . noted, some of the most fundamental assumptions of scientific disciplines have become so taken-for-granted that they no longer come under discussion in public forums. . . . Argyris (1996) argued that keeping some discussions private impeded knowledge creation by inhibiting combination. However, assumptions and premises that are part of the undiscussable domains within communities (Argyris and Schön 1996) may also be at the heart of problems of relevance to the practitioner community. . . . This sanitation of complexities and uncertainties is likely to make research findings less credible to practitioners."

Yet mainstream organizational behavior scholars continue to downplay unconscious processes. Thus Schneider (2007, 589) "found projective techniques like the TAT of little use. . . . While not quite a dead end, this research on the need for achievement, and on the subconscious more generally, has had minor impact on contemporary approaches to the study of personality at work." Landy (2008, 379) says, "My review of the literature suggests that both stereotyping and IAT research study designs (using the unconscious) are sufficiently far removed from real work settings as to render them largely useless." Clearly we are not of one mind on such matters.

CONCLUSIONS

Returning now to what was said at the beginning of this chapter, it would appear that ratios of 1.41 and 1.46 are both justified depending on the phase of the theorizing. Taking an average, which appears justified in instances of this kind, comes to a ratio of 1.44, thus reaching a conclusion that Argyris's theories clearly overestimate the validity achieved to a substantial degree; this result fits well with Porter's (1989) conclusions.

Yet Argyris's theorizing is shown to be predominantly an unconscious process. This is indicated to be the case with regard (1) to skilled unawareness, (2) to an underground organization, and (3) to defenses, defensive routines, and defensive reasoning, all of which—as reflected in the phenomenon of repression—carry unconscious implications. Further evidence derives from the efforts to bringing double-loop learning into being in connection with the bringing-to-consciousness phenomenon and to attempt to change the status quo. Evidence to support unconscious processes is brought to bear from Argyris and, at the opposite pole, from various antithetical mainstream scholars within organizational behavior. The conclusion is that organizational behavior is not of a single mind on such matters.

CHAPTER 35

DYSFUNCTIONS AND VARIANTS ON BUREAUCRACY

In his book *Modern Organization* (1961), Victor Thompson asserts that a major problem for many modern bureaucracies is the imbalance between ability and authority. Increasingly, the knowledge needed to operate the organization is found among specialists and professionals who do not have significant positions of authority. At the same time, bureaucracy by its very nature places the right to exercise authority and the responsibility for outcomes in the hands of hierarchic superiors. The result is continuing confusion and conflict.

The characteristics of bureaucracy listed by Thompson are similar to Max Weber's, but with a somewhat different emphasis:

1. A spirit of rationalism, with science and technology as major contributions
2. Highly trained specialists appointed by merit to a system of assured careers
3. Routinization of organizational activities
4. Factoring of the general goal of the organization into subgoals for units along the lines of differentiation
5. Apparent inversion of ends and means such that the total organizational goal becomes lost to view and the subgoals of units become ends in themselves
6. A formalistic impersonality
7. Categorization of data in accordance with the needs of specialists
8. Classification of clients to minimize discrimination
9. Seeming slowness to act or change as a result of resistance to change and preoccupation with hierarchy
10. Concern with the monistic ideal, including a strong emphasis on legitimizing the superior-subordinate relationship, authority-responsibility, and hierarchy; thus organizational conflict, divergent goals, and divergent interests are precluded as lacking legitimacy.

These themes are perpetuated in a number of books (Thompson 1969, 1975, 1976) and several articles. During the days when the two were together at Illinois Institute of Technology, Thompson helped write a text with Herbert Simon (see Chapter 22 in this volume) on public administration (Simon, Smithburg, and Thompson 1950).

Victor Thompson's theories are discussed in Chapter 19 of Miner (2002) and evaluated in Chapter 17 of Miner (2006b). There the estimated validity is set at three stars and the mean importance rating given by organizational behavior experts is 3.38. See also Epilogue on Bureaucracy (1) in Miner (2007). The most important relevant meta-analysis has been noted previously as Damanpour (1991), although several others in a similar vein have appeared since.

BUREAUTICS AND BUREAUPATHOLOGY

Those who come into contact with bureaucracies must adjust to these characteristics. Certain individuals (Thompson calls them bureautics) are too immature to adjust and react with an overwhelming suspicion. Bureausis is considered a disease that normally prevents people from rising in the hierarchy.

In addition to bureausis (and adaptive bureaucratic behavior), Thompson describes other bureaupathic behavior that is created by anxiety and insecurity. This phenomenon results in large part from the gap between the rights and duties of the hierarchical superior and the specialized ability to solve problems, a gap which in turn makes the superior dependent on specialist subordinates. Oftentimes superiors react to this situation with an excessive need for control, an overemphasis on compliance with rules, exaggerated aloofness, resistance to change, and insistence on the rights of office. Such bureaupathology is a function of the insecurity of authority that is produced in large part by increasing specialization.

Enter in the Unconscious

This is the point at which unconscious considerations become relevant. The pathologies mobilized by bureaucratic exposure operate to introduce various defenses. This is the same phenomenon that Argyris recognized in dubbing employees as infants (see Chapter 34 in this volume), making what is said in Chapter 34 equally appropriate here.

Thompson's Solutions

Although Thompson points out the problems of bureaucracy, he does not give a great deal of attention to solving those problems. What he does suggest are certain variants on the basic bureaucratic theme made necessary when the presence of specialists must be accommodated. These approaches involve changes in processes and in structures, as follows:

1. Give most persons in supervisory positions some specific instrumental functions in addition to the exercise of authority, such as the factory supervisor and the college department chair have.
2. Establish two equal salary scales, one for specialists and one for the hierarchy.
3. Reexamine the division of labor in each organization to bring it into line with the needs of specialization. Wherever machine technology allows, the microdivision of labor should be ended.
4. Ensure that all organizational processes and arrangements have as a manifest purpose the furthering of cooperation (Thompson 1961, 195–197).

ALTERNATIVE ORGANIZATIONAL FORMS

Professional Systems

Much as Blau did (see Chapter 33 in this volume), Thompson considered professionalism an alternative to bureaucracy. Furthermore, he calls professional systems more innovative than bureaucratic systems. This is because they are "pluralistic and collegiate rather than monocratic and hierarchical" (Thompson 1969, 93). Professionalizing an organization decreases administration, top-down command, unquestioning obedience, constriction of communication, and interunit conflict. The associated shift to professional peer control should yield increased flexibility, variety, and receptivity to change, and thus innovation. Structurally there would be greater use of certain project forms.

Innovative professional organizations would dispense with performance ratings by superiors and with most job descriptions. Thompson (1965) views the small technical organization headed by a creative entrepreneur and staffed with a small group of "able and personally loyal" peers as the prototype for innovation. To the extent this structure can be incorporated into or grafted onto them, large organizations might be expected to become more innovative.

Group Systems

Subsequently Thompson (1976) distinguishes more fully between natural (informal) and artificial (bureaucratic) systems. In particular, he is concerned with the relations of each to innovation and change. Following Weber, Thompson develops the idea that artificial systems are tools to carry out the goals of their owners (the charismatic leader, the electorate, etc.). As tools, they are subject to evaluation and control in light of the goals. Artificial systems are monocratic in that only owner goals—not the goals of other possible claimants such as employees—are considered relevant. Norms of rationality prevail.

Natural systems exist alongside the artificial and are an inevitable concomitant of bureaucracy. They are not tools of the owner, but spontaneously emergent entities serving only themselves. They are not rational systems, and their referent is internal—their members. Thus a bureaucratic *organization* is pluralistic, even though the bureaucratic system per se is monocratic. Although the natural and artificial systems have inherent conflicting interests, on occasion and in certain respects the natural system may complement the artificial. Thus the natural system may provide needed redundancy and reliability, flexibility and innovation, and, under certain circumstances, additional rewards and motivation. At the same time, the natural system is primarily devoted to survival-oriented adaptation to the artificial system, and norms of rationality are not relevant for it.

Thompson states in a number of places that the natural system, not the artificial, is the source of innovation, flexibility, and change in bureaucratic organizations:

> Innovative adaptations, if they occur, are largely products of natural system conditions (1976, 19).

> The more organizations are rationalized, the more scientific management is applied to them, the "tauter the ship," and the more romanticism and falsified or erroneous calculations are needed, if there are to be any innovations at all (1976, 90).

Because the artificial system or plan of the organization can only provide extrinsic rewards, it cannot motivate to innovation. (In fact, innovations cannot even be legitimate, because their actual relation to the owner's goal cannot be known in advance.) Innovation for the most part, therefore, must occur outside the formal artificial system (1976, 95).

Entrepreneurial Systems

While working with James Hlavacek during the 1970s, Thompson developed his ideas regarding innovation and venture teams in a series of articles. In the first of these (Hlavacek and Thompson, 1973), the authors start with a statement regarding the environment for innovation: (1) security and freedom are important considerations; (2) a rich and varied background of ideas, at the boundaries of a field, are required and thus a specialist rather than a generalist is needed; (3) a strong personal commitment to the creative process tends to exist. This set of conditions is contrasted with bureaucracy, which is said to yield an environment hostile to innovation and creativity:

> The bureaucratic strategy has a strong tendency to individualize work and to reduce it in scope and responsibility. By these effects on work, reliability, control, and productivity are all increased. . . . Reliability, control, and productivity, *ceteris paribus,* are also promoted by reducing work to simple repetitive *routines*—by avoiding the insecurities and risks of actual problem solving. Routinization, in turn, depends upon stabilizing the organization's conditions of operation. . . . Far from a drive to innovate, the bureaucratic organization has many reasons for fostering the opposite condition—a tendency to stifle innovations (Hlavacek and Thompson, 1973, 364–365).

Product management and venture team structures are hypothesized as a way of modifying bureaucracy to reduce this tendency to stifle innovation.

Another such approach is the joint venture, where two firms combine a portion of their assets to create a new organization intended to engineer, produce, and market a product innovation (Hlavacek and Thompson, 1975). This approach is also favored for the purpose of initial innovation, but steps must be taken to minimize the impact of bureaucracy.

In a final article Hlavacek and Thompson (1978) place greater emphasis on internal venture structures, but they view success as problematic because of venture conflict with more permanent divisions or departments:

> Bureaucratization of authority over venturing would defeat the whole new concept of venture groups—namely, an end run around corporate bureaucratic obstacles by way of a small, inter-disciplinary project group freed from most of the corporate restrictions (Hlavacek and Thompson, 1978, 245).

The key ingredient and dominant motivator in any venture is the freedom to create and operate; if this freedom is lost, the venture will fail.

Commentary

Clearly Victor Thompson was incorrect in his prediction that bureaucracy lacked the capacity to innovate (see Chapter 32 in this volume and in particular the Damanpour [1991] meta-analysis). Whatever the innovation potential of the other forms may be, it cannot be predicated on the assumption that bureaucracy is lacking in this area.

Second, it should be noted that although the bureaupathology hypotheses appear to predominate in invoking unconscious considerations within Thompson's theory, there is evidence that the forms considered here also have this same potential. In this regard I would refer to the evidence from projective techniques (the MSCSs) as presented in Miner (2008). Without question this evidence indicates that considerations extending beyond awareness are implicated in how these alternative forms operate.

ADJUSTING TO BUREAUCRACY

Thompson's theory dealt with the problem of individual adaptation to bureaucracy. Arthur Stinchcombe (1974) and others going back to Weber have maintained that an effective bureaucracy requires certain motivational patterns. The research data indicate that there are people who can and cannot adjust to bureaucratic systems in various roles. Furthermore, based on the personality data, bureaucratic systems differ significantly from professional systems.

Personality Measures

Sally Baker, Amitai Etzioni, Richard Hansen, and Marvin Sontag (1973) developed a measure of worker tolerance for bureaucratic structure based on attitudes toward rules and regulations, attitudes toward the legitimacy of authority, attitudes toward performing limited and structured tasks, and the capacity to delay gratification. This measure differentiates among organizational contexts in a manner that appears to be positively related to their degree of bureaucratization. It also predicts turnover within bureaucracies and performance ratings.

Leonard Gordon (1970) developed a similar instrument that tapped willingness to comply with a superior's wishes, confidence in expert judgment, preference for impersonal relationships, a desire for the security provided by rules and standard procedures, and a desire for the security of organizational identification. Correlations with other measures suggest considerable construct validity. This measure also differentiates among contexts with varying degrees of bureaucratization and predicts turnover in bureaucracies.

I have developed a somewhat different approach of this nature in connection with the specification of managerial role motivation theory (see Chapter 16 in this volume), which focuses on the personality characteristics required of managers in bureaucratic systems. Included are (1) measures of characteristics related to functioning within the hierarchy—positive attitudes upward, competitiveness horizontally with peers, and the exercise of power downward; (2) characteristics related to size of organization—assertiveness and desire to stand out from the group, or be visible; and (3) characteristics related to carrying out the functions of management. Research results indicate that these personality characteristics are a source of behavior and decisions appropriate to the bureaucratic managerial context (Miner 1993b, 2008). However, these results do not mesh nearly as well with nonmanagerial work and nonbureaucratic systems. Apparently there are people who cannot adapt to (and consequently experience considerable anxiety in) bureaucratic managerial roles. Furthermore the kinds of characteristics that make for managerial effectiveness in bureaucracies are generally distinct from those making for professional effectiveness.

On the evidence, although this research does not prove Thompson's specific formulations, it does support his view that there are people who have a great deal of difficulty adjusting to bureaucracy. More broadly, it also appears that certain other individuals have difficulty adjusting to other organizational forms such as the professional and entrepreneurial types (Miner 1993b).

Organizations can produce anxiety and insecurity in their members, and they can arouse resentment and anger in particular individuals as well. Whether bureaucracies produce these emotional reactions more than other types of organizations is an open question, but being larger, they are likely to affect more people in this way.

Unconscious Considerations

"The concept of psychopathy refers to a pattern of chronic antisocial behavior and personality features, such as emotional detachment, lovelessness, and guiltlessness, attributable in part to a temperament deficit. . . . [Such] a deficit . . . involves poor emotional and behavioral control" (Fowles and Dindo 2009, 179). This sounds much like the kind of psychopathology that Thompson describes. It is one of the few publications on the subject that has come out of the new unconscious perspective. There has been a tendency to leave such matters to those with a psychoanalytic orientation, and accordingly psychopathology as a subject matter has been rather neglected by the new unconscious researchers (see Chapter 2 of Miner 2008). To my mind this represents an unfortunate omission; application to the area that Freud originally opened up would seem to represent a goldmine for the new unconscious and its approach to research on the unconscious.

In line with this view, research might extend the following topic:

> The objective of this experiment was to probe the impact of exposure to acute stress on financial decision making and examine the particular influence of stress on decisions with a positive or negative valence. Participants' choices exhibited a stronger reflection effect when participants were under stress than when they were in the no-stress control phase. This suggests that stress modulates risk taking, potentially exacerbating behavioral bias in subsequent decision making. Consistent with dual-process approaches, decision makers fall back on automatized reactions to risk under the influence of disruptive stress (Porcelli and Delgado 2009, 278).

CONCLUSIONS

Victor Thompson describes bureaucracies in somewhat different terms than Weber, and thus introduces certain dysfunctions and variants from the bureaucratic theme presented in Chapter 31 of this volume. His theories have mixed support from the research evidence, although such meta-analyses as have been carried out do not consistently yield results that confirm his theorizing. On balance the ideas presented by Thompson yield a three-star validity and an importance rating of 3.38 at the hands of organizational behavior experts. When the latter value is divided by the validity assigned, the resulting ratio is 1.13, suggesting only a slight overestimation of the presumed validity of the theory by organizational behavior scholars.

Thompson considers bureaucracies to produce a pathology that serves to reflect unconscious factors such as those involved when defenses are activated. His descriptions of this pathology are more extensive than the prescriptions he gives for solving it; these latter tend to be tied to changes in roles and structures. In large part he believes that alternative organizational forms involving professional systems, group or informal systems, and entrepreneurial or venture systems are much more innovative than bureaucracies and thus are to be preferred. He was in fact involved in conducting research on venture teams. His alternative forms all serve to activate roles or role sets that have the potential to yield unconscious motives; this is true of professional, group, and entrepreneurial systems. In addition to the bureaupathologies, then, these alternative forms represent a means to movement into the unconscious realm.

Abundant evidence exists to support Thompson's theories regarding the need for adjustments to the dysfunctions of bureaucracy. This is an area that has been the subject of considerable confirming research. Furthermore, although the new unconscious researchers have done little to consider psychopathologies in their work, some relevant research is available.

COMPLIANCE THEORY

Amitai Etzioni, the author of compliance theory, was primarily a theorist, although he did make occasional research contributions. Compliance theory itself is in large part a dictionary of terms and variables for the study of organizations. That Etzioni defined his terms but did not operationalize them, and thus failed to contribute in the area of measurement, represents a major shortening of his approach. He tended to rely on others in this regard and was only partially successful in adopting this procedure; thus in many respects the theory remains untested. The basic presentation of compliance theory occurs in Etzioni (1961), with a second edition in 1975 that includes the studies operationalized by others and proposed by Etzioni as tests of that theory. A second version of the second edition is Gross and Etzioni (1985), which does not add much to the research pool as a function of the intervening ten years. Thus the limited research on compliance theory extends only over a rather short period, tapered off over time as Etzioni moved to other endeavors, and often consists of qualitative case studies that do not qualify as true tests of the theory.

Yet the theory does have some support. As a result I give compliance theory a three-star validity rating. Organizational behavior as a whole provides an importance rating of 3.95 (see Miner 2006b in Chapter 17). An evaluation of the theory is contained in Miner (2002, Chapter 19). There, no meta-analysis contributes to the result.

ON POWER

Compliance is defined as a relationship that is established both by the power of superiors to control subordinates and by the orientation of subordinates to this power of the superior:

> *Power* is a person's ability to influence or induce someone else to carry out the person's directives or the norms that person supports; power positions give incumbents regular access to some means of power.

Coercive power is based on the use or threat to use physical sanctions (pain, hunger, etc.).

Remunerative power is based on control over material resources and rewards (pay, benefits, etc.).

Normative power is based on the dispensation and manipulation of symbolic rewards (moral involvement, social acceptance, etc.) (Etzioni 1961, 4–5).

Congruence or Fit

Most organizations are assumed to operate from one major means of power (coercive, remunerative, or normative), relying somewhat less on the other two. In response to these types of power, subordinates display some type of involvement, i.e. the cathectic-evaluative orientation of the person, characterized by both intensity and direction. This involvement may take several forms:

Alienative, indicating an intense negative orientation.
Calculative, indicating either a positive or negative orientation of low intensity.
Moral, indicating an intense positive orientation (Etzioni 1961, 10).

The compliance relationship is defined in terms of the type of power applied to the lower participants of an organization and the type of involvement developed by these same lower participants. All nine types of compliance relationships are possible and do occur.

Congruence or fit between type of power and type of involvement occurs as follows:

- Normative—normative, moral
- Utilitarian—remunerative, calculative
- Coercive—coercive, alienative

These are the more effective combinations, and other combinations tend to move toward them over time.

The Operation of Unconscious Factors

Power is subject to the operative of unconscious factors. For prior discussions on this subject see the appropriately labeled sections of Chapters 23 and 31 in this volume. Relevant references are Smith, Dijksterhuis, and Wigboldus (2008), Sivanathan, Pillutla, and Murnighan (2008), and Fast, Gruenfeld, Sivanathan, and Galinsky (2009).

To these should be added the following from Fast and Chen (2009, 1411):

We found that self-perceived competence moderated the relationship between power and aggression. When paired with self-perceived incompetence, power led to generalized aggression (Studies 1 and 4), willingness to expose a stranger to loud and aversive blasts of sound (Study 2), and intentional harming of a subordinate (Study 3). Furthermore, this tendency to aggress among power holders who perceived themselves as incompetent was eliminated among those whose leadership aptitude was affirmed (Study 3), among those who had the chance to affirm an important self-relevant value (Study 4).

These findings offer several important contributions. First, they extend the psychology-of-power literature by showing that power increases reactivity to competency threats. Specifically, a self-perceived lack of competence elicits defensive aggression among power holders, but not among the powerless. This is likely because holding a position of power increases the degree to which one feels one ought to be competent. . . . Second, our findings advance research on the determinants of aggression among power holders. Although some researchers have posited that power always fosters derogatory and aggressive tendencies . . . , our studies corroborate evidence to the contrary. . . . Power led to aggression only when it was paired with perceptions of personal incompetence. . . . Finally, to our knowledge, these studies are the first to document that power holders have an increased, rather than decreased, vulnerability to potential psychological threats.

ON GOALS

Organizational goals are specified as a state of affairs the organization is attempting to realize. They may be either stated or actual, and the two need not be the same. Three types are considered:

> *Order goals* represent attempts to control people who are deviant from the perspective of some social unit the organization is serving, such as society, by segregating these people and blocking further deviant activity.
> *Economic goals* represent efforts to produce commodities and services for outside users.
> *Culture goals* represent attempts to institutionalize conditions required to create and preserve symbolic objects, to apply them, and to reinforce commitment to these objects.
> *Social goals* are a subtype of culture goals (Etzioni 1961, 72–73).

Goals and Type of Compliance

Although organizations may have multiple goals, one is usually predominant. These goals line up with the various compliance structures as follows:

- Culture goals with normative compliance
- Economic goals with utilitarian compliance
- Order goals with coercive compliance

These are the more effective relationships, and organizations that deviate from these patterns tend to strive for relationships of these types.

The Operation of Unconscious Factors

Chapter 2 in this volume on goal-setting theory presents a detailed consideration of how goals may operate unconsciously. From this source one may conclude that "a need for efficiency may lead to goal-related behaviors that are easy, enjoyable, or even automatic to employ. . . . An ever-increasing body of research has found that goals . . . can be automatically activated by the environmental context in which they are pursued" (Shah and Kruglanski 2008, 223). And elsewhere, "Once in place in the cognitive system, goals may be activated and may operate in a thoroughly automatic, nonconscious fashion" (Elliot and Fryer 2008, 246); plus as well "Counteractive control is often an intentional process of committing to high-order goals and eliminating tempting alternatives. . . . Counteractive control may also be an unconscious process" (Fishbach and Trope 2008, 282).

More recent testimonials along these lines are to be found. For instance, "Though human beings embody a unique ability for planned (conscious) behavior, they also often act impulsively. This insight may be important for the study of self-control situations in which people are torn between their long-term goals to restrain behavior and their immediate impulses (automatic) that promise hedonic fulfillment. In the present article we outline a dual-systems perspective of impulse and self-control" (Hofmann, Friese, and Strack 2009, 162).

Other examples also exist, as for instance the following:

It is typically assumed that people always want to feel good. Recent evidence, however, demonstrates that people want to feel unpleasant emotions, such as anger or fear, when the emotions promote the attainment of their long-term goals. . . . People may prefer to feel useful emotions, even if they are unpleasant. . . . Emotional preferences can be conscious and deliberate, yet people may not always be aware of the factors that determine what they want to feel. Although "wanting" typically refers to a conscious desire, it can also refer to an unconscious or implicit process. . . . Expectancies, in particular, can often operate outside of consciousness (Tamir 2009, 101, 104).

ON THE USE OF THE ELITE DESIGNATION

Etzioni is one of those sociologists who uses the elite designation (see Chapter 14 in this volume).

The term *elites* refers to people in organizations who have power. Lower elites are those who possess direct power over lower participants. The source of elite power may be inherent in the position held and accordingly may be coercive, remunerative, or normative; such people are referred to as *officers*. *Leaders* are those who derive power from their personal characteristics. Under crisis conditions only leaders can maintain compliance; however, with only personal power to rely upon, informal leaders remain vulnerable.

Elites control *expressive* activities, thus meeting organizational needs for social and normative integration, as well as *instrumental* activities, thus fulfilling needs of input and allocation. The former is comparable to consideration as measured by the Ohio State scales, and the latter to initiating structure (Gross and Etzioni 1985). Expressive activities tend to require moral involvement on the part of lower participants and thus are appropriately supervised by elites who hold normative power; power based on personal characteristics is particularly appropriate and effective. Instrumental activities tend to require calculative involvement and are best supervised by those with utilitarian power over those who do the performing; here power derived from one's position is most effective.

The effective elite hierarchy is one in which the structure of the elites and the hierarchy of goals, or means, are congruent (Etzioni 1959).

In normative organizations it is functional for the expressive elite to subordinate the instrumental one. . . . In utilitarian organizations, high productivity is associated with subordination of the expressive elite by the instrumental elite, and cooperation between the two. In coercive organizations the antagonism between organizational and informal elites makes for an unstable relationship instead of a clear pattern of subordination (Etzioni 1961, 126).

ON MULTIPLE FORMS WITHIN THE THEORY

Etzioni (1961) subdivides bureaucracy using the nature of the compliance involved to create the basis for his typology. He also subdivides professional systems, differentiating the professions from what he designates as semi-professions (teachers, nurses, and social workers) (Etzioni 1969). In using this type of approach he has been followed by others (see Malhotra and Morris 2009).

ON THE USE OF REMUNERATIVE POWER

Compliance theory uses remunerative power (pay, benefits) as one of its primary variables. The following quote applies to the effective use of remunerative power:

A pernicious paradox in human motivation is the occasional reduced performance associated with tasks and situations that involve larger-than-average rewards. Three broad explanations that might account for such performance decrements are attentional competition (distraction theories), inhibition by conscious processes (explicit-monitoring theories), and excessive drive and arousal (overmotivation theories). Here, we report incentive-dependent performance decrements in humans in a reward-pursuit task; subjects were less successful in capturing a more valuable reward in a computerized maze. Concurrent functional magnetic resonance imaging revealed that increased activity in [the] ventral midbrain, a brain area associated with incentive motivation and basic reward responding, correlated with both reduced number of captures and increased number of near-misses associated with imminent high rewards. These data cast light on the neurobiological basis of choking under pressure and are consistent with overmotivation accounts (Mobbs, Hassabis, Seymour, Marchant, Weiskopf, Dolan, and Frith 2009, 955).

This study is related to the discussions in a number of previous chapters in this volume. First among these is Chapter 1 on expectancy theory. Also of relevance are Chapter 2 on goal-setting theory, Chapter 4 on achievement motivation theory, and perhaps Chapter 11 on self-determination theory.

ON CHARISMA

Previously charisma has been shown to be associated with unconscious processes. This is in Chapter 17 on charismatic leadership theory, in Chapter 21 on the romance of leadership, and in Chapter 31 on Weber's theory of bureaucracy.

Etzioni on Charisma

Weber made charisma, defined as an extraordinary quality of a person, a central concern for bureaucracy. Etzioni defines it as the ability of a person in an organization to exercise diffuse and intense influence over the normative orientations of other participants. This charisma may be developed in a variety of organizational positions:

When charisma is concentrated at the *top*, this is referred to as the *T-Structure*; only utilitarian organizations follow this model (many companies).

Table 36.1

Location of Charisma in Relation to Rank and Compliance Structure

Organizational rank	Type of compliance structure			
	Coercive	Utilitarian	Normative (L)	Normative (R)
Highest	Not charismatic	Charismatic	Charismatic	Not charismatic
Middle	Not charismatic	Not charismatic	Charismatic	Charismatic

Source: Adapted from Amitai Etzioni (1961, 224).

When charisma is characteristic of all *line* positions, this is referred to as the *L-Structure*; normative organizations emphasizing pure normative compliance follow this model (many churches).

When charisma is limited to one or more *ranks* other than the top level, this is referred to as the *R-Structure*; normative organizations stressing social compliance follow this model (many professional organizations).

There are in addition organizations (such as prisons) in which charisma is not required at all (Etzioni 1961, 208–209).

Although Weber tended to emphasize the dysfunctional role of charisma in leading bureaucracies away from their established functions, Etzioni emphasizes the functional role. This functional role for charisma becomes manifest as long as it follows the pattern depicted in Table 36.1.

The use of charisma as a source of compliance strains organizational discipline on occasion, simply because certain members assume a highly personalized type of power. This is less of a problem in the utilitarian T-Structures because charisma is minimal and found in a safe place at the top. It is a problem for L-Structures such as churches and for R-Structures of a professional nature. In these organizations extensive controls must be instituted to keep the personalized power of widespread charisma from contributing to deviance.

Commentary

Etzioni (1975) proposes that in the modern world a clear secular trend—and signs of a similar yearning as well—exists toward increasing reliance on normative organizations and reducing reliance on coercive and utilitarian ones. This trend toward normative dominance in society is discussed at length in Etzioni (1968).

Yet this is where charisma dominates most as well (see Table 36.1). Charisma is more prevalent under compliance theory than even under Weber (see Chapter 31 in this volume). Normative organizations permit more collective action, but guidability is another matter because the relationships are often too expressive and nonrational for this purpose. Clearly, then, Etzioni posits unconscious processes as prevailing in normative organizations, but they are also said to be associated with charisma generally.

However, other types of organizations are not so characterized. Compliance theory is basically about bureaucracies, and as both Weber and Etzioni posit, these are highly rationalized structures. Thus compliance theory would seem to function with both conscious and unconscious factors involved and consequently is best characterized as balanced in nature.

CONCLUSIONS

As indicated at the beginning of this chapter, compliance theory has a validity of three stars and an importance rating (as given by organizational behavior scholars) of 3.95. When the second figure is divided by the first, the result is a value of 1.32, suggesting that the importance rating somewhat overestimates the presumed validity of the theory.

Compliance theory is shown to be a balanced theory in that it possesses rational or conscious elements as well as unconscious components.

Etzioni makes power the essence of compliance theory. It combines with involvement to produce actual compliance. Evidence is presented as to the operation of unconscious factors in power. Goals are also featured in compliance theory, and they too are associated with compliance; they may operate on an unconscious basis as well. Etzioni uses the elite designation, and it in turn operates from a power base. He also advocates multiple forms of both bureaucratic and professional systems. Research on the application of remunerative power suggests that it may be driven by overmotivation forces operating from the ventral midbrain. Consistent with the balanced designation for the theory, Etzioni gives charisma an extensive role in his theory. Further support for unconscious processes comes from Etzioni's extolling of a normative dominance by both extensive use of charisma and what he acknowledges are the largely nonrational functions of normative organizations.

CHAPTER 37

STRUCTURAL CONTINGENCY THEORY

The only relevant meta-analysis that I am aware of regarding structural contingency theory is the one by Donaldson (1996) himself (cited in Chapter 33 of this volume). Based on this and other data to be considered later I give structural contingency theory a three-star evaluation. Organizational behavior as a whole yields an importance rating of 4.33 (see Miner 2006b). A discussion of this specific theory is contained within Miner (2006a) in Chapter 16.

ON THE NATURE OF STRUCTURAL CONTINGENCY THEORY

Structural contingency theory, as the name implies, is a fit or congruence theory. It views the organization as adaptive in its structuring to the particular states of the contingency variables. Changes in structure occur incrementally to achieve this adaptation.

Fit and Nonfit

The causal flow is clearly stated to be from contingency factor to structural factor; there is no equivocating in this regard. Furthermore it takes a fit between contingency and structural variables to achieve positive outcomes. When the two are out of fit, organizational performance will suffer. A structural adaptation to regain fit occurs as follows:

1. There is . . . a fit between the organizational structure and the contingency which affects organizational performance.
2. There is the idea that a change by the organization in its contingency variables causes it to move from fit to misfit.
3. There is the idea that misfit causes structural change.
4. There is also the idea . . . that the organization by changing its organization structure moves from misfit into fit (Donaldson 1995, 33).

At Stage 2 the misfit eventually operates to degrade performance. This triggers an incremental process of structural change to adapt to the new contingency state. The structural changes are in degree of bureaucratization, divisionalization, organicness, and the like, depending on the contingency variable involved. Yet whether this gradually evolving process truly describes the realities of structural change is subject to considerable question (Nickerson and Zenger 2002).

Characteristics

According to Donaldson (1995), structural contingency theory is the base onto which aspects of other theories may be added to fill in holes in the structural contingency formulations; thus a single theory of organization, at least at the macro level, is created. The result is an overarching theoretical integration, which the field needs at the present time. Newer theories would contribute only in limited and localized ways, building on the central core of structural contingency theory.

In discussing the theory thus created, Donaldson (1996, 3) sets forth six characteristics:

1. It is *nomothetic,* meaning that the phenomena are analyzed using a general framework with factors that apply to all organizations, both for the contingency factors (such as size and strategy) and for the organizational structure (like specialization and centralization). General causal relationships in the form of lawlike regularities are sought between contingency and structural factors.
2. The research associated with the theory is *methodologically positivist* in that there is much use of comparative empirical research, often with the measurement of variables and statistical analysis of data.
3. The theory explains organizational structure by *material factors* such as size, technology, and so on, rather than by ideationalist factors such as ideas, ideologies, perceptions, norms, and the like.
4. The theory is *deterministic* in that managers are seen as having to adopt the organizational structure that is required by the contingency factors in order to gain organizational effectiveness.
5. The theory is closely *informed by empirical research* rather than armchair speculation or extended theorizing prior to empirical data collection.
6. The theory is consciously scientific in style with the *aim being to produce scientific knowledge of the type achieved in the natural sciences.*

Structural contingency theory utilizes objective *determinism* to state the causal flow from contingency variables to structural factors. It utilizes *functionalism* and thus holds that structure is determined ultimately by functional necessity and the drive for organizational effectiveness. It utilizes *Cartesianism* in that organizations are seen as taking many different positions in multidimensional space; thus it employs continuous variables rather than types of organizations. It assumes that *generalization* is possible, desirable, and can be demonstrated for organizational structures. Donaldson (2005a) further demonstrates his commitment to science in a discussion of Sumantra Ghoshal's views.

Structural contingency theory was originally influenced by Donaldson's association with the Aston researchers; it was also influenced to a degree by Blau's theorizing (see Chapter 33 in this volume). In both of these instances Weber's theory of bureaucracy was incorporated in the particular theory involved; thus in both instances the relationship to bureaucracy had an influence on how the theory was evaluated. A further influence was Donaldson's (1987) own research on the Chandler (1962) work on strategy and structure.

Table 37.1

Contingency Theories Marshaled by Donaldson (2001) and Evaluative Data

Contingency Theories	Miner's Estimated Validity	OB's Importance Rating
Burns and Stalker (see Chapter 12 of Miner 2006a)	2	5.42
Hage (defined by Donaldson 2001 as similar to Burns and Stalker)	(2)	—
Lawrence and Lorsch (see Chapter 29 of this volume)	3	5.39
Perrow (see Miner 2002, Chapter 16)	2	4.38
Thompson (see Chapter 28 of this volume)	3	5.42
Woodward (see Miner 2002, Chapter 16)	1	4.33
Aston group (see Chapter 32 of this volume)	4	4.28
Blau (see Chapter 33 of this volume)	4	4.31
Chandler (see Miner 1982)	(3)	—
Donaldson	3	4.33
Mean for rated theories	2.7	4.73

The contingency variables emphasized by the theory have changed in different presentations. Another area of change is determinism and its alternative—human choice. At an early point Donaldson adopted a view much like that of Child (1972b), incorporating strategic choice in the contingency process. Over time this has changed to a strict determinism or imperative. It thus extends well beyond the original Aston view that contingency factors set constraints on managerial discretion. Causation from structure to contingency, and consequently the idea of a proactive organization producing changes in its environment, is rejected.

THE THEORIES COVERED

I have noted that at various times structural contingency theory is presumed to deal with different variables and different theories. Which specific theories are invoked has not been consistently indicated, a situation that may be related to the fact that the theory has changed somewhat through a number of statements and restatements. This variability has extended over something like two decades. The most recent definitive position appears to be that of Donaldson (2001).

Table 37.1 lists these theories and where I have discussed them. There I have noted my assessment of their validity, and the importance ratings for each given by organizational behavior scholars (where appropriate). The mean estimated validity is stated as 2.7 and the importance rating assigned by organizational behavior as 4.73. The parenthetic values are estimates derived from the sources cited.

The only high (4+) values I have indicated are for the Aston group and for Blau's theory of differentiation, the places where Donaldson's theory began. These are also the only instances in which my ratings and the importance ratings coincide. Otherwise the two sets of evaluations depart from one another significantly, and always with the performance ratings from organizational behavior being higher. Donaldson (2009) himself laments failures of this latter kind when consensus data are involved, and I have frequently noted similar overestimates throughout this volume (see Chapter 42 to follow).

EVIDENCE

The data of Table 37.1 suggest a deficiency of some sort among certain elements of the list of theories Donaldson (2001) incorporated in his structural contingency theory armamentarium; this is particularly true with regard to the theories set forth by Woodward, Burns and Stalker, and Perrow. The mean rating of 2.7 is consistent with my rating of three stars.

Evaluations by Others

However, there are positive evaluations. Meeus (2002) gives a laudatory evaluation to the basic presentation. Hollenbeck, Moon, Ellis, West, Ilgen, Sheppard, Porter, and Wagner (2002) in a laboratory study of teams seem to provide evidence in support of the theory. Several of the theories listed in Table 37.1 are given lukewarm support at best by Donaldson; this is particularly true of the Burns and Stalker theory (see Donaldson 1995). Van Offenbeek, Sorge, and Knip (2009, 1083) say of the structural contingency approach:

> Whilst this was useful for explaining cross-sectional variety (Pennings 1987), its explanatory value has been contested by longitudinal investigations of organizational dynamics and clinical studies of design. The theory seems to have explained the functional logic of organizational forms well, but less well how individual organizations obtain and change their form over time.

Unconscious Considerations

A question arises as to the involvement of unconscious factors in the Table 37.1 theories. I have considered the theories invoked by the Aston group and by Blau to be balanced because they include the Weber theory of bureaucracy, which utilizes charisma as one of its variables; charisma has been shown to be an unconscious process. These two theories provide the strongest support for structural contingency theory, and are the only instances in which my evaluations and those of organizational behavior scholars are closely aligned.

Another case where unconscious factors emerge is that of the Burns and Stalker theory. This occurs because that theory activates various organizational forms, the hierarchic or mechanistic and the professional or organic (see Miner 2006a, Chapter 12). Chapter 35 in this volume states: "Without question this evidence indicates that considerations that extend beyond awareness are implicated in how these alternative forms operate." The evidence derives primarily from Miner (2008).

I am not convinced that the other theories noted in Table 37.1 invoke unconscious factors, although it is possible to argue that theories such as that of Chandler may involve choice as an individual difference variable, and thus some unconscious activation. In any event structural contingency theory would seem at certain points to bring unconscious considerations into the picture and thus to justify the award of a balanced designation.

CONCLUSIONS

As indicated in Table 37.1, Donaldson's (2001) structural contingency theory yields a three-star rating based on the mean of ratings of theories included (2.7). The actual importance rating at the hands of organizational behavior experts is 4.33, with a ratio of 1.44, although the mean of the theories rated in Table 37.1 is 4.73. In either case organizational behavior appears to substantially overestimate the presumed validity of the theory.

Structural contingency theory is an amalgam of other theories that utilize the fit or congruence notion. The causal flow is from contingency factors to structural factors; the organization continues to seek an appropriate structural fit when a misfit occurs. Structural contingency theory as currently elucidated represents the core on which other contingency theories are to be built. There are six main characteristics of the theory: (1) it is nomothetic, (2) it is methodologically positivist, (3) it explains structure by material factors, (4) it is deterministic, (5) it is informed by empirical research, and (6) it seeks to produce scientific knowledge of the type achieved in the natural sciences. Structural contingency theory was originally developed out of theories that incorporated Weber's theory of bureaucracy (the Aston group and Blau), although a number of other such approaches are now included (see Table 37.1). Using my ratings, the most effective contributors to the amalgam are those from the Aston group and from Blau, although evaluations by others are mixed. Because of their ties to bureaucracy these theories include a degree of unconscious content. The only other such theory in Table 37.1 is the Burns and Stalker approach, dealing with mechanistic and organic forms, which in turn represent hierarchic and professional systems. On these various incorporations of unconscious factors, in addition to conscious factors, I conclude that structural contingency theory is of a balanced nature.

CHAPTER 38

THE THEORY OF ALPHA, BETA, AND GAMMA CHANGE

The theory of alpha, beta, and gamma change is applicable to changes occurring across organization development or in fact any such training evaluation study. Although I am not aware of any meta-analyses on the subject (the Svyantek, Goodman, Benz, and Gard [1999] analysis might be an exception), comprehensive reviews have been conducted (see Day and Lance 2004; Riordan, Richardson, Schaffer, and Vandenberg 2001). I give a three-star rating to the validity of the theory and organizational behavior yields an importance rating of 3.77 (see Miner 2006a, Chapter 18, 347–349; 2006b, Chapter 17; 2007, Epilogue on Bureaucracy 4).

THE NATURE OF ALPHA, BETA, AND GAMMA CHANGE

A question arises as to the specific nature of the changes that occur.

Definitions

Alpha change involves a variation in the level of some existential state, given a constantly calibrated measuring instrument related to a constant conceptual domain.

Beta change involves a variation in the level of some existential state, complicated by the fact that some intervals of the measurement continuum associated with a constant conceptual domain have been recalibrated.

Gamma change involves a redefinition or reconceptualization of some domain, a major change in the perspective or frame-of-reference within which phenomena are perceived and classified, in what is taken to be relevant in some slice of reality (Golembiewski, Billingsley, and Yeager 1976, 134–135).

Interpretation

Alpha changes occur along relatively stable dimensions defined in terms of discrete and constant intervals. Beta changes are characterized by shifts in the intervals used and involve restandardization of a measure in the mind of the respondent. Gamma changes involve a re-defining of the psychological space covered by a measure, such as shifting from one construct to another or expanding the domain envisaged by a given construct; thus new meanings are introduced.

Alpha change is what we normally assume to occur across the process of an intervention when we repeat measurements over time. Yet there is convincing evidence that beta and gamma changes can occur as well—usually without their effects being evident to the researcher; thus we have a potential source of error.

This potentiality for error is particularly pronounced in organization development evaluations for three reasons. First, most interventions are intended to produce gamma change, and probably beta change as well. Typically, organization development is viewed as a process for introducing a new social order or a new culture. It intends to change values and ways of perceiving; concepts of ideal states are expected to shift. If these changes do not occur, then the effort is likely to be considered ineffectual; however, if they do occur, beta and gamma changes are introduced, which in turn confound the measurement process.

Second, beta and gamma change are factors that are most likely to influence self-report measures where meanings and standards within the individual tend to determine the data; this is in contrast to projective measures or hard data outcome measures of productivity. These self-reports are often used to evaluate the results of organization development interventions, either in the form of survey questionnaires or, less often, in standardized interviews. To the extent these approaches are used, conclusions regarding organization development success rates are placed in jeopardy.

Third, procedures of various kinds aimed at detecting beta and gamma change have been developed; some are statistical in nature and some involve innovations in research design. Riordan, Richardson, Schaffer, and Vandenberg (2001) identify a number of such procedures: the Ahmavaara technique (the method endorsed originally by Golembiewski, Billingsley, and Yeager 1976), actual-ideal measures (see Zmud and Armenakis 1978; Bedeian, Armenakis, and Gibson 1980), retrospective accounts (see Terborg, Howard, and Maxwell 1980), confirmatory factor analysis (see Schmitt 1982; Millsap and Hartog 1988), and latent growth modeling (see Chan and Schmitt 2000; Lance, Vandenberg, and Self 2000). The latter two are said to be the most widely supported by researchers.

What then does Golembiewski's theory mean for success rates that are predicated on the incorrect assumption that all change is alpha in nature? The original instigation for the theory came from a deviant case when an evaluation by the usual self-report methods pointed to failure, as indicated by no change from pretest to post-test. Yet participants in the intervention insisted on its overall success. This type of situation would suggest that the research reports may represent underestimates. Others, including Golembiewski (2003) and Golembiewski and Brewer (2008), have reached this same conclusion.

One solution to the problems thus identified is to utilize measures other than those of a self-report nature. This has been done with measures of performance, including productivity, absenteeism, turnover, and the like; positive results have been obtained with these kinds of measures, thus providing confidence in the success rates reported.

There is also the question of whether beta and gamma changes—if they do operate to decrease the amount of recognized change—do so to a meaningful degree. Some beta change and most gamma change would seem to require basic cultural changes before their mechanisms are activated.

CONSCIOUS AND UNCONSCIOUS

Most alpha change, especially when predicated on self-report measures, would appear to be of a conscious nature. Yet Riordan, Richardson, Schaffer, and Vandenberg (2001, 56) note, "We also looked for studies that incorporated techniques for dealing with the complexities of unintentional beta or gamma changes," and go on to explain, "In another line of research, studies that examine organizational culture, and changes to organizational culture, seem inherently to address gamma change. . . . No examples of such studies were found in our sample" (59). Thus beta and gamma changes are a reality; they involve organizational culture change and may well invoke unconscious processes (see in particular Chapter 30 in this volume). Consequently, unconscious considerations, beyond the entirely conscious, need to be given attention in evaluating approaches to dealing with alpha, beta, and gamma change.

The Use of Projective Techniques

One approach to invoking unconscious processes is to use projective techniques in the more traditional training evaluation designs. This has been done in the past, but not widely. Examples derive from McClelland's achievement motivation training (McClelland and Winter 1969; Miron and McClelland 1979; Spencer and Spencer 1993). See as well Chapter 4 in this volume. Other such instances are to use not the Thematic Apperception Test (TAT), but sentence completion measures. This was done using the Miner Sentence Completion Scale (MSCS)—Hierarchic at the Atlantic Refining Company (see Chapter 3 of Miner 2008) and Chapter 13 (from the same Miner [2008] publication) comparing West Point cadets and Ft. Benning, Georgia, officer candidates. Projective approaches of this kind are psychometrically sound, and they work well in opposition to many claims to the contrary (for evidence on this point, see Miner 2008, Chapter 1, and elsewhere in that book).

The Process Dissociation Approach

As shown in Chapter 10 of this volume the process dissociation approach can use projective information as well, but its unique contribution is to help disentangle unconscious phenomena from the conscious. The example I use in Chapter 10 involves dependence, as appropriate to that context (see Bornstein 2002). However, the approach can be extended more widely as well; it would seem to be applicable to gamma-type situations involving organizational culture. As Payne and Stewart (2007, 303) note, "The basic logic of placing intended and unintended influences in concert and in opposition in order to disentangle them can be implemented across many, many domains." The authors also state: "A common way to test that question is to impose a cognitive load, to rush responding, or look for motivational differences. If cognitive load, rush responding, or low motivation interferes with the effect, it is inferred to be resource dependent and therefore likely controlled. In contrast if these variables have no effect (or increase the stereotyping effect), it is inferred that the effect is automatic, because it is not dependent on the investment of cognitive resources" (299).

Expert Predictions under Unconscious and Conscious Conditions

Another approach involves establishing unconscious and conscious conditions to differentiate the two. This is done as follows by Dijksterhuis, Bos, van der Leij, and van Baaren:

> In two experiments, we investigated the effects of expertise and mode of thought on the accuracy of people's predictions. Both experts and nonexperts predicted the results of soccer matches after conscious thought, after unconscious thought (while conscious attention is directed elsewhere), or immediately. In Experiment 1, experts who thought unconsciously outperformed participants in all other conditions. Whereas unconscious thinkers showed a correlation between expertise and accuracy of prediction, no such relation was observed for conscious thinkers, or for immediate decision makers. In Experiment 2, this general pattern was replicated. In addition, experts who thought unconsciously were better at applying diagnostic information than experts who thought consciously or who decided immediately. The results are consistent with unconscious thought theory (Dijksterhuis and Nordgren 2006).

And so again a method is described for separating conscious and unconscious processes, as required by alpha versus certain beta and gamma designs.

UNCONSCIOUS PROCESSES IN ORGANIZATIONAL BEHAVIOR AND CAREER DECISIONS

We are now at a point where unconscious processes are beginning to move from experimental and social psychology, and personality theory, to mainstream applications; however, this latter must be judged as somewhat of a piecemeal procedure. Both organizational behavior and vocational behavior have recently published articles on unconscious processes that I believe represent mainstream applications.

Organizational Behavior

There have been several publications in the organizational behavior literature that I have cited previously, but the only one of these that I would consider of a mainstream nature is the Dane and Pratt (2007) article entitled "Exploring Intuition and Its Role in Managerial Decision Making" in the *Academy of Management Review.* Now, however, Jennifer George (2009) has published an article entitled "The Illusion of Will in Organizational Behavior Research: Nonconscious Processes and Job Design" in the *Journal of Management.* This article deals with job characteristics theory and is not unlike what I wrote here roughly a year earlier as Chapter 5 in this volume. George and I have had no communication on this subject, and I have chosen to leave my presentation of a year earlier unchanged to facilitate comparisons. As the references in George (2009) indicate, the field has seen some development in the interval, but not a great deal. I believe that the George (2009) contribution represents a very useful addition to the literature; I quote several of her alternative propositions on job characteristics theory to make my point:

> Alternative Proposition 1: People respond to the design of their jobs in an automatic fashion based on local cues and the nonconscious activation of knowledge structures (1329).

Alternative Proposition 2: On-the-job behaviors (direction of effort and intensity) are more driven by the local context in which behaviors occur, less driven by global evaluations of the job, and reflect a series of sequential and predominantly automatic choices rather than an overall global approach to the job (1330).

Alternative Proposition 3: High and sustained levels of conscious engagement and deliberation are beneficial for certain kinds of tasks (e.g. acquiring new skills and knowledge) and detrimental for other kinds of tasks (e.g. creativity and complex judgments that rely on existing knowledge and skills) (1332).

Alternative Proposition 4: Job characteristics should be balanced to allow for alternative modes of thinking and behaving (1333).

Alternative Proposition 5: Both positive and negative affective reactions are functional and adaptive (1334).

These alternative propositions are intended to replace the primarily conscious thrust of the original (Hackman and Oldham 1980).

Career Decision Making

At roughly the same time that George (2009) published her article, Krieshok, Black, and McKay (2009) performed a similar function with an article entitled "Career Decision Making: The Limits of Rationality and the Abundance of Non-conscious Processes," published in the *Journal of Vocational Behavior.* This is not focused on any particular theoretical perspective, but it does give considerable attention to unconscious processes as they relate to the career decision-making arena. Let me illustrate with various quotes from the article:

As we examine findings on judgment and decision making, 2-system models of decisional thought, and the neuroanatomy of decision making, we conclude that both rational and intuitive processes are dialectically intertwined in effective decision making (275–276).

Cognitive processes are often confounded by biases and heuristics (Kahneman, Slovic, and Tversky 1982; Simon 1955; Tversky and Kahneman 1974 . . .). An intuitive mode of processing parallels the rational one and is active and influential in decision making (Kahneman 2003) (278).

Our preferences and desires, as well as our pursuit of that which we prefer and desire, are not necessarily dependent on conscious awareness. It is implicit learning . . . that makes this possible (280).

The primacy of rational processing notwithstanding, it appears that automatic cognitive processes do indeed carry out the preponderance of decision making (Bargh and Chartrand 1999, 281).

Dijksterhuis and Nordgren (2006) go even further and propose a model that considers unconscious thought to have analytical capabilities far surpassing those of conscious processing, but only for complex, data-rich tasks (282).

And in the authors' conclusions:

> Vocational psychologists have historically directed their assessments and interventions at the rational aspects of decision making. However, as we have delineated, career decision making is not the exclusively rational practice once imagined. . . . The matter is compounded by the fact that an extensive body of research supports the function of intuition in decision making" (Krieshok, Black, and McKay 2009, 287).

CONCLUSIONS

As noted early in this chapter the theory of alpha, beta, and gamma change is awarded a rating of three stars on validity and has garnered an importance rating of 3.77 from organizational behavior experts. Dividing as appropriate gives a ratio of 1.26, indicative of a minimal overestimation of the presumed validity of the theory from the organizational behavior perspective. This evaluation should be determined relative to positive data from alpha change, indicating as it does conscious processes, and the similar positive data emanating from at least part of beta and gamma change, indicative of unconscious processes and the involvement of organizational cultures. The definitions involved are presented and interpreted. Accordingly the theory appears to represent a balanced view. Next, various procedures for unearthing beta and gamma change are considered; these typically involve certain types of conscious processing. However, unconscious processes are clearly involved when gamma change is introduced to institute new organizational cultural agendas. Thus projective techniques may be applied to measure unconscious change factors, and process dissociation procedures may be used to disentangle conscious and unconscious contributions. Predictions from conscious and unconscious perspective may also be made to measure the extent to which one or the other mode contributes.

The discussion finally shifts to recent publications that acknowledge the role of unconscious processes in organizational behavior and career decision making. These publications serve to mark the entry of these fields into the mainstream literature involved. Their combined impact as of 2009 serves to represent something of a breakthrough at this point in time.

PART VI

SOCIOLOGICAL CONCEPTS OF ORGANIZATION

CHAPTER 39

EXTERNAL CONTROL OF ORGANIZATIONS: RESOURCE DEPENDENCE PERSPECTIVE

Resource dependence theory was originally a product of Jeffrey Pfeffer, who later was joined by Gerald Salancik (Pfeffer and Salancik 1978). I have given this theory an estimated validity evaluation of five stars; the same importance rating is awarded by organizational behavior—5.29 to be exact (see Miner 2006a, Chapter 19; also Miner 2007, Chapter 25). In contradistinction to these high figures, resource dependence theory receives only a three-star evaluation on practical usefulness. It is essentially a sociological theory and, like most other theories of this genre, does not appear to have generated any meta-analyses. However, numerous positive evaluations exist.

INTERDEPENDENCE

Whenever one actor does not fully control all conditions for achieving an action or obtaining the desired outcome, interdependence exists. This interdependence varies with the scarcity of resources, characterizes transactions within the same environment, and is a consequence of the open-systems nature of organizations; it is virtually inevitable. A variety of conditions affect the extent to which an organization is subject to control under these circumstances:

1. The focal organization is aware of the demands.
2. The focal organization obtains some resources from the social actor making the demands.
3. The resource is a critical or important part of the focal organization's operation.
4. The social actor controls the allocation, access, or use of the resource; alternative sources for the resource are not available to the focal organization.
5. The focal organization does not control the allocation, access, or use of other resources critical to the social actor's operation and survival.
6. The actions or inputs of the focal organization are visible and can be assessed by the social actor to judge whether the actions comply with its demands.

7. The focal organization's satisfaction of the social actor's requests is not in conflict with the satisfaction of demands from other components of the environment with which it is interdependent.
8. The focal organization does not control the determination, formulation, or expression of the social actor's demands.
9. The focal organization is capable of developing actions or outcomes that will satisfy the external demands.
10. The organization desires to survive (Pfeffer and Salancik 1978, 44).

The foregoing presents the essence of resource dependence theory. In addition, however, it illustrates the extent to which that theory is characterized by a conscious or rational orientation. That orientation clearly did dominate in the early presentations of the theory.

UNCERTAINTY

Yet Pfeffer and Salancik (1978) do invoke the concept of uncertainty. This is documented in Arthurs, Busenitz, Hoskisson, and Johnson 2009 (see 850–852). The uncertainty concept has been discussed previously in this volume with regard to James Thompson's use of the term (see the appropriate section of Chapter 28), and also with regard to the term's use in connection with Lawrence and Lorsch's contingency theory of differentiation and integration (see the appropriate section of Chapter 29). In both of these instances uncertainty is linked to unconscious processes; thus there does appear to be some inconsistency in the Pfeffer and Salancik treatment with regard to conscious/unconscious considerations.

FURTHER TO PFEFFER'S VIEWS WITH REGARD TO THE NEW UNCONSCIOUS

The New Unconscious perspective (Hassin, Uleman, and Bargh 2005) appeared on the scene in book form at about the same point that Pfeffer began to write on such matters. It is also noteworthy that at this time Pfeffer shifted from his longstanding anti-individual differences position (see for a typical example Pfeffer 2001) to a more favorable disposition toward individual differences (see Pfeffer and Fong 2005, where the authors' argue in favor of the self-enhancement motive).

On the Effects of Priming

Consistent with the adoption of the new unconscious perspective, Pfeffer began to write on the effects of priming. In Pfeffer and Fong (2005, 385) he states: "These types of experiments demonstrate the apparent case in *priming* a feeling of power, a phenomenon that is quite consistent with the tendency to self-enhance." This statement is also consistent with Pfeffer's (1981, 1992) writings on the use of power in organizations. Elsewhere Pfeffer (2005a, 453) indicates: "To the extent that people adhere to a theory and therefore use language derived from and consistent with the theory, the theory can become true because language *primes* both what we see and how we apprehend the world around us." Furthermore DeVoe and Pfeffer (2007, 789) use priming as follows: "We wanted to see to what extent our argument about economic *priming* affecting only or primarily work-related activities held and, therefore, whether or not hourly payment affected decisions about other time use categories." This was with regard to testing the hypothesis that "the economic value of time that is made salient by hourly payment will diminish willingness to undertake work lacking monetary compensation" (785).

Discussions of priming and its effects are distributed throughout this book; this approach is one of the major ways in which unconscious material is activated.

On the Added Influence of Intuitive Processes

Ferraro, Pfeffer, and Sutton (2005) note, "As pressure for accountability increases it activates a wide range of coping strategies in decision makers who become *intuitive* politicians and choose their options with the goal of establishing or preserving a social identity" (17). This follows upon a treatment of another new unconscious aspect, the use of priming, by these same authors who indicate that "the importance of language and *priming* suggest that the study of language should be expanded from the consideration of the rational versus normative dimension to a broader spectrum of linguistic *primes* that can trigger competitive behavior, beliefs in the efficacy of markets, and individual self-interest" (16).

Also consider the following from Pfeffer (2005b, 1105): "There are . . . other notable instances where Donaldson's arguments depart from the evidence. When he talks about the unimportance of *intuition* and the importance and superiority of formal methods of thought and analysis, he ignores the large amount of scholarly research on the power of *intuition,* including evidence cited in Malcolm Gladwell's recently published *Blink.*" (See the Introduction to this volume, but understand that Donaldson's [2005b, 1106] subsequent reply was "I did not choose to ignore the evidence about intuition that Pfeffer cites, because I had never heard of the book he mentions.")

I have dealt with this matter of intuition and with intuitive processes in several previous chapters of this book. In particular I would cite the treatments in Chapter 22 on Simon's views; also the appropriate section of Chapter 23 on image theory and of Chapter 24 on James March's various contributions.

On Mindsets and Unconscious Processes Generally

Pfeffer (2005c) has several things to say that are relevant to this topic. Among these are the following:

> In considering . . . cases of either knowing-doing problems—not implementing what they know they should be doing based on experience and insight—or doing-knowing problems—companies not acting on the basis of the best available evidence—one factor that looms large as an explanation for the difficulties: the mental models or *mind-sets* of senior leaders (124).

> Where do these mental models or *mind-sets* come from? . . . Most of our models of business and behavior are *unconscious* and *implicit* (125).

> Assumptions and *mind-sets* are often deeply embedded *below the surface of conscious thought* (125).

> There may be a potentially even more important activity that human resources might do—the diagnosing and changing of *mind-sets* and mental models. Actually intervening to affect

mental models may be one of the more efficient ways of making the changes that HR so often advocates to build a high-performing culture (127).

Culture is a crucial determinant of many dimensions of organizational performance, and HR's cultural role is significant. . . . Human resources must be concerned with the mental models and *mind-sets* of the people in the company, particularly its leaders (128).

CRITIQUES OF RESOURCE DEPENDENCE THEORY: PRO AND CON

A number of critiques have been offered as to the pluses and minuses of the resource dependence formulations.

The Views of Robert House

Robert House's (1991, 44) views on the subject are particularly informative, although not in and of themselves damning to the theory:

There are several reasons why the [resource dependence] theory is likely to make rather weak predictions. That is, there are several reasons why correlations between the variables are likely to be substantially less than unity. First, the theory appears to apply more to organic than mechanistic organizations. Second, the theory appears to be more relevant to the long term than the short term. Third, the theory appears to apply to non-institutionalized organizations and organizations not embedded in a larger institutionalized network of organizational relationships. Fourth, theoretical predictions of the theory are substantially weakened when the chief operating officer or the dominant coalition has a high degree of power relative to the board of directors, owners, or external agencies intended to exercise stewardship over the organization.

The Views of Amy Hillman

Amy Hillman has consistently reported research that supports Pfeffer's views and those of resource dependence theory (see Hillman, Cannella, and Paetzold 2000; Hillman and Dalziel 2003). In line with this research I would report the following:

Resource dependence theory emphasizes the importance of linking firms with external contingencies that create uncertainty and interdependence. A critical source of external interdependency and uncertainty for business is government. One way to link a firm to the government is appointing ex-politicians to the board of directors. This study ["Politicians on the Board of Directors: Do Connections Affect the Bottom Line?" published in *Journal of Management*] compares the boards of two groups of firms—those from heavily and less regulated industries—and finds the former group has more politician directors. Firms with politicians on the board are associated with better market-based performance across both groups, although the relationships is more pronounced within heavily regulated industries (Hillman 2005, 464).

Thus it appears that resource dependence theory works rather consistently, but better under some circumstances than others.

CONCLUSIONS

The external control of organizations using the resource dependence perspective is a theory developed by Jeffrey Pfeffer and Gerald Salancik; it is in essence a sociological theory. As indicated early in this chapter, this theory supports an estimated validity of five stars and is awarded an importance rating by organizational behavior as a whole of 5.29. Dividing the latter figure by the five stars yields a ratio of 1.06, suggesting that the importance rating of the theory only minimally overestimates its validity. On the evidence there are points at which resource dependence theory exhibits strong conscious characteristics and other points at which Pfeffer espouses unconscious considerations in line with the new unconscious perspective. The net effect is a judgment that the theory is essentially balanced in nature, having both conscious and unconscious aspects that emerge at different points in time.

Resource dependence theory focuses on interdependence and the processes involved in obtaining resources from other organizations. The ultimate goal here is the survival of the organization; this whole process is described in terms of a conscious or rational orientation. Yet the external control of organizations does involve the invoking of uncertainty along the lines specified by James Thompson (Chapter 28) and Lawrence and Lorsch (Chapter 29). As indicated in these previous chapters uncertainty often can activate unconscious processes. Thus even in its early stages resource dependence theory was characterized by some inconsistency on this score.

Later (in 2005 to be exact) Pfeffer began to extol aspects of the new unconscious perspective and to express favorable views of individual difference variables, thus abandoning his previous anti-individual differences position. At this time he invoked repeatedly the concept of priming, especially with regard to power considerations, which represent a key aspect of the theory. Furthermore he brought intuition into his theoretical calculations, noting what Malcolm Gladwell had to say in his book *Blink* about unconscious processes. In one such 2005 publication Pfeffer writes about mindsets that are utilized by top management—specifically how those mindsets exist below the surface of conscious thought. Here he invokes constructs such as the unconscious and implicit processes.

A final emphasis in this chapter is to indicate the views of Robert House in emphasizing certain negative features of resource dependence theory, and of Amy Hillman in providing research support for the propositions advanced by that theory.

NEOINSTITUTIONAL THEORY

Neoinstitutional theory comes in several different versions, three of which tend to stand out. First, there is the position of John Meyer and Richard Scott (see Meyer and Scott 1983; Scott and Meyer 1994, and the initial presentation by Meyer and Rowan 1977). Second, there is Lynne Zucker's version (see Zucker 1977, 1983, 1988; and Meyer and Zucker 1989, which has much in common with the Meyer/Scott approach). Finally, there is the version represented by the DiMaggio and Powell formulation (see DiMaggio and Powell 1983, also DiMaggio 1988). These three versions overlap largely in time and content. I will emphasize the differentiating aspects between them while recognizing the common elements that exist. However, all three are sufficiently different to merit independent recognition and discussion.

META-ANALYSIS

One major meta-analysis stands out in this domain. Rather than attempt to deal with the multitude of propositions inherent in these theories, the authors, Heugens and Lander (2009), propose four hypotheses for testing via the meta-analyses.

Hypotheses

These hypotheses are as follows:

1. The degrees of coercive, normative, and mimetic pressures in an organizational field are positively related to the degrees of isomorphism in that field.
2a. The conformist adoption of isomorphic templates for organizing by focal organizations is positively related to their symbolic performance.
2b. The conformist adoption of isomorphic templates for organizing by focal organizations is negatively related to their substantive performance.
3. Organizational field-level factors moderate the relationship between the degrees of coercive, normative, and mimetic pressures and the degree of isomorphism in a field.

Results

Hypothesis 1: Confirmed
Hypothesis 2a: Confirmed
Hypothesis 2b: Rejected
Hypothesis 3: Supported in four out of five instances—but not where a professional body is involved.

However, note the following as presented in the Discussion section of the Heugens and Lander (2009) report:

> The average effect sizes we identified were very modest, ranging from .07 (coercive and normative pressures) to .09 (mimetic pressures). These effect sizes suggest weak institutional forces. Even though all isomorphic effects hypothesized by DiMaggio and Powell (1983) turned out significant in both the artifact-corrected meta-analysis and vote-counting meta-analysis conducted here, their magnitudes suggest that they hardly represent an institutional iron cage from which no escape is possible. . . . Agency positions, which rest on the assumption that organizations enjoy at least some discretion in crafting responses to institutional processes (Oliver 1991) appear to be fully compatible with our findings (Heugens and Lander 2009, 76).

EVALUATIONS

In line with these meta-analytic results, my reported evaluations of the three theoretical positions of a neoinstitutional nature run as follows:

> For the Meyer and Scott version, an estimated validity of five stars and an importance rating at the hands of organizational behavior of 4.79.

For the Zucker version, an estimated validity of four stars and an importance rating from organizational behavior of 4.51.

For the DiMaggio and Powell version, an estimated validity of three stars and an organizational behavior importance rating of 5.22. This latter figure is in line with these authors' high citation count for references to their "iron cage" article (see Greenwood and Meyer 2008). Yet this version is rated lower on validity because of the heavy reliance on qualitative research, which has proven productive in generating good theory but is clearly lacking insofar as proving and testing validity.

These evaluations are taken from Miner 2006a, Chapter 20; Miner 2006b, Chapter 19; and Miner 2007, Chapter 26. Only the Meyer and Scott vintage achieves an adequate rating on practical usefulness, largely because the authors do indicate some concern with management development and education issues.

THE MEYER AND SCOTT VERSION

Neoinstitutional theory began with an article by Meyer and Rowan (1977) entitled "Institutionalized Organizations: Formal Structures as Myth and Ceremony." Thus Meyer was in fact the originator. This article is reprinted with others in Meyer and Scott (1983).

Organizational structures are said to develop in highly institutionalized contexts. Thus they are influenced to take on the practices and procedures defined by prevailing rationalized ideas about organizational work held in society. When they do this, they increase both their legitimacy and their chances of survival. However, these societal expectations are actually myths and may well conflict with criteria of efficiency. Formal structures and the rules that govern them are in fact reflections of the institutional environment. These institutional effects are quite apart from the effects produced by networks of social behavior and relationships within and around a particular organization. Examples of institutionalized processes are professional rules, business functions, and established technologies. Following these approaches is viewed as appropriate, displays responsibility, and avoids charges of negligence.

These ideas are followed by a series of propositions interspersed with commentary:

1. As rationalized institutional rules arise in given domains of work activity, formal organizations form and expand by incorporating these rules as structural elements.
   1a. As institutionalized myths define new domains of rationalized activity, formal organizations emerge in these domains.
   1b. As rationalized institutional myths arise in existing domains of activity, extant organizations expand their formal structures so as to become isomorphic with these new myths.
2. The more modernized the society, the more extended the rationalized institutional structure in given domains and the greater the number of domains containing rationalized institutions.
   2a. Formal organizations are more likely to emerge in more modernized societies, even with the complexity of immediate relational networks held constant.
   2b. Formal organizations in a given domain of activity are likely to have more elaborated structures in more modernized societies, even with the complexity of immediate relational networks held constant.

Isomorphism with environmental institutions has some crucial consequences: (a) They incorporate elements that are legitimated externally, rather than in terms of efficiency. (b) They employ external or ceremonial assessment criteria to define the value of structural elements. (c) Their dependence on externally fixed institutions reduces turbulence and maintains stability.

3. Organizations that incorporate societally legitimated rationalized elements in their formal structures maximize their legitimacy and increase their resources and survival capabilities.

Organizations may be ordered on a continuum from . . . production organizations under strong output controls . . . to institutionalized organizations whose success depends on the confidence and stability achieved by isomorphism with institutional rules.

Two problems face organizations of the latter type—(a) technical activities and demands for efficiency create conflicts and inconsistencies in an institutionalized organization's efforts to conform to the ceremonial rules of production; and (b) because these ceremonial rules are transmitted by myths that may arise from different parts of the environment, the rules may conflict with one another.

4. Because attempts to control and coordinate activities in institutionalized organizations lead to conflicts and loss of legitimacy, elements of structure are decoupled from activities and from each other.
5. The more an organization's structure is derived from institutionalized myths, the more it maintains elaborate displays of confidence, satisfaction, and good faith, internally and externally.
6. Institutionalized organizations seek to minimize inspection and evaluation by both internal managers and external constituents.

These propositions and arguments lead to three theses for research attention:

1. Environments and environmental domains that have institutionalized a greater number of rational myths generate more formal organization.
2. Organizations that incorporate institutionalized myths are more legitimate, successful, and likely to survive.
3. Organizational control efforts, especially in highly institutionalized contexts, are devoted to ritual conformity, both internally and externally (Meyer and Scott 1983, 26–44).

Further on Organizational Environments

Organizational structures are expected to be generated as technologies and environmental interactions foster the development of bureaucratic systems (this is the technological side); they are also generated in that institutional structures operate to define roles and programs as being rational and legitimate (this is the institutional side).

The following propositions deal with what is involved:

1. Organizations evolving in environments with complex technologies create structures that coordinate and control technical work.
2. Organizations with complex technologies buffer their technical activities from the environment.
3. Organizations with efficient production and coordination structures tend to succeed in environments with complex technologies.
4. Organizations evolving in environments with elaborated institutional rules create structures that conform to those rules.

5. Organizations in institutional environments buffer their organizational structures from their technical activities.
6. Organizations with structures that conform to institutional rules tend to succeed in environments with elaborated institutional structures (Meyer and Scott 1983, 47–48).

These propositions are straightforward enough as long as technology and institutions remain separate, but as Meyer and Scott indicate, ambiguity enters into the theory when, for instance, technologies become institutionalized—as medical technologies do in hospitals. The ambiguities involved here are not resolved.

Societal sectors are said to include all organizations that supply a particular type of product or service together with the suppliers, financial sources, regulators, and the like within the organizational set. The theory then attempts to develop hypotheses as to the effects of sector characteristics on organizational forms. Examples are as follows:

1. Organizations in technical sectors will attempt to control and coordinate their production activities, buffering them from environmental influences.
4. Organizations in institutional sectors will succeed to the extent that they are able to acquire types of personnel and to develop structural arrangements and production processes that conform to the specifications of that sector.
6. Organizations functioning in sectors that are not highly developed technically or institutionally are expected to be relatively small in size and weak in terms of their capacity for survival.
9. The more highly professionalized a sector, the more likely that instrumental and programmatic decisions will be decentralized.
15. The more centralized, unified, and concentrated is the decision making within a sector, the smaller is the number of different organization forms within the sector and the greater is the variance between them.
17. Organizations functioning in sectors that are highly developed institutionally but not technically will be subjected primarily to interlevel controls emphasizing structural measures.
19. The exercise of structural controls is more compatible with the loose coupling of administrative to production tasks than is the exercise of process controls, and the exercise of process controls is more so than the exercise of outcome controls (Meyer and Scott 1983, 141–149).

Elsewhere Scott (1990b) has reemphasized that in sectors where both technical and institutional environments are not well developed, the organizations tend to be small and weak.

Institutional Environments and Organizations

The preceding theoretical statements wrap up what the authors refer to as the first wave. The second wave is reflected in a book with the same title as this section (Institutional Environments and Organizations) and contains a balance of previously published articles (1986–1993) and original papers (Scott and Meyer, 1994).

In Scott and Meyer (1994) *institutions* are defined as cultural rules giving collective meaning (in terms of the collective purposes of progress and justice) and value to particular entities and activities, integrating them into the larger schemes. *Institutionalization,* accordingly, is the process through which a given set of units and a pattern of activities come to be normatively and cognitively held in place, so that they are taken for granted to be lawful (either as a result of formal law, custom, or knowledge). In this view action is not a matter of individual choice but of broad social scripts; individualism loses out in large part to "the massive institutional features of the social system" (Scott and Meyer 1994). These features in turn are part of the culture.

The term *rationalization* is used to refer to purposive or instrumental processes that structure everyday life. This process is dictated by impersonal rules that constitute social organization and lead to collective purpose. Institutions embody universalized claims tied closely to moral purpose and the rules of nature; consequently specific institutional claims and definitions tend to be much the same throughout most of the world.

The essential themes here are:

1. Rationalization . . . leads to the formation of an extraordinary array of legitimated actors reified as purposive and rational—individuals, associations, classes, organizations, ethnic groups, nation-states.
2. Collective actors command greater legitimacy and authority if they are founded on a theory of individual membership and activity, such as the nation-state or the rationalized firm.
3. Organizational entities that are tied into the theories of justice and progress gain special standing above all others.
4. Because they derive from universalistic cultural ideology, dominant organizational forms, including the structure and boundaries of collective action, are relatively standardized across societies (Scott and Meyer 1994, 26–27).

Subsequently a general institutional model is set forth as follows:

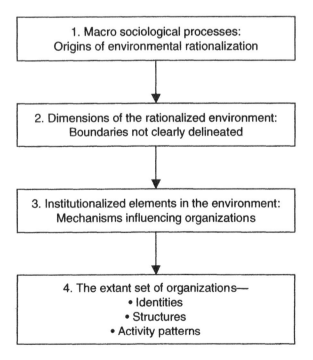

254 SOCIOLOGICAL CONCEPTS OF ORGANIZATION

Figure 40.1 **A Layered Model of Institutional Process**

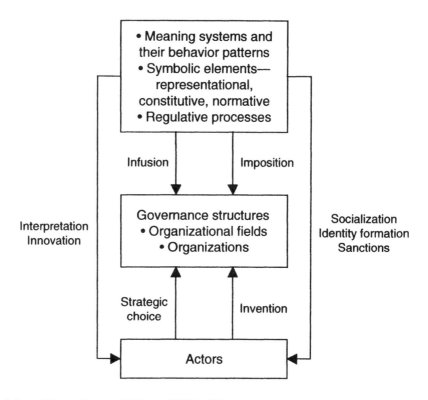

Source: Adapted from Scott and Meyer (1994, 57).

Of these four, the first two are less developed in either a theoretical or a research sense; numbers 3 and 4 are the primary sources of attention. Figure 40.1 focuses on this interaction. The processes through which behavior is shaped may be specified as follows:

- Representational rules that involve shared logics or modes of reasoning that help to create shared understandings of reality—that is, understandings of reality that are "taken for granted"
- Constitutive rules that create social actors—that is, identities linked to specified behaviors and action routines
- Normative rules that stipulate expectations for behavior that are both internalized by actors and reinforced by the beliefs and actions of those with whom they interact
- Enforcement mechanisms, both formal and informal, involving surveillance, assessment, and the application of sanctions rewarding conformity and punishing deviance (Scott and Meyer 1994, 67).

Working from this perspective *institutions* are now defined as symbolic and behavioral systems containing representational, constitutive, and normative rules together with regulatory mechanisms that define a common meaning system and give rise to distinctive actors and action routines. To this is added (somewhat later) that *institutions* operate at a variety of levels, and their elements can be embodied in and carried by cultures, regimes, and formal organizations.

Interpreting Neoinstitutionalism

Scott (1987, 2001) has not only been a contributor to neoinstitutional theory but a purveyor of its history and an interpreter of its development. Much of this is not relevant for present purposes except to show the diversity of approaches. However, a discussion of the role of cognitive, normative, and regulative structures and activities in influencing social behavior provides an addition to what was said previously on this score.

THE PREDOMINANCE OF UNCONSCIOUS PROCESSES IN THE MEYER/SCOTT VERSION

Although the preceding treatment may seem to emphasize conscious and rational considerations in neoinstitutional theory, there is much that would argue for an alternative interpretation. I want to cite a number of references from the authors' writings in this regard to make this point.

On Cooley's Views

In Scott (2001, 10) there is favorable reference to the views of the sociologist Charles Cooley (1956, 313–314) as follows:

> Although the great institutions—language, government, the church, laws and customs of property and of the family—appear to be independent and external to behavior, they are developed and preserved through interactions among individuals and exist "as a habit of mind and of action, largely *unconscious* because largely common to all the group. . . . The individual is always cause as well as effect of the institution."

On Cultural-Cognitive Views

Similarly Scott (2001, 110) offers an opinion on cultural-cognitive views:

> Cultural-cognitive theorists [of which Scott is one] tend to emphasize the important role played by *unconscious,* taken-for-granted assumptions defining social reality. Jepperson (1991, for example) insists that the hallmark of an institution is its capacity for *automatic* maintenance, for self-restoration. Institutional mechanisms are those requiring *no conscious* mobilization of will or effort.

On Naturalistic Narratives

In Scott (2008, 222) the following commentary on naturalistic narratives appears:

> Among proponents of naturalistic narratives are cognitive institutionalists, such as Schutz (1932/1967) and Berger and Luckman (1967) who stress the *unconscious* ways in which activities are habitualized and reciprocally interpreted during social interaction; as well as

social ecologists Carroll and Hannan (1989) who view increasing organizational density as an indicator of their increasing legitimacy and taken-for-grantedness.

On the Multiple Meanings of Rationalization

The dictionary attributes several different meanings to the word *rationalization*. Among these, one utilizes the term *unconscious;* this reflects the meaning as a defense mechanism (see Chapter 34 of this volume).

This multiple meaning phenomenon is inherent in the applications of rationalization within sociology and macro organizational behavior, and thus within neoinstitutional theory. Thus in Drori, Jang, and Meyer (2006) various rationalizations are considered. They say, "Our aim is to show that beyond the technical, narrowly economic and political nature of many pressures and justifications for governance reform, cultural and organizational changes may also serve as important antecedents for changes in governance culture" (206). To indicate that rationalizations come in various forms they note, "Three of the four indicators of rationalization in national governance registered indisputable declines beginning around 1996. . . . One of the indicators of rationalization of national governance—favorable investment profile—resisted the mid- 1990s decade decline and posted steady gains over the last part of the study period" (221). Thus multiple "explanations of government actions were found to exist by the study, not just one true process."

Along this same line Scott (2005) begins his explanation of how neoinstitutional theory came about.

> Institutional theory attends to *the deeper* and more resilient aspects of social structure. It considers the processes by which structures, including schemas, rules, norms, and routines become established as authoritative guidelines for social behavior (460). . . . Organizations were recognized to be "rationalized" systems—sets of roles and associated activities laid out to reflect means-ends relationships oriented to the pursuit of specified goals. The key insight, however, was the recognition that models of rationality are themselves cultural systems, constructed to represent methods for pursuing purposes. . . . Many of the models giving rise to organizations are based on "rationalized myths"—rule-like systems that "depend for their efficacy—for their reality, on the fact that they are widely shared, or have been promulgated by individuals or groups that have been granted the right to determine such matters" (462–463). . . . These and related arguments focusing on "myths," "ceremonial behavior," and *mindless conformity* placed sociological institutionalists in danger of focusing exclusively on the *irrational* and the superficial aspects of organization (469–470).

On the Conscious-Unconscious Duality within Sociology

Scott (2004) has not only written on the history of neoinstitutional theory, but he has chronicled the history of the sociological discipline as well. In doing so he explains:

> The institutionalization of this duality is apparent up to the present. Although occasional scholars present purified models stressing either perfect rationality (posited by assumption) or unadulterated *irrationality* (viewing organizations as a modern curse), most contemporary scholars seem content to work somewhere within the space anchored by these two poles. Concepts as varied as "transaction costs" (Williamson 1975), "rational myths" (Meyer and Rowan 1977), "the social embeddedness of economic action" (Granovetter 1985), and the

juxtaposition of logics of "instrumentality" and "appropriateness" (March and Olsen 1989) continue to reflect a fault line buried deeply within the field (4).

THE IMPLICATIONS OF THE CULTURAL STATUS OF NEOINSTITUTIONAL THEORY

In previous treatments I have emphasized that cultural considerations are frequently involved. Typically, where this happens, unconscious factors have been shown to be operating (see Chapter 7 in this volume and Chapter 11 as well). A more comprehensive discussion is contained in Chapter 30 here, as well as in Chapter 23 in this volume. These contributions repeatedly make the point that cultural contributions may well operate in an unconscious manner. To this conclusion should be added the evidence that culture plays an important role in attuning people to their cultural heritage (Ashton-James, Maddux, Galinsky, and Chartrand 2009), and that a process whereby people seek to establish common ground with their conversation partners causes familiar elements of culture to increase in prominence, independent of performance or quality (Fast, Heath, and Wu 2009).

THE ZUCKER VERSION

The primary statement of the neoinstitutional perspective set forth by Zucker (1977) is in fact an introduction to three experiments conducted to test that perspective. Institutionalization is defined as both a process through which actors transmit what is socially considered to be real, and a property existing at any point in the process, where the meaning of an act can be said to be a taken-for-granted part of the social reality. Such institutionalized acts must be perceived as *objective* (potentially repeatable) and *exterior,* in that they are viewed as part of the world external to the individual.

Objectification and exteriority vary together so that increasing one causes an increase in the other; thus institutionalization can vary from low to high, and acts can possess different degrees of institutionalization. Acts that have ready-made accounts are institutionalized acts. These accounts are socially created and function as objective rules in the absence of direct social control. In fact the invoking of incentives or sanctions may serve to deinstitutionalize the acts involved. Acts performed by occupants of an organizational office tend to be seen as highly objective and exterior, thus institutionalized.

Institutionalization affects three aspects of cultural persistence—transmission, maintenance, and resistance to change. *Transmission* is the process by which cultural understandings are communicated to a succession of actors. The more the objectification and exteriority, the greater the transmission; continuity of the transmission process fosters institutionalization.

The basic assumption is the fact of transmission of acts that are highly institutionalized will be sufficient to cause the *maintenance* of these acts. The institutionalization process serves to define a social reality that will be transmitted, and then maintained, as fact.

Acts high on institutionalization will exhibit *resistance to change,* and attempts to change them through personal influence will face resistance simply because they are viewed as external facts. Failures of influence efforts in such circumstances may well extend to redefining the actor rather than the act.

The higher the level of institutionalization, the higher the transmission, maintenance, and resistance to change of cultural understanding hypothesized. This expectation, which is essentially one of cultural persistence, was tested in the research that we will take up shortly.

Zucker's (1977) theoretical statement is essentially presented at the micro level. Subsequently she began to move toward a theory of organizations as institutions in which organizational power is based not on the control of resources, but on control of institutional structure and process (Zucker 1983). This effort, however, resulted only in the presentation of "the basic outlines which such a theory might take" (37). The objective was to stimulate others to work on a general theory of institutionalization.

In another later approach to macro-level theorizing, Zucker (1988) set forth a view with the following starting principles: (1) social entropy threatens organizational stability, (2) the organization of the social system is characterized by coherence and interconnectedness, (3) the primary change agents are the formally organized collectivity and the power of organizations, (4) institution building is a continual process to foster maintenance, and (5) the key problem is maintaining a degree of stability. Coherence is critical to the stability of the social system but is continually threatened by systemic entropy as well as other factors. This approach too is considered to be "not yet either well developed or tightly interconnected" (45), and is offered in the hope of stimulating the theoretical work of others.

Research Evidence

As indicated previously, Zucker's (1977) theorizing introduced a set of research investigations. These were laboratory studies utilizing the autokinetic effect in which the degree of institutionalization was manipulated by introducing various organizational conditions. The effects on the perceived movement of a light were obtained for transmission, maintenance, and resistance to change conditions. Institutionalization clearly had the anticipated impact under all three conditions; the hypothesized relationships between degree of institutionalization and cultural persistence were supported.

Subsequently Zucker (1983) reported several other investigations that provide evidence for the effects of institutional environments on organizations. An analysis of the spread of civil service reform over a fifty-five-year period showed a gradual institutionalizing process. Although city characteristics were good predictors in the early years, these correlations disappeared later and adoption came to be expected even if not functional for a specific city. An analysis of the establishment of evaluation units in school systems showed a similar development as a function of state regulation and funding. An analysis of city responses to statewide budget cuts in California indicated that institutional forces established parameters for local responses.

In a particularly interesting study Zucker and Kreft (1994) used archival data to study the effects of strike activity on founding rates of union locals. They conclude that institutions (unions) form in response to demand and social conflict (strikes). Thus institutional development does *not* appear always to be a consequence of institutional isomorphism as prior theories had proposed; variance may be added, at least initially, and homogeneity decreased. The data also suggest that institutional structures do not just happen. They evolve over a period of time as a consequence of human agency and demand, and they are maintained as resources to keep them going become available.

Zucker was involved in analyses of organizations that were inefficient but survived for long periods on the basis of their institutional status. Of this work she comments, "The notion that organizations could survive despite very low objective performance implied the possibility of permanently failing organizations (Meyer and Zucker 1989), that is, organizations that survive despite evident inefficiencies that logically should cause them to fail" (Tolbert and Zucker 1996, 178).

Tolbert (in Zucker 1988) studied institutional factors in the operation of large U.S. law firms, specifically the establishment of structures to ensure the socialization of new members. The results showed clearly that professional organizations are affected by institutional processes, as various theorists had indicated previously.

Interpretation (in an Unconscious Mode)

Scott (2001, 110–111) tends to align Zucker's thinking with his own, and thus with cultural-cognitive theorizing. He quotes Zucker (1977, 726) to the following effect: "Internalization, self-reward, or other intervening processes need not be present to ensure cultural persistence because social knowledge once institutionalized exists as a fact, as part of objective reality, and can be transmitted directly on that basis." To substantiate this view Scott then describes the results of Zucker's research with the autokinetic effect. Elsewhere Zucker and Darby (2005, 547–548) state, "Much of the process of institutionalization is tacit and not open to direct measurement. Thus indirect indicators of the social construction process have been used. . . . Social construction does not just build new social structure, it fundamentally changes cognitive conceptions and frames through which we view many aspects of social and economic life."

Cultural factors, which have been shown previously to have an unconscious component, are emphasized in the Zucker theory as attested to by various others (see Scott 2001; Tsui, Zhang, Wang, Xin, and Wu 2006). Similar support exists for the view that institutionalized behaviors/practices are taken-for-granted aspects of social reality (see Staw and Epstein 2000; Wezel and Saka-Helmhout 2006; Fernhaber and Li 2010).

In this same unconscious mode, Cathryn Johnson, Timothy Dowd, and Cecilia Ridgeway (2006, 72) indicate, "We found that the construal of a social object as legitimate in a local situation involves an *implicit* and sometimes explicit process in which widespread consensual beliefs about how things should be or typically are done creates strong expectations for what is likely to occur in that local situation"; Weber and Glynn (2006, 1642) report, "Such roles become *embodied* in actors as *habitus* or tastes and dispositions . . . encoded into action scripts that are enacted . . . or habitually repeated without much mediating process (Zucker 1991)."

THE DIMAGGIO/POWELL VERSION

The seminal publication on this perspective, like Meyer and Rowan (1977) and Zucker (1977) previously, comes from DiMaggio and Powell (1983). Its primary concern is with the mechanisms of institutional isomorphic change, said to be *coercive* isomorphism (stemming from political influence and the problem of legitimacy), *mimetic* isomorphism (resulting from standard, imitative responses to uncertainty), and *normative* isomorphism (associated with professionalization).

A series of hypotheses is then presented dealing with the predictors of isomorphic change, first those operating at the organizational level and then those operating at the field level. Examples follow—

Organizational:

1. The greater the dependence of an organization on another organization, the more similar it will become to that organization in structure, climate, and behavioral focus.

4. The more ambiguous the goals of an organization, the greater the extent to which the organization will model itself after organizations it perceives to be successful.
6. The greater the participation of organizational managers in trade and professional associations, the more likely the organization will be, or will become, like other organizations in the field.

Field:

7. The greater the extent to which an organizational field is dependent upon a single (or several similar) source of support for vital resources, the higher the level of the isomorphism.
10. The greater the extent to which technologies are uncertain or goals are ambiguous within a field, the greater the rate of isomorphic change.
12. The greater the extent of structuration in a field, the greater the degree of isomorphics (DiMaggio and Powell 1983, 154–156).

The authors note that they have not attempted to develop measures of the variables they propose.

Subsequently DiMaggio (1988) attempted to deal theoretically with what he viewed as the failure of institutional theory to handle the matter of self-interest. His central thesis to this end is that:

> institutionalization is a product of the political efforts of actors to accomplish their ends, and the success of an institutionalization project and the form that the institution takes depend on the relative power of the actors who support, oppose, or otherwise strive to influence it. . . . The success of an institutionalization process creates new sets of legitimated actors who, in the course of pursuing distinct interests, tend to delegitimate and deinstitutionalize aspects of the institutional forms to which they owe their own autonomy and legitimacy. . . . Institutionalization as an outcome places organizational structures and practices beyond the reach of interest and politics. By contrast, institutionalization as a process is profoundly political (DiMaggio 1988, 13).

Beyond the writings already noted, both of the theory's authors have contributed in various ways to the literature on institutionalism but not in the form of concerted theoretical formulations. Rather the tendency has been to argue for further development and broadening of the institutional perspective in various ways (see, for example, Powell and DiMaggio 1991) and in various contexts (see DiMaggio, Hargittai, Neuman, and Robinson 2001).

Research Evidence

The DiMaggio/Powell perspective has not been the subject of significant quantitative research by the authors. There have been qualitative studies, referred to by the authors as case studies, dealing with institutional processes as they relate to book publishing, public television, art museums, and the like (see, for example, their articles in Zucker 1988 and Powell and DiMaggio 1991), but these cannot be considered tests of either their or any other institutional theory. This situation exists in spite of the fact that both of these authors have conducted quantitative research in other areas. Yet the qualitative emphasis as promulgated by the authors has exerted a strong influence on subsequent studies. A case in point is a qualitative study intended to provide evidence for the existence of institutional entrepreneurship in the sponsorship of a particular technology by Sun Microsystems (Garud, Jain, and Kumaraswamy 2002).

One area of institutional interest has been the diversification of large firms. Fligstein (in Powell and DiMaggio 1991, 311–336) studied this process among the hundred largest companies over the years 1919 to 1979. He found that diversification put companies in the top 100, while failure to diversify led to more rapid exit. Diversification also institutionalized an elevated role for financial executives (Zorn 2004). In the early period diversification appeared to follow from chief executive characteristics, but this correlation disappeared in the later years. The best index in this later period was the proportion of firms already diversified. The data lend good support to institutional theory and its imitative processes.

Other evidence points to an opposite picture using different data for the years 1980 to 2000 in U.S. industry. Consider the following:

> The picture that emerges from our analysis is very different from that envisioned by DiMaggio and Powell (1983). . . . This pattern of heterogenization was due to the very "field level forces" for isomorphism identified by DiMaggio and Powell, but all of these forces moved in directions opposite of those DiMaggio and Powell anticipated. In most industries, corporate goals became less ambiguous; there was less structuation; the role of the state diminished; resource dependence broadened; the number of legitimate organizational models proliferated; and managerial backgrounds became more diverse (Hambrick, Finkelstein, Cho, and Jackson 2005, 342–343).

Furthermore, the Heugens and Lander (2009) meta-analysis does not list this study as included. I have no explanation for what is involved.

The Case for Conscious Theorizing

In contradistinction to the Meyer/Scott version and the Zucker version of neoinstitutional theory, as discussed previously, the DiMaggio and Powell version appears to marshal considerable belief favoring a conscious interpretation. Let me quote from some of these views:

> The original formulation of neoinstitutional theory has rarely discussed the role of political factors, including agency, interest, power, and conflict. As a number of researchers have pointed out (DiMaggio 1988 and Powell 1991 are among those cited), early studies in this literature often went "overboard with myths and symbols" . . . by concentrating on cognitive and cultural factors, such as taken-for-granted cognitive schemas and intersubjectively shared cultural norms (Kim, Shin, Oh, and Jeong 2007, 287).

> Powell and DiMaggio (1991, 30), lamented that "power and interests have been slighted topics in institutional analysis" (Greenwood 2008, 153).

> DiMaggio and Powell specified "three mechanisms of isomorphism institutional change": *coercive* mechanisms, which occur when external constituents on which an organization is dependent or cultural expectations in the society within which organizations function cajole or force organizations to change in a certain way; *normative* mechanisms, which arise primarily from professional projects; and *mimetic* mechanisms, which occur when

organizations copy successful role models either because their actions are believed to be rational or because of a desire to avoid appearing . . . deviant or backward (see the recent meta-analysis of the empirical strength of the iron cage; Heugens and Lander 2009) (Greenwood and Meyer 2008, 261–262).

Alternatively, other analysts stress an *agent-based* view, which emphasizes the extent to which intentionality and power are at work. This view corresponds with . . . the *enacted* institution, which is the product of rational intervention and intention. Scholars such as DiMaggio (1988, 1991) and Fligstein (2001a; 2001b) embrace this conception. . . . Institutionalization is a product of the political efforts of actors to accomplish their ends. . . . Even 'rational' actors attempting to design and construct institutions that will advance their own interests often fail" (Scott 2008, 223).

These views are reinforced by a number of formulations with regard to institutional entrepreneurship:

Institutional entrepreneurship represents the activities of actors who have an interest in particular institutional arrangements and who leverage resources to create new institutions or to transform existing ones (DiMaggio 1988; Fligstein 1997; Rao, Morrill, and Zald 2000) (Maguire, Hardy, and Lawrence 2004, 657).

Neoinstitutionalists have suggested that institutional activists are *ideological entrepreneurs* who secure constitutive legitimacy for a new industry as routine (DiMaggio 1988, 18; DiMaggio and Powell 1991) (Rao 2004, 262).

This paper redefines institutional change processes. . . . Agency can be not only habitual (Giddens 1984) or strategic (DiMaggio 1988), but also sensemaking (Weick 1995). . . . Leveraging derives from the work of scholars interested in the creation of new organizational forms (DiMaggio 1982, 1991, 1992). . . . *Institutional entrepreneurship* is likely to produce institutional change in opportunity transparent fields (Dorado 2005, 386, 390, 399).

Agency-based explanations of field emergence emphasize the work of *institutional entrepreneurs* who enact new visions, cultivate and capitalize on opportunities for change, and exert political clout to legitimize new institutional arrangements (e.g. DiMaggio 1988; Garud, Jain, and Kumaraswamy 2002; Maguire, Hardy, and Lawrence 2004) (Purdy and Gray 2009, 355).

Previously I discussed the multiple meanings of rationalization and showed how the term may be used by neoinstitutionalists as a defense mechanism, with several different such "explanations" being mobilized to explain the same phenomenon (see Drori, Jang, and Meyer 2006). But within the DiMaggio/Powell context, a more conscious meaning—a single one—appears to emerge. Thus Hwang and Powell (2009) have the following to say:

Nonprofits have to develop consistent accounts. . . . These practices locate rationality inside the organization (strategic planning) and establish specific substantive and financial areas for analysis (272). All four variables loaded strongly on one single general factor, and we obtained one factor with an eigenvalue greater than 1 (279). The prime carriers of rationalization in our study are managerial professionals and foundations. . . . Managerial professionals, rationalization, and foundation initiatives travel together (293).

This is not the message that the Drori, Jang, and Meyer (2006) study carried; clearly the DiMaggio/Powell version of neoinstitutional theory is not the same as the others.

The Case for Unconscious Theorizing

"Logics of action are shared cognitive frameworks related to particular practices or domains that decision makers use to help guide their own behavior (DiMaggio 1997). Of course most firms adopting a practice, whether they are prone to activism or not, will publicly account for their actions using some version of the logic of economic rationality" (Briscoe and Safford 2008, 465). This sounds like the use of rationalization as a defense mechanism, thus tending to mobilize unconscious considerations. It would appear that the consciousness in the DiMaggio/Powell version is mixed with a substantial dose of unconsciousness.

Mimicry as an Unconscious Process

This turns out to be true. I have noted previously that mimicry is one of the mechanisms for institutional change posited by the DiMaggio/Powell theory. Spell and Blum (2005) provide a vivid example—"Drug testing, which arose very rapidly in workplaces, may be adopted first by organizations responding to strategic concerns. . . . Later mimicry variables grow in importance. For more comprehensive innovations, like Employee Assistance Programs, which have a longer and more complicated history, mimicry is more relevant earlier" (1140).

Chapter 5 in this volume and Chapter 14 as well deal with mimicry and similarities, and with how unconscious factors are activated within these contexts. I would recommend in particular from these sources van Baaren, Holland, Kawakami, and van Knippenberg (2004) and Lakin, Chartrand, and Arkin (2008). Further treatment of the research on this subject is contained in the Chartrand, Maddux, and Lakin (2005) chapter of the book *The New Unconscious* and in the section on the mimicry route by Dijsterhuis, Chartrand, and Aarts (2007) in Bargh's recent volume (59–95). That we are dealing with unconscious processes cannot be questioned insofar as mimicry is concerned.

To what has been said previously, I would add the following from Stel, van Dijk, and Olivier (2009, 693):

> Mimicry facilitates the ability to understand what other people are feeling. The present research investigated whether this is also true when the expressions that are being mimicked do not reflect the other person's true emotions. In interactions, targets either lied or told the truth, while observers mimicked or did not mimic the targets' facial and behavioral movements. Detection of deception was measured directly by observers' judgments of the extent to which they thought the targets were telling the truth and indirectly by observers' assessment of targets' emotions. The results demonstrated that nonmimickers were more accurate than mimickers in their estimations of targets' truthfulness and of targets' experienced emotions. The results contradict the view that mimicry facilitates the understanding of people's felt emotions. In the case of deceptive messages, mimicry hinders this emotional understanding.

On Power as an Unconscious Process

Prior discussions have also dealt with the unconscious underpinnings of power, as distinct from the need for power (see Chapter 4 in this volume). These discussions occur in Chapters 23, 28, 31, and 36; they make the point, consistent with the DiMaggio and Powell formulations, that those who hold power obtain added leverage from unconscious considerations. There are, however, distinct differences between social power and personal power (Lammers, Stoker, and Stapel 2009). As with mimicry, the DiMaggio/Powell version of neoinstitutional theory manifests clear unconscious tendencies with regard to power, which with its equally pronounced conscious manifestations, lead to a judgment that this version of the theory is indeed balanced, as distinct from other versions.

FURTHER TO THE GOAL-SETTING LITERATURE

In the recent period several advances in the goal-setting literature of Chapter 2 in this volume have occurred. At least one of these represents a major contribution to the mainstream writing on unconscious processes in organizational behavior (see Chapter 38).

More on the Negative Effects of Goal Setting

In an addendum to Chapter 2 of this volume, I discussed the controversy that has arisen over the negative effects of goal setting. There I called for the incorporation of the unconscious dimension.

Now this controversy has been extended, if not expanded (see Latham and Locke 2009; Ordoñez, Schweitzer, Galinsky, and Bazerman 2009b). I am not sure, however, that much progress has been made; neither set of authors makes any mention of the unconscious factors that would seem to be involved.

On the Relevance and Viability of Subconscious Goals

However, one set of authors (Latham, Stajkovic, and Locke 2010) has returned with a vengeance to the unconscious context that was the subject of their previous research (Stajkovic, Locke, and Blair 2006). This is a major contribution to the mainstream literature on unconscious processes, and it deserves some review here.

They begin with the statement that "most scholars in human resource management and organizational behavior are unaware of or have ignored the programmatic research by a small number of social psychologists on priming subconscious goals (e.g., Bargh 1992; Gollwitzer 1999; Shah 2005)" (Latham, Stajkovic, and Locke 2010, 235). This is followed by a section on early research on the subconscious that considers the contributions of Miner, Bray and Howard, McClelland, and Eden, and features various projective techniques such as the Miner Sentence Completion Scale (MSCS) and the Thematic Apperception Test (TAT).

Next come sections on theories of subconscious goals, activation of subconscious goals, and additive and competing effects of conscious and subconscious goals; priming, as activated by subliminal or supraliminal techniques, is emphasized in these sections. The theories of priming considered are labeled as "mini" theories. Finally, there are sections on unresolved issues, management-related research, research avenues that have yet to be explored, and implications for management practice. Apparently there is considerable research in the works involving these authors, some of which is reviewed in their article (unpublished manuscripts and symposium presentations). Also, as to the time duration of unconscious priming, I would recommend a reading of Mitchell (2006).

CONCLUSIONS

Data on the three versions of neoinstitutional theory considered here are as follows:

Meyer and Scott version	$4.79/5 = .96$
Zucker version	$4.51/4 = 1.13$
DiMaggio and Powell version	$5.22/3 = 1.74$

Only the Meyer and Scott version, which embraces an unconscious perspective, yields a ratio that is close to expectations. The Zucker version, also of an unconscious nature, evidences some degree of overestimation of validity using the average importance rating from organizational behavior. This ratio yields a marked importance rating overestimation on the part of organizational behavior scholars for the DiMaggio and Powell version, which has been shown to be balanced between conscious and unconscious content.

The Meyer and Scott version invokes the concept of myths and thus opens the door to unconscious interpretation. Cultural considerations are also mentioned here, as is the taken-for-granted nature of institutions and the role of rationalization. All of these leave the door to the unconscious wide open. Further incorporation of this position is taken from quotes on Cooley's views, on cultural-cognitive views, on naturalistic narratives, on the multiple meanings of rationalization, and on the conscious-unconscious duality within sociology. The cultural status of neoinstitutional theory also serves to bring evidence of unconscious activation to bear.

In the Zucker version of the theory, "taken-for-granted" wording is used often, as is the invocation of cultural concerns and similarities to the Meyer/Scott formulations. Other indicators of unconscious features are noted as well.

The DiMaggio and Powell version is treated first in its conscious manifestations such as the emphasis on political factors, agency, and interest; institutional entrepreneurship is considered at some length. It is clear that conscious processes are much involved. But so are unconscious processes, particularly as they involve mimetic formulations and mimicry. The use of power also has been shown to have unconscious underpinnings. Both of these are inherent in the DiMaggio and Powell perspective and both have been clearly established by psychological research as unconscious in nature. Putting these conscious and unconscious indicators together I arrive at the conclusion that this version of the theory is indeed balanced.

In a shift of theme, I also consider a further consideration of the mainstream emergence of unconscious treatments within organizational behavior. Here, a recommitment to the research on the unconscious (see Chapter 2 in this volume) on the part of Stajkovic, Latham, and Locke becomes evident. They discuss their experience with the priming technique at considerable length, and evaluate it as well.

CHAPTER 41

ORGANIZATIONAL ECOLOGY AND DEMOGRAPHY

Organizational ecology and demography is a theory concerned with various topical subject matters, a number of which focus on themes within strategic management (see Baum, Dobrev, and van Witteloostuijn 2006). These treatments include entrepreneurship (see Ruef 2006), top management teams (see Boone, Wezel, and van Witteloostuijn 2006), organizational change (see Singh 2006), organizational learning (see Greve and Rao 2006), technology strategy (see Bigelow 2006), competitive strategy (see Negro and Sorenson 2006), cooperative strategy (see Pozner and Rao 2006), scale and scope (see Wezel and van Witteloostuijn 2006), and industry evolution (see Khessina 2006). Such topics may include much from organizational behavior as well, and as we will see, there are other topics that are related more directly to organizational behavior. In any event it is important to recognize that the theory has much to say that is within the purview of strategic management.

The theory of organizational ecology (and to a somewhat lesser extent, demography) is presented in a rather large number of articles and books. Initially in the late 1970s there were Hannan and Freeman (1977, 1978), and then an anthology containing multiple articles (Hannan and Freeman 1989).

Carroll was added to the team subsequently and Freeman largely dropped out (see Hannan and Carroll 1992; Carroll and Hannan 2000b). However, these three researchers were the major contributors to the theory in the early period. Major books written later include those by Harrison and Carroll (2006), Hannan, Pólos, and Carroll (2007), and Barnett (2008).

EVALUATION

To my knowledge there are no meta-analyses to cite; in fact it would be difficult to conduct analyses of this kind, due to the topical, fragmented way in which the theory has been presented. As originally formulated the theory received a validity rating of three stars, but with further development I increased this to four stars (Miner 2006a, Chapter 21). The importance rating given by organizational behavior scholars was 4.88. Estimated usefulness was also raised from one to two stars in recognition of the fact that the authors did make some attempt to deal with matters of this kind as the theory evolved.

THE HANNAN AND FREEMAN (1989) ECOLOGICAL THEORY

The ecological theory seeks to answer the question, Why are there so many (or so few) kinds of organizations? This requires indicating both the sources of increasing diversity, such as new forms, and the sources of decreasing diversity, such as competitive exclusion. The theory thus attempts to achieve an understanding of the rates of new organization and new form founding, the rates of organizational change, and the rates at which organizations and their forms die.

A basic assumption is that organizational variation is a function primarily of the creation of new organizations and forms, and the demise of others; actual change within organizations is rare, slow moving, and occurs early in their histories if at all. Environments change, but inertia prevails within organizations. Examination of such matters involves three levels of complexity:

1. The *demography of organizations*—founding rates, merger rates, disbanding rates.
2. The *population ecology of organizations*—how the existence and density of other populations of organizations affect a focal population.
3. The *community ecology of organizations*—a set of interacting populations; for example, firms, their labor unions, and relevant regulatory agencies (Hannan and Freeman 1989, 14–15).

The current diversity of organizational forms is a consequence of a long history of variation and selection (founding, mortality, and merger processes). Selection processes have general properties that hold across long historical periods. Yet the theory is only partial in its evolutionary treatment of organizational change; it focuses primarily on selection within organizational populations. The theory assumes that change:

> is more Darwinian than Lamarckian. It argues that inertial pressures prevent most organizations from radically changing strategies and structures. Only the most concrete features of technique can be easily copied and inserted into ongoing organizations. Moreover, there are density-dependent constraints on adaptation by individual organizations: although it may be in the interests of the leaders of many organizations to adopt a certain strategy, the carrying capacity for organizations with that strategy is often quite limited. Only a few can succeed in exploiting such a strategy, and those in the vanguard . . . have decided advantages.

Even when actors strive to cope with their environments, action may be random with respect to adaptation as long as the environments are highly uncertain or the connections between means and ends are not well understood. It is the match between action and environmental outcomes that must be random on the average for selection models to apply. In a world of high uncertainty, adaptive efforts by individuals may turn out to be essentially random with respect to future value (Hannan and Freeman 1989, 22).

Four factors are posited that limit managerial potential to create change:

1. The organization's form, which is not easily changed.
2. The scarcity of resources, which provides little slack to devote to change.
3. The competitive pressures, which magnify the effects of other factors.
4. The limitations on rationality, which have been emphasized by decision theorists (Hannan and Freeman 1989, 41).

Organizational forms are defined by technological factors, differences in transaction costs, the closure of social networks, successful collective action, and institutional processes. These segregating processes serve to establish boundaries, which, however, are also subject to blending processes that serve to break down their influences; thus boundaries across organizational forms do change.

In spite of considerable discussion by Hannan and Freeman (1989) of the factors that might be used to build a theoretical typology of organizational forms, and their recognition that further theoretical work in this area will be needed, the authors initially settle upon the "conventional wisdom" of participants and observers to define forms. These "native" classifications appear to have had particular appeal because the data needed for research tend to come bundled in this manner. Thus, at least operationally, the theory at this point is rather unsophisticated in its handling of the types of organizational forms and the boundaries among them. Because the conventional wisdom can change and even be a matter of some dispute, a degree of ambiguity is in fact built into an otherwise quite sophisticated theory.

Once a *complex organization* begins change, the process will be longer lasting; therefore, complexity contributes to a greater mortality risk. The ability to react quickly to new opportunities conflicts with the ability to perform with reliability and accountability here, and so inertia is not always a plus for selection. The theory, although it states a number of specific hypotheses related to inertia and similar matters as noted earlier, has a tendency to respond with statements such as "it is not clear," "is indeterminate in our theory," and "is an open question" at other points. The authors' willingness to admit the limits of their theoretical capabilities is admirable at these points, but logical consistency tends to be lost and ambiguity often prevails (Hannan and Freeman 1989).

The theory as applied to niches focuses on interactions within and between populations of organizations. The argument starts with Hawley's (1968) principle of isomorphism: "Units subjected to the same environmental conditions, or to environmental conditions as mediated through a given key unit, acquire a similar form of organization. They must submit to standard terms of communication and to standard procedures in consequence of which they develop similar internal arrangements within limits imposed by their respective sizes." Thus organizational diversity results from the diversity of agents controlling resources. Hawley's principle does not apply, however, when a large number of resources are involved, as is typically the case. Accordingly the theory turns to niche theory and to the processes of competition and legitimation in search of a solution.

The niche of an organization form consists of the social arrangements whereby a population can grow. To this the theory adds the process of interaction among populations, a process that occurs when one population affects the growth rate of others. The discussion then moves to a series of mathematical equations derived from bioecology. These deal with the carrying capacity of the environment for a given population, the intrinsic growth rate (the speed with which a population grows when there are no resource constraints), and competition coefficients that indicate how the carrying capacity for each population declines with the density of a competitor. The equations involved do not have a known solution, although competition coefficients can be estimated from data; the number of coexisting populations is constrained by the number of resources and constraints operating.

A related approach is to obtain estimates of competition from the overlap of niches and from niche width, which is the variance of the niche's resource utilization. Specialist organizations have less slack and thus less excess capacity than generalists do, but they also are more vulnerable to uncertainty and changing environments. Thus stable environments favor populations of specialists, but under many conditions variable environments favor generalists. Talking about selection on the basis of niche width has the advantage that it takes into account the degree of specialism. A detailed treatment of the niche construct is given in Popielarz and Neal (2007).

Population growth rates may be broken down according to the

1. Intrinsic speed of expansion
2. General environmental limits on growth or carrying capacities
3. Specific competition within and between populations (Hannan and Freeman 1989, 117).

Speed of expansion varies markedly across organizational forms. Life history strategies may vary from *opportunistic* (with many foundings and resources spread thinly) to the opposite (with few foundings and heavy resource investments in each). Life chances vary accordingly, but even so, environments with rapid changes and high uncertainty favor the opportunistic approach. Populations with forms that foster high founding rates tend to continue to exist even though individual organizations do not survive long.

Both speed of founding and carrying capacities—set by time-varying social and material processes—are joined by density dependence in determining vital rates. *Density* serves as a surrogate for features of the social and material environment. *Legitimacy*, which increases as a particular form becomes more prevalent, produces a positive relationship between founding rates and density, while competition produces a negative relationship. Dense environments are characterized by limited resources and crowded markets. Legitimacy processes dominate when N is small, and competition processes dominate when N is large; as a result, the function as a whole is nonmonotonic (does change). The authors developed formulas to show this. Disbanding rates fall with increasing density, up to the limits set by carrying capacity, after which they begin to rise. Merger processes, however, are more complicated and beyond the capabilities of the theory to explain at this point (Hannan and Freeman 1989, 139).

In many respects, organizational ecology as treated by Hannan and Freeman is not so much an integrated theory as an exercise in applying a rich variety of formal models to the subject matter. One such area for formal modeling is the dynamics of organizational populations. This area has been reworked and restated several times (see Hannan and Carroll 1992).

ENTER DEMOGRAPHY (CARROLL AND HANNAN 2000A, 2000B)

The shift from a theoretical focus on ecology to a focus on demography occurred at the turn of the twenty-first century. It brought with it new constructs and new emphases, but the result has been primarily a continuation of the prior approach to theory development. Many of the additions within the demography thrust represent attempts to rectify previous theoretical shortcomings; in this regard the new theory has been eminently successful.

The Carroll and Hannan (2000b) book contains at least five major extensions of the theory. These five are recognized by Rao (2002) as follows:

1. The established axiom of age dependence in death rates is reconsidered in a fresh light with the use of logical formalization, a powerful new weapon in the arsenal of organizational ecology. Carroll and Hannan lucidly discuss how initial endowments, imprinting effects, and positional advantage underlie age dependence in death rates and formalize the scope conditions of the liabilities of newness, adolescence, obsolescence, and senescence. . . .
2. Carroll and Hannan revisit the nettlesome issue of organizational forms and outline a new account of organizational forms. *Organizational Ecology* emphasized the boundaries of forms and directed attention to segregating and blending mechanisms. By contrast Carroll and Hannan assert that forms are organizational identities based on genetic and penal codes that are enforced by external and internal observers who respond to code violations with sanctions. . . . Industry persistence may conceal extraordinary turnover in organizational forms.
3. There is a striking difference in the two books' accounts of segregating processes. While *Organizational Ecology* gave prominence to how institutional processes were critical in the segregation of organizations, Carroll and Hannan depict resource partitioning and size-localized competition as segregating processes, but they are careful to show how resource partitioning may be premised on identity movements and institutional dynamics.
4. *The Demography of Corporations and Industries* describes the effects of corporate demography on the social structure of individual careers and, in particular, the effects of vital rates on job creation, dissolution, and individual mobility. In doing so, it opens up promising avenues for invigorating contact between corporate demography and the study of labor markets and inequality.
5. *Organizational Ecology* presents theory discursively, but Carroll and Hannan (2000b, 585) present theory through the adroit use of logical formalization.

Rao (2002) seems much enamored of these new contributions to theory.

The distinction that Carroll and Hannan (2000b) now make within their theoretical domain should also be noted:

- *Organizational demography*—processes that apply at the levels of populations of organizations.
- *Population ecology*—interactions between localized sets of populations.
- *Community ecology*—processes that follow from the full set of population interactions in some system (xx).

Forms and Populations Revisited

In the reconstructed theory of organizational forms Carroll and Hannan (2000b) posit that forms and identities are closely related concepts. A form is a recognizable pattern that acquires rule-like qualities. It is based on judgments made by outsiders and involves both *cognitive recognition* and *imperative standing*. Thus it is a cultural aspect. An identity becomes a form only if certain conditions apply:

1. The identity applied to and was satisfied by a form-specific constant number of organizations at the beginning of the interval; and
2. Violation of the applicable identity causes the outsider evaluation functions to drop sharply (73).

Defining forms in this way still permits the use of the same research data as previously, but it is somewhat more precise. Ideally it would call for an operationalization that relied upon the actual judgments of outsiders who reflect the culture.

This identity-based treatment of organizational forms is given a major endorsement in Hsu and Hannan (2005). Nothing has changed in the definition of organizational populations, except as implied by the new way of establishing forms. Accordingly an organizational population is now established "as the set consisting of the organizations defined by a given minimal external identity in a bounded system in some period" (75). This concept of population, embedded in an identity-based theory of form, is explained further and illustrated in an article by McKendrick, Jaffee, Carroll, and Khessina (2003). There it is shown that disk array production does not attain the "minimal external identity" necessary to constitute an organizational form.

Segregating Processes and Resource Partitioning

Among the theoretical developments stressed in the Carroll and Hannan (2000b) volume is the concept of resource partitioning, which appears to have been introduced in large part to explain certain inconsistencies in prior theory when subjected to research tests. Resource partitioning says that differences in niche width come to play a determining role in that specialist forms react differently to competition than large generalist forms. In the later stages of population age, a segregating process sets in that produces discontinuity on some dimension such as size, niche width, or status. A set of hypotheses is generated to deal with these phenomena as follows:

1. Under conditions of resource partitioning, as market concentration rises, the founding rates of specialist organizations will rise and the mortality rates of specialists will fall (266).
2. Under conditions of resource partitioning, as the number of dimensions in resource space increases, the founding rates of specialist organizations will rise and the mortality rates of specialist organizations will decline (268).
3. Under such competition, the greater the aggregate distance of larger competitors, the higher the generalist mortality rate (271).
4. Under resource partitioning based on identity, the legitimating effects of specialist organizational identity depend on (a) the normative status of the specialist form and (b) the social visibility of the specialist form (274).

Generally small specialist organizations do not compete with one another; however, intense competition among large generalist organizations tends to be characteristic. As a result specialists proliferate and generalists are few in number.

These views are elaborated further in a subsequent publication (Carroll, Dobrev, and Swaminathan 2002), and the following hypotheses are proposed:

1. An organization's hazard of mortality increases as a function of its position distance away from the market center (13).
2. Among scale-based (generalist) competitors within an organizational population, the greater the sum of distances of a firm from each of its larger (generalist) competitors, the higher its mortality hazard (14).
3. As market concentration rises, the mean amount of resource space covered by surviving individual generalists will expand (15).
4. As market concentration rises, the amount of unique resource space covered by the combination of all generalist organizations contracts (16).
5. The more concentrated the environmental resource distribution, the more concentrated the scale-based organizations serving the market (16).
6. As market concentration rises, the total amount of resource space open to specialist organizations expands (17).
7. As the number of dimensions in resource space increases, the total amount of space open to specialist organizations expands (18).
8. As the resource space open to specialists expands, the founding rates of specialist organizations will rise (18).
9. As the resource space open to specialists expands, the mortality rates of specialist organizations will fall (18).

These hypotheses place primary emphasis on the location of an organization in resource space. Other factors such as customization, anti-mass-production cultural sentiment, and conspicuous status consumption may operate in the same manner, however (Carroll, Dobrev, and Swaminathan 2002).

Initial Mobilizing

Most start-ups of new organizations involve a period of planning and in many cases preproduction operations that result in either failure or mobilization prior to actual entry into production. Hypotheses have been formulated in this regard also:

1. Preproducer density has an inverted-U-shaped relationship with the rate of entry into production.
2. Producer density has a greater impact on the rate of entry into production than does preproducer density.
3. The rate of preproducer initiation has an inverted-U-shaped relationship with the density of producers.
4. The rate of successful movement from preproduction into production declines monotonically with the time spent in [preproduction] organizing mode (Carroll and Hannan, 2000b, 345–346).

These hypotheses represent attempts to tie what happens in the pre-startup period to the larger body of theory dealing with density dependence.

Organizational Transformation and Inertia

The idea that inertia follows from the theory is modeled in various ways, stressing that organizations that are favored by selection tend to be resistant to change. Thus organizations attempting structural transformation should be more predisposed to failure. The models proposed in Carroll and Hannan (2000b) reach this conclusion in new ways but achieve the same result as in the ecological theory.

An instance of organizational inertia occurs in the case of *environmental imprinting,* under which specific environmental characteristics are mapped onto an organization, thus influencing its subsequent development and life chances. This is particularly likely to occur in the founding period; the imprinted features continue to hold over long periods.

Driven by inconsistent research findings the theory continues to be elaborated with regard to change and inertia (Hannan, Pólos, and Carroll 2003a, 2003b). The idea thus advanced is that architectural changes in an organization prompt additional alterations that reverberate through the firm, generating what amounts to a cascade of changes. Organizations undergoing change tend to concentrate on the change process and as a result miss opportunities to acquire resources. Consequently, long cascades increase the risk of failure. This risk is accentuated by limited foresight that creates a systematic inclination to underestimate both the length of an organizational transformation and the costs associated with it.

Note that concepts such as inertia and the deleterious affects of cascading change appear to contradict a number of other theoretical positions in the literature. These include (1) the idea that organizations should adapt to environmental changes by transforming themselves in some way, the general thrust of organization development, and (2) the concept of structural modulation, whereby efficiency is fostered by frequent changes even in the absence of environmental prompting (see Nickerson and Zenger 2002).

The Core Event-History Research and Relevant Studies

The preferred approach to conducting research on organizational ecology and demography theory is to collect information on the life histories of organizational populations and in particular on the occurrence of certain theory-relevant events of the type discussed previously; thus to use a kind of event-history procedure (Hannan and Tuma 1979). This retrospective approach differs from the modal methodology in organizational behavior by emphasizing populations rather than focal organizations and longitudinal analyses stretched out over extended time periods. It has been at the core of research on the Hannan/Freeman/Carroll theory from the beginning, although there are both major benefits and some drawbacks associated with it. Examples of the use of such an approach applied to academic rules at Stanford University indicates how these rules are born, revised, and suspended (March, Schulz, and Zhou 2000, 84). Another such application is Lange, Boivie, and Henderson (2009). Clearly such studies have a degree of feasibility.

The benefits are that by using archival data, events in the life histories of organizations of a given form and in a particular niche can be reconstructed. The only readily apparent alternatives are to start at the founding of the first organization and collect data forward until the last such organization dies (not a very parsimonious or perhaps even tenable procedure, although some truncation at the extremes might prove feasible) and to develop and run simulations of the processes involved (not the kind of approach one would want to rely on exclusively for evidence regarding a subject). So the event-history procedure clearly does lend itself to testing this type of theory.

The problem is that events and theoretical constructs do not always match perfectly. For instance, archival data may differ in the way organizational foundings are defined, thus resulting in construct invalidity (Hannan and Freeman 1989). Other features of organizations may be used in different ways in different studies because the available information differs. Published histories and data sources may vary in the precision used to define events. Certain types of information may be unavailable for periods of time or even completely lacking on a particular population (see Carroll and Hannan 2000b for an extended discussion of these issues).

The difficulties inherent in conducting research with archival, retrospective data sources constructed for purposes completely different from the theory they are used to test are problem enough. However, there is an even greater threat in that a theory constructed to be tested in this way might be driven in both its definition of variables and its specification of relationships by a knowledge of the available research data sets. That Hannan and Freeman (1989) often note their inability to formulate theory on a particular subject suggests that they are not forcing theory in this way and gives reason for optimism on this score. However, the real test is to look into studies conducted at a time and by researchers far removed from the original theorists. But first we need to consider the research that has involved participation by Hannan, Freeman, and Carroll themselves.

Initial Studies by the Theory Authors

The book *Organizational Ecology* (Hannan and Freeman 1989) draws upon three primary organizational populations to test its theory. These are all populations that had been utilized and discussed to some extent in previous publications during the 1980s, and they include:

1. The 479 U.S. labor unions founded in the period 1836–1985; foundings per year were close to zero until the Civil War (see also Hannan and Freeman 1987).
2. The 1,197 entries into the semiconductor manufacturing industry between 1946 and 1984; a number were new entries with a prior organizational existence (see also Brittain and Freeman 1980).
3. The 2,170 newspapers founded in the San Francisco Bay area in the 1840–1975 period; this is part of a wider study of seven urban newspaper populations in the United States (see Carroll 1987).

For all three populations, founding rates were related to density, usually rising with increasing density to a point and then declining with further increases in density. This theoretically specified, nonmonotonic pattern was characteristic of all but the independent foundings in the semiconductor industry; the latter do not appear to have encountered a carrying capacity in the same way as the other organizations. As predicted, failure rates were consistently a monotonic function of age, the liability of newness phenomenon (see also Freeman, Carroll, and Hannan 1983). Mortality rates were also a function of density, with rates falling with increasing density to a point and then rising. This consistency across populations was not maintained for the effects of competition on mortality rates; competitive pressures were particularly pronounced for the unions. Overall, across three very different populations, the theory received extensive, but not universal, support.

Hannan has continued to publish research with a variety of coauthors focusing on a multi-population approach similar to that used in the initial studies. One such analysis used three populations of newspapers, the San Francisco Bay population noted previously, an Irish population for the 1800 to 1975 period, and an Argentinean population from 1800 to 1900, as well as the U.S. labor union data and a population of brewing firms in the United States covering the period from 1633 to 1988 (Carroll and Hannan 1989). The question to be resolved was whether density at founding affects mortality rates. The conclusion was that it does in all five instances. However, whether this was a function primarily of resource scarcity or niche packing remains unresolved, requiring size-related data for its solution.

A subsequent study by Ranger-Moore, Banaszak-Holl, and Hannan (1991) extended the density dependence research to Manhattan banks (1791–1980) and American life insurance companies (1759–1937). The nonmonotonic function noted previously involving legitimacy and competition was again attained, confirming the theory in both instances. Furthermore, these data indicate that the theory is not merely applicable to small firms that are relatively free of regulation.

More recently Hannan and his colleagues have become involved in event-history studies of the automobile industry, particularly for the 1886 to 1981 period in Europe (Hannan, Carroll, Dundon, and Torres 1995). Again, the predictions of the theory hold, and for all five countries studied, insofar as density dependence is concerned. In addition there is evidence that the legitimation process is driven by density in Europe as a whole, while competition is a function of specific country densities. The generality of this apparently industry-specific finding is unclear.

One failure in this long list of research successes, other than what was noted earlier, involves the role of organizational size. This has been an area of considerable theoretical uncertainty; attempts to deal with it using the bank and insurance company data have proved to be only partially effective (Hannan, Ranger-Moore, and Banaszak-Holl 1990). Some theoretical developments to deal with these matters are contained in Carroll and Hannan (2000b).

The same volume presents reports on other research of interest. One such study dealt with initial mobilizing in the U.S. automobile industry from 1886 to 1982, where data on the subject were available. The results indicated some weak support for the first hypothesis on the inverted-U-shaped relationship between preproducer density and the rate of entry into production, and much stronger support for the effect of producer density in this regard. The other two hypotheses noted previously do not appear to have been confirmed.

Also the Carroll and Hannan (2000b) book contains a summary of studies on the effects of organizational change on mortality. Some fifteen investigations are noted, two of which involved Carroll as an author; the types of changes considered spread over a wide range. The two studies with Carroll as author supported the theory in indicating a positive relationship between change and mortality, but a number of studies did not. As Carroll and Hannan indicated, "The pattern of findings is far from uniform" (370). There are some signs of design problems in certain of the nonconfirming studies. All in all, however, the theory is not consistently supported by this line of research.

Yet Dobrev, Kim, and Carroll (2003), working with the automobile industry data, found that change elevates the potential for failure. The fact that instances of change that do not have these negative effects occur is also acknowledged, and explained using the niche width of generalist organizations as a moderator. It becomes increasingly evident that the theory of organizational transformation and inertia holds only under certain circumstances and that relationships in this area are exceedingly complex (see Dobrev, Kim, and Carroll 2002).

Findings That Give Reason for Pause

The research involving the authors provides considerable positive evidence in support of the theory. There are points at which exceptions appear, but these are commonly attributed to imperfections in the research data. Numerous studies by others yield an equally positive picture. Carroll's (1987) analysis of various newspaper populations, a particularly propitious setting for the conduct of event-histories, provides a good example of this positive set of findings.

Yet there are findings that introduce problems for the theory. I will start with a treatment of research on the theory of ecology. A study of voluntary social service organizations in Toronto from 1970 to 1982 obtained information on organizational changes from interviews (Singh, House, and Tucker 1986). The data indicated that changes did not necessarily result in an increase in organizational death rates. Ecological theory best described core changes, but peripheral changes were best described by an adaptation perspective. Thus a truly comprehensive theory of change would require the incorporation of both selection and adaptation processes. A subsequent study of the same population focused on specialist and generalist organizations and found substantial differences between the two forms (Tucker, Singh, and Meinhard 1990). Both ecological dynamics and institutional changes appeared to influence specialists more.

An analysis of organizational failures in the California wine industry between 1940 and 1985 fails to support the Hannan/Freeman ecological theory (Delacroix, Swaminathan, and Solt 1989). That theory, as it applies to the density dependence of mortality, consistently overstates the negative effects of a lack of legitimacy. In a number of instances, overcrowding was avoided by migrating to a new niche or by enlarging the initial niche. A follow-up analysis of information from the wine industry indicated that both businesses founded in the table wine niche and those that diversified into it had lower failure rates (Swaminathan and Delacroix 1991). Organizations appear to be more flexible in a strategic sense and environments less rigid than the density dependence concept of organizational demise would indicate.

An event-history analysis of newspapers in Finland over the period from 1771 to 1963 indicated that certain factors reduced failures, increased organizational transformations, and changed the chances of failure subsequent to transformation (Miner, Amburgey, and Stearns 1990). These factors operated in conjunction with interorganizational linkages that served to buffer against failure, influence the likelihood of organizational transformation, and change the effects of transformation on failure. Thus interorganizational linkages introduced a degree of flexibility in avoiding failures.

Petersen and Koput (1991) provide evidence that the decreasing mortality rate in the early part of a population's history is not necessarily a function of increasing legitimacy, but can be explained as a result of unresolved heterogeneity. There appears no need to invoke the process of legitimation, and, if legitimacy is to be invoked, direct measures are needed to support it rather than the inferential procedures of the Hannan/Freeman theory. These findings are based on various simulations and accordingly are not definitive, but they do underscore the need for hard measures of legitimacy rather than proxies more readily derivable from archival data.

Taken as a whole the research prior to 2000 emphasizes greater adaptability and flexibility on the part of organizations than the Hannan/Freeman theory seems to permit. It also raises questions as to whether the event-history approach to research alone is adequate to the task of validating the theory.

With the publication of the Carroll and Hannan (2000b) volume, and the theoretical extensions contained therein, however, a number of the earlier questions are given theoretical answers. In particular the advent of resource partitioning theory helps to explain the differential between generalist and specialist organizations. Swaminathan (2001) presents further evidence from the wine industry that yields considerable support for resource partitioning and accordingly places that industry in much closer alignment with the revised demographic theory. Also this study indicates that identity plays an important role in the evolution of specialist forms, thus adding credibility to the new definition of organizational form.

On the other hand, research continues to emphasize the importance of adaptability and flexibility. Analyses of Spanish savings and loan organizations

> support the validity of the different evolutionary patterns of the model and reveal the existence of different strategies for organizational adaptation in the population studied. In some cases, SS&L institutions resorted to strategic adjustment (internal adaptation), whereas in other cases, they stood inert or disappeared. . . . We also arrived at the following conclusion: on the one hand, business strategy is capable of leading organizational evolution and, on the other hand, the firm and its environment are clearly interrelated. . . . We found that organizational resources conditioned the path of organizational evolution. In short, organizational resources and routines linked to expansion policies clearly determined whether an institution died or adapted to the new competitive environment. . . . In summary, our results highlight the existence of different ways in which organizational evolutionary processes may operate (Alvarez and Merino 2003, 1449–1450).

Along these same lines, Kukalis (2010, 453) found that "enthusiasm for cluster theory shown by scholars, practitioners, and policy makers may need to be tempered." A study of 194 firms from the semiconductor and pharmaceutical industries indicated no significant differences between clustered and nonclustered firms in the early stages of the industry life cycle. However, support was found for the following hypotheses:

- The financial performance of nonclustered laggards (located outside the industry cluster) is higher than that of geographically clustered firms late in the industry life cycle (isolated laggards vs. clustered laggards).
- During periods of economic contraction, the financial performance of nonclustered firms is higher than that of clustered firms in the late stages of the industry life cycle (474).

Thus "clusters may have a dampening, rather than enhancing, effect on firm performance" (475). "Ecology theorists have emphasized that once industry growth reaches a saturation point, at which too many firms compete for the same resources in the same location, the ever-increasing competition could result in a dramatic reduction in the birthrate of new firms while hastening the demise of established, yet vulnerable firms (Hannan and Freeman 1977, 1989)" (Kukalis 2010, 475). Perhaps the greater influence of residential mobility is a factor here (see Oishi 2010); it should be considered in the theorizing.

CULTURE AND DEMOGRAPHY IN ORGANIZATIONS (HARRISON AND CARROLL 2006)

Harrison and Carroll's *Culture and Demography in Organizations* (2006) has two characteristics: It is *first* of all a computer simulation, which as I have indicated previously is somewhat suspect in its methodology. Although a reviewer, Burton (2007), endorses this approach and the book as a whole, the authors indicate their own concerns on this score (Harrison, Lin, Carroll, and Carley 2007, 1243):

Simulation analysis offers a variety of benefits. It can be useful in developing theory and in guiding empirical work. It can provide insight into the operation of complex systems and can explore their behaviors. It can examine the consequences of theoretical arguments and assumptions. By relying on formal modeling, simulation imposes theoretical rigor and promotes scientific progress.

But in spite of these benefits, the authors conclude as follows:

Simulation research, like any other research method, also suffers from problems and limitations. The value of simulation findings rests on the validity of the simulation model, which frequently must be constructed with little guidance from previous work and can be prone to problems of misspecification. Simulation work can be technically demanding and susceptible to errors in computer programming. The data generated by simulations do not represent real observations, and techniques for their analysis are limited. And it is risky to attempt generalizing simulation findings to areas of the parameter space not examined in the simulation. So claims based on simulation findings are necessarily qualified.

The *second* characteristic of the Harrison and Carroll (2006) book is that it is explicitly concerned with the effects of cultures, and thus introduces considerations of this kind into the theory; such matters have been noted previously, but here they are given major billing.

As noted in Chapter 40 of this volume, this emphasis leads to the incorporation as well of unconscious considerations into ecological and demographic theory. To what is said in Chapter 40, I would add numerous discussions in Chapters 7, 11, 23, and 30, which continue to make the point that cultural factors are often unconscious in nature. In Chapter 11 the study by Oyserman and Lee (2008) is considered. Commenting on this study, Varnum, Grossman, Kitayama, and Nisbett (2010, 11) say, "Although the effects of social orientation priming on cognition have been demonstrated primarily in Western societies, preliminary evidence suggests that comparable effects can be observed among East Asians and Asian Americans. Oyserman and Lee (2008) report comparable effect sizes for both Western and Asian samples."

LOGICS OF ORGANIZATION THEORY (HANNAN, PÓLOS, AND CARROLL 2007)

This book starts with a listing of theory fragments inherent in organizational ecology. These are:

- Organizational forms and populations
- Structural inertia and change
- Age dependence
- Dynamics of social movements
- Density dependence
- Niche structure
- Resource partitioning
- Diversity of organizations (Hannan, Pólos, and Carroll 2007, 18–20)

The present book involves a reworking of four of these—age dependence, forms and populations, niche structure and resource partitioning, and structural inertia and change.

On the Use of Nonmonotonic Logic

In this process the theory uses some unusual approaches; thus nonmonotonic logic "allows for rules—with exceptions—which the authors argue are more appropriate than simpler forms of logic in a social science context" (Kuilman 2007, 1587). But another reviewer (Kamps 2009, 352) states: "Changing the rules of a game, especially while playing the game, is rather risky." This logic form is used in an attempt to reconcile the disparities between the liability-of-newness, the liability of adolescence, and the theory of obsolescence in dealing with age dependence. "A nonmonotonic logic allows for a happier marriage" (Hannan, Pólos, and Carroll 2007, 152). Yet "among younger entrepreneurial firms, a dearth of top management industry experience is offset by the presence of outside directors with significant managerial industry experience, providing evidence of experience supplementing by outside directors. Our study highlights that the notion of experience supplementing at the upper echelons prevails in young firms as they try to alleviate the burdens of the liability of newness" (Kor and Misangyi 2008, 1345). Such considerations are not incorporated in the ecological theory proposed, even though doing so would seem to be warranted.

Further to the Activation of Unconscious Factors

I have already noted how unconscious considerations are activated by the incorporation of culture in the theory. There are, however, other ways in which unconsciousness is broached in the formulations. In the Hannan, Pólos, and Carroll (2007) book similarities are typically invoked (see pages 41, 58, and 293), and the evidence with regard to unconscious activation is discussed in Chapters 5 and 14 of this volume, as well as in Chapter 40. The latter treatment also invokes taken-for-granted formulations, and these are inherent as well in the Hannan, Pólos, and Carroll (2007) theory (see pages 78, 84–85, 97, 103, 197, 294, 306, and 312). Additionally, cultural resistances, organizational forms, and architectural codes (role prescriptions) may operate to bring about unconscious activations. All of these are now inherent in ecological theory.

Elsewhere Worley (2009) says with regard to the population ecology literature that it is "met with all manner of defensive routines" (55). "These organization behaviors are not some normal sort of 'resistance' but a much deeper pathology that exists in most (all?) organizations. It is part of the deep cultural assumptions that Schein (1992) describes" (55). Thus it is apparent that others perceive ecology theory as predominantly of an unconscious nature.

Furthermore intuition is noted within the Hannan, Pólos, and Carroll (2007) theory as an operative process, as is automatic cognition (48). Intuition is invoked on pages 180 and 246. The matter of bounded rationality introduces some uncertainty here. Hannan, Pólos, and Carroll (2007) do use the term *intuition* (see pages 238 and 256), but it is not exactly clear how they use it (see Chapter 22 and 24 in this volume). It would seem entirely possible that using this term as Hannan, Pólos, and Carroll do allows conscious processes into the theory. However, this is not entirely certain, and the term is invoked only on limited occasions. In contrast to the use of unconscious constructs (which may include nonmonotonic formulations), this activation would seem to be somewhat miniscule; thus I view the balance in the theory as distinctly unconscious in nature. In any event the reviewers (Kuilman 2007 and Kamps 2009), who do not commit themselves as to the unconscious versus conscious perspective of the theory, do give this presentation high marks; they describe it as "a remarkable and praiseworthy achievement" (Kuilman 2007, 1590) and as "a monumental achievement" (Kamps 2009, 353).

THE RED QUEEN AMONG ORGANIZATIONS (BARNETT 2008)

This last book, *The Red Queen among Organizations* (Barnett 2008), is not authored by the previously noted theorists, but it is relevant nonetheless. Barnett has written extensively on ecological theory (see Barnett 1990; Barnett and Woywode 2004). His 2008 book is subtitled *How Competitiveness Evolves*. It presents a number of hypotheses and their research tests.

The Hypotheses

Let us start with what constitutes a logic of competition and what the Red Queen reference means.

> A logic of competition is a system of principles in a given context that determines who can compete, how they compete, on what criteria they succeed or fail, and what are the consequences of success or failure. . . . A broad range of environmental factors potentially affect logics of competition—both technical factors featured in the economic analysis of "market structure" such as market demand or the availability of inputs, as well as factors in the institutional environment such as social norms, political forces, and legal constraints. These environmental factors comprise the playing field within which logics of competition develop and function. By identifying these forces explicitly in any given context, one can consider how they shape the process of *Red Queen* competition over time and across places (Barnett 2008, 14, 23). Through this process, both rivalry and viability increase in a system of reciprocal causality: the *Red Queen* (51). The *Red Queen* reference here is to Lewis Carroll's *Through the Looking Glass* (1871/1960).

Red Queen competition depends on the historical timing of experience:

> *Competitive Hysteresis Hypothesis:* Organizations with more exposure to a recent history of competition are more viable and generate stronger competition (Barnett 2008, 60).

The predicted hysteretic effect can be expected to reverse as an organization's competitive history becomes outdated:

> *Competency-Trap Hypothesis:* Organizations with more exposure to competition in the distant past are less viable and generate weaker competition (Barnett 2008, 62).

The Red Queen allows for the costs of adaptation to be estimated as a function of the number of distinct rivals faced over time by an organization:

> *Costly Adaptation Hypothesis:* For a given amount of historical competition, an organization's viability falls with the number of distinct historical rivals it has faced (Barnett 2008, 64).
> I [Barnett] propose to measure dispersion in two different ways:
> 1. Dispersion over market conditions
> 2. Dispersion over the features of an organization's rivals
> Measured either through dispersion of density or dispersion among competitor's cohorts:

Myopic Learning Hypothesis: The greater the dispersion of historical exposure to competition, the more viable the organization (Barnett 2008, 68).

1. Dispersion over market conditions (density)
2. Dispersion over historical rivals (competitors' cohorts)

I conclude that acquiring one's rivals carries harmful compositional and process effects, although this strategy also has clear benefits in terms of lessened competition and increased scale:

Costly Predation Hypothesis: Controlling for the current-time position of an organization, an organization's viability falls with the number of distinct historical rivals it has acquired (Barnett 2008, 72).

I propose that disruption is stronger the more adapted an organization is to some other context's logic of competition:

Competition-Inertia Hypothesis: The more an organization experiences a history of competition in one context, the more hazardous it will be for the organization to move into another context (Barnett 2008, 220).

Findings

Table 41.1 yields 15 results that appear to be consistent with predictions, 19 that are not significant (*NS*), and 5 reversals from among the findings that could be determined. The myopic learning hypothesis clearly does not hold up very well, and the competitive hysteresis hypothesis is particularly supported. Thus the balance of the findings is consistently positive, although the nonsignificant results are substantial and thus somewhat troublesome.

The Illinois Banks were studied in a period when branch banking was severely restricted in the state of Illinois, and accordingly most banks operated in a very limited market. The computer firms were studied in three waves matching the technology involved in the period.

All of the Red Queen studies were carried out using the net effects of competitive endeavors among the organizations involved; there is no analysis of discrete competitive moves within the samples studied, and consequently there is a missing link that is not considered. This would appear to represent a shortcoming of the Table 41.1 data.

The Derfus, Maggitti, Grimm, and Smith (2008) Analysis

The Derfus, Maggitti, Grimm, and Smith (2008) analysis attempts to deal with this shortcoming, although it is sprinkled with disclaimers such as "a complete analysis is beyond the scope of our current study" (77) and "more research is required" (77). Yet there are positive findings—"all the relationships in our baseline model were supported and showed that even though a focal firm's actions do increase performance, they also increase the number and speed of rivals' actions which, at least partially, negatively impact the focal firm's performance" (73).

In this context Swaminathan (2009, 690–691), as a reviewer of the Barnett (2008) book, has the following to say:

> Red Queen competition as a sequence of discrete competitive moves and responses in a sample of large firms (see e.g. Derfus et al. 2008) is inconsistent with the population-level theory developed in this book. While Derfus et al.'s (2008) research design is inconsistent with Barnett's theory of Red Queen competition, it does raise questions about the missing

Table 41.1

Summary of Evidence on Red Queen Evolution

Hypotheses Dates Studied	Predicted Effect	Illinois Banks (1900–1993)	Mainframe Computers (1951–1994)	Midrange Computers (1963–1994)	Micro Computers (1975–1994)
Founding Rates					
Competitive Hysteresis	−	−	−	NS	−
Competency Trap	+	+	+	NS	NS
Costly Adaptation					
Myopic Learning					
Inequality of Past Rivalry	+	−	−	NS	NS
Inequality of Past Rival Cohorts	+	−	NS	NS	+
Costly Predation	+	+			
Competition-Inertia	+				
Failure Rates					
Competitive Hysteresis	−	−	−	NS	−
Competency Trap	+	−	+	NS	NS
Costly Adaptation	+	NS	NS	NS	+
Myopic Learning					
Inequality of Past Rivalry	+	−	NS	NS	NS
Inequality of Past Rival Cohorts	+	NS	NS		NS
Costly Predation	+	+		+	
Competition-Inertia	+				+

Source: Adapted from Swaminathan (2009, 690) based on Barnett (2008).

link in empirical tests of the theory. Red Queen competition involves a self-exciting process in which firms respond to competition in ways that exert competitive pressure on other firms, causing them to respond, and so on. Barnett's tests of the theory do not explicitly model this intermediate stage of organizational action. Instead, he directly models the effects of exposure to competitive pressures on the viability of firms. The evidence in support of Red Queen competition will be the more convincing if the missing link of organizational action is explicitly taken into account.

It does indeed appear that much remains to be untangled.

OTHER CRITIQUES

In addition to the above, one major critique of the organizational ecology and demography theory—with origins in the Baum and Singh (1994) volume—involves Davis and Swaminathan (1996), who come down hard on the theory for failing to deal effectively with the concept of organizational form. The problem is that the theory is based on a research methodology—the event-history approach—that forces researchers to use groupings of organizations for which archival data sources are available. These groupings then become the forms of which populations are composed. The forms and their populations are thus made up anew for each study, depending on the requirements of those who created the data, not the theorists. There is no overarching typology; the theory simply accepts what is given in whatever grouping is available. Accordingly, there is not an unambiguous statement of what constitutes a form; nor is there any basis for determining when an organization changes its form and enters another population. The idea that organizations of considerable size might contain within them multiple forms is rarely entertained. This is not an issue that has been given much attention, but it needs to be addressed.

MORE CONTRIBUTIONS TO THE USE OF UNCONSCIOUS CONSTRUCTS IN ORGANIZATIONAL BEHAVIOR

I want to acknowledge here one other contribution to the burgeoning mainstream literature on unconscious constructs within organizational behavior. Previously I have discussed in this regard the Dane and Pratt (2007), the George (2009), and the Krieshok, Black, and McKay (2009) articles (within Chapter 38 of this volume); also the Latham, Stajkovic, and Locke (2010) article (within Chapter 40 of this volume). Now I wish to add to this list the article by Grant and Wade-Benzoni (2009) in the *Academy of Management Review* titled "The Hot and Cool of Death Awareness at Work: Mortality Cues, Aging, and Self-Protective and Prosocial Motivations." This article draws upon the research dealing with terror management (see Greenberg, Solomon, and Pyszczynski 1997). I have discussed this research in Chapters 11 and 17 of this volume.

This article focuses on certain major topics (with some characteristic subtopics) as follows:

The Nature of Death Awareness (Terror Management Theory: Death Awareness Increases Self-Protective Motivation; Reconciling Terror Management and Generativity: Death Anxiety versus Death Reflection)

The Emergence of Death Awareness at Work (The Effects of Mortality Cues on Death Anxiety and Death Reflection; The Moderating Role of Aging Processes)

Behavioral Consequences of Death Awareness at Work

Discussion (Theoretical Contributions; Practical Implications)

Grant and Wade-Benzoni (2009, 616) conclude as follows:

Because of its "hot" nature, death anxiety may be difficult to measure accurately with self-reports. To transcend this limitation we recommend that researchers consider linguistic analyses of expressive writing, which are well suited to the assessment of the intense emotions that can accompany death anxiety (e.g. Cohn, Mehl, and Pennebaker 2004). In this connection I wonder whether techniques originally applied to the Thematic Apperception Test (TAT), as for instance Tomkins (1947) or Stein (1948), might not be applicable.

CONCLUSIONS

As indicated earlier in this chapter organizational ecology and demography theory has a validity (as corrected in terms of the more recent writings) of four stars and an importance rating as given by organizational behavior scholars of 4.88. When the second value is divided by the former, the consequence is a ratio of 1.22, indicating that the importance rating somewhat overestimates the presumed validity of the theory.

Given that the theory is judged to be predominantly unconscious in nature, this ratio appears to be comparable to that of other macro theories of this type.

Ecology and demography theory has its closest affinity with strategic management, although it is relevant for organizational behavior as well. It is presented in a long series of books. However, there are important articles as well. The key early books of Hannan and Freeman (1989) focused on ecological theory and dealing with new forms, rates of organizational change, the death rates of organizations, and niche competition. Carroll and Hannan (2000b) focused on demography and dealing with age dependence, organizational forms and identities, resource partitioning, initial mobilizing, and inertia. The use of event-history data is given considerable attention. Research in this early period raises some important questions, including the need for greater flexibility and adaptability than the theory incorporates.

Later books include those by Harrison and Carroll (2006), a simulation emphasizing cultural factors; by Hannan, Pólos, and Carroll (2007), dealing with age dependence, forms and populations, niche structure, and inertia and change; and by Barnett (2008), representing research on the Red Queen theory of competitiveness. By and large all of these books have received favorable reviews, although there have been a few exceptions.

I consider the treatment of cultural factors as providing evidence for the existence of unconscious considerations in the theory; the use of similarities, taken-for-granted formulations, organizational forms and codes, defensive routines, intuition, bounded rationality, and perhaps nonmonotonic logic would also appear to carry the same unconscious message. On balance the theory seems to be more heavily weighted on the unconscious side than on the rational or conscious—in certain respects much more heavily weighted.

The chapter ends with a salute to the Grant and Wade-Benzoni (2009) article on terror management and death awareness, as a mainstream manifestation within the organizational behavior literature (in the *Academy of Management Review*) of writing on the unconscious.

CHAPTER 42

CONCLUSIONS ON CONCLUSIONS

Evaluations of Organizational Behavior's Micro Theories
Evaluations of Organizational Behavior's Macro Theories
Evaluations of Organizational Behavior's Combined Micro and Macro Theories
    (Tables 42.1 and 42.2)
Addendum to Unconscious Motivation as Viewed from the Projective Perspective
    Del Giudice (2010) on the Use of the Rorschach
    The Johnson, Tolentino, Rodopman, and Cho (2010) Research Using an Implicit
        Measure (A Word Fragment Completion Index)
Consciousness: The Science of Subjectivity (Revonsuo 2010)

In the past chapters I have presented in the Conclusions sections various ratios when the importance ratings assigned by organizational behavior scholars are divided by validity evaluations. My purpose in doing this has been to determine whether organizational behavior overestimates or underestimates the validity of each theory; this, in turn, helps shed light on whether some bias may be inherent in the averages reported by organizational behavior's assessments of the theories. In addition I have assigned a rating of conscious, balanced, or unconscious to each theory. Remember that the performance ratings made by the organizational behavior scholars were typically snap judgments made based on their memory of a theory and its research findings, while my validity assessments were based on extensive study and review of the data, which have been documented in writing at the time, often in several different books (thus on multiple occasions). There is reason to believe that my judgments may be more veridical; this is contrary to much of the existing lore on such matters, but I believe it to be the case.

EVALUATIONS OF ORGANIZATIONAL BEHAVIOR'S MICRO THEORIES

Table 42.1 presents the results of the relative assessments from the two sources for those theories judged to be of an essentially conscious nature, those judged to be coequal or balanced, and those judged to be predominantly of an unconscious nature, based on the literature that has accumulated on the new unconscious perspective, and on an up-to-date consideration of each theory itself.

I present first of all a chi-square analysis using a median split:

Ratio values	Conscious	Balanced	Unconscious
.89–1.25	2	2	8
1.26–	7	1	2

$\chi^2 = 6.51 \ (< .05)$
$df = 2$

Table 42.1

Value of Importance Ratings Divided by Estimated Validity for Various Types of Theory Dealing with Motivation and Leadership

Chapter Title	Type of Theory		
	Conscious	Balanced	Unconscious
1. Expectancy Theories	1.19		1.19
2. Goal-Setting Theory	1.33		
3. Kurt Lewin's Social Psychology			1.29
4. Achievement Motivation Theory	1.40		
5. Job Characteristics Theory			
6. Theories Based on B.F. Skinner and Organizational Behavior Modification	1.48	1.08	
7. Equity Theory and Distributive Justice			
8. Attribution Theory as Applied to Managerial Perceptions			1.05
9. Existence, Relatedness, and Growth Theory			1.19
10. Psychoanalytic Theory as Applied to Organizations			.95
11. Self-Determination Theory	1.42		
12. Theory of Behavior in Organizations	1.31		
13. Normative Decision Process Theory	.89		
14. Leader-Member Exchange Theory		1.17	
15. Information Processing Theory of Leadership			.96
16. Role Motivation Theory of Leadership			1.01
17. Charismatic Leadership Theory			
House			1.19
Bass			1.27
18. Contingency Theory of Leadership Theory		1.44	
19. Substitutes for Leadership	1.49		
20. Path-Goal Theory	1.53		
21. The Romance of Leadership			1.15

Then I obtained an analysis of variance:

Source of variation	Sum of squares	df	Mean of squares	F
Between groups	.215	2	.107	3.90 (< .05)
Within groups	.523	19	.028	
Total	.738	21		

For the three groups the findings were:

	N	$\bar{x}$
Conscious	9	1.34 (< .05)
Balanced	3	1.23 (< .05)
Unconscious	10	1.125 (< .02)

EVALUATIONS OF ORGANIZATIONAL BEHAVIOR'S MACRO THEORIES

Using a median split with the macro theories, the chi-square looked like this:

Ratio values	Conscious	Balanced	Unconscious
.89–1.25	0	5	6
1.26–	4	5	2

$\chi^2 = 6.00 \ (< .05)$
$df = 2$

The computed analysis of variance was as follows:

Source of variation	Sum of squares	df	Mean of squares	F
Between groups	1.031	2	.516	9.69 (<.01)
Within groups	1.011	19	.053	
Total	2.042	21		

For the three groups the findings were:

	N	$\bar{x}$
Conscious	4	1.79 (< .01)
Balanced	10	1.25 (< .10)
Unconscious	8	1.20 (< .10)

Table 42.2

Value of Importance Ratings Divided by Estimated Validity for Various Types of Theory Dealing with Process and Structure

Chapter Title	Type of Theory		
	Conscious	Balanced	Unconscious
22. Administrative Behavior and Organizations			1.16
23. Image Theory			.91
24. Behavioral Theory of the Firm, Organizational Learning, and the Garbage Can Model: Theories Involving James March			1.67
25. Control Theory (Using the Control Graph)		.90	
26. Katz and Kahn's Social Psychology of Organizations	1.78		
27. Sociotechnical Systems Theory	1.70		
28. Sociological Open Systems Theory	1.87		
29. Contingency Theory of Organizations: Differentiation and Integration	1.80		
30. Ralph Stogdill's Group-Focused Systems Theory		1.15	
31. Weber's Theory of Bureaucracy		1.48	
32. The Theory Undergirding the Aston Studies		1.07	
33. Peter Blau's Theory of Differentiation		1.08	
34. Goal Congruence Theory and Organization Development			1.44
35. Dysfunctions and Variants on Bureaucracy			1.13
36. Compliance Theory		1.32	
37. Structural Contingency Theory		1.44	
38. The Theory of Alpha, Beta, and Gamma Change		1.26	
39. External Control of Organizations: Resource Dependence Perspective		1.06	
40. Neoinstitutional Theory			
Meyer/Scott			.96
Zucker			1.13
DiMaggio/Powell		1.74	
41. Organizational Ecology and Demography			1.22

EVALUATIONS OF ORGANIZATIONAL BEHAVIOR'S COMBINED MICRO AND MACRO THEORIES (TABLES 42.1 AND 42.2)

Combining Tables 42.1 and 42.2, and thus obtaining a result for all theories contained in this book—both micro and macro—yields the following chi-square:

Ratio values	Conscious	Balanced	Unconscious
.89–1.25	2	7	14
1.26–	11	6	4

$\chi^2 = 11.84$
$df = 2$

For the combined theories ($N = 44$) the analysis of variance findings were:

Source of variation	Sum of squares	df	Mean of squares	F
Between groups	.777	2	.389	7.51 ($p < .01$)
Within groups	2.121	41	.052	
Total	2.898	43		

For the three groups the results were:

	N	$\bar{x}$
Conscious	13	1.48 ($< .10$)
Balanced	13	1.25 ($< .10$)
Unconscious	18	1.16 ($< .05$)

The results of these analyses are consistently and significantly positive for the overall findings; it would seem that there is indeed, as hypothesized, a clear bias among the organizational behavior scholars, consistent with what Kahneman, Slovic, and Tversky (1982) found. This holds for both micro (motivation and leadership) theories and theories of a macro (process and structure) type. Both exhibit a distinct preference for conscious, rational theories as opposed to those theories that are characterized by some degree of unconscious process.

ADDENDUM TO UNCONSCIOUS MOTIVATION AS VIEWED FROM THE PROJECTIVE PERSPECTIVE

In book five of this series (Miner 2008) I provided a treatment (see Chapter 1) that argued for the value of projective techniques as opposed to self-report measures. This argument has been supported by numerous citations in the present volume. However, I want to add to these sources by discussing certain materials from the very recent literature on the subject.

Del Giudice (2010) on the Use of the Rorschach

In the chapter of Miner (2008) noted previously, I discussed the Piotrowski and Rock (1963) research with the Rorschach test, which was applied in selecting top managers. There it was noted that the failure to cross-validate the findings obtained served to undermine acceptance of this research; Del Giudice (2010) has also noted this deficiency. However, in his recent article he has relied on the Piotrowski and Rock (1963) findings, plus others of a related nature, and on Exner's (2003) Rorschach Comprehensive System to develop a revised scoring system for the Rorschach to be used in selecting corporate leaders.

Among the studies cited by Del Giudice (2010) on how Rorschach variables predict within the corporate world are Gibb (1949), Phelan (1962), Hampton (1960), deVillemor-Amaral (2007), and Bach (2006). However, of these studies in general, Del Giudice (2010, 80) notes, "The limitations and inconsistencies of existing research studies with organizational populations have made it challenging to determine the Rorschach's viability in selection contexts."

Thus he suggests another approach to identifying Rorschach variables; these are as follows:

Cognitive Capacities
Social perceptiveness   X+%
   Wolff, Pescosolido, and Druskat (2002)
   Zaccaro, Foti, and Kenny (1991)
Intelligence; cognitive complexity   DQ+
   Brown, Scott, and Lewis (2004)   Zf
   Schmidt and Hunter (1998)
Strategic thinking abilities;
analytical reasoning   EII, EII-2
   Hughes and Beatty (2005)
Interpersonal Functioning
Interpersonal adeptness   COP
   Rosete and Ciarrochi (2005)
   Goleman (1998)
Psychological adjustment   MOA
   Judge, Bono, Ilies, and Gerhardt (2002)
   Van Velsor and Leslie (1995)   ROD
Capacity for Self-Improvement
Change management skills   EA
   Kotter (1999)
Continuous self-improvement   RPRS
   London (2002)

As is apparent, these variables are from the organizational behavior literature; they are matched with Rorschach's indexes selected as measuring the designated characteristics and having substantial reliability; the lowest reported reliability value is .67, with most in the .80s ranging up into the high .90s. The median reported reliability would appear to be in the upper .80s.

Information on the Rorschach indexes is given by the author as follows:

X+% . . . assesses the inclination to perceive and interpret information accurately . . . consistent with social norms (82).

Developmental Quality Synthesis (DQ+) score is coded for . . . responses that meaningfully organize and integrate the stimulus field. . . . (82).

Organizational Activity (Zf) scores are coded when the respondent articulates a relationship between elements of the stimulus field, uses the entire . . . field, or integrates white space with ink . . . an index of intellectual engagement and a willingness to tackle complexity. (82).

EII (Ego Impairment Index) is an index of psychological impairment and thinking problems. . . . (83).

COP score (Cooperative Movement) . . . responses with Movement involving two or more objects in which the interaction is . . . positive and cooperative. . . . portend good leader performance (83).

MOA (Mutuality of Autonomy Score) is a thematic Content scale assessing . . . interaction responses . . . (83).

. . . Oral Dependency Scale (ROD) is a content-based measure of interpersonal dependency . . . to assess needs . . . that respondents are . . . unable or unwilling to disclose on self-report tests. . . . (84).

EA (Experience Actual) is a composite scale derived from scores of human action and responsiveness to color to indicate cognitive and emotionally based psychological resources related to coping with life challenges. . . . (84).

Prognostic Rating Scale (RPRS) [was] developed to identify individuals . . . inclined to succeed in psychotherapy . . . generated from the quality of multiple . . . variables including Movement, Shading, and Color scores. . . . (84).

Del Giudice (2010) summarizes a number of practical considerations that argue against the use of the Rorschach in organizational settings, including the lack of face validity, skepticism regarding the instrument's controversial history, and the time (or costliness) involved. He is aware that his approach (like Piotrowski and Rock 1963) has not been subjected to actual or adequate research test. Yet he has developed a measure that involves Rorschach indexes and taps unconscious factors; he has used relevant foundational research to make the case for using the Rorschach as a method of moving beyond the shortcomings of self-report approaches. For this he is to be applauded. I hope he, or others, will take the next step and carry out the needed research.

The Johnson, Tolentino, Rodopman, and Cho (2010) Research Using an Implicit Measure (A Word Fragment Completion Index)

This research deficiency is not in evidence in the Johnson, Tolentino, Rodopman, and Cho (2010) study using an approximation to the sentence completion format (see Miner 2008), an implicit measure of trait affectivity and thus an index of unconscious process. The hypotheses of this study were:

1. Positive affect will be positively related to task performance.
2. Negative affect will be negatively related to task performance.
3. Positive affect will be positively related to organizational citizenship behavior.
4. Negative affect will be positively related to counterproductive work behavior.
5. An implicit measure of trait affectivity will contribute more to the prediction of (a) task performance, (b) organizational citizenship behavior, and (c) counterproductive work behavior than an explicit measure.

These hypotheses were either supported in most cases or partially supported in a few instances; pilot studies were consistent with the main body of the research. The authors conclude: "We extended previous research by demonstrating that an implicit measure of trait affectivity predicted job performance and appeared to do so more effectively than an explicit measure. We believe that paying further attention to processes and constructs at implicit levels will provide a more comprehensive understanding of organizational attitudes and behavior" (Johnson, Tolentino, Rodopman, and Cho 2010, 215).

CONSCIOUSNESS: THE SCIENCE OF SUBJECTIVITY (REVONSUO 2010)

Revonsuo's 2010 book *Consciousness: The Science of Subjectivity* is a thoroughly up-to-date treatment of consciousness and its relationship to unconscious considerations. Its approach is multidisciplinary and objective. I present the Table of Contents below in the hope that a reader may find something of interest in this book:

I. Background to the Science of Consciousness
    1. The Philosophical Foundations of Consciousness Science
    2. The Historical Foundations of Consciousness Science
    3. The Conceptual Foundations of Consciousness Science
II. Central Domains of Consciousness Science
    4. Neuropsychological Deficits of Visual Consciousness
    5. Neuropsychological Dissociations of Visual Consciousness from Behavior
    6. Neuropsychological Disorders of Self-Awareness
    7. Methods and Design of Neural Correlates of Consciousness Experiments
    8. Studies on the Neural Basis of Consciousness as a State
    9. Studies on the Neural Basis of Visual Consciousness
    10. Philosophical Theories of Consciousness
    11. Empirical Theories of Consciousness
    12. What Is an Altered State of Consciousness?
    13. Dreaming and Sleep
    14. Hypnosis
    15. Higher States of Consciousness

Revonsuo (2010) notes in his epilogue, "In a nutshell, my approach to consciousness can be summarized like this: Phenomenal consciousness is a higher biological level of organization in the brain that firstly enables the inner presence of phenomenal qualities and secondly organizes those qualities into a coherent world simulation, with a self or a body image in the centre of the virtual world" (289).

Thus, this volume comes to an end, as all books must. However, research and theory dealing with unconscious processes is continuing, extending well beyond what has been said here. I hope, nevertheless, that sufficient has been said to make the point that previous conclusions to the effect that unconscious processes and projective techniques do *not* meet the test of research evidence are substantially in error. What is said in Miner (2008) is indeed in line with the realities of a considerable body of research data. It is in this sense as vindicating the role of the unconscious that this book is concerned with integrated development.

REFERENCES

Aarts, Henk, Chartrand, Tanya L., Custers, R., Danner, U., Dik, G., and Jefferis, V. (2005). Social Stereotypes and Automatic Goal Pursuit. *Social Cognition,* 23, 464–489.

Aarts, Henk, Dijksterhuis, Ap, and Dik, Giel (2008). Goal Contagion: Inferring Goals from Others' Actions—And What It Leads To. In James Y. Shah and Wendi L. Gardner (Eds.), *Handbook of Motivation Science.* New York: Guilford Press, 265–280.

Adams, J. Stacy. (1965). Inequity in Social Exchange. In Leonard Berkowitz (Ed.), *Advances in Experimental Social Psychology,* Vol. 2. New York: Academic Press, 267–299.

Adler, Paul S., Kwon, Seok-Woo, and Heckscher, Charles. (2008). Professional Work: The Emergence of Collaborative Community. *Organization Science,* 19, 359–376.

Agle, Bradley R., Nagarajan, Nandu J., Sonnenfeld, Jeffrey A., and Srinivasan, Dhinu. (2006). Does CEO Charisma Matter? An Empirical Analysis of the Relationships among Organizational Performance, Environmental Uncertainty, and Top Management Team Perceptions of CEO Charisma. *Academy of Management Journal,* 49, 161–174.

Ajzen, Icek. (2001). Nature and Operation of Attitudes. *Annual Review of Psychology,* 52, 27–58.

Alderfer, Clayton P. (1972). *Existence, Relatedness, and Growth: Human Needs in Organizational Settings.* New York: Free Press.

Allen, Natalie J., and Hecht, Tracy D. (2004). The "Romance of Teams": Toward an Understanding of Its Psychological Underpinnings and Implications. *Journal of Occupational and Organizational Psychology,* 77, 439–461.

Allison, Scott T., Eylon, Dafna, Beggan, James K., and Bachelder, Jennifer (2009). The Demise of Leadership: Positivity and Negativity Biases in Evaluations of Dead Leaders. *Leadership Quarterly,* 20, 115–129.

Alvarez, Valle S., and Merino, Teresa G. (2003). The History of Organizational Renewal: Evolutionary Models of Spanish Savings and Loan Institutions. *Organization Studies,* 24, 1437–1461.

Amabile, Teresa M., Barsade, Sigal G., Mueller, Jennifer S., and Staw, Barry M. (2005). Affect and Creativity at Work. *Administrative Science Quarterly,* 50, 367–403.

Ambady, Nalini, and Skowronski, John J. (2008). *First Impressions.* New York: Guilford Press.

Andersen, Susan M., Reznik, Inga, and Glassman, Noah S. (2005). The Unconscious Relational Self. In Ran R. Hassin, James S. Uleman, and John A. Bargh (Eds.), *The New Unconscious.* New York: Oxford University Press, 421–481.

Anderson, Michael C. (2003). Rethinking Interference Theory: Executive Control and the Mechanisms of Forgetting. *Journal of Memory and Language,* 49, 415–445.

———. (2005). The Role of Inhibitory Control in Forgetting Unwanted Memories: A Consideration of Three Methods. In C. MacLeod and B. Uttl (Eds.), *Dynamic Cognitive Processes.* Tokyo, Japan: Springer-Verlag, 159–190.

———. (2006). Repression: A Cognitive Neuroscience Approach. In M. Mancia (Ed.), *Neuroscience and Psychoanalysis.* Milan, Italy: Springer, 327–350.

Anderson, Michael C., and Green, Collin. (2001). Suppressing Unwanted Memories by Executive Control. *Nature,* 410, 366–369.

Anderson, Michael C., and Levy, Benjamin J. (2002). Repression Can (and Should) Be Studied Empirically. *Trends in Cognitive Science,* 6, 502–503.

———. (2006). Encouraging the Nascent Cognitive Neuroscience of Repression. *Behavioral and Brain Sciences,* 29, 511–513.

———. (2009). Suppressing Unwanted Memories. *Current Directions in Psychological Science,* 18, 189–194.

Anderson, Michael C., Ochsner, K. N., Kuhl, B., Cooper, J., Robertson, E., Gabrieli, S. W., Glover, G. H., Gabrieli, J. D. E. (2004). Neural Systems Underlying the Suppression of Unwanted Memories. *Science,* 303, 232–235.

Andreas, Joel. (2007). The Structure of Charismatic Mobilization: A Case Study of Rebellion during the Chinese Cultural Revolution. *American Sociological Review,* 72, 434–458.

Andriessen, Daniel, and Gubbins, Claire. (2009). Metaphor Analysis as an Approach for Exploring Theoretical Concepts: The Case of Social Capital. *Organization Studies,* 30, 845–863.

Argote, Linda, and Greve, Henrich R. (2007). A Behavioral Theory of the Firm—40 Years and Counting: Introduction and Impact. *Organization Science,* 18, 337–349.

Argote, Linda, and Todorova, Gergana (2007). Organizational Learning. *International Review of Industrial and Organizational Psychology,* 22, 193–234.

Argyris, Chris. (1957). *Personality and Organization.* New York: Harper and Row.

———. (1964). *Integrating the Individual and the Organization.* New York: Wiley.

———. (1972). *The Applicability of Organizational Sociology.* London, UK: Cambridge University Press.

———. (1973). Personality and Organization Theory Revisited. *Administrative Science Quarterly,* 18, 141–167.

———. (1985). *Strategy, Change, and Defensive Routines.* Boston, MA: Pitman.

———. (1990). *Overcoming Organizational Defenses: Facilitating Organizational Learning.* Boston, MA: Allyn and Bacon.

———. (1992). *On Organizational Learning.* Cambridge, MA: Blackwell.

———. (1996). Unrecognized Defenses of Scholars: Impact on Theory and Research. *Organization Science,* 7, 79–87.

———. (2004). *Reasons and Rationalizations: The Limits to Organizational Knowledge.* Oxford, UK: Oxford University Press.

———. (2005). Double-Loop Learning in Organizations: A Theory of Action Perspective. In Ken G. Smith and Michael A. Hitt (Eds.), *Great Minds in Management: The Process of Theory Development.* Oxford, UK: Oxford University Press, 261–279.

———. (2008). Learning in Organizations. In Thomas G. Cummings (Ed.), *Handbook of Organization Development.* Thousand Oaks, CA: Sage, 53–67.

Argyris, Chris, and Schön, Donald A. (1996). *Organizational Learning II: Theory, Method, and Practice.* Reading, MA: Addison-Wesley.

Arthurs, Jonathan D., Busenitz, Lowell W., Hoskisson, Robert E., and Johnson, Richard A. (2009). Firm-Specific Human Capital and Governance in IPO Firms: Addressing Agency and Resource Dependence Concerns. *Entrepreneurship Theory and Practice,* 33, 845–865.

Ashforth, Blake E. (2001). *Role Transitions in Organizational Life: An Identity-Based Perspective.* Mahwah, NJ: Lawrence Erlbaum.

Ashton-James, Claire E., Maddux, William W., Galinsky, Adam D., and Chartrand, Tanya L. (2009). Who I Am Depends on How I Feel: The Role of Affect in the Expression of Culture. *Psychological Science,* 20, 340–346.

Augier, Mie. (2004). James March on Education, Leadership, and Don Quixote: Introduction and Interview. *Academy of Management Learning and Education,* 3, 169–177.

Augier, Mie, and Teece, David J. (2005). Reflections on (Schumpeterian) Leadership: A Report on a Seminar on Leadership and Management Education. *California Management Review,* 47(2), 114–136.

Aviezer, Hillel, Hassin, Ran R., Bentin, Shlomo, and Trope, Yaacov. (2008). Putting Facial Expressions Back in Context. In Nalini Ambady and John J. Skowronski (Eds.), *First Impressions.* New York: Guilford Press, 255–286.

Avolio, Bruce J. (2004). Examining the Full Range Model of Leadership: Looking Back to Transform Forward. In David V. Day, Stephen J. Zaccaro, and Stanley M. Halpin (Eds.), *Leader Development for Transforming Organizations: Growing Leaders for Tomorrow.* Mahwah, NJ: Lawrence Erlbaum, 71–98.

Avolio, Bruce J., and Locke, Edwin E. (2002). Contrasting Different Philosophies of Leader Motivation— Altruism versus Egoism. *Leadership Quarterly,* 13, 169–191.

Avolio, Bruce J., Walumbwa, Fred O., and Weber, Todd J. (2009). Leadership: Current Theories, Research, and Future Directions. *Annual Review of Psychology,* 60, 421–449.

Ayman, Roya. (2002). Contingency Model of Leadership Effectiveness: Challenges and Achievements. In Linda L. Neider and Chester Schriesheim (Eds.), *Leadership.* Greenwich, CT: Information Age Publishing, 197–228.

Ayman, Roya, Chemers, Martin M., and Fiedler, Fred E. (1995). The Contingency Model of Leadership Effectiveness: Its Levels of Analysis. *Leadership Quarterly,* 6, 147–167.

Bach, P. L. (2006). A Descriptive Rorschach Study of Senior Business Executives. *Dissertation Abstracts International,* 66(8), 4526B.

Baker, Sally H., Etzioni, Amitai, Hansen, Richard A., and Sontag, Marvin (1973). Tolerance for Bureaucratic Structure: Theory and Measurements. *Human Relations,* 26, 775–786.

Baltes, Paul B., and Smith, Jacqui (2008). The Fascination of Wisdom: Its Nature, Ontogeny, and Function. *Perspectives on Psychological Science,* 3, 56–64.

Bamberger, Peter, and Biron, Michael. (2007). Group Norms and Excessive Absenteeism: The Role of Peer Referent Others. *Organizational Behavior and Human Decision Processes,* 103, 179–196.

Bandura, Albert. (1977). *Social Learning Theory.* Englewood Cliffs, NJ: Prentice-Hall.

———. (1982). Self-Efficacy Mechanism in Human Agency. *American Psychologist,* 37, 122–147.

———. (1997). *Self-Efficacy: The Exercise of Control.* New York: Freeman.

Bandura, Albert, and Locke, Edwin A. (2003). Negative Self-Efficacy and Goal Effects Revisited. *Journal of Applied Psychology,* 88, 87–99.

Bargh, John A. (1990). Auto-Motives: Preconscious Determinants of Social Interaction. In E. T. Higgins and R. M. Sorrentino (Eds.), *Handbook of Motivation and Cognition, Vol. 2: Foundations of Social Behavior.* New York: Guilford Press, 93–130.

———. (1992). The Ecology of Automaticity—Toward Establishing the Conditions Needed to Produce Automatic Processing Effects. *American Journal of Psychology,* 150, 181–199.

———. (1994). The Four-Horseman of Automaticity: Awareness, Intention, Efficiency, and Control in Social Cognition. In R. S. Wyer, and T. K. Srull (Eds.), *Handbook of Social Cognition: Vol. 1. Basic Processes; Vol. 2. Applications.* Hillsdale, NJ: Lawrence Erlbaum, 1–40.

———. (2005). Bypassing the Will: Toward Demystifying the Nonconscious Control of Social Behavior. In Ran R. Hassin, James S. Uleman, and John A. Bargh (Eds.), *The New Unconscious.* New York: Oxford University Press, 37–58.

———. (2007). Introduction. In John A. Bargh (Ed.), *Social Psychology and the Unconscious: The Automaticity of Higher Mental Processes.* New York: Psychology Press, 1–9.

Bargh, John A., and Chartrand, Tanya L. (1999). The Unbearable Automaticity of Being. *American Psychologist,* 54, 462–479.

Bargh, John A., Gollwitzer, Peter M., Lee-Chai, Annette, Barndollar, Kimberly, and Trötschel, Roman. (2001). The Automated Will: Nonconscious Activation and Pursuit of Behavioral Goals. *Journal of Personality and Social Psychology,* 81, 1014–1029.

Bargh, John A., and Morsella, Ezequiel. (2008). The Unconscious Mind. *Perspectives on Psychological Science,* 3, 73–79.

Bargh, John A., and Williams, Erin L. (2006). The Automaticity of Social Life. *Current Directions in Psychological Science,* 15, 1–4.

Barnard, Chester I. (1938). *The Functions of the Executive.* Cambridge, MA: Harvard University Press.

Barnett, William P. (1990). The Organizational Ecology of a Technological System. *Administrative Science Quarterly,* 35, 31–60.

———. (2008). *The Red Queen among Organizations: How Competitiveness Evolves.* Princeton, NJ: Princeton University Press.

Barnett, William P., and Woywode, Michael. (2004). From Red Vienna to the Anschluss: Ideological Competition among Viennese Newspapers during the Rise of National Socialism. *American Journal of Sociology,* 109, 1452–1499.

Baron, Andrew S., and Banaji, Mahzarin. (2006). The Development of Implicit Attitudes: Evidence of Race Evaluations from Age 6 and 10 and Adulthood. *Psychological Science,* 17, 53–58.

Baron, Robert A. (2004). The Cognitive Perspective: A Valuable Tool for Answering Entrepreneurship's Basic "Why" Questions. *Journal of Business Venturing,* 19, 221–239.

———. (2007a). Behavioral and Cognitive Factors in Entrepreneurship: Entrepreneurs as the Active Element in New Venture Creation. *Strategic Entrepreneurship Journal,* 1, 167.

———. (2007b). Entrepreneurship: A Process Perspective. In J. Robert Baum, Michael Frese, and Robert A. Baron (Eds.), *The Psychology of Entrepreneurship.* Mahwah, NJ: Lawrence Erlbaum, 19–39.

Baron, Robert A., and Ward, Thomas B. (2004). Expanding Entrepreneurial Cognition's Toolbox: Potential Contributions from the Field of Cognitive Science. *Entrepreneurship Theory and Practice,* 28, 553–573.

Barrett, Lisa F. (2005). Feeling Is Perceiving: Core Affect and Conceptualization in the Experience of Emotion. In Lisa F. Barrett, Paula M. Niedenthal, and Piotr Winkielman (Eds.), *Emotion and Consciousness.* New York: Guilford Press, 255–284.

Barrett, Lisa F., Mesquita, Batja, Ochsner, Kevin N., and Gross, James J. (2007). The Experience of Emotion. *Annual Review of Psychology*, 58, 373–403.

Barrett, Lisa F., Niedenthal, Paula M., and Winkielman, Piotr. (2005). Introduction. In Lisa F. Barrett, Paula M. Niedenthal, and Piotr Winkielman (Eds.), *Emotion and Consciousness*. New York: Guilford Press, 1–18.

Barrett, Lisa F., Ochsner, Kevin N., and Gross, James J. (2007). On the Automaticity of Emotion. In John A. Bargh (Ed.), *Social Psychology and the Unconscious: The Automaticity of Higher Mental Processes*. New York: Psychology Press, 173–217.

Barrett, Lisa F., Tugade, Michele M., and Engle, Randall W. (2004). Individual Differences in Working Memory Capacity and Dual-Process Theories of the Mind. *Psychological Bulletin*, 130, 553–573.

Barry, Heather, and Tyler, Tom R. (2009). The Other Side of Injustice: When Unfair Procedures Increase Group-Serving Behavior. *Psychological Science*, 20, 1026–1032.

Bartol, Kathryn M., and Locke, Edwin A. (2000). Incentives and Motivation. In Sara L. Rynes and Barry Gerhart (Eds.), *Compensation in Organizations: Current Research and Practice*. San Francisco, CA: Jossey-Bass, 104–147.

Bass, Bernard M. (1985). *Leadership and Performance Beyond Expectations*. New York: Free Press.

Baum, Joel A. C., Dobrev, Stanislav D., and van Witteloostuijn, Arjen. (2006). *Ecology and Strategy*. Oxford, UK: Elsevier.

Baum, Joel A. C., and Singh, Jitendra V. (1994). *Evolutionary Dynamics of Organizations*. New York: Oxford University Press.

Baumeister, Roy F. (2002). Ego-Depletion and Self-Control Failure: An Energy Model of the Self's Executive Function. *Self and Identity*, 1, 129–136.

———. (2008). Free Will in Scientific Psychology. *Perspectives on Psychological Science*, 3, 14–19.

Beach, Lee Roy (1990). *Image Theory: Decision Making in Personal and Organizational Contexts*. West Sussex, UK: John Wiley & Sons.

———. (1993). *Making the Right Decision: Organizational Culture, Vision, and Planning*. Englewood Cliffs, NJ: Prentice-Hall.

———. (2006). *Leadership and the Art of Change: A Practical Guide to Organizational Transformation*. Thousand Oaks, CA: Sage.

Beach, Lee Roy, and Mitchell, Terence R. (2005). Image Theory. In Ken G. Smith and Michael A. Hitt (Eds.), *Great Minds in Management: The Process of Theory Development*. New York: Oxford University Press, 36–54.

Bedeian, Arthur G., Armenakis, Achilles A., and Gibson, R. W. (1980). The Measurement and Control of Beta Change. *Academy of Management Review*, 5, 561–566.

Bedell-Avers, Katrina E., Hunter, Samuel T., and Mumford, Michael D. (2008). Conditons of Problem-Solving and the Performance of Charismatic, Ideological, and Pragmatic Leaders: A Comparative Experimental Study. *Leadership Quarterly*, 19, 89–106.

Benjamin, Lily, and Flynn, Francis J. (2006). Leadership Style and Regulatory Mode: Value from Fit. *Organizational Behavior and Human Decision Processes*, 100, 216–230.

Berger, Peter L., and Luckman, Thomas. (1967). *The Social Construction of Reality*. New York: Doubleday Anchor.

Bigelow, Lyda S. (2006). Technology Choice, Transaction Alignment, and Survival: The Impact of Subpopulation Organizational Structure. In Joel A. C. Baum, Stanislav D. Dobrev, and Arjen van Witteloostuijn (Eds.), *Ecology and Strategy*. Oxford, UK: Elsevier, 301–333.

Bing, Mark N., Stewart, Susan M., Davison, H. Kristl, Green, Philip D., McIntyre, Michael D., and James, Lawrence R. (2007). An Integrative Typology of Personality Assessment for Aggression: Implications for Predicting Counterproductive Workplace Behavior. *Journal of Applied Psychology*, 92, 722–744.

Blair, I. V., and Banaji, Mahzarin R. (1996). Automatic and Controlled Processes in Stereotype Priming. *Journal of Personality and Social Psychology*, 70, 1142–1163.

Blankenship, Virginia, Vega, Christopher M., Ramos, Erica, Romero, Katherine, Warren, Kenneth, Keenan, Kathleen, Rosenow, Valery, Vasquez, Jennifer, and Sullivan, Amanda. (2006). Using the Multifaceted Rasch Model to Improve the TAT/PSE Measure of Need for Achievement. *Journal of Personality Assessment*, 86, 100–114.

Blanton, Hart, and Jaccard, James. (2006). Arbitrary Metrics in Psychology. *American Psychologist*, 61, 27–41.

Blau, Peter M. (1955). *The Dynamics of Bureaucracy: A Study of Interpersonal Relations in Two Government Agencies.* Chicago, IL: University of Chicago Press.
———. (1956). *Bureaucracy in Modern Society.* New York: Random House.
———. (1964). *Exchange and Power in Social Life.* New York: Wiley.
———. (1973). *The Organization of Academic Work.* New York: Wiley.
———. (1974). *On the Nature of Organizations.* New York: Wiley.
———. (1977). *Inequality and Heterogeneity.* New York: Free Press.
———. (1995). A Circuitous Path to Macrostructural Theory. *Annual Review of Sociology.* 21, 1–19.
Blau, Peter M., Falbe, Cecilia M., McKinley, William, and Tracy, Phelps K. (1976). Technology and Organization in Manufacturing. *Administrative Science Quarterly,* 21, 20–40.
Blau, Peter M., and Schoenherr, Richard A. (1971). *The Structure of Organizations.* New York: Basic Books.
Bligh, Michelle C., and Kohles, Jeffrey C. (2009). The Enduring Allure of Charisma: How Barack Obama Won the 2008 Presidential Election. *Leadership Quarterly,* 20, 483–492.
Bligh, Michelle C., Kohles, Jeffrey C., and Meindl, James R. (2004). Charisma under Crisis: Presidential Leadership, Rhetoric, and Media Responses before and after the September 11th Terrorist Attacks. *Leadership Quarterly,* 15, 211–239.
Bluedorn, Allen C. (1993). Pilgrim's Progress: Trends and Convergence in Research on Organizational Size and Environments. *Journal of Management,* 19, 163–191.
Bono, Joyce E., and Ilies, Remus. (2006). Charisma, Positive Emotions, and Mood Contagion. *Leadership Quarterly,* 17, 317–334.
Bontis, Nick, Crossan, Mary M., and Hulland, John. (2002). Managing an Organizational Learning System by Aligning Stocks and Flows. *Journal of Management Studies,* 39, 437–469.
Boone, Christophe, Wezel, Filippo C., and van Witteloostuijn, Arjen. (2006). Top Management Team Composition and Organizational Ecology: A Nested Hierarchical Selection Theory of Team Reproduction and Organizational Diversity. In Joel A. C. Baum, Stanislav Dobrev, and Arjen van Witteloostuijn (Eds.), *Ecology and Strategy.* Oxford, UK: Elsevier, 103–135.
Boring, Edwin G. (1950). *A History of Experimental Psychology.* New York: Appleton-Century-Crofts.
Bornstein, Robert F. (2002). A Process Dissociation Approach to Objective-Projective Test Score Interrelationships. *Journal of Personality Assessment,* 78, 47–68.
———. (2007). Might the Rorschach be a Projective Test after All? Social Projection of an Undesired Trait Alters Rorschach Oral Dependency Scores. *Journal of Personality Assessment,* 88, 354–367.
Brigham, Keith H., and DeCastro, Julio O. (2003). Entrepreneurial Fit: The Role of Cognitive Misfit. *Advances in Entrepreneurship, Firm Emergence, and Growth,* 6, 37–71.
Briscoe, Forrest, and Safford, Sean (2008). The Nixon-in-China Effect: Activism, Imitation, and the Institutionalization of Contentious Practices. *Administrative Science Quarterly,* 53, 460–491.
Brittain, Jack W., and Freeman, John H. (1980). Organizational Proliferation and Density Dependent Selection. In John R. Kimberly and Robert H. Miles (Eds.), *The Organizational Life Cycle: Issues in the Creation, Transformation, and Decline of Organizations.* San Francisco, CA: Jossey-Bass, 291–338.
Brown, D. J., Scott, K. A., and Lewis, H. (2004). Information Processing and Leadership. In J. Antonakis, A. T. Cianciolo, and R. J. Sternberg (Eds.), *The Nature of Leadership.* Thousand Oaks, CA: Sage, 125–147.
Bryan, Judith A., and Locke, Edwin A. (1967). Parkinson's Law as a Goal-Setting Phenomenon. *Organizational Behavior and Human Performance,* 2, 258–275.
Burke, C. Shawn, Stagl, Kevin C., Klein, Cameron, Goodwin, Gerald F., Salas, Eduardo, and Halpin, Stanley M. (2006). What Type of Leadership Behaviors Are Functional in Teams? A Meta-Analysis. *Leadership Quarterly,* 17, 288–307.
Burke, Lisa A., and Sadler-Smith, Eugene (2006). Instructor Intuition in the Educational Setting. *Academy of Management Learning and Education,* 5, 169–181.
Burke, Michael J., and Day, Russell R. (1986). A Cumulative Study of the Effectiveness of Managerial Training. *Journal of Applied Psychology,* 71, 232–245.
Burnes, Bernard. (2007). Kurt Lewin and the Harwood Studies: The Foundation of O.D. *Journal of Applied Behavioral Science,* 43, 213–231.
Burns, Tom, and Stalker, G.M. (1961, 1997). *The Management of Innovation.* Chicago: Quadrangle.
Burton, Richard M. (2007). Review of *Culture and Demography in Organizations. Administrative Science Quarterly,* 52, 152–155.
Busenitz, Lowell W. (1999). Entrepreneurial Risk and Strategic Decision Making: It's a Matter of Perspective. *Journal of Applied Behavioral Science,* 35, 325–340.

Busenitz, Lowell W., and Arthurs, Jonathan D. (2007). Cognition and Capabilities in Entrepreneurial Ventures. In J. Robert Baum, Michael Frese, and Robert A. Baron (Eds.), *The Psychology of Entrepreneurship.* Mahwah, NJ: Lawrence Erlbaum, 131–150.

Busenitz, Lowell W., and Barney, Jay B. (1997). Differences between Entrepreneurs and Managers in Large Organizations: Biases and Heuristics in Strategic Decision Making. *Journal of Business Venturing,* 12, 9–30.

Cahn, B. Rael, and Polich, John (2006). Meditation States and Traits: EEG, ERP, and Neuroimaging Studies. *Psychological Bulletin,* 132, 180–211.

Cameron, Judy, and Pierce, W. David (2002). *Rewards and Intrinsic Motivation: Resolving the Controversy.* Westport, CT: Bergin & Garvey.

Cameron, Kim (2008). *Positive Leadership: Strategies for Extraordinary Performance.* San Francisco, CA: Berrett-Koehler Publishers.

Camisón-Zornoza, César, Lapiedra-Alcamí, Rafael, Segarra-Ciprés, Mercedes, and Boronat-Navarro, Montserrat. (2004). A Meta-analysis of Innovation and Organizational Size. *Organization Studies,* 25, 331–361.

Campbell, Andrew, Whitehead, Jo, and Finkelstein, Sydney. (2009). Why Good Leaders Make Bad Decisions. *Harvard Business Review,* 87(2), 60–66.

Carmeli, Abraham, and Sheaffer, Zachary. (2008). How Learning Leadership and Organizational Learning from Failures Enhance Perceived Organizational Capacity to Adapt to the Task Environment. *Journal of Applied Behavioral Science,* 44, 468–489.

Carr, Adrian. (2002). Managing in a Psychoanalytically Informed Manner. *Journal of Managerial Psychology,* 17, 343–347.

Carroll, Glenn R. (1987). *Publish and Perish: The Organizational Ecology of Newspaper Industries.* Greenwich, CT: JAI Press.

Carroll, Glenn R., Dobrev, Stanislav D., and Swaminathan, Anand. (2002). Organizational Processes of Resource Partitioning. *Research in Organizational Behavior,* 24, 1–40.

Carroll, Glenn R., and Hannan, Michael T. (1989). Density Delay in the Evolution of Organizational Populations: A Model and Five Empirical Tests. *Administrative Science Quarterly,* 34, 411–430.

———. (2000a). Why Corporate Demography Matters: Policy Implications of Organizational Diversity. *California Management Review,* 42(3), 148–163.

———. (2000b). *The Demography of Corporations and Industries.* Princeton, NJ: Princeton University Press.

Carroll, Lewis. (1871/1960). *Through the Looking Glass.* New York: New American Library.

Carsten, Melissa K., and Bligh, Michelle C. (2007). Here Today, Gone Tomorrow: Follower Perceptions of a Departing Leader and a Lingering Vision. In Boas Shamir, Rajnandini Pillai, Michelle C. Bligh, and Mary Uhl-Bien (Eds.), *Follower-Centered Perspectives on Leadership: A Tribute to the Memory of James R. Meindl.* Greenwich, CT: Information Age Publishing, 211–241.

Carver, Charles S., and Scheier, Michael F. (2008). Feedback Processes in the Simultaneous Regulation of Action and Affect. In James Y. Shah and Wendi L. Gardner (Eds.), *Handbook of Motivation Science.* New York: Guilford Press, 308–324.

Certo, S. Trevis, Connelly, Brian L., and Tihanyi, Laszlo. (2008). Managers and Their Not-So-Rational Decisions. *Business Horizons,* 51, 113–119.

Certo, S. Trevis, Lester, Richard H., Dalton, Catherine M., and Dalton, Dan R. (2006). Top Management Teams, Strategy and Financial Performance: A Meta-analytic Examination. *Journal of Management Studies,* 43, 813–839.

Chan, D., and Schmitt, Neal. (2000). Interindividual Differences in Intraindividual Changes in Proactivity during Organizational Entry: A Latent Growth Modeling Approach to Understanding Newcomer Adaptation. *Journal of Applied Psychology,* 85, 190–210.

Chan, Kim-Yin, and Drasgow, Fritz. (2001). Toward a Theory of Individual Differences and Leadership: Understanding the Motivation to Lead. *Journal of Applied Psychology,* 86, 481–498.

Chan, Kim-Yin, Rounds, James, and Drasgow, Fritz. (2000). The Relation between Vocational Interests and the Motivation to Lead. *Journal of Vocational Behavior,* 57, 226–245.

Chandler, Alfred D. (1962). *Strategy and Structure: Chapters in the History of the American Industrial Enterprise.* Cambridge, MA: MIT Press.

Chapman, Benjamin P. (2008). Edith Weisskopf's Transcendence Index. In Sharon R. Jenkins (Ed.), *A Handbook of Clinical Scoring Systems for Thematic Apperceptive Techniques.* New York: Lawrence Erlbaum, 89–102.

Charland, Louis C. (2005). Emotion Experience and the Indeterminacy of Valance. In Lisa F. Barrett, Paula M. Niedenthal, and Piotr Winkielman (Eds.), *Emotion and Consciousness*. New York: Guilford Press, 231–254.

Chartrand, Tanya L., Dalton, Amy N., and Cheng, Clara M. (2008). The Antecedents and Consequences of Nonconscious Goal Pursuit. In James Y. Shah and Wendi I. Gardner (Eds.), *Handbook of Motivation Science*. New York: Guilford Press, 342–355.

Chartrand, Tanya L., Maddux, William W., and Lakin, Jessica L. (2005). Beyond the Perception-Behavior Link: The Ubiquitous Utility and Motivational Moderators of Nonconscious Mimicry. In Ran R. Hassin, James S. Uleman, and John A. Bargh (Eds.), *The New Unconscious*. New York: Oxford University Press, 334–361.

Chen, Chao C., Belkin, Liuba Y., and Kurtzberg, Terri R. (2007). Organizational Change, Member Emotion, and Construction of Charismatic Leadership: A Follower-centric Contingency Model. In Boas Shamir, Rajnandini Pillai, Michelle C. Bligh, and Mary Uhl-Bien (Eds.), *Follower-Centered Perspectives on Leadership: A Tribute to the Memory of James R. Meindl*. Greenwich, CT: Information Age Publishing, 115–134.

Chen, Serena, Fitzsimons, Gráinne M., and Andersen, Susan M. (2007). Automaticity in Close Relationships. In John A. Bargh (Ed.), *Social Psychology and the Unconscious: The Automaticity of Higher Mental Processes*. New York: Psychology Press, 133–172.

Child, John (1972a). Organization Structure and Strategies of Control: A Replication of the Aston Study. *Administrative Science Quarterly*, 17, 163–177.

———. (1972b). Organizational Structure, Environment, and Performance—The Role of Strategic Choice. *Sociology*, 6, 1–22.

Choi, Y. Susan, Gray, Heather M., and Ambady, Nalini. (2005). The Glimpsed World: Unintended Communication and Unintended Perception. In Ran R. Hassin, James S. Uleman, and John A. Bargh (Eds.), *The New Unconscious*. New York: Oxford University Press, 309–333.

Choi, Young R., and Shepherd, Dean A. (2004). Entrepreneurs? Decisions to Exploit Opportunities. *Journal of Management*, 30, 377–395.

Clore, Gerald L., Storbeck, Justin, Robinson, Michael D., and Centerbar, David B. (2005). Seven Sins in the Study of Unconscious Affect. In Lisa F. Barrett, Paula M. Niedenthal, and Piotr Winkielman (Eds.), *Emotion and Consciousness*. New York: Guilford Press, 384–408.

Coghlan, David, and Jacobs, Claus. (2005). Kurt Lewin on Reeducation: Foundations for Action Research. *Journal of Applied Behavioral Science*, 41, 444–457.

Cogliser, Claudia C., and Schriesheim, Chester A. (2006). Conflict among Subordinates and Conflict-Handling Styles as Predictors of Managers' Anticipated Power-Sharing: An Experimental Investigation. In Chester A. Schriesheim and Linda L. Neider (Eds.), *Power and Influence in Organizations: New Empirical and Theoretical Perspectives*. Greenwich, CT: Information Age Publishing, 155–173.

Cogswell, Alex. (2008). Explicit Rejection of an Implicit Dichotomy: Integrating Two Approaches to Assessing Dependency. *Journal of Personality Assessment*, 90, 26–35.

Cohen, Florette, Solomon, Sheldon, Maxfield, Molly, Pyszczynski, Tom, and Greenberg, Jeff. (2004). Fatal Attraction: The Effects of Mortality Salience on Evaluations of Charismatic, Task-Oriented, and Relationship-Oriented Leaders. *Psychological Science*, 15, 846–851.

Cohen, Michael D., March, James G., and Olsen, Johan P. (1972). A Garbage Can Model of Organizational Choice. *Administrative Science Quarterly*, 17, 1–25.

Cohn, Michael A., Mehl, Matthias R., and Pennebaker, James W. (2004). Linguistic Markers of Psychological Change Surrounding September 11, 2001. *Psychological Science*, 15, 687–693.

Collins, Christopher J., Hanges, Paul J., and Locke, Edwin A. (2004). The Relationship of Need for Achievement to Entrepreneurial Behavior: A Meta-Analysis. *Human Performance*, 17, 95–117.

Cooley, Charles H. (1956). *Social Organization*. Glencoe, IL: Free Press.

Coutu, Dianne, and Hackman, J. Richard (2009). Why Teams Don't Work. *Harvard Business Review*, 87(5), 99–105.

Cozolino, Louis (2008). *The Healthy Aging Brain: Sustaining Attachment, Attaining Wisdom*. New York: W. W. Norton.

Crano, William D., and Prislin, Radmila. (2006). Attitudes and Persuasion. *Annual Review of Psychology*, 57, 345–374.

Crisp, Richard J., and Turner, Rhiannon N. (2009). Can Imagined Interactions Produce Positive Perceptions? Reducing Prejudices through Simulated Social Contact. *American Psychologist*, 64, 231–240.

Cronshaw, Stephen F., and Lord, Robert G. (1987). Effects of Categorization, Attribution, and Encoding Processes on Leadership Perceptions. *Journal of Applied Psychology*, 72, 97–106.

Csikszentmihalya, Mihaly, and Nakamura, Jeanne. (2005). The Role of Emotions in the Development of Wisdom. In Robert J. Sternberg and Jennifer Jordan (Eds.), *A Handbook of Wisdom: Psychological Perspectives*. New York: Cambridge University Press, 220–242.

Cue, Alexandra, Koppel, Jonathan, and Hirst, William. (2007). Silence Is Not Golden: A Case for Socially Shared Retrieval-Induced Forgetting. *Psychological Science*, 18, 727–733.

Cummings, Larry L. (1981). Review of *A Theory of Behavior in Organizations*. *Contemporary Psychology*, 26, 661–663.

Cummings, Thomas G., ed. (2008). *Handbook of Organization Development*. Los Angeles, CA: Sage.

Cunningham, William A., Van Bavel, Jay J., and Johnsen, Ingrid R. (2008). Affective Flexibility: Evaluative Processing Goals Shape Amygdala Activity. *Psychological Science*, 19, 152–160.

Currie, Graeme, and Proctor, Stephen J. (2005). The Antecedents of Middle Managers' Strategic Contribution: The Case of a Professional Bureaucracy. *Journal of Management Studies*, 42, 1325–1356.

Cyders, Melissa A., and Smith, Gregory T. (2008). Emotion-Based Dispositions to Rash Action: Positive and Negative Urgency. *Psychological Bulletin*, 134, 807–828.

Cyert, Richard M., and March, James G. (1963). *A Behavioral Theory of the Firm*. Englewood Cliffs, NJ: Prentice-Hall.

———. (1992). *A Behavioral Theory of the Firm*. Oxford, UK: Blackwell Business.

Dalgleish, Tim, Hauer, Beatrijs, and Kuyken, Willem. (2008). The Mental Regulation of Autobiographical Recollection in the Aftermath of Trauma. *Current Directions in Psychological Science*, 17, 259–263.

Damanpour, Fariborz. (1991). Organizational Innovation: A Meta-analysis of Effects of Determinants and Moderators. *Academy of Management Journal*, 34, 555–590.

Dane, Erik, and Pratt, Michael G. (2007). Exploring Intuition and Its Role in Managerial Decision Making. *Academy of Management Review*, 32, 33–54.

Davis, Gerald F., and Swaminathan, Anand. (1996). Review Symposium—*Evolutionary Dynamics of Organizations*. *Administrative Science Quarterly*, 41, 538–550.

Davis, Stanley M., and Lawrence, Paul R. (1977). *Matrix*. Reading, MA: Addison-Wesley.

Davis, Walter D., and Gardner, William L. (2004). Perceptions of Politics and Organizational Cynicism: An Attributional and Leader-Member Exchange Perspective. *Leadership Quarterly*, 15, 439–465.

Day, David V., Gronn, Peter, and Salas, Eduardo (2006). Leadership in Team-Based Organizations: On the Threshold of a New Era. *Leadership Quarterly*, 17, 211–216.

Day, David V., and Lance, Charles E. (2004). Understanding the Development of Leadership Complexity through Latent Growth Modeling. In David V. Day, Stephen J. Zaccaro, and Stanley M. Halpin (Eds.), *Leader Development for Transforming Organizations: Growing Leaders for Tomorrow*. Mahwah, NJ: Lawrence Erlbaum, 41–69.

Deci, Edward L. (1975). *Intrinsic Motivation*. New York: Plenum.

———. (1980). *The Psychology of Self-Determination*. Lexington, MA: Heath.

Deci, Edward L., Koestner, Richard, and Ryan, Richard M. (1999). A Meta-Analytic Review of Experiments Examining the Effects of Extrinsic Rewards on Intrinsic Motivation. *Psychological Bulletin*, 125, 627–668.

Deci, Edward L., and Ryan, Richard M. (1985). *Intrinsic Motivation and Self-Determination in Human Behavior*. New York: Plenum.

———. (1991). A Motivational Approach to Self: Integration in Personality. In R. Dienstbier (Ed.), *Nebraska Symposium on Motivation: Vol. 38. Perspectives on Motivation*. Lincoln: University of Nebraska Press, 237–288.

———. (2000). The "What" and "Why" of Goal Pursuits: Human Needs and the Self-Determination of Behavior. *Psychological Inquiry*, 11, 227–268.

deGelder, Beatrice. (2005). Nonconscious Emotions: New Findings and Perspectives on Nonconscious Facial Expression Recognition and Its Voice and Whole-Body Contexts. In Lisa F. Barrett, Paula M. Niedenthal, and Piotr Winkielman (Eds.), *Emotion and Consciousness*. New York: Guilford Press, 123–149.

De Houwer, Jan, and Moors, Agnes. (2007). How to Define and Examine the Implicitness of Implicit Measures. In Bernd Wittenbrink and Norbert Schwarz (Eds.), *Implicit Measures of Attitudes*. New York: Guilford Press, 179–194.

De Houwer, Jan, Teige-Mocigemba, Sarah, Spruyt, Adriaan, and Moors, Agnes. (2009). Implicit Measures: A Normative Analysis and Review. *Psychological Bulletin,* 135, 347–368.

Delacroix, Jacques, Swaminathan, Anand, and Solt, Michael E. (1989). Density Dependence versus Population Dynamics: An Ecological Study of Failings in the California Wine Industry. *American Sociological Review,* 54, 245–262.

Del Giudice, Matthew J. (2010). What Might This Be? Rediscovering the Rorschach as a Tool for Personnel Selection in Organizations. *Journal of Personality Assessment,* 92, 78–89.

Delmar, Frédéric, and Shane, Scott. (2004). Legitimating First: Organizing Activities and the Survival of New Ventures. *Journal of Business Venturing,* 19, 385–410.

Den Hartog, Deanne N., DeHoogh, Annabel H. B., and Keegan, Anne E. (2007). The Interactive Effects of Belongingness and Charisma on Helping and Compliance. *Journal of Applied Psychology,* 92, 1131–1139.

De Neys, Wim. (2006). Dual Processing in Reasoning: Two Systems but One Reasoner. *Psychological Science,* 17, 428–433.

Derfus, Pamela J., Maggitti, Patrick G., Grimm, Curtis M., and Smith, Ken G. (2008). The Red Queen Effect: Competitive Actions and Firm Performance. *Academy of Management Journal,* 51, 61–80.

deVillemor-Amaral, E. (2007). Executive Performance on the Rorschach Comprehensive System. *Rorschachiana,* 18, 119–133.

DeVoe, Sanford, and Pfeffer, Jeffrey. (2007). Hourly Payment and Volunteering: The Effect of Organizational Practices on Decisions about Time Use. *Academy of Management Journal,* 50, 783–798.

deVries, Reinout E., and van Gelder, Jean-Louis. (2005). Leadership and Need for Leadership: Testing an Implicit Followership Theory. In Birgit Schyns and James R. Meindl (Eds.), *Implicit Leadership Theories: Essays and Explorations.* Greenwich, CT: Information Age Publishing, 277–303.

DeWall, C. Nathan, and Baumeister, Roy F. (2007). From Terror to Joy: Automatic Tuning to Positive Affective Information Following Mortality Salience. *Psychological Science,* 18, 984–990.

Diamond, Michael A. (1986). Resistance to Change: A Psychoanalytic Critique of Argyris and Schön's Contributions to Organization Theory and Intervention. *Journal of Management Studies,* 23, 543–562.

Diekman, Amanda B., and Eagly, Alice H. (2008). Of Men, Women, and Motivation: A Role Congruity Account. In James Y. Shah and Wendi L. Gardner (Eds.), *Handbook of Motivation Science.* New York: Guilford Press, 434–447.

Dierdorff, Erich C., and Morgeson, Frederick P. (2007). Consensus in Work Role Requirements: The Influence of Discrete Occupational Context on Role Expectations. *Journal of Applied Psychology,* 92, 1228–1241.

Dijksterhuis, Ap, Aarts, Henk, and Smith, Pamela K. (2005). The Power of the Subliminal: On Subliminal Persuasion and Other Potential Applications. In Ran R. Hassin, James S. Uleman, and John A. Bargh (Eds.), *The New Unconscious.* New York: Oxford University Press, 77–106.

Dijksterhuis, Ap, Bos, Maarten W., van der Leij, Andries, and van Baaren, Rick B. (2009). Predicting Soccer Matches after Unconscious and Conscious Thought as a Function of Expertise. *Psychological Science,* 20, 1381–1387.

Dijksterhuis, Ap, Chartrand, Tanya L., and Aarts, Henk. (2007). Effects of Priming and Perception on Social Behavior and Goal Pursuit. In John A. Bargh (Ed.), *Social Psychology and the Unconscious: The Automaticity of Higher Mental Processes.* New York: Psychology Press, 51–131.

Dijksterhuis, Ap, and Nordgren, Loran F. (2006). A Theory of Unconscious Thought. *Perspectives on Psychological Science,* 1, 95–109.

DiMaggio, Paul J. (1982). Cultural Entrepreneurship in Nineteenth-Century Boston: The Creation of an Organizational Base for High Culture in America. *Media, Culture, and Society,* 4, 33–50.

———. (1988). Interest and Agency in Institutional Theory. In Lynne G. Zucker (Ed.), *Institutional Patterns and Organizations: Culture and Environment.* Cambridge, MA: Ballinger, 3–21.

———. (1991). Constructing an Organizational Field as a Professional Project: U.S. Art Museums, 1920–1940. In Walter W. Powell and Paul J. Di Maggio (Eds.), *The New Institutionalism in Organizational Analysis.* Chicago: University of Chicago Press, 267–292.

———. (1992). Nadel's Paradox Revisited: Relational and Cultural Aspects of Organizational Structure. In N. Nohria and R. G. Eccles (Eds.), *Networks and Organizations: Structure, Form, and Action.* Boston, MA: Harvard Business School Press, 118–142.

———. (1997). Culture and Cognition. *Annual Review of Sociology,* 23, 263–287.

DiMaggio, Paul J., Hargittai, Eszter, Neuman, W. Russell, and Robinson, John P. (2001). Social Implications of the Internet. *Annual Review of Sociology,* 27, 307–336.

DiMaggio, Paul J., and Powell, Walter W. (1983). The Iron Cage Revisited: Institutional Isomorphism and Collective Rationality in Organizational Fields. *American Sociological Review,* 48, 147–160.

Dobrev, Stanislav D., Kim, Tai-Young, and Carroll, Glenn R. (2002). The Evolution of Organizational Niches: U.S. Automobile Manufacturers, 1885–1981. *Administrative Science Quarterly,* 47, 233–264.

———. (2003). Shifting Gears, Shifting Niches, Organizational Inertia and Change in the Evolution of the U.S. Automobile Industry, 1885–1981. *Organization Science,* 14, 264–282.

Donaldson, Lex. (1976). Woodward, Technology, Organization Structure and Performance—A Critique of the Universal Generalization. *Journal of Management Studies,* 13, 255–273.

———. (1987). Strategy and Structural Adjustment to Regain Fit and Performance: In Defense of Contingency Theory. *Journal of Management Studies,* 24, 1–24.

———. (1995). *American Antimanagement Theories of Organization: A Critique of Paradigm Proliferation.* Cambridge, UK: Cambridge University Press.

———. (1996). *For Positivist Organization Theory: Proving the Hard Core.* London, UK: Sage.

———. (2001). *The Contingency Theory of Organizations.* Thousand Oaks, CA: Sage.

———. (2005a). For Positive Management Theories While Retaining Science: Reply to Ghoshal. *Academy of Management Learning and Education,* 4, 109–113.

———. (2005b). Reply to Pfeffer. *Organization Studies,* 26, 1106–1109.

———. (2009). Where Is the Jury: The Failures in the Scientific Evaluation Processes in Organizational Science. *Journal of Management Inquiry,* 18, 97–99.

Dorado, Silvia. (2005). Institutional Entrepreneurship, Partaking, and Convening. *Organization Studies,* 26, 385–414.

Dorfman, Peter W., Hanges, Paul J., and Brodbeck, Felix C. (2004). Leadership and Cultural Variation: The Identification of Culturally Endorsed Leadership Profiles. In Robert J. House, Paul J. Hanges, Mansour Javidan, Peter W. Dorfman, and Vipin Gupta (Eds.), *Culture, Leadership, and Organizations: The GLOBE Study of 62 Societies.* Thousand Oaks, CA: Sage, 669–719.

Drori, Gili S., Jang, Yong S., and Meyer, John W. (2006). Sources of Rationalized Governance: Cross-National Longitudinal Analyses. *Administrative Science Quarterly,* 51, 205–229.

Dumdum, Uldarico R., Lowe, Kevin B., and Avolio, Bruce J. (2002). A Meta-Analysis of Transformational and Transactional Correlates of Effectiveness and Satisfaction: An Update and Extension. In Bruce J. Avolio and Francis J. Yammarino (Eds.), *Transformational and Charismatic Leadership: The Road Ahead.* Oxford, UK: Elsevier Science, 35–66.

Dunning, David, Heath, Chip, and Suls, Jerry M. (2004). Flawed Self-Assessment: Implications for Health, Education, and the Workplace. *Psychological Science in the Public Interest,* 5, 69–106.

Dweck, C. S., and Leggett, E. L. (1988). A Social-Cognitive Approach to Motivation and Personality. *Psychological Review,* 95, 256–273.

Eagly, Alice H., Johannesen-Schmidt, Mary C., and van Engen, Marloes L. (2003). Transformational, Transactional, and Laissez-Faire Leadership Styles: A Meta-analysis Comparing Women and Men. *Psychological Bulletin,* 129, 569–591.

Eitam, Baruch, Hassin, Ran R., and Schul, Yaacov. (2008). Nonconscious Goal Pursuit in Novel Environments: The Case of Implicit Learning. *Psychological Science,* 19, 261–267.

Elkins, Teri, and Keller, Robert T. (2003). Leadership in Research and Development Organizations: A Literature Review and Conceptual Framework. *Leadership Quarterly,* 14, 587–606.

Elliott, Andrew J., and Fryer, James W. (2008). The Goal Construct in Psychology. In James Y. Shah and Wendi L. Gardner (Eds.), *Handbook of Motivation Science.* New York: Guilford Press, 235–250.

Elsbach, Kimberly D., and Hargadon, Andrew B. (2006). Enhancing Creativity through "Mindless" Work: A Framework of Workday Design. *Organization Science,* 17, 470–483.

Emery, Fred E., and Trist, Eric L. (1973). *Toward a Social Ecology.* London, UK: Plenum.

Ephraim, David. (2008). Psychocultural System Manual. In Sharon R. Jenkins (Ed.), *A Handbook of Clinical Scoring Systems for Thematic Apperceptive Techniques.* New York: Lawrence Erlbaum, 739–760.

Epitropaki, Olga, and Martin, Robin. (2004). Implicit Leadership Theories in Applied Settings: Factor Structure, Generalizability, and Stability over Time. *Journal of Applied Psychology,* 89, 293–310.

———. (2005). From Ideal to Real: A Longitudinal Study of the Role of Implicit Leadership Theories in Leader-Member Exchanges and Employee Outcomes. *Journal of Applied Psychology,* 90, 659–676.

Erdogan, Berrin, Liden, Robert C., and Kraimer, Maria L. (2006). Justice and Leader-Member Exchange: The Moderating Role of Organizational Culture. *Academy of Management Journal,* 49, 395–406.

Erez, Amir, Misangyi, Vilmos F., Johnson, Diane F., LePine, Marcie A., and Halverson, Kent C. (2008). Stirring the Hearts of Followers; Charismatic Leadership as the Transferral of Affect. *Journal of Applied Psychology,* 93, 602–615.

Etzioni, Amitai. (1959). Authority Structure and Organizational Effectiveness. *Administrative Science Quarterly,* 4, 43–67.

———. (1961, 1975). *A Comparative Analysis of Complex Organizations: On Power, Involvement, and Their Correlates.* New York: Free Press.

———. (1968). *The Active Society: A Theory of Societal and Political Processes.* New York: Free Press.

———. (1969). *The Semi-Professions and Their Organization: Teachers, Nurses, and Social Workers.* New York: Free Press.

Evans, Jonathan St. B. T. (2008). Dual-Processing Accounts of Reasoning, Judgment, and Social Cognition. *Annual Review of Psychology,* 59, 255–278.

Evans, Martin G. (1970a). The Effects of Supervisory Behavior on the Path-Goal Relationship. *Organizational Behavior and Human Performance,* 5, 277–298.

———. (1970b). Leadership and Motivation: A Core Concept. *Academy of Management Journal,* 13, 91–102.

———. (2002). Path-Goal Theory of Leadership. In Linda L. Neider and Chester A. Schriesheim (Eds.), *Leadership.* Greenwich, CT: Information Age Publishing, 115–138.

Evans, Richard I. (1968). *B. F. Skinner: The Man and His Ideas.* New York: E. P. Dutton.

Exner, John E. (2003). *The Rorschach: A Comprehensive System.* Hoboken, NJ: Wiley.

Fast, Nathanael J., and Chen, Serena (2009). When the Boss Feels Inadequate: Power, Incompetence, and Aggression. *Psychological Science,* 20, 1406–1413.

Fast, Nathanael J., Gruenfeld, Deborah H., Sivanathan, Niro, and Galinsky, Adam D. (2009). Illusory Control: A Generative Force behind Power's Far-Reaching Effects. *Psychological Science,* 20, 502–508.

Fast, Nathanael J., Heath, Chip, and Wu, George. (2009). Common Ground and Cultural Prominence: How Conversation Reinforces Culture. *Psychological Science,* 20, 904–911.

Fazio, R. H., Sanbonmatsu, D. M., Powell, M. C., and Kardes, F. R. (1986). On the Automatic Activation of Attitudes. *Journal of Personality and Social Psychology,* 50, 229–238.

Feinberg, Barbara J., Ostroff, Cheri, and Burke, W. Warner. (2005). The Role of Within-Group Agreement in Understanding Transformational Leadership. *Journal of Occupational and Organizational Psychology,* 78, 471–488.

Felfe, Jörg. (2005). Personality and Romance of Leadership. In Birgit Schyns and James R. Meindl (Eds.), *Implicit Leadership Theories: Essays and Explorations.* Greenwich, CT: Information Age Publishing, 199–225.

Felps, Will, Mitchell, Terence R., and Byington, Eliza. (2006). How, When, and Why Bad Apples Spoil the Barrel: Negative Group Members and Dysfunctional Groups. *Research in Organizational Behavior,* 27, 175–222.

Ferguson, Melissa J. (2007). The Automaticity of Evaluation. In John A. Bargh (Ed.), *Social Psychology and the Unconscious: The Automaticity of Higher Mental Processes.* New York: Psychology Press, 219–264.

Ferguson, Melissa J., and Bargh, John A. (2007). Beyond the Attitude Object: Implicit Attitudes Spring from Object-Centered Contexts. In Bernd Wittenbrink and Norbert Schwarz (Eds.), *Implicit Measures of Attitudes.* New York: Guilford Press, 216–246.

Ferguson, Melissa J., Hassin, Ran, and Bargh, John A. (2008). Implicit Motivation: Past, Present, and Future. In James Y. Shah and Wendi L. Gardner (Eds.), *Handbook of Motivation Science.* New York: Guilford Press, 150–166.

Fernet, Claude, Guay, Frédéric, and Senécal, Caroline. (2004). Adjusting to Job Demands: The Role of Work Self-Determination and Job Control in Predicting Burnout. *Journal of Vocational Behavior,* 65, 39–56.

Fernhaber, Stephanie A., and Li, Dan. (2010). The Impact of Interorganizational Imitation on New Venture International Entry and Performance. *Entrepreneurship Theory and Practice,* 34, 1–30.

Ferraro, Fabrizio, Pfeffer, Jeffrey, and Sutton, Robert I. (2005). Economics Language and Assumptions: How Theories Can Become Self-Fulfilling. *Academy of Management Review,* 30, 8–24.

Ferrier, Walter J., Smith, Ken G., Rediker, Kenneth J., and Mitchell, Terence R. (1995). Distributive Justice Norms and Attributions for Performance Outcomes as a Function of Power. In Mark J. Martinko (Ed.), *Attribution Theory: An Organizational Perspective.* Delray Beach, FL: St. Lucie Press, 315–330.

Fiedler, Fred E. (1967). *A Theory of Leadership Effectiveness.* New York: McGraw-Hill.

————. (1972). Personality, Motivational Systems, and Behavior of High and Low LPC Persons. *Human Relations*, 25, 391–412.

————. (1973). Personality and Situational Determinants of Leader Behavior. In Edwin A. Fleishman and James G. Hunt (Eds.), *Current Developments in the Study of Leadership*. Carbondale: Southern Illinois University Press, 41–61.

————. (1978). The Contingency Model and the Dynamics of the Leadership Process. In Leonard Berkowitz (Ed.), *Advances in Experimental Social Psychology, Vol. 11*. New York: Academic Press, 59–112.

————. (2002). The Curious Role of Cognitive Resources in Leadership. In Ronald E. Riggio and Susan E. Murphy (Eds.), *Multiple Intelligences and Leadership*. Mahwah, NJ: Lawrence Erlbaum, 91–104.

Fiedler, Fred E., and Chemers, Martin M. (1974). *Leadership and Effective Management*. Glenview, IL: Scott, Foresman.

————. (1984). *Improving Leadership Effectiveness: The Leader Match Concept*. New York: John Wiley.

Fiedler, Fred E., and Garcia, Joseph E. (1987). *New Approaches to Effective Leadership: Cognitive Resources and Organizational Performance*. New York: John Wiley.

Fiedler, Fred E., and Senior, K. (1952). An Exploratory Study of Unconscious Feeling Reactions in Fifteen Patient-Therapist Pairs. *Journal of Abnormal and Social Psychology*, 47(2), 446–453.

Fiedler, Fred E., and Siegel, S. M. (1949). The Free Drawing Test as a Predictor of Nonimprovement in Psychotherapy. *Journal of Clinical Psychology*, 5(4), 386–389.

Fiedler, Klaus. (2008). Language: A Toolbox for Sharing and Influencing Social Reality. *Perspectives on Psychological Science*, 3, 38–47.

Finkbeiner, Matthew, and Palermo, Romina. (2009). The Role of Spatial Attention in Nonconscious Processing: A Comparison of Face and Nonface Stimuli. *Psychological Science*, 20, 42–51.

Fishbach, Ayelet, and Trope, Yaacov. (2008). Implicit and Explicit Counteractive Self-Control. In James Y. Shah and Wendi L. Gardner (Eds.), *Handbook of Motivation Science*. New York: Guilford Press, 281–294.

Fiske, Susan T. (2008). Core Social Motivations: Views from the Couch, Consciousness, Classroom, Computers, and Collectives. In James Y. Shah and Wendi L. Gardner (Eds.), *Handbook of Motivation Science*. New York: Guilford Press, 3–22.

Fitzsimons, Gráinne M., and Bargh, John A. (2004). Automatic Self-Regulation. In R. F. Baumeister and K. D. Vohs (Eds.), *Handbook of Self-Regulation*. New York: Guilford Press, 151–170.

Fligstein, Neil. (1997). Social Skill and Institutional Theory. *American Behavioral Scientist*, 40, 397–405.

————. (2001a). *The Architecture of Markets: An Economic Sociology of Twenty-first Century Capitalist Societies*. Princeton, NJ: Princeton University Press.

————. (2001b). Social Skill and the Theory of Fields. *Social Theory*, 19, 105–125.

Flynn, Francis J., and Staw, Barry, M. (2004). Lend Me Your Wallets: The Effect of Charismatic Leadership on External Support for an Organization. *Strategic Management Journal*, 25, 309–330.

Foa, Uriel G., Mitchell, Terence R., and Fiedler, Fred E. (1971). Differentiation Matching. *Behavioral Science*, 16, 130–142.

Folger, Robert. (2005). The Road to Fairness and Beyond. In Ken G. Smith and Michael A. Hitt (Eds.), *Great Minds in Management: The Process of Theory Development*. New York: Oxford University Press, 55–83.

Fong, Christina T. (2006). The Effects of Emotional Ambivalence on Creativity. *Academy of Management Journal*, 49, 1016–1030.

Forbes, Daniel P. (2005). Are Some Entrepreneurs More Overconfident Than Others? *Journal of Business Venturing*, 20, 623–640.

Foti, Roseanne J., and Miner, John B. (2003). Individual Differences and Organizational Forms in the Leadership Process. *Leadership Quarterly*, 14, 83–112.

Fowles, Don C., and Dindo, Lilian. (2009). Temperament and Psychopathy: A Dual-Pathway Model. *Current Directions in Psychological Science*, 18, 179–183.

Frank, Michael J., O'Reilly, Randall C., and Curran, Tim. (2006). When Memory Fails, Intuition Reigns: Midazolam Enhances Implicit Inference in Humans. *Psychological Science*, 17, 700–707.

Franke, Nikolaus, Gruber, Marc, Harhoff, Dietmar, and Henkel, Joachim. (2006). What You Are Is What You Like—Similarity Biases in Venture Capitalists' Evaluations of Start-Up Teams. *Journal of Business Venturing*, 21, 802–826.

Freeman, John H., Carroll, Glenn R., and Hannan, Michael T. (1983). The Liability of Newness: Age Dependence in Organizational Death Rates. *American Sociological Review*, 48, 692–710.

Freud, Anna. (1946). *The Ego and the Mechanisms of Defense*. New York: International Universities Press.

Freud, Sigmund. (1930). *Civilization and Its Discontents.* New York: Norton.

———. (1931). Libidinal Types. In *Collected Papers. Vol. V.* London, UK: Hogarth Press, 247–251.

———. (1938). *The Basic Writings of Sigmund Freud.* New York: The Modern Library/Random House.

———. (1950). *Collected Papers, Vol. I.* London, UK: Hogarth Press.

Fried, Yitzhak, Levi, Ariel S., and Laurence, Gregory. (2007). The Job Characteristics Model and LMX-MMX Leadership. In George B. Graen and Joni A. Graen (Eds.), *New Multinational Network Sharing.* Charlotte, NC: Information Age Publishing, 157–196.

Frost, Brian C., Ko, Chia-Huei E., and James, Lawrence R. (2007). Implicit and Explicit Personality: A Test of a Channeling Hypothesis for Aggressive Behavior. *Journal of Applied Psychology, 92,* 1299–1319.

Frost, Peter J. (1997). Bridging Academia and Business: A Conversation with Steve Kerr. *Organization Science, 8,* 332–347.

Fulk, Janet, and Wendler, Eric R. (1982). Dimensionality of Leader-Subordinate Interactions: A Path-Goal Investigation. *Organizational Behavior and Human Performance, 30,* 241–264.

Furnham, A. (1988). *Lay Theories: Everyday Understanding of Problems in the Social Sciences.* Oxford, UK: Pergamon.

Gable, Shelly L., and Strachman, Amy. (2008). Approaching Social Rewards and Avoiding Social Punishments: Appetitive and Aversive Social Motivation. In James Y. Shah and Wendi L. Gardner (Eds.), *Handbook of Motivation Science.* New York: Guilford Press, 561–575.

Gabriel, Yiannis. (1999). *Organizations in Depth: The Psychoanalysis of Organizations.* Thousand Oaks, CA: Sage.

Gailliot, Matthew T. (2008). Unlocking the Energy Dynamics of Executive Functioning: Linking Executive Functioning to Brain Glycogen. *Perspectives on Psychological Science, 3,* 245–263.

Galbraith, Jay R. (2009). *Designing Matrix Organizations That Actually Work: How IBM, Procter & Gamble, and Others Design for Success.* San Francisco, CA: Jossey-Bass.

Garud, Raghu, Jain, Sanjay, and Kumaraswamy, Arun. (2002). Institutional Entrepreneurship in the Sponsorship of Common Technological Standards: The Case of Sun Microsystems and Java. *Academy of Management Journal, 45,* 196–214.

Gavetti, Giavanni, Levinthal, Daniel, and Ocasio, William. (2007). Neo-Carnegie: The Carnegie School's Past, Present, and Reconstructing for the Future. *Organization Science, 18,* 523–536.

Gawronski, Bertram, and Bodenhausen, Galen V. (2006). Associative and Propositional Processes in Evaluation: An Integrative Review of Implicit and Explicit Attitude Change. *Psychological Bulletin, 132,* 692–730.

———. (2007). What Do We Know about Implicit Attitude Measures and What Do We Have to Learn? In Bernd Wittenbrink and Norbert Schwarz (Eds.), *Implicit Measures of Attitudes.* New York: Guilford Press, 265–286.

Gawronski, Bertram, LeBel, Etienne P., and Peters, Kurt R. (2007). What Do Implicit Measures Tell Us? *Perspectives on Psychological Science, 2,* 181–193.

George, Jennifer M. (2008). Creativity in Organizations. In James P. Walsh and Arthur P. Brief (Eds.), *The Academy of Management Annals, 1,* 439–477.

———. (2009). The Illusion of Will in Organizational Behavior Research: Nonconscious Processes and Job Design. *Journal of Management, 35,* 1318–1339.

George, Jennifer, and Zhou, Jing. (2007). Dual Tuning in a Supportive Context: Joint Contributions of Positive Mood, Negative Mood, and Supervisory Behaviors to Employee Creativity. *Academy of Management Journal, 50,* 605–622.

Georgopoulos, Basil S., Mahoney, Gerald M., and Jones, Nyle W. (1957). A Path-Goal Approach to Productivity. *Journal of Applied Psychology, 41,* 345–353.

Gergen, Kenneth J., and Thatchenkery, Tojo J. (2004). Organization Science as Social Construction: Postmodern Potentials. *Journal of Applied Behavioral Science, 40,* 228–249.

Gerstner, Charlotte R., and Day, David V. (1997). Meta-Analytic Review of Leader-Member Exchange Theory: Correlates and Construct Issues. *Journal of Applied Psychology, 82,* 827–844.

Gianotti, Lorena R., Knoch, Daria, Faber, Pascal L., Lehmann, Dietrich, Pascual-Marqui, Roberto D., Diezi, Christa, Schoch, Cornelia, Eisenegger, Christoph, and Fehr, Ernst. (2009). Tonic Activity Level in the Right Prefrontal Cortex Predicts Individuals' Risk Taking. *Psychological Science, 20,* 33–38.

Gibb, C. A. (1949). Some Tentative Comments Concerning Group Rorschach Pointers to the Personality Traits of Leaders. *Journal of Social Psychology, 30,* 251–263.

Gibbons, F. X., Gerrard, M., and Lane, D. J. (2003). A Social-Reaction Model of Adolescent Health Risk. In J. J. Suls and K. A. Wallston (Eds.), *Social Psychological Foundations of Health and Illness.* Oxford, UK: Blackwell, 107–136.

Gibson, Donald E. (2003). Developing the Professional Self-Concept: Role Model Constructs in Early, Middle, and Late Career Stages. *Organization Science,* 14, 591–610.

Giddens, Anthony. (1984). *The Constitution of Society.* Berkeley: University of California Press.

Gigerenzer, Gerd. (2008). Why Heuristics Work. *Perspectives on Psychological Science,* 3, 20–29.

Gilovich, Thomas, Griffin, Dale, and Kahneman, Daniel. (2002). *Heuristics and Biases: The Psychology of Intuitive Judgment.* Cambridge, UK: Cambridge University Press.

Gladwell, Malcolm. (2005). *Blink: The Power of Thinking without Thinking.* New York: Little, Brown.

Glaser, Jack, and Kihlstrom, John F. (2005). Compensatory Automaticity: Unconscious Volition Is Not an Oxymoron. In Ran R. Hassin, James S. Uleman, and John A. Bargh (Eds.), *The New Unconscious.* New York: Oxford University Press, 171–195.

Golden-Biddle, Karen, and Rao, Hayagreeva. (2004). Breaches in the Boardroom: Organizational Identity and Conflict of Commitment in a Nonprofit Organization. In Mary Jo Hatch and Majken Schultz (Eds.), *Organizational Identity: A Reader.* New York: Oxford University Press, 313–345.

Goldstein, Kurt. (1939). *The Organism.* New York: American Book.

Goleman, D. (1998). *Working with Emotional Intelligence.* New York: Bantam Books.

Golembiewski, Robert T. (2003). *Ironies in Organization Development.* New York: Marcel Dekker.

Golembiewski, Robert T., Billingsley, Keith, and Yeager, Samuel. (1976). Measuring Change and Persistence in Human Affairs: Types of Change Generated by OD Designs. *Journal of Applied Behavioral Science,* 12, 133–157.

Golembiewski, Robert T., and Brewer, Gene A. (2008). *The Status of OD in Public Administration: Another Case of Practice Being Ahead of Theory.* In Thomas G. Cummings (Ed.), *Handbook of Organization Development.* Los Angeles, CA: Sage, 541–551.

Gollwitzer, Peter M. (1999). Implementation Intentions and Effective Goal Pursuit: Strong Effects of Simple Plans. *American Psychologist,* 54, 493–503.

Gollwitzer, Peter M., and Bargh, John A. (2005). Automaticity in Goal Pursuit. In Andrew J. Elliott and C. Dweck (Eds.), *Handbook of Competence and Motivation.* New York: Guilford Press.

Gollwitzer, Peter M., Bayer, Ute C., and McCulloch, Kathleen C. (2005). The Control of the Unwanted. In Ran R. Hassin, James S. Uleman, and John A. Bargh (Eds.), *The New Unconscious.* New York: Oxford University Press, 485–515.

Gollwitzer, Peter M., Parks-Stamm, Elizabeth J., Jaudas, Alexander, and Sheeran, Paschel. (2008). Flexible Tenacity in Goal Pursuit. In James Y. Shah and Wendi I. Gardner (Eds.), *Handbook of Motivation Science.* New York: Guilford Press, 325–341.

Gordon, Leonard V. (1970). Measurement of Bureaucratic Orientation. *Personnel Psychology,* 23, 1–11.

Graen, George B. (1969). Instrumentality Theory of Work Motivation: Some Experimental Results and Suggested Modifications. *Journal of Applied Psychology Monograph,* 53(2), 1–25.

———. (1989). *Unwritten Rules for Your Career: 15 Secrets for Fast-Track Success.* New York: John Wiley.

———. (2003). *Dealing with Diversity.* Greenwich, CT: Information Age Publishing.

———. (2004). *New Frontiers of Leadership.* Greenwich, CT: Information Age Publishing.

———. (2005). Three Dyadic Leadership Theories: Comparative Multiple Hypotheses Testing. In George B. Graen and Joni A. Graen (Eds.), *Global Organizing Designs.* Greenwich, CT: Information Age Publishing, 205–215.

———. (2006). In the Eye of the Beholder: Cross-Cultural Lessons in Leadership from Project Globe: A Response Viewed from the Third Cultural Bonding (TCB) Model of Cross-Cultural Leadership. *Academy of Management Perspectives,* 20(4), 95–101.

———. (2007a). Integrating Graen's LMX Leadership Theory and Hackman's Job Characteristics Model. In George B. Graen and Joni A. Graen (Eds.), *New Multinational Network Sharing.* Charlotte, NC: Information Age Publishing, 197–209.

———. (2007b). Letter to the Editor. *Academy of Management Perspectives,* 21(1), 5–6.

Graen, George B., and Graen, Joni A. (2005). *Global Organizing Designs.* Greenwich, CT: Information Age Publishing.

———. (2006). *Sharing Network Leadership.* Greenwich, CT: Information Age Publishing.

———. (2007). *New Multinational Network Sharing.* Charlotte, NC: Information Age Publishing.

————. (2008). *Knowledge-Driven Corporation: Complex Creative Destruction.* Charlotte, NC: Information Age Publishing.

Graen, George B., Novak, Michael A., and Sommerkamp, Patricia. (1982). The Effect of Leader-Member Exchange and Job Design on Productivity and Satisfaction: Testing a Dual Attachment Model. *Organizational Behavior and Human Performance,* 30, 109–131.

Graen, George B., Scandura, Terri A., and Graen, Michael A. (1986). A Field Experimental Test of the Moderating Effects of Growth Need Strength on Productivity. *Journal of Applied Psychology,* 71, 484–491.

Granovetter, M. (1985). Economic Action and Social Structure: The Problem of Embeddedness. *American Journal of Sociology,* 91, 481–510.

Grant, Adam M., and Wade-Benzoni, Kimberly A. (2009). The Hot and Cool of Death Awareness at Work: Mortality Cues, Aging, and Self-Protective and Prosocial Motivations. *Academy of Management Review,* 34, 600–622.

Gray, Heather M. (2008). To What Extent, and Under What Conditions Are First Impressions Valid? In Nalini Ambady and John J. Skowrouski (Eds.), *First Impressions.* New York: Guilford Press, 106–128.

Green, Stephen G., and Mitchell, Terence R. (1979). Attributional Processes of Leaders in Leader-Member Interactions. *Organizational Behavior and Human Performance,* 23, 429–458.

Greenberg, Jeff. (2008). Understanding the Vital Human Quest for Self-Esteem. *Perspectives on Psychological Science,* 3, 48–55.

Greenberg, Jeff, Solomon, Sheldon, and Arndt, Jamie. (2008). A Basic but Uniquely Human Motivation: Terror Management. In James Y. Shah and Wendi I. Gardner (Eds.), *Handbook of Motivation Science.* New York: Guilford Press, 114–134.

Greenberg, Jeff, Solomon, Sheldon, and Pyszczynski, Tom. (1997). Terror Management Theory of Self-Esteem and Cultural Worldviews: Empirical Assessments and Conceptual Refinements. *Advances in Experimental Social Psychology,* 29, 309–347.

Greenberg, Jerald. (2006). Losing Sleep over Organizational Injustice: Attenuating Insomniac Reactions to Underpayment Inequity with Supervisory Training in Interactional Justice. *Journal of Applied Psychology,* 91, 58–69.

Greenwald, Anthony G., Nosek, Brian A., and Sriram, N. (2006). Consequential Validity of the Implicit Association Test: Comment on Blanton and Jaccard (2006). *American Psychologist,* 61, 56–61.

Greenwood, Royston. (2008). Focusing the Asteroid Belt of Organizations. *Journal of Management Inquiry,* 17, 152–156.

Greenwood, Royston, and Devine, Kay. (1997). Inside Aston: A Conversation with Derek Pugh. *Journal of Management Inquiry,* 6, 200–208.

Greenwood, Royston, and Meyer, Renate F. (2008). Influencing Ideas: A Celebration of DiMaggio and Powell (1983). *Journal of Management Inquiry,* 17, 258–264.

Greguras, Gary J., and Ford, John M. (2006). An Examination of the Multidimensionality of Supervisor and Subordinate Perceptions of Leader-Member Exchange. *Journal of Occupational and Organizational Psychology,* 79, 433–465.

Greiner, Larry E., and Cummings, Thomas G. (2004). Wanted: OD More Alive Than Dead. *Journal of Applied Behavioral Science,* 40, 374–391.

Greve, Henrich R., and Rao, Hayagreeva. (2006). If It Doesn't Kill You: Learning from Ecological Competition. In Joel A. C. Baum, Stanislav D. Dobrev, and Arjen van Witteloostuijn (Eds.), *Ecology and Strategy.* Oxford, UK: Elsevier, 243–271.

Grinyer, Peter H., and Yasai-Ardekani, Masoud. (1980). Dimensions of Organizational Structure: A Critical Replication. *Academy of Management Journal,* 23, 405–431.

Gross, Edward, and Etzioni, Amitai. (1985). *Organizations in Society.* Englewood Cliffs, NJ: Prentice-Hall.

Gruber, Daniel A. (2006). The Craft of Translation: An Interview with Malcolm Gladwell. *Journal of Management Inquiry,* 15, 397–403.

Gupta, Vipin, deLuque, Mary, and House, Robert J. (2004). Multisource Construct Validity of GLOBE Scales. In Robert J. House, Paul J. Hanges, Mansour Javidan, Peter W. Dorfman, and Vipin Gupta (Eds.), *Culture, Leadership, and Organizations: The GLOBE Study of 62 Societies.* Thousand Oaks, CA: Sage, 152–177.

Gupta, Vipin, MacMillan, Ian C., and Surie, Gita. (2004). Entrepreneurial Leadership: Developing and Managing a Cross-Cultural Construct. *Journal of Business Venturing,* 19, 241–260.

Hackman, J. Richard. (1978). The Design of Self-Managing Work Groups. In Bert King, Siegfried Streufert, and Fred E. Fiedler (Eds.), *Managerial Control and Organizational Democracy.* New York: Wiley, 61–91.

Hackman, J. Richard, and Oldham, Greg R. (1976). Motivation through the Design of Work: Test of a Theory. *Organizational Behavior and Human Performance,* 16, 250–279.

———. (1980). *Work Redesign.* Reading, MA: Addison-Wesley.

Haidt, Jonathan. (2008). Morality. *Perspectives on Psychological Science,* 3, 65–71.

Halbesleben, Jonathon R. B. (2006). Sources of Social Support and Burnout: A Meta-Analytic Test of the Conservation of Resources Model. *Journal of Applied Psychology,* 91, 1134–1145.

Halbesleben, Jonathon R. B., and Buckley, M. Ronald. (2004). Burnout in Organizational Life. *Journal of Management,* 30, 859–879.

Halbesleben, Jonathon R. B., Osburn, Holly K., and Mumford, Michael D. (2006). Action Research as a Burnout Intervention: Reducing Burnout in the Federal Fire Service. *Journal of Applied Behavioral Science,* 42, 244–266.

Hall, Calvin S., and Lindzey, Gardner. (1957). *Theories of Personality.* New York: Wiley.

Hall, Crystal C., Ariss, Lynn, and Todorov, Alexander. (2007). The Illusion of Knowledge: When More Information Reduces Accuracy and Increases Confidence. *Organizational Behavior and Human Decision Processes,* 103, 277–290.

Hall, Douglas T. (2002). *Careers In and Out of Organizations.* Thousand Oaks, CA: Sage.

Hall, Judith A., and Andrzejewski, Susan A. (2008). Who Draws Accurate First Impressions? Personal Correlates of Sensitivity to Nonverbal Cues. In Nalini Ambady and John J. Skowronski (Eds.), *First Impressions.* New York: Guilford Press, 87–105.

Hambrick, Donald C., Finkelstein, Sydney, Cho, Theresa S., and Jackson, Eric M. (2005). Isomorphism in Reverse: Institutional Theory as an Explanation for Recent Increases in Intraindustry Heterogeneity and Managerial Discretion. *Research in Organizational Behavior,* 26, 307–350.

Hampton, P. J. (1960). Use of Rorschach Test in Selecting Factory Supervisors. *Personnel Journal,* 39, 46–48.

Hanges, Paul J., and Dickson, Marcus W. (2004). The Development and Validation of the GLOBE Culture and Leadership Scales. In Robert J. House, Paul J. Hanges, Mansour Javidan, Peter W. Dorfman, and Vipin Gupta (Eds.), *Culture, Leadership, and Organizations: The GLOBE Study of 62 Societies.* Thousand Oaks, CA: Sage, 122–151.

Hannan, Michael T., and Carroll, Glenn R. (1992). *Dynamics of Organizational Populations: Density, Legitimation, and Competition.* New York: Oxford University Press.

Hannan, Michael T., Carroll, Glenn R., Dundon, Elizabeth A., and Torres, John C. (1995). Organizational Evolution in a Multinational Context: Entries of Automobile Manufacturers in Belgium, Britain, France, Germany, and Italy. *American Sociological Review,* 60, 509–528.

Hannan, Michael T., and Freeman, John H. (1977). The Population Ecology of Organizations. *American Journal of Sociology,* 82, 929–964.

———. (1978). The Population Ecology of Organizations. In Marshall W. Meyer and Associates (Eds.), *Environments and Organizations.* San Francisco, CA: Jossey-Bass, 131–171.

———. (1987). The Ecology of Organizational Founding: American Labor Unions, 1836–1985. *American Journal of Sociology,* 92, 910–943.

———. (1989). *Organizational Ecology.* Cambridge, MA: Harvard University Press.

Hannan, Michael T., Pólos, László, and Carroll, Glenn R. (2003a). Cascading Organizational Change. *Organization Science,* 14, 463–482.

———. (2003b). The Fog of Change: Opacity and Asperity in Organizations. *Administrative Science Quarterly,* 48, 399–432.

———. (2007). *Logics of Organization Theory: Audiences, Codes, and Ecologies.* Princeton, NJ: Princeton University Press.

Hannan, Michael T., Ranger-Moore, James, and Banaszak-Holl, Jane. (1990). Competition and the Evolution of Organizational Size Distributions. In Jitendra V. Singh (Ed.), *Organizational Evolution: New Directions.* Newbury Park, CA: Sage, 246–268.

Hannan, Michael T., and Tuma, Nancy B. (1979). Methods for Temporal Analysis. *Annual Review of Sociology,* 5, 303–328.

Hansbrough, Tiffany. (2005). Cognition Matters: Leader Images and Their Implications for Organizational Life. In Birgit Schyns and James R. Meindl (Eds.), *Implicit Leadership Theories: Essays and Explorations.* Greenwich, CT: Information Age Publishing, 63–77.

Harder, David W., and Greenwald, Deborah F. (2008). Scoring Manual for the TAT Ambitious-Narcissistic Scale. In Sharon R. Jenkins (Ed.), *A Handbook of Clinical Scoring Systems for Thematic Apperceptive Techniques*. New York: Lawrence Erlbaum, 437–446.

Harmon-Jones, Eddie, and Harmon-Jones, Cindy. (2008). Cognitive Dissonance Theory: An Update with a Focus on the Action-Based Model. In James Y. Shah and Wendi L. Gardner (Eds.), *Handbook of Motivation Science*. New York: Guilford Press, 71–83.

Harris, Monica J., and Garris, Christopher P. (2008). You Never Get a Second Chance to Make a First Impression: Behavioral Consequences of First Impressions. In Nalini Ambady and John J. Skowronski (Eds.), *First Impressions*. New York: Guilford Press, 147–168.

Harrison, J. Richard, and Carroll, Glenn R. (2006). *Culture and Demography in Organizations*. Princeton, NJ: Princeton University Press.

Harrison, J. Richard, Lin, Zhiang, Carroll, Glenn R., and Carley, Kathleen M. (2007). Simulation Modeling in Organizational and Management Research. *Academy of Management Review*, 32, 1229–1245.

Hassin, Ran R. (2005). Nonconscious Control and Implicit Working Memory. In Ran R. Hassin, James S. Uleman, and John A. Bargh (Eds.), *The New Unconscious*. New York: Oxford University Press, 196–222.

Hassin, Ran R., Uleman, James S., and Bargh, John A. (2005). *The New Unconscious*. New York: Oxford University Press.

Hawley, Amos. (1968). Human Ecology. In David Sills (Ed.), *International Encyclopedia of the Social Sciences, Vol. 4*. New York: Free Press, 328–337.

Heath, Chip, and Staudenmayer, Nancy (2000). Coordination Neglect: How Lay Theories of Organizing Complicate Coordination in Organizations. *Research in Organizational Behavior*, 22, 153–191.

Hertzog, Christopher, Kramer, Arthur F., Wilson, Robert S., and Lindenberger, Ulman. (2008). Enrichment Effects on Adult Cognitive Development: Can the Functional Capacity of Older Adults be Preserved and Enhanced? *Psychological Science in the Public Interest*, 9, 1–65.

Heugens, Pursey P. M. A. R., and Lander, Michel W. (2009). Structure! Agency! (and Other Quarrels): A Meta-Analysis of Institutional Theories of Organization. *Academy of Management Journal*, 52, 61–85.

Hickson, David J., Hinings, C. Robert, McMillan, Charles J., and Schwitter, J. P. (1974). The Culture-Free Context of Organization Structure: A Trinational Comparison. *Sociology*, 8, 59–80.

Hickson, David J., and McMillan, Charles J. (1981). *Organization and Nation: The Aston Programme IV*. Westmead, Farnborough, Hampshire, UK: Gower.

Hickson, David J., Pugh, Derek S., and Pheysey, Diana C. (1969). Operations Technology and Organization Structure: An Empirical Reappraisal. *Administrative Science Quarterly*, 14, 378–397.

Higgins, E. Tory. (2000). Making a Good Decision: Value from Fit. *American Psychologist*, 55, 1217–1230.

———. (2005). Motivational Sources of Unintended Thought: Irrational Intrusions of Side Effects of Rational Strategies? In Ran R. Hassin, James S. Uleman, and John A. Bargh (Eds.), *The New Unconscious*. New York: Oxford University Press, 516–536.

———. (2008). Regulatory Fit. In James Y. Shah and Wendi G. Gardner (Eds.), *Handbook of Motivation Science*. New York: Guilford Press, 356–372.

Higgins, E. Tory, Kruglanski, A. W., and Pierro, A. (2003). Regulatory Mode: Locomotion and Assessment on Distinct Orientations. In M. P. Zanna (Ed.), *Advances in Experimental Social Psychology*. New York: Academic Press, 293–344.

Hillman, Amy J. (2005). Politicians on the Board of Directors: Do Connections Affect the Bottom Line? *Journal of Management*, 31, 464–481.

Hillman, Amy J., Cannella, Albert A., and Paetzold, Romona L. (2000). The Resource Dependence Role of Corporate Directors: Strategic Adaptation of Board Composition in Response to Environmental Change. *Journal of Management*, 37, 235–255.

Hillman, Amy J., and Dalziel, Thomas. (2003). Boards of Directors and Firm Performance: Integrating Agency and Resource Dependence Perspectives. *Academy of Management Review*, 28, 383–396.

Hinkin, Timothy R., and Schriesheim, Chester A. (2008). An Examination of "Nonleadership": From Laissez-Faire Leadership to Leader Reward Omission and Punishment Omission. *Journal of Applied Psychology*, 93, 1234–1248.

Hisrich, Robert, Langan-Fox, Janice, and Grant, Sharon. (2007). Entrepreneurship Research and Practice: A Call to Action for Psychology. *American Psychologist*, 62, 575–589.

Hlavacek, James D., and Thompson, Victor A. (1973). Bureaucracy and New Product Innovation. *Academy of Management Journal*, 16, 361–372.

———. (1975). The Joint Venture Approach to Technology Utilization. *IEEE Transactions on Engineering Management,* EM 23(1), 35–41.

———. (1978). Bureaucracy and Venture Failures. *Academy of Management Review,* 3, 242–248.

Hofmann, Wilhelm, Friese, Malte, and Strack, Fritz (2009). Impulse and Self-Control from a Dual-Systems Perspective. *Perspectives on Psychological Science,* 4, 162–176.

Hofstede, Geert. (1980). *Culture's Consequences: International Differences in Work-Related Values.* London, UK: Sage.

Hollenbeck, John R., Moon, Henry, Ellis, Aleksander P. J., West, Bradley J., Ilgen, Daniel R., Sheppard, Lori, Porter, Christopher O. L. H., and Wagner, John A. (2002). Structural Contingency Theory and Individual Differences: Examination of External and Internal Person-Team Fit. *Journal of Applied Psychology,* 87, 599–606.

Hough, Leaetta M., and Oswald, Frederick L. (2008). Personality Testing and Industrial-Organizational Psychology: Reflections, Progress, and Prospects. *Industrial and Organizational Psychology—Perspectives on Science and Practice,* 1, 272–290.

Houkes, Inge, Winants, Yvonne H. W. M., and Twellaar, Mascha (2008). Specific Determinants of Burnout among Male and Female General Practitioners: A Cross-Lagged Panel Analysis. *Journal of Occupational and Organizational Psychology,* 81, 249–276.

House, Robert J. (1971). A Path-Goal Theory of Leader Effectiveness. *Administrative Science Quarterly,* 16, 321–338.

———. (1977). A 1976 Theory of Charismatic Leadership. In James G. Hunt and Lars L. Larson (Eds.), *Leadership: The Cutting Edge.* Carbondale: Southern Illinois University Press.

———. (1991). The Distribution and Exercise of Power in Complex Organizations: A Meso Theory. *Leadership Quarterly,* 2, 23–58.

———. (1995). Leadership in the Twenty-First Century: A Speculative Inquiry. In Ann Howard (Ed.), *The Changing Nature of Work.* San Francisco, CA: Jossey-Bass, 411–450.

———. (1996). Path-Goal Theory of Leadership: Lessons, Legacy, and a Reformulated Theory. *Leadership Quarterly,* 7, 323–352.

House, Robert J., and Aditya, Ram N. (1997). The Social Scientific Study of Leadership: Quo Vadis. *Journal of Management,* 23, 409–473.

House, Robert J., and Howell, Jane M. (1992). Personality and Charismatic Leadership. *Leadership Quarterly,* 3, 81–108.

House, Robert J., and Javidan, Mansour. (2004). Overview of GLOBE. In Robert J. House, Paul J. Hanges, Mansour Javidan, Peter W. Dorfman, and Vipin Gupta (Eds.), *Culture, Leadership, and Organizations: The GLOBE Study of 62 Societies.* Thousand Oaks, CA: Sage, 9–28.

House, Robert J., Javidan, Mansour, Dorfman, Peter W., and de Luque, Mary S. (2006). A Failure of Scholarship: Response to George Graen's Critique of GLOBE. *Academy of Management Perspectives,* 20(4), 102–114.

House, Robert J., and Mitchell, Terence R. (1974). Path-Goal Theory of Leadership. *Journal of Contemporary Business,* 3(4), 81–97.

House, Robert J., and Rizzo, John R. (1972). Role Conflict and Ambiguity as Critical Variables in a Model of Organizational Behavior. *Organizational Behavior and Human Performance,* 7, 467–505.

House, Robert J., Spangler, William D., and Woycke, James (1991). Personality and Charisma in the U.S. Presidency: A Psychological Theory of Leader Effectiveness. *Administrative Science Quarterly,* 36, 364–396.

House, Robert J., Woycke, James, and Fodor, Eugene M. (1988). Charismatic and Noncharismatic Leaders: Differences in Behavior and Effectiveness. In Jay A. Conger and Rabindra N. Kenungo (Eds.), *Charismatic Leadership: The Elusive Factor in Organizational Effectiveness.* San Francisco, CA: Jossey-Bass, 98–121.

Howell, Jon P., Bowen, David E., Dorfman, Peter W., Kerr, Steven, and Podsakoff, Philip M. (1990). Substitutes for Leadership: Effective Alternatives to Ineffective Leadership. *Organizational Dynamics,* 19(1), 21–38.

Howell, Jon P., Dorfman, Peter W., and Kerr, Steven. (1986). Moderator Variables in Leadership Research. *Academy of Management Review,* 11, 88–102.

Hsu, Greta, and Hannan, Michael T. (2005). Identities, Genres, and Organizational Forms. *Organization Science,* 16, 474–490.

Huang, Julie Y., and Bargh, John A. (2008). Peak of Desire: Activating the Mating Goal Changes Life-Stage Preferences across Living Kinds. *Psychological Science,* 19, 573–578.

Huang, Xu, Wright, Robert P., Chiu, Warren C. K., and Wang, Chao. (2008). Relational Schemas as Sources of Evaluation and Misevaluation of Leader-Member Exchanges: Some Initial Evidence. *Leadership Quarterly,* 19, 266–282.

Huffman, Michael A., Nahallage, Charmalie A. D., and Leca, Jean-Baptiste. (2008). Cultural Monkeys: Social Learning Cast in Stones. *Current Directions in Psychological Science,* 17, 410–414.

Hughes, R. L., and Beatty, K. C. (2005). *Becoming a Strategic Leader: Your Role in Your Organization's Enduring Success.* San Francisco, CA: Jossey-Bass.

Hülsheger, Ute R., Anderson, Neil, and Salgado, Jesus F. (2009). Team-Level Predictors of Innovation at Work: A Comprehensive Meta-analysis Spanning Three Decades of Research. *Journal of Applied Psychology,* 94, 1128–1145.

Hunt, James G. (1996). Citation Classics. *Leadership Quarterly,* 7, 303–304.

Hunt, James G., Boal, Kimberly B., and Sorenson, Ritch L. (1990). Top Management Leadership: Inside the Black Box. *Leadership Quarterly,* 1, 41–65.

Hwang, Hokyu, and Powell, Walter W. (2009). The Rationalization of Charity: The Influence of Professionalization in the Nonprofit Sector. *Administrative Science Quarterly,* 54, 268–298.

Iacoboni, Marco. (2009). Imitation, Empathy, and Mirror Neurons. *Annual Review of Psychology,* 60, 653–670.

Indvik, Julie. (1986). Path-Goal Theory of Leadership: A Meta-analysis. *Academy of Management Proceedings,* 46, 189–192.

Ito, Tiffany A., and Cacioppo, John T. (2007). Attitudes as Mental and Neural States of Readiness: Using Physiological Measures to Study Implicit Attitudes. In Bernd Wittenbrink and Norbert Schwarz (Eds.), *Implicit Measures of Attitudes.* New York: Guilford Press, 125–158.

Izard, Carroll E. (2009). Emotion Theory and Research: Highlights, Unanswered Questions, and Emerging Issues. *Annual Review of Psychology,* 60, 1–25.

Jago, Arthur G., and Ragan, James W. (1986). The Trouble with Leader Match Is That It Doesn't Match Fiedler's Contingency Model. *Journal of Applied Psychology,* 71, 555–559.

James, Lawrence R., and LeBreton, James M. (2010). Assessing Aggression Using Conditional Reasoning. *Current Directions in Psychological Science,* 19, 30–35.

James, Lawrence R., and Mazerolle, Michelle D. (2002). *Personality in Work Organizations.* Thousand Oaks, CA: Sage.

James, William. (1890). *The Principles of Psychology.* New York: Henry Holt.

———. (1892). *Psychology.* New York: Henry Holt.

———. (1921). *Talks to Teachers on Psychology: and to Students on Some of Life's Ideals.* New York: Henry Holt.

Jansen, Justin J. P., Tempelaar, Michiel P., van den Bosch, Frans A. J., and Volberda, Henk W. (2009). Structural Differentiation and Ambidexterity: The Mediating Role of Integrating Mechanisms. *Organization Science,* 20, 797–811.

Javidan, Mansour. (2004). Performance Orientation. In Robert J. House, Paul J. Hanges, Mansour Javidan, Peter W. Dorfman, and Vipin Gupta (Eds.), *Culture, Leadership, and Organizations: The GLOBE Study of 62 Societies.* Thousand Oaks, CA: Sage, 239–281.

Jenkins, Sharon R. (2008). *A Handbook of Clinical Scoring Systems for Thematic Apperceptive Techniques.* New York: Lawrence Erlbaum.

Jepperson, Ronald L. (1991). Institutions, Institutional Effects, and Institutionalization. In Walter W. Powell and Paul J. DiMaggio (Eds.), *The New Institutionalism in Organizational Analysis.* Chicago: University of Chicago Press, 204, 231.

Jermier, John M., and Kerr, Steven. (1997). Substitutes for Leadership: Their Meaning and Measurement—Contextual Recollections and Current Observations. *Leadership Quarterly,* 8, 95–101.

Jiang, Bin, and Murphy, Patrick J. (2007). Do Business School Professors Make Good Executive Managers? *Academy of Management Perspectives,* 21(3), 29–50.

Johnson, Cathryn, Dowd, Timothy J., and Ridgeway, Cecilia L. (2006). Legitimacy as a Social Process. *Annual Review of Sociology,* 32, 53–78.

Johnson, Russell E., Chang, Chu-Hsiang, and Lord, Robert G. (2006). Moving from Cognition to Behavior: What the Research Says. *Psychological Bulletin,* 132, 381–415.

Johnson, Russell E., Selenta, Christopher, and Lord, Robert G. (2006). When Organizational Justice and the Self-Concept Meet: Consequences for the Organization and Its Members. *Organizational Behavior and Human Decision Processes,* 99, 175–201.

Johnson, Russell E., Tolentino, Anna L. Rodopman, Ozgun B., and Cho, Eunae. (2010). We (Sometimes) Know Not How We Feel: Predicting Job Performance with an Implicit Measure of Trait Affectivity. *Personnel Psychology,* 63, 197–219.

Johnson, Sarah K., and Anderson, Michael C. (2004). The Role of Inhibitory Control in Forgetting Semantic Knowledge. *Psychological Science,* 15, 448–453.

Johnson, Stefanie K., Murphy, Susan E., Zewdie, Selamawit, and Reichard, Rebecca J. (2008). The Strong Sensitive Type: Effects of Gender Stereotypes and Leadership Prototypes on the Evaluation of Male and Female Leaders. *Organizational Behavior and Human Decision Processes,* 106, 39–60.

Jordan, Jennifer. (2005). The Quest for Wisdom in Adulthood. In Robert J. Sternberg and Jennifer Jordan (Eds.), *A Handbook of Wisdom: Psychological Perspectives.* New York: Cambridge University Press, 160–188.

Jost, John T., Pietrzak, Janina, Liviatan, Ido, Mandisodza, Anesu N., and Napier, Jaime L. (2008). System Justification as Conscious and Nonconscious Goal Pursuit. In James Y. Shah and Wendi L. Gardner (Eds.), *Handbook of Motivation Science.* New York: Guilford Press, 591–605.

Judge, Timothy A., Bono, J. E., Ilies, Remus, and Gerhardt, M. W. (2002). Personality and Leadership: A Qualitative and Quantitative Review. *Journal of Applied Psychology,* 87, 765–780.

Judge, Timothy A., and Ilies, Remus. (2002). Relationship of Personality to Performance Motivation: A Meta-analytic Review. *Journal of Applied Psychology,* 87, 797–807.

Judge, Timothy A., and Piccolo, Ronald F. (2004). Transformational and Transactional Leadership: A Meta-analytic Test of Their Relative Validity. *Journal of Applied Psychology,* 89, 755–768.

Jung, Dongil, Wu, Anne, Chow, Chee W. (2008). Towards Understanding the Direct and Indirect Effects of CEOs' Transformational Leadership on Firm Innovation. *Leadership Quarterly,* 19, 582–594.

Kahn, Robert L., Wolfe, Donald M., Quinn, Robert P., Snoek, J. Diedrick, and Rosenthal, Robert A. (1964). *Organizational Stress: Studies in Role Conflict and Ambiguity.* New York: Wiley.

Kahneman, Daniel. (2003). A Perspective on Judgment and Choice: Mapping Bounded Rationality. *American Psychologist,* 58, 697–720.

Kahneman, Daniel, Slovic, Paul, and Tversky, A. (1982). *Judgment under Uncertainty: Heuristics and Biases.* New York: Cambridge University Press.

Kahneman, Daniel, and Tversky, A. (1984). Choices, Values, and Frames. *American Psychologist,* 39, 341–350.

Kamps, Jaap. (2009). Review of *Logics of Organization Theory: Audiences, Codes, and Ecologies. Administrative Science Quarterly,* 54, 350–353.

Kaplan, Seth, Bradley, Jill C., Luchman, Joseph N., and Haynes, Douglas. (2009). On the Role of Positive and Negative Affectivity in Job Performance: A Meta-analytic Investigation. *Journal of Applied Psychology,* 94, 162–176.

Kark, Ronit, and Van Dijk, Dina. (2007). Motivation to Lead, Motivation to Follow: The Role of the Self-Regulatory Focus in Leadership Processes. *Academy of Management Review,* 32, 500–528.

Karon, Bertram P. (2008). Pathogenesis Index. In Jenkins, Sharon R. (Ed.), *A Handbook of Clinical Scoring Systems for Thematic Apperceptive Techniques.* New York: Lawrence Erlbaum, 347–364.

Katz, Daniel, and Kahn, Robert L. (1966, 1978). *The Social Psychology of Organizations.* 2 eds. New York: Wiley.

Kawada, Christie L. K., Oettingen, Gabriele, Gollwitzer, Peter M., and Bargh, John A. (2004). The Projection of Implicit and Explicit Goals. *Journal of Personality and Social Psychology,* 86, 545–559.

Kay, Aaron C., Wheeler, S. Christian, Bargh, John A., and Ross, Lee. (2004). Material Priming: The Influence of Mundane Physical Objects on Situational Construal and Competitive Behavioral Choice. *Organizational Behavior and Human Decision Processes,* 94, 83–96.

Kayes, D. Christopher. (2005). The Destructive Pursuit of Idealized Goals. *Organizational Dynamics,* 34, 391–401.

Kearney, Eric, and Gebert, Diether. (2009). Managing Diversity and Enhancing Team Outcomes: The Promise of Transformational Leadership. *Journal of Applied Psychology,* 94, 77–89.

Kehr, Hugo M. (2004). Integrating Implicit Motives, Explicit Motives, and Perceived Abilities: The Compensatory Model of Work Motivation and Volition. *Academy of Management Review,* 29, 479–499.

Keller, Robert T. (2006). Transformational Leadership, Initiating Structure, and Substitutes for Leadership: A Longitudinal Study of Research and Development Team Performance. *Journal of Applied Psychology,* 91, 202–210.

Kennedy, John K., and Gallo, D. D. (1986). Test-Retest Properties of the Least Preferred Coworker (LPC) Score. *Journal of Psychology,* 120, 607–612.

Kensinger, Elizabeth A. (2007). Negative Emotion Enhances Memory Accuracy: Behavioral and Neuroimaging Evidence. *Current Directions in Psychological Science,* 16, 213–218.

Kerr, Steven. (1977). Substitutes for Leadership: Some Implications for Organizational Design. *Organization and Administrative Sciences,* 8, 135–146.

Kerr, Steven, Hill, Kenneth D., and Broedling, Laurie. (1986). The First-Line Supervisor: Phasing Out or Here to Stay? *Academy of Management Review,* 11, 103–117.

Kerr, Steven, and Jermier, John M. (1978). Substitutes for Leadership: Their Meaning and Measurement. *Organizational Behavior and Human Performance,* 22, 375–403.

Kerr, Steven, and Slocum, John W. (1981). Controlling the Performance of People in Organizations. In Paul C. Nystrom and William H. Starbuck (Eds.), *Handbook of Organizational Design, Vol. 2.* New York: Oxford University Press, 116–134.

Ketchum, Lyman D., and Trist, Eric L. (1992). *All Teams Are Not Created Equal: How Employee Empowerment Really Works.* Newbury Park, CA: Sage.

Keys, Daniel J., and Schwartz, Barry. (2007). "Leaky" Rationality—How Research on Behavioral Decision Making Challenges Normative Standards of Rationality. *Perspectives on Psychological Science,* 2, 162–180.

Khessina, Olga M. (2006). Direct and Indirect Effects of Product Portfolio on Firm Survival in the Worldwide Optical Disk Drive Industry, 1983–1999. In Joel A. C. Baum, Stanislav D. Dobrev, and Arjen van Witteloostuijn (Eds.), *Ecology and Strategy.* Oxford, UK: Elsevier, 591–630.

Kihlstrom, John F. (2002). No Need for Repression. *Trends in Cognitive Science,* 6, 502.

Kim, Tai-Young, Shin, Dongyouk, Oh, Hongseok, and Jeong, Young-Chul (2007). Inside the Iron Cage: Organizational Political Dynamics and Institutional Changes in Presidential Selection Systems in Korean Universities, 1985–2002. *Administrative Science Quarterly,* 52, 286–323.

Kirkpatrick, Shelley A., Wofford, J. C., and Baum, J. Robert. (2002). Measuring Motive Imagery Contained in the Vision Statement. *Leadership Quarterly,* 13, 139–150.

Kirsch, Irving. (2004). Conditioning, Expectancy, and the Placebo Effect: Comment on Stewart-Williams and Podd (2004). *Psychological Bulletin,* 130, 341–343.

Koole, Sander L., and Kuhl, Julius. (2008). Dealing with Unwanted Feelings: The Role of Affect Regulation in Voluntary Action Control. In James Y. Shah and Wendi L. Gardner (Eds.), *Handbook of Motivation Science.* New York: Guilford Press, 295–307.

Kor, Yasemin Y., and Misangyi, Vilmos F. (2008). Outside Directors' Industry-Specific Experience and Firms' Liability of Newness. *Strategic Management Journal,* 29, 1345–1355.

Kotter, John P. (1999). *John P. Kotter on What Leaders Really Do.* Boston, MA: Harvard Business School Press.

Kouider, Sid, and Dupoux, Emmanuel. (2004). Partial Awareness Creates the "Illusion" of Subliminal Semantic Priming. *Psychological Science,* 15, 75–81.

Kozhevnikov, Maria, Louchakova, Olga, Josipovic, Zoran, and Motes, Michael A. (2009). The Enhancement of Visuospatial Processing Efficiency through Buddhist Deity Meditation. *Psychological Science,* 20, 645–653.

Kozlowski, Steve W. J., and Bell, Bradford S. (2006). Disentangling Achievement Orientation and Goal Setting: Effects on Self-Regulatory Processes. *Journal of Applied Psychology,* 91, 900–916.

Kradin, Richard. (2008). *The Placebo Response and the Power of Unconscious Healing.* New York: Routledge.

Kretschmer, Tobias, and Puranam, Phanish. (2008). Integration through Incentives within Differentiated Organizations. *Organization Science,* 19, 860–875.

Krieshok, Thomas S., Black, Michael D., and McKay, Robyn A. (2009). Career Decision Making: The Limits of Rationality and the Abundance of Non-Conscious Processes. *Journal of Vocational Behavior,* 75, 275–290.

Krizan, Zlatan, and Windschitl, Paul D. (2007). The Influence of Outcome Desirability on Optimism. *Psychological Bulletin,* 133, 95–121.

Kroon, Brigitte. (2005). The Role of Implicit Organization Theory in the Start-up Phase of New Firms. In Birgit Schyns and James R. Meindl (Eds.), *Implicit Leadership Theories: Essays and Explorations.* Greenwich, CT: Information Age Publishing, 333–348.

Kruglanski, Arie W., and Duchesne, Mark. (2006). Are Associative and Propositional Processes Qualitatively Distinct? Comment on Gawronski and Bodenhausen (2006). *Psychological Bulletin,* 132, 736–739.

Kruglanski, Arie W., and Pierro, Antonio. (2008). Night and Day, You Are the One: On Circadian Mismatches and the Transference Effect in Social Perception. *Psychological Science,* 19, 296–301.

Kuilman, Jeroen G. (2007). Review of *Logics of Organization Theory: Audiences, Codes, and Ecologies. Organization Studies,* 28, 1587–1590.

Kukalis, Sal. (2010). Agglomeration Economies and Firm Performance: The Case of Industry Clusters. *Journal of Management,* 36, 453–481.

Lakin, Jessica L., Chartrand, Tanya L., and Arkin, Robert M. (2008). I Am Too Just Like You: Nonconscious Mimicry as an Automatic Behavioral Response to Social Exclusion. *Psychological Science,* 19, 816–822.

Lammers, Joris, Stoker, Janka I., and Stapel, Diederik A. (2009). Differentiating Social and Personal Power: Opposite Effects on Stereotyping, but Parallel Effects on Behavioral Approach Tendencies. *Psychological Science,* 20, 1543–1549.

Lance, Charles E., Vandenberg, Robert J., and Self, Robin M. (2000). Latent Growth Models of Individual Change: The Case of Newcomer Adjustment. *Organizational Behavior and Human Decision Processes,* 83, 107–140.

Landau, M. J., Solomon, Sheldon, Greenberg, Jeff, Cohen, Florette, Pyszczynski, Tom, Arndt, Jamie et al. (2004). Deliver Us from Evil: The Effects of Mortality Salience and Reminders of 9/11 on Support for President George W. Bush. *Personality and Social Psychology Bulletin,* 30, 1136–1150.

Landy, Frank. (2008). Stereotypes, Bias, and Personnel Decisions: Strange and Stranger. *Industrial and Organizational Psychology: Perspectives on Science and Practice,* 1, 379–392.

Lane, Kristin A., Banaji, Mahzarin R., Nosek, Brian A., and Greenwald, Anthony G. (2007). Understanding and Using the Implicit Association Test: IV—What We Know (So Far) about the Method. In Bernd Wittenbrink and Norbert Schwarz (Ed.), *Implicit Measures of Attitudes.* New York: Guilford Press, 59–102.

Langan-Fox, Janice, and Grant, Sharon. (2006). The Thematic Apperception Test: Toward a Standard Measure of the Big Three Motives. *Journal of Personality Assessment,* 87, 277–291.

Lange, Donald, Boivie, Steven, and Henderson, Andrew D. (2009). The Parenting Paradox: How Multibusiness Diversifiers Endorse Disruptive Technologies While Their Corporate Children Struggle. *Academy of Management Journal,* 52, 179–198.

Langfred, Claus W. (2004). Too Much of a Good Thing? Negative Effects of High Trust and Individual Autonomy in Self-Managing Teams. *Academy of Management Journal,* 47, 385–399.

Lankau, Melenie J., Carlson, Dawn S., and Nielson, Troy R. (2006). The Mediating Influence of Role Stressors in the Relationship between Mentoring and Job Attitudes. *Journal of Vocational Behavior,* 68, 308–322.

Lapierre, Laurent M., and Hackett, Rick D. (2007). Trait Conscientiousness, Leader-Member Exchange, Job Satisfaction, and Organizational Citizenship Behavior: A Test of an Integrative Model. *Journal of Occupational and Organizational Behavior,* 80, 539–554.

Lassiter, G. Daniel, Lindberg, Matthew J., González-Vallejo, Claudia, Bellezza, Francis S., and Phillips, Nathaniel D. (2009). The Deliberation-Without-Attention Effect: Evidence for an Artifactual Interpretation. *Psychological Science,* 20, 671–675.

Latham, Gary P. (2007). *Work Motivation: History, Theory, Research, and Practice.* Thousand Oaks, CA: Sage.

Latham, Gary P., and Locke, Edwin A. (2006). Enhancing the Benefits and Overcoming the Pitfalls of Goal Setting. *Organizational Dynamics,* 35, 332–340.

———. (2009). Science and Ethics: What Should Count as Evidence against the Use of Goal Setting? *Academy of Management Perspectives,* 23(3), 88–91.

Latham, Gary P., and Pinder, Craig C. (2005). Work Motivation Theory and Research at the Dawn of the Twenty-first Century. *Annual Review of Psychology,* 56, 485–516.

Latham, Gary P., Stajkovic, Alexander D., and Locke, Edwin A. (2010). The Relevance and Viability of Subconscious Goals in the Workplace. *Journal of Management,* 36, 234–255.

Lawrence, Paul R., and Dyer, Davis. (1983). *Renewing American Industry: Organizing for Efficiency and Innovation.* New York: Free Press.

Lawrence, Paul R., and Lorsch, Jay W. (1967a). *Organization and Environment: Managing Differentiation and Integration.* Boston, MA: Graduate School of Business Administration, Harvard University.

———. (1967b). New Management Job: The Integrator. *Harvard Business Review,* 45(6), 142–151.

Le, Huy, Oh, In-Sue, Shaffer, Jonathan, and Schmidt, Frank. (2007). Implications of Methodological Advances for the Practice of Personnel Selection: How Practitioners Benefit from Meta-Analysis. *Academy of Management Perspectives* 21(3), 6–15.

Leary, Mark R. (2007). Motivational and Emotional Aspects of the Self. *Annual Review of Psychology*, 58, 317–344.

Leary, Mark R., and Cox, Cody B. (2008). Belongingness Motivation: A Mainspring of Social Action. In James Y. Shah and Wendi L. Gardner (Eds.), *Handbook of Motivation Science*. New York: Guilford Press, 27–40.

LeBreton, James M., Barksdale, Cheryl D., Robin, Jennifer, and James, Lawrence R. (2007). Measurement Issues Associated with Conditional Reasoning Tests: Indirect Measurement and Test Faking. *Journal of Applied Psychology*, 92, 1–16.

Leung, Angela K., Maddux, William W., Galinsky, Adam D., and Chiu, Chi-yue. (2008). Multicultural Experience Enhances Creativity: The When and How. *American Psychologist*, 63, 169–181.

Levinson, Harry. (1968). *The Exceptional Executive: A Psychological Conception*. Cambridge, MA: Harvard University Press.

———. (1970). *Executive Stress*. New York: Harper and Row.

———. (1973). *The Great Jackass Fallacy*. Boston, MA: Graduate School of Business Administration, Harvard University.

———. (1981). *Executive*. Cambridge, MA: Harvard University Press.

———. (1994). Why the Behemoths Fell: Psychological Roots of Corporate Failure. *American Psychologist*, 49, 428–436.

———. (1998). A Clinical Approach to Executive Selection. In Richard Jeanneret and Rob Silzer (Eds.), *Individual Psychological Assessment: Predicting Behavior in Organizational Settings*. San Francisco, CA: Jossey-Bass, 228–242.

Levinthal, Daniel A., and March, James G. (1993). The Myopia of Learning. *Strategic Management Journal*, 14, 95–112.

Levinthal, Daniel, and Rerup, Claus. (2006). Crossing an Apparent Chasm: Bridging Mindful and Less-Mindful Perspectives on Organizational Learning. *Organization Science*, 17, 502–513.

Levy, Becca R., Zonderman, Alan B., Slade, Martin D., and Ferrucci, Luigi. (2009). Age Stereotypes Held Earlier in Life Predict Cardiovascular Events in Later Life. *Psychological Science*, 20, 296–298.

Levy, Benjamin J., and Anderson, Michael C. (2002). Inhibitory Processes and the Control of Memory Retrieval. *Trends in Cognitive Sciences*, 6, 299–305.

———. (2008). Individual Differences in the Suppression of Unwanted Memories: The Executive Deficit Hypothesis. *Acta Psychologica*, 127, 623–635.

Levy, Benjamin J., McVeigh, Nathan D., Marful, Alejandra, and Anderson, Michael C. (2007). Inhibiting Your Native Language: The Role of Retrieval-Induced Forgetting During Second-Language Acquisition. *Psychological Science*, 18, 29–34.

Levy, D. A., Stark, C. E. L., and Squire, L. R. (2004). Intact Conceptual Priming in the Absence of Declarative Memory. *Psychological Science*, 15, 680–686.

Lewig, Kerry A., Xanthopoulou, Despoina, Bakker, Arnold B., Dollard, Maureen F., and Metzer, Jacques C. (2007). Burnout and Connectedness among Australian Volunteers: A Test of the Job Demands-Resources Model. *Journal of Vocational Behavior*, 71, 429–445.

Lewin, Kurt. (1948). *Resolving Social Conflicts: Selected Papers on Group Dynamics*. In Gertrude W. Lewin (Ed.). New York: Harper.

———. (1951). *Field Theory in Social Science*. Chicago: University of Chicago Press.

Liden, Robert C., Wayne, Sandy J., and Kraimer, Maria L. (2001). Managing Individual Performance in Work Groups. *Human Resource Management*, 40, 63–72.

Ligon, Gina S., Hunter, Samuel T., and Mumford, Michael D. (2008). Development of Outstanding Leadership: A Life Narrative Approach. *Leadership Quarterly*, 19, 312–334.

Likert, Rensis, and Likert, Jane G. (1976). *New Ways of Managing Conflict*. New York: McGraw-Hill.

Lillard, Angeline S., and Skibbe, Lori. (2005). Theory of Mind: Conscious Attribution and Spontaneous Trait Inference. In Ran R. Hassin, James S. Uleman, and John A. Bargh (Eds.), *The New Unconscious*. New York: Oxford University Press, 277–305.

Ling, Yan, Simsek, Zeki, Lubatkin, Michael H., and Veiga, John F. (2008). The Impact of Transformational CEOs on the Performance of Small-to-Medium-Sized Firms: Does Organizational Context Matter? *Journal of Applied Psychology*, 93, 923–934.

Linnenbrink-Garcia, Lisa, and Fredericks, Jennifer A. (2008). Developmental Perspective on Achievement Motivation: Personal and Contextual Influences. In James Y. Shah and Wendi L. Gardner (Eds.), *Handbook of Motivation Science*. New York: Guilford Press, 448–464.

Lipman-Blumen, Jean. (2007). Toxic Leaders and the Fundamental Vulnerability of Being Alive. In Boas Shamir, Rajnandini Pillai, Michelle Bligh, and Mary Uhl-Bien (Eds.), *Follower-Centered Perspectives on Leadership: A Tribute to the Memory of James R. Meindl*. Greenwich, CT: Information Age Publishing, 1–17.

Lipman-Blumen, Jean, and Leavitt, Harold J. (2009). Beyond Typical Teams: Hot Groups and Connective Leaders. *Organizational Dynamics*, 38, 225–233.

Liu, Wei, Lepak, David P., Takeuchi, Riki, and Sims, Henry P. (2003). Matching Leadership Styles with Employment Modes: Strategic Human Resource Management Perspective, *Human Resource Management Review*, 13, 127–152.

Locke, Edwin A. (2003). Foundations for a Theory of Leadership. In Susan E. Murphy and Ronald E. Riggio (Eds.), *The Future of Leadership Development*. Mahwah, NJ: Lawrence Erlbaum, 29–46.

———. (2004). Linking Goals to Monetary Incentives. *Academy of Management Executive*, 18, 130–133.

———. (2007). The Case for Inductive Theory Building. *Journal of Management*, 33, 867–890.

Locke, Edwin A., Alavi, Maryam, and Wagner, John A. (1997). Participation in Decision Making: An Information Exchange Perspective. *Research in Personnel and Human Resources Management*, 15, 293–331.

Locke, Edwin A., and Baum, J. Robert. (2007). Entrepreneurial Motivation. In J. Robert Baum, Michael Frese, and Robert Baron (Eds.), *The Psychology of Entrepreneurship*. Mahwah, NJ: Lawrence Erlbaum, 93–112.

Locke, Edwin A., and Latham, Gary P. (1990). *Goal Setting: A Motivational Technique That Works*. Englewood Cliffs, NJ: Prentice-Hall.

———. (2002). Building a Practically Useful Theory of Goal Setting and Task Motivation: A 35-Year Odyssey. *American Psychologist*, 57, 705–717.

———. (2004). What Should We Do about Motivation Theory? Six Recommendations for the Twenty-First Century. *Academy of Management Review*, 29, 388–403.

———. (2005). Goal-Setting Theory: Theory Building by Induction. In Ken G. Smith and Michael A. Hitt (Eds.), *Great Minds in Management: The Process of Theory Development*. New York: Oxford University Press, 128–150.

———. (2006). New Directions in Goal-Setting Theory. *Current Directions in Psychological Science*, 15, 265–268.

———. (2009). Has Goal Setting Gone Wild, or Have Its Attackers Abandoned Good Scholarship? *Academy of Management Perspectives*, 23(1), 17–23.

Lockwood, Penelope, and Pinkus, Rebecca T. (2008). The Impact of Social Comparisons on Motivation. In James Y. Shah and Wendi L. Gardner (Eds.), *Handbook of Motivation Science*. New York: Guilford Press, 251–264.

London, Manual. (2002). *Leadership Development: Paths to Insight and Professional Growth*. Mahwah, NJ: Lawrence Erlbaum.

Lord, Robert G. (1995). An Alternative Perspective on Attributional Processes. In Mark J. Martinko (Ed.), *Attribution Theory: An Organizational Perspective*. Delray Beach, FL: St. Lucie Press, 333–350.

———. (2005). Preface: Implicit Leadership Theory. In Birgit Schyns and James R. Meindl (Eds.), *Implicit Leadership Theories: Essays and Explorations*. Greenwich, CT: Information Age Publishing, ix–xiv.

Lord, Robert G., and Brown, Douglas J. (2004). *Leadership Processes and Follower-Self-Identity*. Mahwah, NJ: Lawrence Erlbaum.

Lord, Robert G., DeVader, C. L., and Alliger, G. M. (1986). A Meta-Analysis of the Relation between Personality Traits and Leadership Perceptions: An Application of Validity Generalization Procedures. *Journal of Applied Psychology*, 71, 402–410.

Lord, Robert G., Foti, Roseanne J., and DeVader, Christy L. (1984). A Test of Leadership Categorization Theory: Internal Structure, Information Processing, and Leadership Perceptions. *Organizational Behavior and Human Performance*, 34, 343–378.

Lord, Robert G., and Levy, P. E. (1994). Moving from Cognition to Action: A Control Theory Perspective. *Applied Psychology: An International Review*, 43, 335–367.

Lord, Robert G., and Maher, Karen J. (1991). *Leadership and Information Processing: Linking Perceptions and Performance*. Boston, MA: Unwin Hyman.

Lord, Robert G., and Smith, Wendy G. (1999). Leadership and the Changing Nature of Performance. In Daniel R. Ilgen and Elaine D. Pulakos (Eds.), *The Changing Nature of Performance: Implications for Staffing, Motivation, and Development*. San Francisco, CA: Jossey-Bass, 192–239.

Lorsch, Jay W., and Allen, Stephen A. (1973). *Managing Diversity and Interdependence: An Organizational*

Study of Multidivisional Forms. Boston, MA: Graduate School of Business Administration, Harvard University.

Lorsch, Jay W., and Morse, John J. (1974). *Organizations and Their Members: A Contingency Approach.* New York: Harper and Row.

Lowe, Kevin B., Kroeck, K. Galen, and Sivasubramaniam, Nagaraj (1996). Effective Correlates of Transformational and Transactional Leadership: A Meta-analytic Review of the MLQ Literature. *Leadership Quarterly,* 7, 385–425.

Luthans, Fred, and Kreitner, Robert. (1975). *Organizational Behavior Modification.* Glenview, IL: Scott, Foresman.

———. (1985). *Organizational Behavior Modification and Beyond: An Operant and Social Learning Approach.* Glenview, IL: Scott, Foresman.

Luthans, Fred, Youssef, Carolyn M., and Avolio, Bruce J. (2007). *Psychological Capital: Developing the Human Competitive Edge.* New York: Oxford University Press.

Maccoby, Michael. (2004). Why People Follow the Leader: The Power of Transference. *Harvard Business Review,* 82(9), 76–85.

MacLeod, Malcolm D., and Saunders, Jo. (2008). Retrieval Inhibition and Memory Distortion. *Current Directions in Psychological Science,* 17, 26–30.

Maddox, Keith B., and Dukes, Kristin N. (2008). Social Categorization and Beyond: How Facial Features Impact Social Judgment. In Nalini Ambady and John J. Skowronski (Eds.), *First Impressions.* New York: Guilford Press, 205–233.

Maddux, William W., Leung, Angela K., Chiu, Chi-yue, and Galinsky, Adam D. (2009). Toward a More Complete Understanding of the Link between Multicultural Experience and Creativity. *American Psychologist,* 64, 156–158.

Madjar, Nora, and Shalley, Christina E. (2008). Multiple Tasks' and Multiple Goals' Effect on Creativity: Forced Incubation or Just a Distraction? *Journal of Management,* 34, 786–805.

Maguire, Steve, Hardy, Cynthia, and Lawrence, Thomas B. (2004). Institutional Entrepreneurship in Emerging Fields: HIV/AIDS Treatment Advocacy in Canada. *Academy of Management Journal,* 47, 657–679.

Maitlis, Sally, and Ozcelik, Hakan. (2004). Toxic Decision Processes: A Study of Emotion and Organizational Decision Making. *Organization Science,* 15, 375–393.

Malhotra, Namrata, and Morris, Timothy. (2009). Heterogeneity in Professional Service Firms. *Journal of Management Studies,* 46, 895–922.

Malle, Bertram F. (2005). Folk Theory of Mind: Conceptual Foundations of Human Social Cognition. In Ran R. Hassin, James S. Uleman, and John A. Bargh (Eds.), *The New Unconscious.* New York: Oxford University Press, 225–255.

Mansfield, Roger. (1973). Bureaucracy and Centralization: An Examination of Organizational Structure. *Administrative Science Quarterly,* 18, 477–488.

March, James G. (1991). Exploration and Exploitation in Organizational Learning. *Organization Science,* 2, 71–87.

———. (1994). *A Primer on Decision Making: How Decisions Happen.* New York: Free Press.

———. (1999). *The Pursuit of Organizational Intelligence.* Oxford, UK: Blackwell Business.

———. (2006). Rationality, Foolishness, and Adaptive Intelligence. *Strategic Management Journal,* 27, 201–214.

———. (2007a). The Study of Organizations and Organizing since 1945. *Organization Studies,* 28, 9–19.

———. (2007b). Ibsen, Ideals, and the Subordination of Lies. *Organization Studies,* 28, 1277–1285.

March, James G., and Coutu, Diane. (2006). Ideas as Art. *Harvard Business Review,* 84(10), 83–89.

March, James G., and Olsen, Johan P. (1976). *Ambiguity and Choice in Organizations.* Bergen, Norway: Universitetsforlaget.

———. (1989). *Rediscovering Institutions: The Organizational Basis of Politics.* New York: Free Press.

March, James G., Schulz, Martin, and Zhou, Xueguang. (2000). *The Dynamics of Roles: Change in Written Organizational Codes.* Stanford, CA: Stanford University Press.

March, James G., and Simon, Herbert A. (1958). *Organizations.* New York: John Wiley & Sons.

March, James G., Sproull, Lee S., and Tamuz, Michael. (1991). Learning from Samples of One or Fewer. *Organization Science,* 2, 1–13.

Markman, Arthur B., and Gentner, Dedre. (2005). Nonintentional Similarity Processing. In Ran R. Hassin, James S. Uleman, and John A. Bargh (Eds.), *The New Unconscious.* New York: Oxford University Press, 107–137.

Martin, R., Thomas, G., Charles, K., Epitropaki, O., and McNamara, R. (2005). The Role of Leader-Member Exchanges in Mediating the Relationship between Locus of Control and Work Reactions. *Journal of Occupational and Organizational Psychology*, 78, 141–147.

Martinko, Mark J., Douglas, Scott C., and Harvey, Paul. (2006). Attribution Theory in Industrial and Organizational Psychology: A Review. *International Review of Industrial and Organizational Psychology*, 21, 127–187.

Martinko, Mark J., Harvey, Paul, and Douglas, Scott C. (2007). The Role, Function and Contribution of Attribution Theory to Leadership: A Review. *Leadership Quarterly*, 18, 561–585.

Martinko, Mark J., Moss, Sherry E., Douglas, Scott C., and Borkowski, Nancy. (2007). Anticipating the Inevitable: When Leader and Member Attribution Styles Clash. *Organizational Behavior and Human Decision Processes*, 104, 158–174.

Maslach, Christina. (2003). Job Burnout: New Directions in Research and Intervention. *Current Directions in Psychological Science*, 12, 189–196.

Maslach, Christina, and Jackson, S. E. (1986). *MBI Maslach Burnout Inventory Manual*. Palo Alto, CA: Consulting Psychologists Press.

Maslach, Christina, Schaufeli, Wilmar B., and Leiter, Michael P. (2001). Job Burnout. *Annual Review of Psychology*, 52, 397–422.

Maslow, Abraham H. (1943). A Theory of Human Motivation. *Psychological Review*, 50, 370–396.

———. (1954). *Motivation and Personality*. New York: Harper & Row.

———. (1955). Deficiency Motivation and Growth Motivation. In M. Jones (Ed.), *Nebraska Symposium on Motivation: Vol. 3*. Lincoln: University of Nebraska Press, 1–30.

———. (1987). *Motivation and Personality*, 3d ed. New York: Harper & Row.

Maslyn, John M., and Uhl-Bien, Mary. (2005). *LMX* Differentiation: Key Concepts and Related Empirical Findings. In George B. Graen and Joni A. Graen (Eds.), *Global Organizing Designs*. Greenwich, CT: Information Age Publishing, 73–98.

Matzler, Kurt, Bailom, Franz, and Mooradian, Todd A. (2007). Intuitive Decision Making. *MIT Sloan Management Review*, 49(1), 13–15.

May, Cynthia P., Hasher, Lynn, and Foong, Natalie. (2005). Implicit Memory, Age, and Time of Day: Paradoxical Priming Effects. *Psychological Science*, 16, 96–100.

Mayo, Margarita, and Pastor, Juan Carlos. (2007). Leadership Embedded in Social Networks: Looking at Interfollower Processes. In Boas Shamir, Rajnandini Pillai, Michelle C. Bligh, and Mary Uhl-Bien (Eds.), *Follower-Centered Perspectives on Leadership: A Tribute to the Memory of James R. Meindl*. Greenwich, CT: Information Age Publishing, 93–113.

McAdams, Dan P., and Pals, Jennifer L. (2006). A New Big Five: Fundamental Principles for an Integrative Science of Personality. *American Psychologist*, 61, 204–217.

McClelland, David C. (1965). N-Achievement and Entrepreneurship: A Longitudinal Study. *Journal of Personality and Social Psychology*, 1, 389–392.

———. (1980). Motive Dispositions: The Merits of Operant and Respondent Measures. In L. Wheeler (Ed.), *Review of Personality and Social Psychology, Vol. 1*. Beverly Hills, CA: Sage, 10–41.

———. (1985). *Human Motivation*. Glenview, IL: Scott, Foresman.

———. (1987). *Human Motivation*. New York: Cambridge University Press.

McClelland, David C., Atkinson, John W., Clark, Russell A., and Lowell, Edgar L. (1953). *The Achievement Motive*. New York: Appleton-Century-Crofts.

McClelland, David C., Koestner, Richard, and Weinberger, Joel. (1989). How Do Self-Attributed and Implicit Motives Differ? *Psychological Review*, 96, 690–702.

McClelland, David C., and Winter, David G. (1969). *Motivating Economic Achievement*. New York: Free Press.

McCrae, Robert R., and Terracciano, Antonio. (2006). National Character and Personality. *Current Directions in Psychological Science*, 15, 156–161.

McGrath, Robert E. (2008). The Rorschach in the Context of Performance-Based Personality Assessment. *Journal of Personality Assessment*, 90, 465–475.

McKendrick, David G., Jaffee, Jonathan, Carroll, Glenn R., and Khessina, Olga M. (2003). In the Bud? Disk Array Producers as a (Possibly) Emergent Organizational Form. *Administrative Science Quarterly*, 48, 60–93.

McKenna, Bernard, Rooney, David, and Boal, Kimberly B. (2009). Wisdom Principles as a Meta-theoretical Basis for Evaluating Leadership. *Leadership Quarterly*, 20, 177–190.

McMullen, Jeffrey S., Shepherd, Dean A., and Patzelt, Holger. (2009). Managerial In(attention) to Competitive Threats. *Journal of Management Studies,* 46, 157–181.

Meckler, Mark, Drake, Bruce H., and Levinson, Harry. (2003). Putting Psychology Back into Psychological Contracts. *Journal of Management Inquiry,* 12, 217–228.

Medvedeff, Megan E., and Lord, Robert G. (2007). Implicit Leadership Theories as Dynamic Processing Structures. In Boas Shamir, Rajnandini Pillai, Michelle C. Bligh, and Mary Uhl-Bien (Eds.), *Follower-Centered Perspectives on Leadership: A Tribute to the Memory of James R. Meindl.* Greenwich, CT: Information Age Publishing, 19–50.

Meeus, Marius T. H. (2002). Review of Lex Donaldson's *The Contingency Theory of Organizations. Organization Studies,* 23, 986.

Meier, Brian P., Robinson, Michael D., and Clore, Gerald L. (2004). Why Good Guys Wear White: Automatic Inferences about Stimulus Valence Based on Brightness. *Psychological Science,* 15, 82–87.

Meier, Brian P., Robinson, Michael D., and Wilkowski, Benjamin M. (2006). Turning the Other Cheek: Agreeableness and the Regulation of Aggression-Related Primes. *Psychological Science,* 17, 136–142.

Meindl, James R. (1990). On Leadership: An Alternative to the Conventional Wisdom. *Research in Organizational Behavior,* 12, 159–203.

———. (1995). The Romance of Leadership as a Follower-centric Theory: A Social Constructionist Approach. *Leadership Quarterly,* 6, 329–341.

———. (2004). The Romance of Teams: Is the Honeymoon Over? *Journal of Occupational and Organizational Psychology,* 77, 463–466.

Meindl, James R., and Ehrlich, Sanford B. (1987). The Romance of Leadership and the Evaluation of Organizational Performance. *Academy of Management Journal,* 30, 91–109.

Meindl, James R., Ehrlich, Sanford B., and Dukerich, Janet M. (1985). The Romance of Leadership. *Administrative Science Quarterly,* 30, 78–102.

Melamed, Samuel, Shirom, Arie, Toker, Sharon, Berliner, Shlomo, and Shapira, Itzhak. (2006). Burnout and Risk of Cardiovascular Disease: Evidence, Possible Causal Paths, and Promising Research Directions. *Psychological Bulletin,* 132, 327–353.

Meyer, John W., and Rowan, Brian. (1977). Institutionalized Organizations: Formal Structures as Myth and Ceremony. *American Journal of Sociology,* 83, 340–363.

Meyer, John W., and Scott, W. Richard. (1983). *Organizational Environments: Ritual and Rationality.* Beverly Hills, CA: Sage.

Meyer, Marshall W., and Zucker, Lynne G. (1989). *Permanently Failing Organizations.* Newbury Park, CA: Sage.

Michel, A. Alexandra. (2007). A Distributed Cognition Perspective on Newcomers' Change Processes: The Management of Cognitive Uncertainty in Two Investment Banks. *Administrative Science Quarterly,* 52, 507–557.

Milkman, Katherine L., Chugh, Dolly, and Bazerman, Max H. (2009). How Can Decision Making Be Improved? *Perspectives on Psychological Science,* 4, 379–383.

Miller, George A. (1987). Meta-analysis and the Culture-Free Hypothesis. *Organization Studies,* 8, 309–326.

Miller, Kent D. (2008). Simon and Polanyi on Rationality and Knowledge. *Organization Studies,* 29, 933–955.

Miller, Kent D., and Chen, Wei-Ru. (2004). Variable Organizational Risk Preferences: Tests of the March-Shapira Model. *Academy of Management Journal,* 47, 105–115.

Miller, Lynn E., and Grush, Joseph E. (1988). Improving Predictions in Expectancy Theory Research: Effects of Personality, Expectancies, and Norms. *Academy of Management Journal,* 31, 107–122.

Millsap, R. E., and Hartog, S. B. (1988). Alpha, Beta, and Gamma Change in Evaluation Research: A Structural Equation Approach. *Journal of Applied Psychology,* 73, 574–584.

Miner, Anne S., Amburgey, Terry L., and Stearns, Timothy M. (1990). Interorganizational Linkages and Population Dynamics: Buffering and Transformational Shields. *Administrative Science Quarterly,* 35, 689–713.

Miner, Jennifer L. (2008). Factor Analysis of the Miner Sentence Completion Scales. In John B. Miner (Ed.), *Organizational Behavior 5: From Unconscious Motivation to Role-Motivated Leadership.* Armonk, NY: M.E. Sharpe, 421–435.

Miner, John B. (1956). Motion Perception, Time Perspective, and Creativity. *Journal of Projective Techniques,* 20, 405–413.

———. (1962). Personality and Ability Factors in Sales Performance. *Journal of Applied Psychology*, 46, 6–13.

———. (1971). Success in Management Consulting and the Concept of Eliteness Motivation. *Academy of Management Journal*, 14, 367–378.

———. (1982). *Theories of Organizational Structure and Process*. Hinsdale, IL: Dryden.

———. (1993a). Pursuing Diversity in an Increasingly Specialized Organizational Science. In Arthur G. Bedeian (Ed.), *Management Laureates: A Collection of Autobiographical Essays, Vol. 2*. Greenwich, CT: JAI Press, 283–319.

———. (1993b). *Role Motivation Theories*. London, UK: Routledge.

———. (2002). *Organizational Behavior: Foundations, Theories, and Analyses*. New York: Oxford University Press.

———. (2005). *Organizational Behavior 1: Essential Theories of Motivation and Leadership*. Armonk, NY: M.E. Sharpe.

———. (2006a). *Organizational Behavior 2: Essential Theories of Process and Structure*. Armonk, NY: M. E. Sharpe.

———. (2006b). *Organizational Behavior 3: Historical Origins, Theoretical Foundations, and the Future*. Armonk, NY: M. E. Sharpe

———. (2006c). Role Motivation Theories. In Jay C. Thomas and Daniel L. Segal (Eds.), *Comprehensive Handbook of Personality and Psychopathology, Vol. 1: Personality and Everyday Functioning*. Hoboken, NJ: John Wiley & Sons, 233–250.

———. (2007). *Organizational Behavior 4: From Theory to Practice*. Armonk, NY: M.E. Sharpe.

———. (2008). *Organizational Behavior 5: From Unconscious Motivation to Role-Motivated Leadership*. Armonk, NY: M. E. Sharpe.

Miner, John B., and Anderson, James K. (1958). The Postwar Occupational Adjustment of Emotionally Disturbed Soldiers. *Journal of Applied Psychology*, 42, 317–322.

Miner, John B., and Miner, Mary G. (1978). *Employee Selection within the Law*. Washington, DC: BNA Books.

Miner, John B., and Raju, Nambury, S. (2004). Risk Propensity Differences between Managers and Entrepreneurs and between Low- and High-Growth Entrepreneurs: A Reply in a More Conservative Vein. *Journal of Applied Psychology*, 89, 3–13.

Minssen, Heiner. (2006). Challenges of Teamwork in Production: Demands of Communication. *Organization Studies*, 27, 103–124.

Miron, David, and McClelland, David C. (1979). The Impact of Achievement Motivation Training on Small Business. *California Management Review*, 21(4), 13–28.

Mitchell, David B. (2006). Nonconscious Priming after 17 Years. *Psychological Science*, 17, 925–929.

Mitchell, J. Robert, Friga, Paul N., and Mitchell, Ronald K. (2005). Untangling the Intuition Mess: Intuition as a Construct in Entrepreneurship Research. *Entrepreneurship Theory and Practice*, 29, 653–679.

Mitchell, Ronald K., Busenitz, Lowell W., Bird, Barbara, Gaglio, Connie M., McMullen, Jeffery S., Morse, Eric A., and Smith, J. Brock. (2007). The Central Question in Entrepreneurial Cognition Research 2007. *Entrepreneurship Theory and Practice*, 31, 1–27.

Mitchell, Terence R. (1982). Attributions and Action: A Note of Caution. *Journal of Management*, 8, 65–74.

Mitchell, Terence R., and Beach, Lee Roy. (1990). "Do I Love Thee? Let Me Count . . ." Toward an Understanding of Intuitive and Automatic Decision Making. *Organizational Behavior and Human Decision Processes*, 47, 1–20.

Mitchell, Terence R., and Wood, Robert E. (1980). Supervisor's Responses to Subordinate Poor Performance: A Test of an Attributional Model. *Organizational Behavior and Human Performance*, 25, 123–138.

Mobbs, Dean, Hassabis, Demis, Seymour, Ben, Marchant, Jennifer L., Weiskopf, Nikolaus, Dolan, Raymond J., and Frith, Christopher D. (2009). Choking on the Money: Reward-Based Performance Decrements Are Associated with Midbrain Activity. *Psychological Science*, 20, 955–962.

Moeller, Sara K., Robinson, Michael D., and Zabelina, Darya L. (2008). Personality Dominance and Preferential Use of the Vertical Dimension of Space: Evidence from Spatial Attention Paradigms. *Psychological Science*, 19, 355–361.

Molden, Daniel C., Lee, Angela Y., and Higgins, E. Tory. (2008). Motivations for Promotion and Prevention. In James Y. Shah and Wendi L. Gardner (Eds.), *Handbook of Motivation Science*. New York: Guilford Press, 169–187.

Moore, Don A., Oesch, John M., and Zietsma, Charlene. (2007). What Competition? Myopic Self-Focus in Market-Entry Decisions. *Organization Science,* 18, 440–454.

Moors, Agnes, and De Houwer, Jan. (2006). Automaticity: A Theoretical and Conceptual Analysis. *Psychological Bulletin,* 132, 297–326.

———. (2007). What Is Automaticity? An Analysis of Its Component Features and Their Interrelations. In John A. Bargh (Ed.), *Social Psychology and the Unconscious: The Automaticity of Higher Mental Processes.* New York: Psychology Press, 11–50.

Morling, Beth, and Kitayama, Shinobu. (2008). Culture and Motivation. In James Y. Shah and Wendi L. Gardner (Eds.), *Handbook of Motivation Science.* New York: Guilford Press, 417–433.

Moskowitz, Gordon B., and Grant, Heidi. (2009). *The Psychology of Goals.* New York: Guilford Press.

Moskowitz, Gordon B., Solomon, A. R., and Taylor, C. M. (2000). Implicit Control of Stereotype Activation through the Preconscious Operation of Egalitarian Goals. *Social Cognition,* 18, 151–177.

Motowidlo, Stephan J., Hooper, Amy C., and Jackson, Hannah L. (2006). Implicit Policies about Relations between Personality Traits and Behavioral Effectiveness in Situational Judgment Items. *Journal of Applied Psychology,* 91, 749–761.

Muchinsky, Paul (2007). Avoiding Undergraduate Teaching Burnout. *The Industrial-Organizational Psychologist,* 45(2), 73–76.

Müller, Andreas, and Schyns, Birgit. (2005). The Perception of Leadership—Leadership as Perception. In Birgit Schyns and James R. Meindl (Eds.), *Implicit Theories of Leadership: Essays and Explorations.* Greenwich, CT: Information Age Publishing, 81–101.

Mumford, Michael D. (2006). *Pathways to Outstanding Leadership: A Comparative Analysis of Charismatic, Ideological, and Pragmatic Leaders.* Mahwah, NJ: Lawrence Erlbaum.

Mumford, Michael D., Antes, Alison L., Caughron, Jay J., and Friedrich, Tamara L. (2008). Charismatic, Ideological, and Pragmatic Leadership: Multilevel Influences on Emergence and Performance. *Leadership Quarterly,* 19, 144–160.

Murphy, S. T. (2001). Feeling without Thinking: Affective Primacy and Nonconscious Processing of Emotion. In John A. Bargh and Apsley, D. K. (Eds.), *Unravel the Complexities of Social Life: A Festschrift in Honor of Robert B. Zajonc.* Washington, DC: American Psychological Association, 39–53.

Naylor, James C., and Ilgen, Daniel R. (1984). Goal Setting: A Theoretical Analysis of a Motivational Technology. *Research in Organizational Behavior,* 6, 95–140.

Naylor, James C., Pritchard, Robert D., and Ilgen, Daniel R. (1980). *A Theory of Behavior in Organizations.* New York: Academic Press.

Negro, Giacomo, and Sorenson, Olav. (2006). The Competitive Dynamics of Vertical Integration: Evidence from U.S. Motion Picture Producers, 1912–1970. In Joel A. C. Baum, Stanislav D. Dobrev, and Arjen van Witteloostuijn (Eds.), *Ecology and Strategy.* Oxford, UK: Elsevier, 363–398.

Neubert, Mitchell J., Kacmar, K. Michele, Carlson, Dawn S., Chonko, Lawrence B., and Roberts, James A. (2008). Regulatory Focus as a Mediator of the Influence of Initiating Structure and Servant Leadership on Employee Behavior. *Journal of Applied Psychology,* 93, 1220–1233.

Ng, Kok-Yee, Koh, Christine S-K, and Goh, Hock-Chye. (2008). The Heart of the Servant Leader: Leader's Motivation-to-Serve and Its Impact on LMX and Subordinates' Extra-Role Behaviors. In George B. Graen and Joni A. Graen (Eds.), *Knowledge-Driven Corporation: Complex Creative Destruction.* Charlotte, NC: Information Age Publishing, 125–144.

Nicholson, Christy. (2006). Memory and Consciousness—Consciousness to Unconsciousness and Back Again. *Observer,* 19(8), 25–26.

Nickerson, Jack A., and Zenger, Todd R. (2002). Being Efficiently Fickle: A Dynamic Theory of Organizational Choice. *Organization Science,* 13, 547–566.

———. (2004). A Knowledge-Based Theory of the Firm—The Problem-Solving Perspective. *Organization Science,* 15, 617–632.

Nosek, Brian A. (2007). Implicit-Explicit Relations. *Current Directions in Psychological Science,* 16, 65–69.

Nosek, Brian A., Greenwald, Anthony G., and Banaji, Mahzarin R. (2007). The Implicit Association Test at Age 7: A Methodological and Conceptual Review. In John A. Bargh (Ed.), *Social Psychology and the Unconscious: The Automaticity of Higher Mental Processes.* New York: Psychology Press, 265–292.

Novotney, Amy. (2008). Psychology for the Masses. *Monitor on Psychology,* 39(5), 62–63.

O'Connor, Anahad. (2004). Theory Given on Burying of Memories by People. *New York Times,* January 9.

Offerman, Lynn R., and Scuderi, Noelle F. (2007). Sharing Leadership: Who, What, When, and Why. In Boas Shamir, Rajnandini Pillai, Michelle C. Bligh, and Mary Uhl-Bien (Eds.), *Follower-Centered Perspectives on Leadership: A Tribute to the Memory of James R. Meindl.* Greenwich, CT: Information Age Publishing, 71–91.

Oishi, Shigehiro. (2010). The Psychology of Residential Mobility: Implications for the Self, Social Relationships, and Well-Being. *Perspectives on Psychological Science,* 5, 5–19.

Oldham, Greg R. (2003). Stimulating and Supporting Creativity in Organizations. In Susan E. Jackson, Michael A. Hitt, and Angelo S. DeNisi (Eds.), *Managing Knowledge for Sustained Competitive Advantage: Designing Strategies for Effective Human Resource Management.* San Francisco, CA: Jossey-Bass, 243–273.

Oldham, Greg R., and Hackman, J. Richard. (2005). How Job Characteristics Theory Happened. In Ken G. Smith and Michael A. Hitt (Eds.), *Great Minds in Management: The Process of Theory Development.* New York: Oxford University Press, 151–170.

Oliver, Christine. (1991). Strategic Responses to Institutional Processes. *Academy of Management Review,* 16, 145–179.

Olson, Michael A., Fazio, Russell H., and Hermann, Anthony D. (2007). Reporting Tendencies Underlie Discrepancies between Implicit and Explicit Measures of Self-Esteem. *Psychological Science,* 18, 287–291.

Olsson, Andreas, and Phelps, Elizabeth A. (2004). Learned Fear of "Unseen Faces" after Pavlovian, Observational, and Instructed Fear. *Psychological Science,* 15, 822–828.

———. (2007). Understanding Social Evaluations: What We Can (and Cannot) Learn from Neuroimaging. In Bernd Wittenbrink and Norbert Schwarz (Eds.), *Implicit Measures of Attitudes.* New York: Guilford Press, 159–175.

Ordóñez, Lisa D., Schweitzer, Maurice E., Galinsky, Adam D., and Bazerman, Max H. (2009a). Goals Gone Wild: The Systematic Side Effects of Overprescribing Goal Setting. *Academy of Management Perspectives,* 23(1), 6–16.

———. (2009b). On Good Scholarship, Goal Setting and Scholars Gone Wild. *Academy of Management Perspectives,* 23(3), 82–87.

Osbeck, Lisa M., and Robinson, Daniel N. (2005). Philosophical Theories of Wisdom. In Robert J. Sternberg and Jennifer Jordan (Eds.), *A Handbook of Wisdom: Psychological Perspectives.* New York: Cambridge University Press, 61–83.

Overskeid, Geir. (2007). Looking for Skinner and Finding Freud. *American Psychologist,* 62, 590–595.

Oyserman, Daphna, and Lee, Spike W. S. (2008). Does Culture Influence What and How We Think? Effects of Priming Individualism and Collectivism. *Psychological Bulletin,* 134, 311–342.

Pablo, Zelinna, and Hardy, Cynthia. (2009). Merging, Masquerading and Morphing: Metaphors and the World Wide Web. *Organization Studies,* 30, 821–843.

Pascalis, Olivier, and Kelly, David J. (2009). The Origins of Face Processing in Humans. *Perspectives on Psychological Science,* 4, 200–209.

Pastor, Juan Carlos, Mayo, Margarita, and Shamir, Boas. (2007). Adding Fuel to Fire: The Impact of Followers' Arousal on Ratings of Charisma. *Journal of Applied Psychology,* 92, 1584–1596.

Patall, Erika A., Cooper, Harris, and Robinson, Jorgianne C. (2008). The Effects of Choice on Intrinsic Motivation and Related Outcomes: A Meta-analysis of Research Findings. *Psychological Bulletin,* 134, 270–300.

Payne, B. Keith, Jacoby, Larry L., and Lambert, Alan J. (2005). Attitudes as Accessibility Bias: Dissociating Automatic and Controlled Processes. In Ran R. Hassin, James S. Uleman, and John A. Bargh (Eds.), *The New Unconscious.* New York: Oxford University Press, 393–420.

Payne, B. Keith, and Stewart, Brandon D. (2007). Automatic and Controlled Components of Social Cognition: A Process Dissociation Approach. In John A. Bargh (Ed.), *Social Psychology and the Unconscious: The Automaticity of Higher Mental Processes.* New York: Psychology Press, 293–315.

Pearce, Craig L., Manz, Charles C., and Sims, Henry P. (2008). The Roles of Vertical and Shared Leadership in the Enactment of Executive Corruption: Implications for Research and Practice. *Leadership Quarterly,* 19, 353–359.

Pelham, Brett N., Carvallo, Mauricio, and Jones, John T. (2005). Implicit Egotism. *Current Directions in Psychological Science,* 14(2), 106–110.

Pennings, Johannes M. (1987). Structural Contingency Theory: A Multivariant Test. *Organization Studies,* 8, 223–240.

Pentland, Alex. (2008). *Honest Signals: How They Shape Our World*. Cambridge, MA: MIT Press.

Pentland, Alex, and Heibeck, Tracy. (2008). Understanding "Honest Signals' in Business. *MIT Sloan Management Review*, 50(1), 70–75.

Perrewé, Pamela L., Zellars, Kelly L., Ferris, Gerald R., Rossi, Ana Maria, Kacmar, Charles J., and Ralston, David A. (2004). Neutralizing Job Stressors: Political Skill as an Antidote to the Dysfunctional Consequences of Role Conflict. *Academy of Management Journal*, 47, 141–152.

Perrow, Charles. (1976). Review of Rushing and Zald's *Organizations and Beyond*. *Administrative Science Quarterly*, 21, 718–721.

Peters, Ellen, Hess, Thomas M., Västfjäll, Daniel, and Auman, Corinne. (2007). Adult Age Differences in Dual Information Processes: Implications for the Role of Affective and Deliberative Processes in Older Adults' Decision Making. *Perspectives on Psychological Science*, 2, 1–23.

Peters, Lawrence H., Hartke, Darell D., and Pohlman, John T. (1985). Fiedler's Contingency Theory of Leadership: An Application of the Meta-analysis Procedures of Schmidt and Hunter. *Psychological Bulletin*, 97, 274–285.

Petersen, Trond, and Koput, Kenneth W. (1991). Density Dependence in Organizational Mortality: Legitimacy or Unobserved Heterogeneity? *American Sociological Review*, 56, 399–409.

Peterson, Mark F. (2004). Review of *Culture, Leadership, and Organizations: The GLOBE Study of 62 Societies*. Thousand Oaks, CA: Sage.

Peterson, Suzanne J., Walumbwa, Fred O., Byron, Kristin, and Myrowitz, Jason. (2009). CEO Positive Psychological Traits, Transformational Leadership, and Firm Performance in High-Technology Startup and Established Firms. *Journal of Management*, 35, 348–368.

Pfeffer, Jeffrey (1981). *Power in Organizations*. Marshfield, MA: Pitman.

———. (1992). *Managing with Power: Politics and Influences in Organizations*. Boston, MA: Harvard Business School Press.

———. (2001). Fighting the War for Talent Is Hazardous to Your Organization's Health. *Organizational Dynamics*, 29, 248–259.

———. (2005a). Developing Resource Dependence Theory: How Theory Is Affected by Its Environment. In Ken G. Smith and Michael A. Hitt (Eds.), *Great Minds in Management: The Process of Theory Development*. New York: Oxford University Press, 436–459.

———. (2005b). Response to Donaldson. *Organization Studies*, 26, 1105–1106.

———. (2005c). Changing Mental Models: HR's Most Important Task. *Human Resource Management*, 44, 123–128.

Pfeffer, Jeffrey, and Fong, Christina. (2005). Building Organization Theory from First Principles: The Self-Enhancement Motive and Understanding Power and Influence. *Organization Science*, 16, 372–388.

Pfeffer, Jeffrey, and Salancik, Gerald. (1978). *The External Control of Organizations: A Resource Dependence Perspective*. New York: Harper and Row.

Phelan, J. G. (1962). Projective Techniques in the Selection of Management Personnel. *Journal of Projective Techniques*, 4, 102–110.

Phelps, Elizabeth A. (2006). Emotion and Cognition: Insights from Studies of the Human Amygdala. *Annual Review of Psychology*, 57, 27–53.

Phillips, Katherine W., Rothbard, Nancy P., and Dumas, Tracy L. (2009). To Disclose or Not to Disclose? Status Distance and Self-Disclosure in Diverse Environments. *Academy of Management Review*, 34, 710–732.

Piccolo, Ronald F., and Colquitt, Jason A. (2006). Transformational Leadership and Job Behaviors: The Mediating Role of Core Job Characteristics. *Academy of Management Journal*, 49, 327–340.

Pillai, Rajnandini, Kohles, Jeffrey C., and Bligh, Michelle C. (2007). Through Thick and Thin? Follower Constructions of Presidential Leadership amidst Crisis, 2001–2005. In Boas Shamir, Rajnandini Pillai, Michelle C. Bligh, and Mary Uhl-Bien (Eds.), *Follower-Centered Perspectives on Leadership: A Tribute to the Memory of James R. Meindl*. Greenwich, CT: Information Age Publishing, 135–165.

Piotrowski, Zygmunt A., and Rock, Milton R. (1963). *The Perceptanalytic Executive Scale: A Tool for the Selection of Top Managers*. New York: Grune and Stratton.

Podsakoff, Philip M., MacKenzie, Scott B., and Bommer, William H. (1996). Meta-analysis of the Relationships between Kerr and Jermier's Substitutes for Leadership and Employee Job Attitudes, Role Perceptions, and Performance. *Journal of Applied Psychology*, 81, 380–399.

Podsakoff, Philip M., Todor, William D., Grover, Richard A., and Huber, Vandra L. (1984). Situational Moderators of Leader Reward and Punishment Behaviors: Fact or Fiction. *Organizational Behavior and Human Performance*, 34, 21–63.

Pondy, Louis R., and Mitroff, Ian I. (1979). Beyond Open Systems Models of Organization. *Research in Organizational Behavior,* 1, 3–39.

Popielarz, Pamela A., and Neal, Zachary P. (2007). The Niche as a Theoretical Tool. *Annual Review of Sociology,* 33, 65–84.

Porcelli, Anthony J., and Delgado, Maurice R. (2009). Acute Stress Modulates Risk Taking in Financial Decision Making. *Psychological Science,* 20, 278–283.

Porter, Lyman. (1989). A Retrospective Review: Argyris' *Personality and Organization. Academy of Management Review,* 14, 284–285.

Porter, Lyman W., and Lawler, Edward E. (1968). *Managerial Attitudes and Performance.* Homewood, IL: Irwin.

Powell, Walter W. (1991). Expanding the Scope of Institutional Analysis. In Walter W. Powell and Paul J. DiMaggio (Eds.), *The New Institutionalism in Organizational Analysis.* Chicago: University of Chicago Press, 183–203.

Powell, Walter W., and DiMaggio, Paul J. (Eds.) (1991). *The New Institutionalism in Organizational Analysis.* Chicago, IL: University of Chicago Press.

Pozner, Jo-Ellen, and Rao, Hayagreeva. (2006). Fighting a Common Foe: Enmity, Identity and Collective Strategy. In Joel A. C. Baum, Stanislav D. Dobrev, and Arjen van Wittelootuijn (Eds.), *Ecology and Strategy.* Oxford, UK: Elsevier, 445–479.

Pratch, Leslie, and Levinson, Harry. (2002). Understanding the Personality of the Executive. In Rob Silzer (Ed.), *The 21st Century Executive: Innovative Practices for Building Leadership at the Top.* San Francisco, CA: Jossey-Bass, 43–74.

Price, Donald D., Finniss, Damien G., and Benedetti, Fabrizio. (2008). A Comprehensive Review of the Placebo Effect: Recent Advances and Current Thought. *Annual Review of Psychology,* 57, 565–290.

Prinz, Jesse J. (2005). Emotions, Embodiment, and Awareness. In Lisa F. Barrett, Paula M. Niedenthal, and Piotr Winkielman (Eds.), *Emotion and Consciousness.* New York: Guilford Press, 363–383.

Pugh, Derek S. (1976). The Aston Approach to the Study of Organizations. In Geert Hofstede and M. Sami Kassem (Eds.), *European Contributions to Organization Theory.* Amsterdam, The Netherlands: Van Gorcum, Assen, 62–78.

Pugh, Derek S., and Hickson, David J. (1976). *Organizational Structure in Its Context: The Aston Programme I.* Westmead, Farnborough, Hants, UK: Saxon House.

Pugh, Derek S., and Hinings, C. Robert. (1976). *Organizational Structure Extensions and Replications: The Aston Programme II.* Westmead, Farnborough Hampshire, UK: Saxon House.

Pugh, Derek S., and Payne, Roy L. (1977). *Organizational Behavior in Its Context: The Aston Programme III.* Westmead, Farnborough, Hants, UK: Saxon House.

Purdy, Jill M., and Gray, Barbara. (2009). Conflicting Logics, Mechanisms of Diffusion, and Multilevel Dynamics in Emerging Institutional Fields. *Academy of Management Journal,* 52, 355–380.

Pyszczynski, Tom, Greenberg, Jeff, Solomon, Sheldon, Arndt, Jamie, and Schimel, Jeff. (2004). Why Do People Need Self-Esteem? A Theoretical and Empirical Review. *Psychological Bulletin,* 130, 435–472.

Quigley, Narda R., Tesluk, Paul E., Locke, Edwin A., and Bartol, Kathryn M. (2007). A Multilevel Investigation of the Motivational Mechanisms Underlying Knowledge Sharing Performance. *Organization Science,* 18, 71–88.

Raelin, Joe. (2006). Does Action Learning Promote Collaborative Leadership? *Academy of Management Learning and Education,* 5, 152–168.

Ranganath, Kate A., and Nosek, Brian A. (2008). Implicit Attitude Generalization Occurs Immediately; Explicit Attitude Generalization Takes Time. *Psychological Science,* 19, 249–254.

Ranger-Moore, James, Banaszak-Holl, Jane, and Hannan, Michael T. (1991). Density-Dependent Dynamics in Regulated Industries: Founding Rates of Banks and Life Insurance Companies. *Administrative Science Quarterly,* 36, 36–65.

Rao, Hayagreeva. (2002). Review of *The Demography of Corporations and Industries. Administrative Science Quarterly,* 47, 584–586.

———. (2004). Institutional Activism in the Early American Automobile Industry. *Journal of Business Venturing,* 19, 359–384.

Rao, Hayagreeva, Morrill, C., and Zald, M. N. (2000). Power Plays: How Social Movements and Collective Action Create New Organizational Forms. *Research in Organizational Behavior,* 22, 239–282.

Rauch, Andreas, and Frese, Michael. (2000). Psychological Approaches to Entrepreneurial Success: A

General Model and an Overview of Findings. *International Review of Industrial and Organizational Psychology,* 15, 101–141.

———. (2007). Born to Be an Entrepreneur? Revisiting the Personality Approach to Entrepreneurship. In J. Robert Baum, Michael Frese, and Robert A. Baron (Eds.), *The Psychology of Entrepreneurship.* Mahwah, NJ: Lawrence Erlbaum, 41–65.

Reis, Harry T., and Collins, W. Andrew. (2004). Relationships, Human Behavior, and Psychological Science. *Current Directions in Psychological Science,* 13, 233–237.

Revonsuo, Antti. (2010). *Consciousness: The Science of Subjectivity.* New York: Psychology Press.

Richards, Jane. (2004). The Cognitive Consequences of Concealing Feelings. *Current Directions in Psychological Science,* 13, 131–134.

Richardson, Astrid M., and Martinussen, Monica. (2004). The Maslach Burnout Inventory: Factorial Validity and Consistency across Occupational Groups in Norway. *Journal of Occupational and Organizational Psychology,* 77, 377–384.

Riordan, Christine M., Richardson, Hettie A., Schaffer, Bryan S., and Vandenberg, Robert J. (2001). Alpha, Beta, and Gamma Change: A Review of Past Research and Recommendations for New Directions. In Chester R. Schriesheim and Linda L. Neider (Eds.), *Equivalence in Measurement.* Greenwich, CT: Information Age Publishing, 57–97.

Ritter, Barbara A., and Lord, Robert G. (2007). The Impact of Previous Leaders on the Evaluation of New Leaders: An Alternative to Prototype Matching. *Journal of Applied Psychology,* 92, 1683–1695.

Rizzo, John R., House, Robert J., and Lirtzman, Sidney I. (1970). Role Conflict and Ambiguity in Complex Organizations. *Administrative Science Quarterly,* 15, 150–163.

Roch, Sylvia G. (2007). Avoiding Undergraduate Teaching Burnout. *The Industrial-Organizational Psychologist,* 45(2), 73.

Román, Patricia, Soriano, M. Falipa, Gómez-Ariza, Carlos J., and Bajo, M. Teresa. (2009). Retrieval-Induced Forgetting and Executive Control. *Psychological Science,* 20, 1053–1058.

Rorschach, Hermann (1942). *Psychodiagnostics.* Berne: Hans Huber.

Rosenthal, R., and DiMatteo, M. R. (2001). Meta-Analysis: Recent Developments in Quantitative Methods for Literature Reviews. *Annual Review of Psychology,* 52, 59–82.

Rosenthal, Seth A., and Pittinsky, Todd L. (2006). Narcissistic Leadership. *Leadership Quarterly,* 17, 617–633.

Rosete, D., and Ciarrochi, J. (2005). Emotional Intelligence and its Relationship to Workplace Performance Outcomes of Leadership Effectiveness. *Leadership and Organizational Development Journal,* 26, 388–389.

Rowold, Jens, and Heinitz, Kathrin. (2007). Transformational and Charismatic Leadership: Assessing the Convergent, Divergent, and Criterion Validity of the MLQ and CKS. *Leadership Quarterly,* 18, 121–133.

Roy, S. K. (1969). A Re-Examination of the Methodology of A. K. Rice's Indian Textile Mill Work Reorganization. *Indian Journal of Industrial Relations,* 5(2), 170–191.

Rudman, Laurie A. (2004). Sources of Implicit Attitudes. *Current Directions in Psychological Science,* 13, 79–82.

Ruef, Martin (2006). Boom and Bust: The Effect of Entrepreneurial Inertia on Organizational Populations. In Joel A. C. Baum, Stanislav D. Dobrev, and Arjen van Witteloostuijn (Eds.), *Ecology and Strategy.* Oxford, UK: Elsevier, 29–72.

Rule, Nicholas O., and Ambady, Nalini. (2008). First Impressions: Peeking at the Neural Underpinnings. In Nalini Ambady and John J. Skowronski (Eds.), *First Impressions.* New York: Guilford Press, 35–56.

Rushing, William A., and Zald, Mayer N. (1976). *Organizations and Beyond: Selected Essays of James D. Thompson.* Lexington, MA: D. C. Heath.

Ruys, Kirsten I., and Stapel, Diederik A. (2008). The Secret Life of Emotions. *Psychological Science,* 19, 385–391.

Ryan, Richard M., and Deci, Edward L. (2000). Self-Determination Theory and the Facilitation of Intrinsic Motivation, Social Development, and Well-Being. *American Psychologist,* 55, 68–78.

———. (2004). Avoiding Death or Engaging Life as Accounts of Meaning and Culture: Comments on Pyszczynski et al. (2004). *Psychological Bulletin,* 130, 473–477.

Rynes, Sara L., Bartunek, Jean M., and Daft, Richard L. (2001). Across the Great Divide: Knowledge Creation and Transfer between Practitioners and Academics. *Academy of Management Journal,* 44, 340–355.

Sadler-Smith, Eugene, and Shefy, Erella. (2004). The Intuitive Executive: Understanding and Applying "Gut Feel" in Decision Making. *Academy of Management Executive,* 18, 76–91.

———. (2007). Developing Intuitive Awareness in Management Education. *Academy of Management Learning and Education*, 6, 186–205.

Sagie, Abraham. (1994). Participative Decision Making and Performance: A Moderator Analysis. *Journal of Applied Behavioral Science*, 30, 227–246.

Salancik, Gerald R., and Pfeffer, Jeffrey. (1977). An Examination of Need-Satisfaction Models of Job Attitudes. *Administrative Science Quarterly*, 22, 427–456.

———. (1978). A Social Information Processing Approach to Job Attitudes and Task Design. *Administrative Science Quarterly*, 23, 224–253.

Sanchez, Rudolph J., and Byrne, Zinta S. (2004). Leader-Member Exchange and Organizational Justice. In George B. Graen (Ed.), *New Frontiers of Leadership*. Greenwich, CT: Information Age Publishing, 193–223.

Satow, Roberta L. (1975). Value-Rational Authority and Professional Organizations: Weber's Missing Type. *Administrative Science Quarterly*, 20, 526–531.

Sayegh, Lisa, Anthony, William P., and Perrewé, Pamela L. (2004). Managerial Decision Making under Crisis: The Role of Emotion in an Intuitive Decision Process. *Human Resource Management Review*, 14, 179–199.

Schein, Edwin. (1992). *Organizational Culture and Leadership*. San Francisco, CA: Jossey-Bass.

Scherer, Klaus R. (2005). Unconscious Processes in Emotion: The Bulk of the Iceberg. In Lisa F. Barrett, Paula M. Niedenthal, and Piotr Winkielman (Eds.), *Emotion and Consciousness*. New York: Guilford Press, 312–334.

Schmalt, Heinz-Dieter. (2005). Validity of a Short Form of the Achievement-Motive Grid (AMG-S): Evidence for the Three-Factor Structure Emphasizing Active and Passive Forms of Fear of Failure. *Journal of Personality Assessment*, 84, 172–184.

Schmidt, Frank L., and Hunter, John E. (1998). The Validity and Utility of Selection Methods in Personnel Psychology: Practical and Theoretical Implications of 85 Years of Research Findings. *Psychological Bulletin*, 124, 262–274.

Schmitt, Neal. (1982). The Use of Analysis of Covariance Structure to Assess Beta and Gamma Change. *Multivariate Behavioral Research*, 17, 343–358.

Schnall, Simone, Benton, Jennifer, and Harvey, Sophie. (2008). With a Clean Conscience: Cleanliness Reduces the Severity of Moral Judgments. *Psychological Science*, 19, 1219–1227.

Schneider, Benjamin. (2007). Evolution of the Study and Practice of Personality at Work. *Human Resource Management*, 46, 583–610.

Schriesheim, Chester A. (1997). Substitutes for Leadership Theory: Development and Basic Concepts. *Leadership Quarterly*, 8, 103–108.

Schriesheim, Chester A., Castro, Stephanie L., Zhou, Xiaohua, and DeChurch, Leslie A. (2006). An Investigation of Path-Goal and Transformational Leadership Theory Predictions at the Individual Level of Analysis. *Leadership Quarterly*, 17, 21–38.

Schriesheim, Chester A., Tepper, Bennett J., and Tetrault, Linda A. (1994). Least Preferred Coworker Score, Situational Control, and Leadership Effectiveness: A Meta-analysis of Contingency Model Performance Predictions. *Journal of Applied Psychology*, 79, 561–573.

Schultheiss, Oliver, C., and Brunstein, Joachim C. (2001). Assessment of Implicit Motives with a Research Version of the TAT: Picture Profiles, Gender Differences, and Relations to Other Personality Measures. *Journal of Personality Assessment*, 77, 71–86.

Schultheiss, Oliver C., Yankova, Diana, Dirlikov, Benjamin, and Schad, Daniel J. (2009). Are Implicit and Explicit Motive Measures Statistically Independent? A Fair and Balanced Test Using the Picture Story Exercise and a Cue- and Response-Matched Questionnaire Measure. *Journal of Personality Assessment*, 91, 72–81.

Schutte, Nico, Toppinen, Salla, Kalimo, Raija, and Schaufeli, Wilmar. (2000). The Factorial Validity of the Maslach Burnout Inventory-General Survey (MBI-GS) across Organizational Groups and Nations. *Journal of Occupational and Organizational Psychology*, 73, 53–66.

Schutz, Alfred. (1932/1967). *The Phenomenology of the Social World*. First published in German. Trans. George Walsh and Frederick Lehnert. Evanston, IL: Northwestern University Press.

Schwab, Andreas, and Miner, Anne S. (2008). Learning in Hybrid-Project Systems: The Effects of Project Performance on Repeated Collaboration. *Academy of Management Journal*, 51, 1117–1149.

Schyns, Birgit, Felfe, Jörg, and Blank, H. (2007). Is Charisma Hyper-romanticism? Empirical Evidence from New Data and a Meta-analysis. *Applied Psychology: An International Review*, 56, 505–527.

Schyns, Birgit, and Meindl, James R. (2005a). *Implicit Leadership Theories: Essays and Explorations.* Greenwich, CT: Information Age Publishing.

————. (2005b). An Overview of Implicit Leadership Theories and Their Application in Organizational Practice. In Birgit Schyns and James R. Meindl (Eds.), *Implicit Leadership Theories: Essays and Explorations.* Greenwich, CT: Information Age Publishing, 15–36.

Schyns, Birgit, and Paul, Tina. (2005). Dyadic Leadership and Organizational Outcomes: Different Results for Different Instruments? In George B. Graen and Joni A. Graen (Eds.), *Global Organizing Designs.* Greenwich, CT: Information Age Publishing, 173–203.

Scott, Kristyn A., and Brown, Douglas J. (2006). Female First, Leader Second? Gender Bias in the Encoding of Leadership Behavior. *Organizational Behavior and Human Decision Processes,* 101, 230–242.

Scott, W. Richard. (1987). The Adolescence of Institutional Theory. *Administrative Science Quarterly,* 32, 493–511.

————. (1990a). Introduction to Part II: Formal Theory. In Craig Calhoun, Marshall W. Meyer, and W. Richard Scott (Eds.), *Structures of Power and Constraint: Papers in Honor of Peter M. Blau.* Cambridge, UK: Cambridge University Press, 181–189.

————. (1990b). Symbols and Organizations: From Barnard to the Institutionalists. In Oliver E. Williamson (Ed.), *Organization Theory: From Chester Barnard to the Present and Beyond.* New York: Oxford University Press, 38–55.

————. (2001). *Institutions and Organizations.* Thousand Oaks, CA: Sage.

————. (2004). Reflections on a Half-Century of Organizational Sociology. *Annual Review of Sociology,* 30, 1–21.

————. (2005). Institutional Theory: Contributing to a Theoretical Research Program. In Ken G. Smith and Michael A. Hitt (Eds.), *Great Minds in Management: The Process of Theory Development.* Oxford, UK: Oxford University Press, 460–484.

————. (2008). Lords of the Dance: Professionals as Institutional Agents. *Organization Studies,* 29, 219–238.

Scott, W. Richard, and Meyer, John W. (1994). *Institutional Environments and Organizations: Structural Complexity and Individualism.* Thousand Oaks, CA: Sage.

Senko, Corwin, Durik, Amanda M., and Harackiewicz, Judith M. (2008). Historical Perspectives and New Directions in Achievement Goal Theory: Understanding the Effects of Mastery and Performance-Approach Goals. In James Y. Shah and Wendi L. Gardner (Eds.), *Handbook of Motivation Science.* New York: Guilford Press, 100–113.

Sergent, Claire, and Dehaene, Stanislas. (2004). Is Consciousness a Gradual Phenomenon? Evidence for an All-or-None Bifurcation during the Attentional Blink. *Psychological Science,* 15, 720–728.

Seyranian, Viviane, and Bligh, Michelle C. (2008). Presidential Charismatic Leadership: Exploring the Rhetoric of Social Change. *Leadership Quarterly,* 19, 54–76.

Shah, Anuj K., and Oppenheimer, Daniel M. (2008). Heuristics Made Easy: An Effort-Reduction Framework. *Psychological Bulletin,* 134, 207–222.

Shah, James Y. (2005). The Automatic Pursuit and Management of Goals. *Current Directions in Psychological Science,* 14, 10–13.

Shah, James Y., and Gardner, Wendi L. (2008). *Handbook of Motivation Science.* New York: Guilford Press.

Shah, James Y., and Kruglanski, Arie W. (2008). Structural Dynamics: The Challenge of Change in Goal Systems. In James Y. Shah and Wendi L. Gardner (Eds.), *Handbook of Motivation Science.* New York: Guilford Press, 217–229.

Shamir, Boas. (2007). From Passive Recipients to Active Co-Producers: Followers' Roles in the Leadership Process. In Boas Shamir, Rajnandini Pillai, Michelle C. Bligh, and Mary Uhl-Bien (Eds.), *Follower-Centered Perspectives on Leadership: A Tribute to the Memory of James R. Meindl.* Greenwich, CT: Information Age Publishing, ix–xxxvii.

Shamir, Boas, Pillai, Rajnandini, Bligh, Michelle C., and Uhl-Bien, Mary. (2007). *Follower-Centered Perspectives on Leadership: A Tribute to the Memory of James R. Meindl.* Greenwich, CT: Information Age Publishing.

Shane, Scott, Locke, Edwin A., and Collins, Christopher J. (2003). Entrepreneurial Motivation. *Human Resource Management Review,* 13, 257–279.

Shantz, Amanda, and Latham, Gary R. (2009). An Exploratory Field Experiment of the Effect of Subconscioius and Conscious Goals on Employee Performance. *Organizational Behavior and Human Decision Processes,* 109, 9–17.

Shariff, Azim F., and Norenzayan, Ara. (2007). God Is Watching You: Priming God Concepts Increases Prosocial Behavior in an Anonymous Economic Game. *Psychological Science,* 18, 803–809.

Shepherd, Dean A., Zacharakis, Andrew, and Baron, Robert A. (2003). VC's Decision Processes: Evidence Suggesting More Experience May Not Always Be Better. *Journal of Business Venturing,* 18, 381–401.

Shin, Shung J., and Zhou, Jing. (2007). When Is Educational Specialization Heterogeneity Related to Creativity in Research and Development Teams? Transformational Leadership as a Moderator. *Journal of Applied Psychology,* 92, 1709–1721.

Shirom, Arie, Melamed, Samuel, Toker, Sharon, Berliner, Shlomo, and Shapira, Itzhak. (2005). Burnout and Health Review: Current Knowledge and Future Research Directions. *International Review of Industrial and Organizational Psychology,* 20, 269–308.

Siegall, Marc. (2000). Putting the Stress Back into Role Stress: Improving the Measurement of Role Conflict and Role Ambiguity. *Journal of Managerial Psychology,* 15, 427–435.

Silva, Paul J. (2008). Interest—The Curious Emotion. *Current Directions in Psychological Science,* 17, 57–60.

Simon, Herbert A. (1947, 1957, 1976, 1997). *Administrative Behavior: A Study of Decision-Making Processes in Administrative Organizations.* 4 eds. New York: Free Press.

———. (1955). A Behavioral Model of Rational Choice. *Quarterly Journal of Economics,* 69, 99–118.

———. (1962). The Architecture of Complexity. *Proceedings of the American Philosophic Society,* 106(6), 467–482.

———. (1965). *The Shape of Automation for Men and Management.* New York: Harper and Row.

———. (1967). Motivational and Emotional Controls of Cognition. *Psychological Review,* 74, 29–39.

———. (1977). *The New Science of Management Decision.* Englewood Cliffs, NJ: Prentice-Hall.

———. (1978). Rationality as a Process and Product of Thought. *American Economic Review,* 68, 1–16.

———. (1987). Making Management Decisions: The Role of Intuition and Emotion. *Academy of Management Executive,* 1, 57–64.

———. (1991). Bounded Rationality and Organizational Learning. *Organization Science,* 2, 125–134.

Simon, Herbert A., Smithburg, Donald A., and Thompson, Victor A. (1950). *Public Administration.* New York: Knopf.

Sims, Henry P., Faraj, Samer, and Yun, Seokhwe. (2009). When Should a Leader Be Directive, or Empowering? How to Develop Your Own Situational Theory of Leadership. *Business Horizons,* 52, 149–158.

Singh, Jitendra V. (2006). Ecology, Strategy and Organizational Change. In Joel A. C. Baum, Sanislav D. Dobrev, and Arjen van Witteloostuijn (Eds.), *Ecology and Strategy.* Oxford, UK; Elsevier, 177–214.

Singh, Jitendra V., House, Robert J., and Tucker, David J. (1986). Organizational Change and Organizational Mortality. *Administrative Science Quarterly,* 31, 587–611.

Sio, Ut Na, and Ormerod, Thomas C. (2009). Does Incubation Enhance Problem Solving? A Meta-analytic Review. *Psychological Bulletin,* 135, 94–120.

Sivanathan, Niro, Pillutla, Madan M., and Murnighan, J. Keith. (2008). Power Gained, Power Lost. *Organizational Behavior and Human Decision Processes,* 105, 135–146.

Skinner, B. F. (1953). *Science and Human Behavior.* New York: Macmillan.

———. (1971). *Beyond Freedom and Dignity.* Harmondsworth, UK: Penguin.

Skowronski, John J., Carlston, Donal E., and Hartnett, Jessica. (2008). Spontaneous Impressions Derived from Observations of Behavior: What a Long, Strange Trip It's Been (and It's Not Over Yet). In Nalini Ambady and John J. Skowronski (Eds.), *First Impressions.* New York: Guilford Press, 313–333.

Smith, Eliot R., and Conrey, Frederica R. (2007). Mental Representations Are States, Not Things: Implications for Implicit and Explicit Measurement. In Bernd Wittenbrink and Norbert Schwarz (Eds.), *Implicit Measures of Attitudes.* New York: Guilford Press, 247–264.

Smith, Pamela K., Dijksterhuis, Ap, and Wigboldus, Daniël H. J. (2008). Powerful People Make Good Decisions Even When They Consciously Think. *Psychological Science,* 19, 1258–1259.

Smith, Pamela K., Jostmann, Nils B., Galinsky, Adam D., and van Dijk, Wilco W. (2008). Lacking Power Impairs Executive Functions. *Psychological Science,* 19, 441–447.

Smith, Steven M., and Moynan, Sarah C. (2008). Forgetting and Recovering the Unforgettable. *Psychological Science,* 19, 462–468.

Sonenshein, Scott. (2007). The Role of Construction, Intuition, and Justification in Responding to Ethical Issues at Work: The Sensemaking-Intuition Model. *Academy of Management Review,* 32, 1022–1040.

Spangler, William D. (1992). Validity of Questionnaire and TAT Measures of Need for Achievement: Two Meta-analyses. *Psychological Bulletin,* 112, 140–154.

Sparrowe, Raymond T., and Liden, Robert C. (2005). Two Routes to Influence: Integrating Leader-Member Exchange and Social Network Perspectives. *Administrative Science Quarterly,* 50, 505–535.

Spell, Chester S., and Blum, Terry C. (2005). Adoption of Workplace Substance Abuse Prevention Programs: Strategic Choice and Institutional Perspectives. *Academy of Management Journal,* 48, 1125–1142.

Spencer, Lyle M., and Spencer, Signe M. (1993). *Competence at Work: Models for Superior Performance.* New York: Wiley.

Spreier, Scott W., Fontaine, Mary H., and Malloy, Ruth L. (2006). Leadership Run Amok: The Destructive Potential of Overachievers. *Harvard Business Review,* 84(6), 72–82.

Stajkovic, Alexander D., Locke, Edwin A., and Blair, Eden S. (2006). A First Examination of the Relationship between Primed Subconscious Goals, Assigned Conscious Goals, and Task Performance. *Journal of Applied Psychology,* 91, 1172–1180.

Stanley, Damian, Phelps, Elizabeth, and Banaji, Mahzarin. (2008). The Neural Basis of Implicit Attitudes. *Current Directions in Psychological Science,* 17, 164–170.

Staw, Barry M., and Epstein, Lisa D. (2000). What Bandwagons Bring: Effects of Popular Management Techniques on Corporate Performance, Reputation, and CEO Pay. *Administrative Science Quarterly,* 45, 523–556.

Stein, Morris I. (1948). *The Thematic Apperception Test: An Introductory Manual for its Clinical Use with Adult Males.* Cambridge, MA: Addison-Wesley.

Stel, Mariëlle, van Dijk, Eric, and Olivier, Einar. (2009). You Want to Know the Truth: Then Don't Mimic. *Psychological Science,* 20, 693–699.

Sternberg, Robert J. (2005). Foolishness. In Robert J. Sternberg and Jennifer Jordan (Eds.), *A Handbook of Wisdom: Psychological Perspectives.* New York: Cambridge University Press, 331–352.

Stewart, Greg L. (2006). A Meta-Analytic Review of Relationships between Team Design Features and Team Performance. *Journal of Management,* 32, 29–55.

Stewart, Wayne H., and Roth, Philip L. (2001). Risk Propensity Differences between Entrepreneurs and Managers: A Meta-analytic Review. *Journal of Applied Psychology,* 86, 145–153.

———. (2004). Data Quality Affects Meta-analytic Conclusions: A Response to Miner and Raju (2004) Concerning Entrepreneurial Risk Propensity. *Journal of Applied Psychology,* 89, 14–21.

Stewart-Williams, Steve, and Podd, John. (2004a). The Placebo Effect: Dissolving the Expectancy Versions Conditioning Debate. *Psychological Bulletin,* 130, 324–340.

———. (2004b). Placebo Psychotherapies and Nonconscious Learning in the Placebo Effect: Reply to Kirsch (2004). *Psychological Bulletin,* 130, 344–345.

Stinchcombe, Arthur L. (1974). *Creating Efficient Industrial Administrations.* New York: Academic Press.

Stogdill, Ralph M. (1959). *Individual Behavior and Group Achievement.* New York: Oxford University Press.

———. (1962). Intragroup-Intergroup Theory and Research. In Muzafer Sherif (Ed.), *Intergroup Relations and Leadership.* New York: Wiley, 48–65.

———. (1965). *Managers, Employees, Organizations.* Columbus: Bureau of Business Research, Ohio State University.

———. (1966). Dimensions of Organization Theory. In James D. Thompson (Ed.), *Approaches to Organizational Design.* Pittsburgh, PA: University of Pittsburgh Press, 3–56.

———. (1972). Group Productivity, Drive, and Cohesiveness. *Organizational Behavior and Human Performance,* 8, 26–43.

Strube, Michael J., and Garcia, Joseph E. (1981). A Meta-analytic Investigation of Fiedler's Contingency Model of Leader Effectiveness. *Psychological Bulletin,* 90, 307–321.

Sui, Jie, and Han, Shihui. (2007). Self-Construal Priming Modulates Neural Substrates of Self-Awareness. *Psychological Science,* 18, 861–866.

Svyantek, Daniel J., Goodman, Scott A., Benz, Lori L., and Gard, Julia A. (1999). The Relationship between Organizational Characteristics and Team Building Success. *Journal of Business and Psychology,* 14, 265–283.

Swaminathan, Anand. (2001). Resource Partitioning and the Evolution of Specialist Organizations: The Role of Location and Identity in the U.S. Wine Industry. *Academy of Management Journal,* 44, 1169–1185.

———. (2009). Review of *The Red Queen among Organizations: How Competiveness Evolves. Administrative Science Quarterly,* 54, 689–691.

Swaminathan, Anand, and Delacroix, Jacques. (1991). Differentiation within an Organizational Population: Additional Evidence from the Wine Industry. *Academy of Management Journal,* 34, 679–692.

Sweeny, Kate. (2008). Crisis Decision Theory: Decisions in the Face of Negative Events. *Psychological Bulletin,* 134, 61–76.

Taggar, Simon, and Neubert, Mitchell. (2004). The Impact of Poor Performers on Team Outcomes: An Empirical Examination of Attribution Theory. *Personnel Psychology,* 57, 935–968.

Takahashi, Masami, and Overton, Willis F. (2005). Cultural Foundations of Wisdom: An Integrated Developmental Approach. In Robert J. Sternberg and Jennifer Jordan (Eds.), *A Handbook of Wisdom: Psychological Perspectives.* New York: Cambridge University Press, 32–60.

Tamir, Maya. (2009). What Do People Want to Feel and Why? Pleasure and Utility in Emotion Regulation. *Current Directions in Psychological Science,* 18, 101–105.

Tannenbaum, Arnold S. (1968). *Control in Organizations.* New York: McGraw-Hill.

Tannenbaum, Arnold S., and Cooke, Robert A. (1979). Organizational Control: A Review of Studies Employing the Control Graph Method. In Cornelis J. Lammers and David Hickson (Eds.), *Organizations Alike and Unlike.* London, UK: Routledge and Kegan Paul, 183–210.

Tannenbaum, Arnold S., and Kahn, Robert L. (1957). *Participation in Union Locals.* Evanston, IL: Row, Peterson.

Tannenbaum, Arnold S., Kavčič, Bogdan, Rosner, Menachem, Vianello, Mino, and Wieser, Georg. (1974). *Hierarchy in Organizations: An International Comparison.* San Francisco, CA: Jossey-Bass.

Tannenbaum, Arnold S., and Rozgonyi, Tomás (1986). *Authority and Reward in Organizations: An International Research.* Ann Arbor: Survey Research Center, Institute for Social Research, University of Michigan.

Taylor, Alva, and Helfat, Constance E. (2009). Organizational Linkages for Surviving Technological Change: Complementary Assets. Middle Management, and Ambidexterity. *Organization Science,* 20, 718–739.

Taylor, Shelley E., and Sherman, David K. (2008). Self-Enhancement and Self-Affirmation: The Consequences of Positive Self-Thoughts for Motivation and Health. In James Y. Shah and Wendi L. Gardner (Eds.), *Handbook of Motivation Science.* New York: Guilford Press, 57–70.

Terborg, James R., Howard, G. S., and Maxwell, S. E. (1980). Evaluating Planned Organizational Change: A Method for Assessing Alpha, Beta, and Gamma Change. *Academy of Management Review,* 5, 109–121.

Thomas, Christopher H., and Lankau, Melenie J. (2009). Preventing Burnout: The Effects of LMX and Mentoring on Socialization, Role Stress, and Burnout. *Human Resource Management,* 48, 417–432.

Thompson, James D. (1967). *Organizations in Action.* New York: McGraw-Hill.

Thompson, Suzanne C., and Schlehofer, Michèle M. (2008). The Many Sides of Control Motivation: Motives for High, Low, and Illusory Control. In James Y. Shah and Wendi L. Gardner (Eds.), *Handbook of Motivation Science.* New York: Guilford Press, 41–56.

Thompson, Victor A. (1961). *Modern Organization.* New York: Knopf.

———. (1965). Bureaucracy and Innovation. *Administrative Science Quarterly,* 10, 1–20.

———. (1969). *Bureaucracy and Innovation.* Tuscaloosa: University of Alabama Press.

———. (1975). *Without Sympathy or Enthusiasm: The Problem of Administrative Compassion.* Tuscaloosa: University of Alabama Press.

———. (1976). *Bureaucracy and the Modern World.* Morristown, NJ: General Learning Press.

Thoresen, Carl J., Kaplan, Seth A., Barsky, Adam P., Warren, Christopher R., and de Chermont, Kelly. (2003). The Affective Underpinning of Job Perceptions and Attitudes: A Meta-Analytic Review and Integration. *Psychology Bulletin,* 129, 914–945.

Tierney, Pamela, Farmer, Steven M., and Graen, George B. (1999). An Examination of Leadership and Employee Creativity: The Relevance of Traits and Relationships. *Personnel Psychology,* 52, 591–620.

Tolbert, Pamela S., and Zucker, Lynne G. (1996). The Institutionalization of Institutional Theory. In Stewart R. Clegg, Cynthia Hardy, and Walter R. Nord (Eds.), *Handbook of Organizations.* London, UK: Sage, 175–190.

Tomkins, Silvan S. (1947). *The Thematic Apperception Test: The Theory and Technique of Interpretation.* New York: Grune & Stratton.

———. (1949). The Present Status of the Thematic Apperception Test. *American Journal of Orthopsychiatry,* 19, 358–362.

Tomkins, Silvan S., and Miner, John B. (1957). *The Tomkins-Horn Picture Arrangement Test.* New York: Springer Publishing.

———. (1959). *Picture Arrangement Test Interpretation: Scope and Technique.* New York: Springer.

Tosi, Henry L., Misangyi, Vilmos F., Fanelli, Angelo, Waldman, David A., and Yammarino, Francis J. (2004). CEO Charisma, Compensation, and Firm Performance. *Leadership Quarterly,* 15, 405–420.

Triandis, Harry C. (1995). *Individualism and Collectivism.* Boulder, CO: Westview Press.

Trist, Eric L., and Bamforth, K. W. (1951). Some Social and Psychological Consequences of the Longwall Method of Coal-Getting. *Human Relations,* 4, 3–38.

Trist, Eric L., Emery, Fred, and Murray, Hugh (1997). *The Social Engagement of Social Science: A Tavistock Anthology, Vol. 3, The Socio-Ecological Perspective.* Philadelphia: University of Pennsylvania Press.

Trist, Eric L., Higgin, G. W., Murray, Hugh, and Pollack, A. B. (1963). *Organizational Choice: Capabilities of Groups at the Coal Face under Changing Technologies.* London, UK: Tavistock.

Trist, Eric L., and Murray, Hugh. (1993). *The Social Engagement of Social Science: A Tavistock Anthology, Vol. 2, The Socio-Technical Perspective.* Philadelphia: University of Pennsylvania Press.

Trope, Yaacov, and Fishbach, Ayelet. (2005). Going Beyond the Motivation Given: Self-Control and Situational Control over Behavior. In Ran R. Hassin, James S. Uleman, and John A. Bargh (Eds.), *The New Unconscious.* New York: Oxford University Press, 537–565.

Troyer, Lisa. (2004). Democracy in a Bureaucracy: The Legitimacy Paradox of Teamwork in Organizations. *Research in the Sociology of Organizations,* 22, 49–87.

Tsui, Anne S., Zhang, Zhi-Xue, Wang, Hui, Xin, Katherine R., and Wu, Joshua B. (2006). Unpacking the Relationship between CEO Leadership Behavior and Organization Culture. *Leadership Quarterly,* 17, 113–137.

Tucker, David J., Singh, Jitendra V., and Meinhard, Agnes G. (1990). Organizational, Forms, Population Dynamics, and Institutional Change: The Founding Patterns of Voluntary Organizations. *Academy of Management Journal,* 33, 151–178.

Turner, Stephen P. (1977). Blau's Theory of Differentiation: Is It Explanatory? In J. Kenneth Benson (Ed.), *Organizational Analysis: Critique and Innovation.* Beverly Hills, CA: Sage, 19–34.

Tversky, A., and Kahneman, Daniel (1974). Judgment under Uncertainty: Heuristics and Biases. *Science,* 185, 1124–1131.

———. (1984). Extensional Versus Intuitive Reasoning: The Conjunction Fallacy in Probability Judgment. *Psychological Review,* 91, 293–315.

Uhl-Bien, Mary. (2003). Relationship Development as a Key Ingredient for Leadership Development. In Elaine Murphy and Ronald E. Riggio (Eds.), *The Future of Leadership Development.* Mahwah, NJ: Lawrence Erlbaum, 129–147.

Uhl-Bien, Mary, and Pillai, Rajnandini. (2007). The Romance of Leadership and the Social Construction of Followership. In Boas Shamir, Rajnandini Pillai, Michelle C. Bligh, and Mary Uhl-Bien (Eds.), *Follower-Centered Perspectives on Leadership: A Tribute to the Memory of James R. Meindl.* Greenwich, CT: Information Age Publishing, 187–209.

Uhlmann, Eric L., and Cohen, Geoffrey L. (2007). "I Think It, Therefore It's True": Effects of Self-Perceived Objectivity on Hiring Discrimination. *Organizational Behavior and Human Decision Processes,* 104, 207–223.

Uleman, James S. (2005). Introduction: Becoming Aware of the New Unconscious. In Ran S. Hassin, James S. Uleman, and John A. Bargh (Eds.), *The New Unconscious.* New York: Oxford University Press, 3–15.

Uleman, James S., Blader, Steven L., and Todorov, Alexander. (2005). Implicit Impressions. In Ran R. Hassin, James S. Uleman, and John A. Bargh (Eds.), *The New Unconscious.* New York: Oxford University Press, 362–392.

Vaish, Amrisha, Grossmann, Tobias, and Woodward, Amanda. (2008). Not All Emotions Are Created Equal: The Negativity Bias in Social-Emotional Development. *Psychological Bulletin,* 134, 383–403.

Vaitl, Dieter, Birbaumer, Niels, Gruzelier, John, Jamieson, Graham A., Kotchoubey, Boris, Kübler, Andrea, Lehmann, Dietrich, Miltner, Wolfgang H. R., Ott, Ulrich, Pütz, Peter, Sammer, Gebhard, Strauch, Inge, Strehl, Ute, Wackermen, Jiri, and Weiss, Thomas. (2005). Psychobiology of Altered States of Consciousness. *Psychological Bulletin,* 131, 98–127.

van Baaren, Rick B., Holland, Rob W., Kawakami, Kerry, and van Knippenberg, Ad. (2004). Mimicry and Prosocial Behavior. *Psychological Science,* 15, 71–74.

Vance, Charles M., Groves, Kevin S., Paik, Yongsun, and Kindler, Herb. (2007). Understanding and Measuring Linear-Nonlinear Thinking Style for Enhanced Management Education and Professional Practice. *Academy of Management Learning and Education,* 6, 167–185.

Vancouver, Jeffrey B., Thompson, Charles M., Tischner, E. Casey, and Putka, Dan J. (2002). Two Studies Examining the Negative Effect of Self-Efficacy on Performance. *Journal of Applied Psychology*, 87, 506–516.

Vancouver, Jeffrey B., Thompson, Charles M., and Williams, Amy A. (2001). The Changing Signs in the Relationship among Self-Efficacy, Personal Goals, and Performance. *Journal of Applied Psychology*, 86, 605–620.

Van den Bussche, Eva, Van den Noortgate, Wim, and Reynvoet, Bert. (2009). Mechanism of Masked Priming: A Meta-Analysis. *Psychological Bulletin*, 135, 452–472.

van Knippenberg, Barbara, and van Knippenberg, Daan. (2005). Leader Self-Sacrifice and Leader Effectiveness: The Moderating Role of Leader Prototypicality. *Journal of Applied Psychology*, 90, 25–37.

van Offenbeek, Marjolein, Sorge, Arndt, and Knip, Marrig. (2009). Enacting Fit in Work Organization and Occupational Structure Design: The Case of Intermediary Occupations in Dutch Hospitals. *Organization Studies*, 30, 1083–1114.

Van Velsor, E., and Leslie, J. B. (1995). Why Executives Derail: Perspective across Time and Culture. *Academy of Management Executive*, 9, 62–72.

Vargas, Patrick T., Sekaquaptewa, Denise, and von Hippel, William. (2007). Armed Only with Paper and Pencil: "Low-Tech" Measures of Implicit Attitudes. In Bernd Wittenbrink and Norbert Schwarz (Eds.), *Implicit Measures of Attitudes*. New York: Guilford Press, 103–124.

Varnum, Michael E. W., Grossman, Igor, Kitayama, Shinobu, and Nisbett, Richard E. (2010). The Origin of Cultural Differences in Cognition: The Social Orientation Hypothesis. *Current Directions in Psychological Science*, 19, 9–13.

Vecchio, Robert P. (2003). Entrepreneurship and Leadership: Common Trends and Common Threads. *Human Resource Management Review*, 13, 303–327.

von Hippel, William. (2007). Aging, Executive Functioning, and Social Control. *Current Directions in Psychological Science*, 16, 240–244.

Vroom, Victor H. (1964). *Work and Motivation*. New York: Wiley.

———. (2005). On the Origins of Expectancy Theory. In Ken G. Smith and Michael A. Hitt (Eds.), *Great Minds in Management: The Process of Theory Development*. New York: Oxford University Press, 239–258.

Vroom, Victor H., and Deci, Edward L. (1971). The Stability of Post-decision Dissonance: A Follow-up Study of the Job Attitudes of Business School Graduates. *Organizational Behavior and Human Performance*, 6, 36–49.

Vroom, Victor H., and Jago, Arthur G. (1988). *The New Leadership: Managing Participation in Organizations*. Englewood Cliffs, NJ: Prentice-Hall.

Vroom, Victor H., and Yetton, Philip W. (1973). *Leadership and Decision Making*. Pittsburgh, PA: University of Pittsburgh Press.

Wageman, Ruth, Fisher, Colin M., and Hackman, J. Richard (2009). Leading Teams When the Time Is Right: Finding the Best Moments to Act. *Organizational Dynamics*, 38, 192–203.

Waldman, David A., Javidan, Mansour, and Varella, Paul. (2004). Charismatic Leadership at the Strategic Level: A New Application of Upper Echelons Theory. *Leadership Quarterly*, 15, 355–380.

Wall, Toby D., Michie, Jonathan, Patterson, Malcolm, Wood, Stephen J., Sheehan, Maura, Clegg, Chris W., and West, Michael. (2004). On the Validity of Subjective Measures of Company Performance. *Personnel Psychology*, 57, 95–118.

Walsh, Kate (2004). Interpreting the Impact of Culture on Structure: The Role of Change Processes. *Journal of Applied Behavioral Science*, 40, 302–322.

Walton, Eric J. (2005). The Persistence of Bureaucracy: A Meta-Analysis of Weber's Model of Bureaucratic Control. *Organization Studies*, 26, 569–600.

Wansink, Brian, Payne, Collin R., and van Ittersum, Koert. (2008). Profiling the Heroic Leader: Empirical Lessons from Combat-Decorated Veterans of World War II. *Leadership Quarterly*, 19, 547–555.

Webb, Thomas L., and Sheeran, Paschal. (2006). Does Changing Behavioral Intentions Engender Behavior Change: A Meta-analysis of the Experimental Evidence. *Psychological Bulletin*, 132, 249–268.

Weber, Elke U., and Johnson, Eric J. (2009). Mindful Judgment and Decision Making. *Annual Review of Psychology*, 60, 53–85.

Weber, Klaus, and Glynn, Mary A. (2006). Making Sense with Intuitions: Context, Thought, and Action in Karl Weick's Theory. *Organization Studies*, 27, 1639–1660.

Weber, Max. (1930). *The Protestant Ethic and the Spirit of Capitalism*. Trans. Talcott Parson. London, UK: Allen and Unwin.

———. (1946). *From Max Weber: Essays in Sociology*. Trans. and ed. Hans H. Gerth and C. Wright Mills. New York: Oxford University Press.

————. (1947). *The Theory of Social and Economic Organization.* Trans. and ed. Talcott Parsons and A. M. Henderson. New York: Free Press.

————. (1968). *Economy and Society, Vols. I–III.* Trans. and ed. Guenther Roth and Claus Wittich. New York: Bedminster.

Wegner, Daniel M., Wenzlaff, Richard M., and Kozak, Megan. (2004). Dream Rebound: The Return of Suppressed Thoughts in Dreams. *Psychological Science,* 232–236.

Weick, Karl E. (1995). *Sensemaking in Organizations.* Thousand Oaks, CA: Sage.

————. (2007). Romancing, Following, and Sensemaking: James Meindl's Legacy. In Boas Shamir, Rajnandini Pillai, Michelle C. Bligh, and Mary Uhl-Bien (Eds.), *Follower-Centered Perspectives on Leadership: A Tribute to the Memory of James R. Meindl.* Greenwich, CT: Information Age Publishing, 279–291.

Weick, Karl E., and Putnam, Ted. (2006). Organizing for Mindfulness: Eastern Wisdom and Western Knowledge. *Journal of Management Inquiry,* 15, 275–287.

Weiner, Bernard. (1985). An Attributional Theory of Achievement Motivation and Emotion. *Psychological Review,* 92, 548–573.

Weiner, Bernard, and Sierad, Jack. (1975). Misattribution for Failure and Enhancement of Achievement Strivings. *Journal of Personality and Social Psychology,* 31, 415–421.

Weisbuch, Max, Unkelbach, Christian, and Fiedler, Klaus. (2008). Remnants of the Recent Past: Influences of Priming on First Impressions. In Nalini Ambady and John J. Skowronski (Eds.), *First Impressions.* New York: Guilford Press, 289–312.

Wentura, Dirk, and Rothermund, Klaus. (2007). Paradigms We Live By: A Plea for More Basic Research on the Implicit Association Test. In Bernd Wittenbrink and Norbert Schwarz (Eds.), *Implicit Measures of Attitude.* New York: Guilford Press, 194–215.

Westen, Drew. (1998). The Scientific Legacy of Sigmund Freud: Toward a Psychodynamically Informed Psychological Science. *Psychological Bulletin,* 124, 333–371.

Westen, Drew, and Weinberger, John. (2004). When Clinical Description Becomes Statistical Prediction. *American Psychologist,* 59, 595–613.

Wezel, Filippo C., and Saka-Helmhout, Ayse. (2006). Antecedents and Consequences of Organizational Change: "Institutionalizing" the Behavioral Theory of the Firm. *Organization Studies,* 27, 265–286.

Wezel, Filippo C., and van Witteloostuijn, Arjen. (2006). Scale and Scope Economies in the British Motorcycle Industry, 1899–1993. In Joel A. C. Baum, Stanislav D. Dobrev, and Arjen van Witteloostuijn (Eds.), *Ecology and Strategy.* Oxford, UK: Elsevier, 523–548.

White, Roderick E., Thornhill, Stewart, and Hampson, Elizabeth. (2006). Entrepreneurs and Evolutionary Biology: The Relationship between Testosterone and New Venture Creation. *Organizational Behavior and Human Decision Processes,* 100, 21–34.

Wilkowski, Benjamin M., Robinson, Michael D., and Friesen, Chris K. (2009). Gaze-Triggered Orienting as a Tool of the Belongingness Self-Regulation System. *Psychological Science,* 20, 495–501.

Williams, Ethalyn A., Pillai, Rajnandini, Lowe, Kevin B., Jung, Dongil, and Herst, David. (2009). Crisis, Charisma, Values, and Voting Behavior in the 2004 Presidential Election. *Leadership Quarterly,* 20, 70–86.

Williams, Lisa A., and DeSteno, David. (2009). Pride: Adaptive Social Emotion or Seventh Sin? *Psychological Science,* 20, 284–288.

Williamson, Oliver E. (1975). *Markets and Hierarchies: Analysis and Antitrust Implications.* New York: Free Press.

Willis, Janine, and Todorov, Alexander. (2006). First Impressions: Making Up Your Mind after a 100-Ms Exposure to a Face. *Psychological Science,* 17, 592–598.

Wilson, Timothy D. (2009). Know Thyself. *Perspectives on Psychological Science,* 4, 384–389.

Winerman, Lea. (2005). Can You Force Yourself to Forget? *Monitor on Psychology,* 36(8), 52–57.

Winkielman, Piotr, and Berridge, Kent C. (2004). Unconscious Emotion. *Current Directions in Psychological Science,* 13, 120–123.

Winkielman, Piotr, Berridge, Kent C., and Wilbarger, Julia L. (2005). Emotion, Behavior, and Conscious Experience: Once More without Feeling. In Lisa F. Barrett, Paula M. Niedenthal, and Piotr Winkielman (Eds.), *Emotion and Consciousness.* New York: Guilford Press, 335–362.

Winkielman, Piotr, Halbertstadt, Jamin, Fazendeiro, Tedra, and Catty, Steve. (2006). Prototypes Are Attractive Because They Are Easy on the Mind. *Psychological Science,* 17, 799–806.

Winter, David G. (2002). The Motivational Dimensions of Leadership: Power, Achievement, and Affiliation. In Ronald E. Riggio, Susan E. Murphy, and Francis J. Pirozzolo (Eds.), *Multiple Intelligences and Leadership.* Mahwah, NJ: Lawrence Erlbaum, 119–137.

Wittenbrink, Bernd. (2007). Measuring Attitudes through Priming. In Bernd Wittenbrink and Norbert Schwarz (Eds.), *Implicit Measures of Attitudes*. New York: Guilford Press, 17–58.

Wittenbrink, Bernd, and Schwarz, Norbert. (2007). Introduction. In Bernd Wittenbrink and Norbert Schwarz (Eds.), *Implicit Measures of Attitudes*. New York: Guilford Press, 1–13.

Wofford, J. C., and Liska, Laurie Z. (1993). Path-Goal Theories of Leadership: A Meta-Analysis. *Journal of Management*, 19, 857–876.

Wolff, S. B., Pescosolido, A. T., and Druskat, V. U. (2002). Emotional Intelligence as the Basis of Leadership Emergence in Self-Managing Teams. *Leadership Quarterly*, 12, 505–522.

Wong, Kin Fai E., Yik, Michelle, and Kwong, Jessica Y. Y. (2006). Understanding the Emotional Aspects of Escalation of Commitment: The Role of Negative Affect. *Journal of Applied Psychology*, 91, 282–297.

Woodward, Joan. (1958). *Management and Technology: Problems of Progress in Industry, No. 3*. London, UK: Her Majesty's Stationery Office.

Worley, Christopher G. (2009). A Response to "Defixation" as Intervention Perspective: Understanding Wicked Problems at the Dutch Ministry of Foreign Affairs. *Journal of Management Inquiry*, 18, 55–57.

Worley, Christopher G., and Lawler, Edward E. (2006). Designing Organizations That Are Built to Change. *MIT Sloan Management Review*, 48(1), 19–23.

Wu, Tsung-Yu, and Hu, Changya. (2009). Abusive Supervision and Employee Emotional Exhaustion: Dispositional Antecedents and Boundaries. *Group and Organization Management*, 34, 143–169.

Xu, Hongwei, and Ruef, Martin. (2004). The Myth of the Risk-Tolerant Entrepreneur. *Strategic Organization*, 2, 331–355.

Zaccaro, S. J., Foti, Roseanne J., and Kenny, D.A. (1991). Self-Monitoring and Trait-Based Variance in Leadership: An Investigation of Leader Flexibility across Multiple Situations. *Journal of Applied Psychology*, 76, 308–315.

Zárraga, Celia, and Bonache, Jaime. (2005). The Impact of Team Atmosphere on Knowledge Outcomes in Self-Managed Teams. *Organization Studies*, 26, 661–681.

Zenger, Todd R., Lazzarini, Sergio G., and Poppo, Laura. (2002). Informal and Formal Organization in New Institutional Economics. *Advances in Strategic Management*, 19, 277–305.

Zhao, Hao, and Seibert, Scott E. (2006). The Big Five Personality Dimensions and Entrepreneurial Status: A Meta-analytic Review. *Journal of Applied Psychology*, 91, 259–271.

Zhong, Chen-Bo, Dijksterhuis, Ap, and Galinsky, Adam D. (2008). The Merits of Unconscious Thought in Creativity. *Psychological Science*, 19, 912–918.

Zhong, Chen-Bo, and Leonardelli, Geoffrey J. (2008). Cold and Lonely: Does Social Exclusion Literally Feel Cold? *Psychological Science*, 19, 838–842.

Zhu, Weichun, Chew, Irene K. H., and Spangler, William D. (2005). CEO Transformational Leadership and Organizational Outcomes: The Mediating Role of Human-Capital-Enhancing Human Resource Management. *Leadership Quarterly*, 16, 39–52.

Zmud, Robert W., and Armenakis, Achilles A. (1978). Understanding the Measurement of Change. *Academy of Management Review*, 3, 661–669.

Zorn, Dirk M. (2004). Here a Chief, There a Chief: The Rise of the CFO in the American Firm. *American Sociological Review*, 69, 345–364.

Zucker, Lynne G. (1977). The Role of Institutionalization in Cultural Persistence. *American Sociological Review*, 42, 726–743.

———. (1983). Organizations as Institutions. *Research in the Sociology of Organizations*, 2, 1–47.

———. (1988). *Institutional Patterns and Organizations: Culture and Environment*. Cambridge, MA: Ballinger.

———. (1991). The Role of Institutionalization in Cultural Persistence. In Walter W. Powell and Paul J. DiMaggio (Eds.), *The New Institutionalism in Organizational Analysis*. Chicago: University of Chicago Press, 83–107.

Zucker, Lynne G., and Darby, Michael R. (2005). An Evolutionary Approach to Institutions and Social Construction Process and Structure. In Ken G. Smith and Michael A. Hitt (Eds.), *Great Minds in Management: The Process of Theory Development*. New York: Oxford University Press, 547–571.

Zucker, Lynne G., and Kreft, Ita G. G. (1994). The Evolution of Socially Contingent Rational Action: Effects of Labor Strikes on Change in Union Founding in the 1980s. In Joel A. C. Baum and Jitendra V. Singh (Eds.), *Evolutionary Dynamics of Organizations*. New York: Oxford University Press, 194–313.

Zyphur, Michael J. (2009). When Mindsets Collide: Switching Analytical Mindsets to Advance Organizational Science. *Academy of Management Review*, 34, 677–688.

NAME INDEX

SUBJECT INDEX

ABOUT THE AUTHOR

An expert in the field of organizational behavior, **John B. Miner** has a professional practice in Eugene, Oregon. He held the Donald S. Carmichael Chair in Human Resources at the State University of New York–Buffalo and was faculty director of the Center for Entrepreneurial Leadership there. Previously he served as Research Professor of Management at Georgia State University. He has written 57 books and over 140 other publications.

For Product Safety Concerns and Information please contact our EU representative GPSR@taylorandfrancis.com Taylor & Francis Verlag GmbH, Kaufingerstraße 24, 80331 München, Germany

T - #0103 - 230425 - C0 - 254/178/21 - PB - 9780765619938 - Gloss Lamination